Fear and Faith in Paradise

Fear and Faith in Paradise

Exploring Conflict and Religion in the Middle East

Phil Karber

ROWMAN & LITTLEFIELD PUBLISHERS, INC.
Lanham • Boulder • New York • Toronto • Plymouth, UK

Published by Rowman & Littlefield Publishers, Inc.
A wholly owned subsidiary of The Rowman & Littlefield Publishing Group, Inc.
4501 Forbes Boulevard, Suite 200, Lanham, Maryland 20706
www.rowman.com

10 Thornbury Road, Plymouth PL6 7PP, United Kingdom

British Library Cataloguing in Publication Information Available

Library of Congress Cataloging-in-Publication Data

Karber, Phil, 1951–
  Fear and faith in paradise : exploring conflict and religion in the Middle East /
Phil Karber.
    p. cm.
  Includes bibliographical references and index.
  ISBN 978-1-4422-1477-4 (cloth : alk. paper) — ISBN 978-1-4422-1479-8 (electronic)
1. Middle East—Description and travel. 2. Karber, Phil, 1951—Travel—Middle East.
3. Fear—Middle East—Religious aspects. 4. Violence—Middle East—Religious aspects.
5. United States—Foreign relations—Middle East. 6. Middle East—Foreign relations—
United States. I. Title.
  DS49.7.K336 2012
  956.05'3—dc23

                                                                 2012003032

Printed in the United States of America

In memory of
brothers John and Greg,
and dear friend Dennis,
inspirations all

"When I was coming up, it was a dangerous world. And we knew exactly who 'they' were. It was us versus them, and it was clear who them was. Today we're not sure who the 'they' are but we know they're there."

—George W. Bush

"Now faith is the substance of things hoped for, the evidence of things not seen."

—Hebrews 11:1

"Almost every culture has developed a myth of a lost paradise from which men and women were ejected at the beginning of time. . . . This nostalgia informed the cult of 'sacred geography,' one of the oldest and most universal religious ideas."

—Karen Armstrong, *The Case for God*

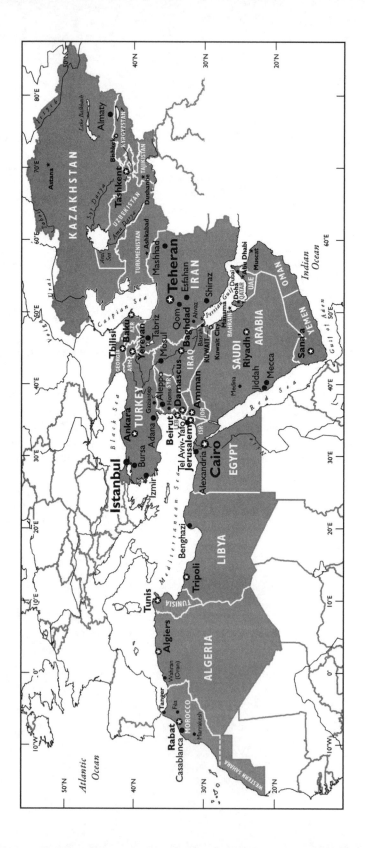

Contents

Acknowledgments

I would like to thank the many individuals who have smiled on this project. David Holdridge, as director of Mercy Corps in the Middle East, hosted me in his home in Beirut, and his staff welcomed me at the Mercy Corps facilities in Iraq. Those trips, which included several visits to project sites, became the backbone of the book.

Along the road, I came into contact with many remarkable people who generously gave their time to this story: Farid Chrabieh in Lebanon, Nilay Ornek in Turkey, Amar Galaly and Ammar Zakri in Kurdistan and Iraq, Abdel Ovederni in Tunisia, Idder Mounier in Morocco, Mira Mahdavi in Iran, and Ghoussoon Arnouk in Syria are but a few.

Routine clippings from the *New York Times* aside, the books and blogs of religious scholar Karen Armstrong and Middle East experts such as Juan Cole and Robin Wright were invaluable resources, giving me guidance in framing my subject. Living in Cambridge has allowed me access to Harvard's Middle East Initiative and MIT's Center for International Studies, where visiting experts such as Husam Zomlot, Gene Sharp, Wael Ghonim, Mona Eltahawy, Michele Angrist, and Aboubakr Jamai have provided invaluable insights and analysis.

Faithful friends Billy Higgins, John Lancaster, and Mike Boulden read the first and last drafts, providing worthy suggestions and saving me from many embarrassing mistakes.

Many, many thanks go to Susan McEachern at Rowman & Littlefield for recognizing the worth of my manuscript and showing me the way. Thanks to assistant editor Grace Baumgartner for answering all my questions and providing sound editorial input. Thanks also to copyeditor Naomi Burns and to senior production editor Alden Perkins, who presided over the organization and editing.

Finally, my greatest debt is to my wife, Joellen Lambiotte, who, from day one, tirelessly provided moral and editorial support. All her time is not forgotten.

There are a few characters in the book whose names and personal circumstances I chose to change. The reasons for this vary but mostly had to do with their residency in countries where freedom of expression can be hazardous to one's health. The bibliography was a stockpile for many ideas, facts, and events, but in the end, I vouch for the accuracy of all details in the book.

~

Prologue

A Moment of Opportunity

We had arrived in Marrakech only hours before on the express train from Casablanca. The afternoon heat had been stifling, shops were shuttered, and Moroccans of the medina were sheltering themselves, as I had been, in fountain-cooled courtyards, shaded by crimson bougainvillea and branching oleanders. I had entered the 17th-century *riad* through a short cedar doorway protected from the evil eye by the hand of Fatima, a rabbit-hole-like transition from chaos and external influences to family and meditation (the hijab is but a fashion expression for this pivot from public to private).

Now, it was evening, and from our sky perch, people and swallows awakened. Like Miro's birds, swallows blotted the orange-red sky with black silhouettes. We were the highest terrace, only the Atlas Mountains and Marrakech's venerated minarets stood taller. Those towers had now turned wine dark from their pinkish plaster facades of day. Joellen (my wife) and I sat with friends on Berber carpets, drinking Meknes cabernet and fig brandy, and smoking a hookah, all ears cocked. First a lone muezzin sounded in Arabic, and then another, followed by many more, until it became a chorus of tenor voices, the evening call to prayer, rolling across the medina and up the Atlas slopes like a comforting breeze. Beneath the majestic 12th-century Koutoubia Mosque, smoke clouded the twilight air. In the night food stalls of Djemma el-Fna, Marrakech's main square and medieval theater, vendors fired up their grills. We would soon make our way there, taking in the pungent aromas and the fierce swarm of medina nightlife: snake charmers and Gnoui dancers, fez-spinning music men and fire-eaters, monkey handlers and henna girls, and storytellers and red-costumed water sellers. Stall number 20, cooking up sides of sardines, mashed aubergine, and fish brochettes, was our favorite, located just steps from the Argana café.

Hauntingly, only two weeks before, the Argana had been percussion shocked and shredded from an al-Qaeda-inspired bombing that killed 16 people and wounded at least 20. Tourism was in tatters: not since the 2003 Casablanca bombings had Morocco fallen victim like this to the jihad jitters. Four days after the Argana bombing, U.S. Navy Seals killed Osama bin Laden in Abbottabad, Pakistan. It wasn't the end of al-Qaeda (or the idea of it), but bin Laden's death, coupled with the more temperate tone of the Arab Spring, has forced its cold-blooded adherents back into the primitive shadows where they belong.

In the rising din of Marrakech nightlife, from the nearby Ali ben Youssef Mosque, the last voice of the evening prayers fell silent. We reveled in the theater of Djemma el-Fna.

Since my last visit to the region, voices of discontent—infinitely more resonant and reality based than al-Qaeda's scorched-earth nihilism—have been ratcheted up, in the streets and through social media. Not since the post–World War II decolonization of Africa and Asia has such a "great pageant of political progress" played out in the region. With the exception of Libya and Syria, in almost a dozen countries in North Africa and the Middle East autocrats and extremists are now in the crosshairs of grassroots reform and independence movements focused on nonviolent protest but compelled by a sudden break from decades of oppression and frustration. Political expression for young people in the Middle East and North Africa is now defined less by ideological hatred and more by a yearning for equity and jobs. One-third of the Arab world is between 15 and 29 years old. Morocco has a youth unemployment rate of 40 percent, while 40 percent of Egyptians live on less than two dollars a day. As President Barack Obama noted in his May 19 speech titled "A Moment of Opportunity," if you take out oil exports, this region of over 400 million people exports roughly the same amount as Switzerland.

For eight weeks I traveled the roads and rails of Morocco and Tunisia, listening to those voices and their hopes and fears; their struggles for women's rights, equity, and justice; their stories about life under corrupt politicians; and their aspirations that passive resistance and civil disobedience campaigns were replacing jihadism. With the normalization of Islamic political parties, they now seem to be taking back religion and a culture hijacked so long ago by martyrs and extremists. After all, Ayman al-Zawahiri and Egypt's Islamic Jihad couldn't oust President Hosni Mubarak, but in a mere 18 days a people's revolution of nonviolent protestors put their future into their own hands and did. Tunisia provided the first spark of the Arab Spring when the Jasmine Revolution took down President Zine al-Abidine Ben Ali, a dictator of 23 years, in 28 days.

Robin Wright, in her new book *Rock the Casbah*, describes the Arab Spring as the fourth in a series of pivotal turning points of the Middle East over a century: the collapse of the Ottoman Empire and the formation of Turkey and the Arab states; the 1948 creation of Israel and displacement of Palestinians; and Iran's Islamic revolution that codified fundamentalist dogma. The Arab Spring, it seems, is the swan song for the Ottoman legacy of despots—a transition of power from the old guard to a younger, more democratic-minded generation.

Yet a virtual community of youth and street protests in Tunisia or Morocco are much different from a civil war in Libya or an armed revolt in Syria. "No revolution is executed like a ballet," wrote Martin Luther King Jr. in his book *Why We Can't Wait*. "Its steps and gestures are not neatly designed and precisely performed. In our movement the spontaneity of its pattern was particularly in evidence." But what made the Middle East and North Africa so ripe for this revolutionary improvisation—the Arab Spring?

~

Introduction

Terror in the Name of God

As I was preparing to move from Arkansas to Kenya, I received a call from my mother, Joyce Wilson, shortly after nine o'clock on the morning of April 19, 1995. Her neighborhood in Oklahoma City had just been shaken by a seismic shock wave, from the bombing of the Alfred P. Murrah Federal Building. Perhaps by chance, it was the tenth anniversary of the siege by 300 federal agents of the Arkansas compound of The Covenant, the Sword, and the Arm of the Law, a racist, anti-Semitic group of Christian end-timers. My mother feared, as did I and others, including former CIA head James Woolsey and a spate of news agencies that hastened to hypothesize, that it was the handiwork of Islamic extremists. Our collective fears caused immediate blowback against Muslim Americans.

In Oklahoma City, as the debris was cleared, 168 were dead, including 19 preschoolers who had just arrived at the Murrah building daycare center. Some 450 others were wounded. Like other victims of modern terrorism, their only crime was to be in the wrong place at the wrong time.

Timothy McVeigh, a 27-year-old, transient meth-head and Gulf War vet was arrested for the most deadly terrorist act ever committed in the United States (until September 11). The television images of the devastation reminded us all more of Beirut than the middle of America. In the days that followed, everyone asked how it could happen here.

McVeigh, they say, was inspired by *The Turner Diaries*, a racist, Jew-hating manifesto written by a white supremacist that, among other things, served as a how-to manual for radiological, nuclear, and chemical and biological weapons. The diaries were a second bible for adherents of Identity Christianity. Believers see "Anglo-Saxons as the 'true Israel,' America as a sacred land, and the

1

Declaration of Independence and the Constitution as a God-inspired, Christian inheritance," wrote Jessica Stern in *Terror in the Name of God*.

Identity Christians expect to be present during the Apocalypse but first must "attack the Antichrist, who will become the leader of the world during the end-times," Stern writes. "He will offer the people a false religion and a single world government. The strength of international institutions promoting world government, including the United Nations and the international banks, are indications that the Antichrist is already here, they believe." Al-Qaeda would later describe the same institutions as tools of the "new crusades."

McVeigh was not "born again," but at his trial it came out that he wanted to exact revenge on the federal government for what he saw as big brother over-reach during the Branch Davidian siege in Waco, Texas. Christian, Jewish, and Muslim terrorists all think alike: they use religion to legitimize acts of violence; the end, they believe, always justifies the means. "Every single fundamentalist movement that I have studied in Judaism, Christianity, and Islam is rooted in profound fear," wrote religious scholar Karen Armstrong. McVeigh had accomplished what all terrorists set out to do: instill fear and dread in the target population. But surely no one sees the fringe movements that Timothy McVeigh was aligned with as representative of America or Christianity.

～

The World Trade Center bombing of 1993 made it apparent there was, at least in certain countries and cultures, a rising hostility toward the United States. Even so, for me, the level of anger and agitation didn't really crystallize until the midnineties, when I moved to Nairobi and, with events leading to events, got a foretaste of things to come. Sudan was one of the first places I traveled to from Nairobi, following my wife, who worked in partnership there with the Ministry of Health to reduce the practice of female genital mutilation.

In 1989, field marshal Omar al-Bashir came to power in a military coup, joined at the hip with radical cleric Hassan al-Turabi, the leader of the National Islamic Front. Together they ousted the inept but democratically elected Sadiq al-Mahdi. Subsequently, the dictator and cleric set upon making Sudan the world headquarters for the *ummah*—the international body of Islamists. From Khartoum, they believed, *ummah* would spread to the rest of the world.

Al-Bashir acted swiftly to ban political parties, dissolve parliament, quash the press, and impose the laws of Sharia. He made a public display of emptying into the Nile River all the alcohol from bars, hotels, and homes. Drawn by the promise of a rising Islamic state, in 1992 Osama bin Laden, who had been living in Pakistan and Afghanistan, arrived in Khartoum. He brought along 4 wives,

17 children, a stable of Arabian horses, and bulldozers. Bin Laden promised the people of Sudan an airport at Port Sudan and a 200-mile road in the eastern desert. Al-Bashir and al-Turabi welcomed him with open arms.

Bin Laden settled in on Mek Nimr Street, across from the Ministry of Islamic Affairs, and near the Acropole Hotel, where Joellen and I often stayed. There, between breeding and riding horses on his farm, and going to the racetrack, bin Laden held a *jirga*, a tribal-like assembly, of 50 or more Arab fundamentalists every afternoon. Each evening, bin Laden would slaughter a lamb for these rising jihadists, one of whom would have been Ayman al-Zawahiri, whom bin Laden had befriended in Peshawar, Pakistan.

By April of 1996, the U.S. State Department had placed Sudan on the list of state sponsors of terror. The American embassy in Khartoum had shut its doors, withdrawing staff to Nairobi. Feeling the U.S. pressure over harboring international terrorists, President al-Bashir ordered the expulsion of bin Laden and al-Zawahiri, who had just attempted to assassinate President Hosni Mubarak of Egypt.[1]

As Americans coming and going to Sudan, our being harassed by police and military at the airport was business as usual—heavy on the alcohol searches, always last in and last out. But these slights, unless we were with my wife's colleagues, also happened often in Khartoum. The tension was ratcheted up every Friday after the noon prayer, when mobs of Arabs and Sudanese, wearing djellabas and turbans, would circle the Acropole, chanting and brandishing hate America signs. The first time I heard the annoying commotion I was having lunch with an Australian agricultural aid worker, who spoke Arabic. I remember being taken aback when I found out what the jihadists, a word barely familiar to me at the time, were saying: "Death to America." "But don't worry," my companion said. "They will be finished in another hour."

⌁

The next year, 1997, marked my first trip to Egypt, where Joellen and I spent a couple of weeks before traveling across the Gulf of Aqaba to Jordan and Israel. While in Luxor, by pure chance we learned of an international performance of *Aida*, Verdi's opera of ancient Egypt. It was the 125th anniversary of its world premiere, which had been commissioned by Ismail Pasha in celebration of the opening of the Suez Canal. The stakes were high for Egypt: tourism drives their economy, their main source of hard currency. Suzanne Mubarak, the president's wife, sponsored the event and attended the first night with her husband.

---

1. Although the State Department denies it, there is evidence that Sudan offered to hand bin Laden over to the United States at this time.

Meantime, Ayman al-Zawahiri, who had by now become stateless and fled to Afghanistan, saw the *Aida* performance as an opportunity to decimate Egypt's tourist industry. The Islamic Group, one of the terrorist organizations with which al-Zawahiri was associated, saw tourism as responsible for introducing "alien customs and morals which offend Islam."

Al-Zawahiri had come by his radicalism from the writings of Sayyid Qutb, some say the most influential ideologue the "Islamic revival" has produced. Oddly enough it was an exchange program in the late '40s to the University of Northern Colorado in Greeley, a town meant to be a utopia of family values, that inspired Qutb's extremism. Couples dancing at the college socials, he thought, lacked appropriate modesty, and sexual desire was far too apparent. Nearby Garden City was full of liquor stores and bars, where, to Qutb's dismay, students often quenched their thirst. At the time, the America he saw and the self-image of Americans were substantially different. But that gap narrowed, among many Americans, a few decades later when the same behavior that disgusted Qutb became the target of a fundamentalist Christian movement that has swept the United States.

Qutb's American experience set off an anger that led him to become the voice of the Muslim Brotherhood, an Islamic fundamentalist organization that would spawn Fatah, Hamas, al-Qaeda, the Islamic Group, and dozens of others like them. Imprisoned and executed in the '60s by Gamal Nasser while blaming America and the West for the oppression of Muslims, the martyred Qutb is bin Laden and al-Zawahiri's ideological godfather.

That day in Luxor, due to a recent attack on German tourists in front of the Cairo Museum, there had been cancellations for *Aida*, which meant there were extra tickets. Joellen and I bought a couple of scalped ones at our hotel for the final night. Security was heavy: a brigade of 3,000 police and military spread over Luxor. A special pontoon bridge was built across the Nile to handle the heavy traffic. The route to Hapshepsut's Temple, where the opera was held, was lined with flags and fairy lights and military types in full dress. They stood at attention with that upward-canted, dead-fish-hand salute they do in that part of the world.

Deterred by the massive security, a terrorist attack was averted that week, which would prove to be the luck of the draw for *Aida* attendees. Less than three weeks later, though, six men dressed in black with red headbands, symbolic of the Islamic Group, came over the mountain and entered Hapshepsut's Temple. There was no security to turn them back. Before the massacre was over, 58 foreigners and 4 Egyptians perished. Many bodies were mutilated, while others were shot multiple times in the head at close range. Women, children, and honeymooners—no one was spared in the 45 minutes of uninterrupted slaughter.

When the police arrived, the fleeing attackers were either killed or committed suicide in a nearby cave. No survivors; gone to paradise.

A Swiss investigation determined that al-Zawahiri had planned the massacre and bin Laden had financed it. Egypt was in a state of shock, as were friends of ours who arrived a few days later to an empty, bloodstained temple, the cleanup still ongoing. In Egypt during the '90s, all told over 1,200 people were killed in terrorist attacks. The nexus of a sock hop in Greeley, Colorado, and this kind of carnage is mind-boggling, if not an inscrutable chapter in modern chaos theory.

~

We moved from Nairobi to Hanoi in late August of 1998, but not before the Dar es Salaam and Nairobi embassy bombings. The attacks were the first documented that were al-Qaeda sponsored. Joellen and I were in Madagascar on August 7, the day of the bombings and the eighth anniversary of the arrival of American troops in Saudi Arabia. We returned to Nairobi a few days later with the rubble still smoking.

Joellen had lived there six years and I for more than two; we had both been on numerous occasions to the American embassy on Moi Avenue. While 12 Americans paid the price in the Nairobi embassy, it was innocent Africans who suffered most: over 200 Kenyans were murdered and 4,500 injured, overloading Nairobi's hospitals for weeks. Ordinary Kenyans blamed America as much as they did the Islamic terrorists—as allies they were caught in the middle. Years later, residents of London and Madrid would feel the same when their cities fell under attack.

Gathering with friends on our last nights in Nairobi, we listened to their separate accounts of victims and vaporized bodies: "No bones, no shirts, no hair, no burial," said a psychiatrist friend who counseled victims' families. A lawyer friend working in a downtown firm described the sonic boom that collapsed buildings and blew broken glass for blocks. "Plumes of smoke rose in the air, and shredded paper fell like confetti for half a mile," he said. We talked about why they hated us and of the vulnerability of American embassies worldwide. Bin Laden would later say he wanted to give Americans a dose of what we had been dishing out to Muslims. Yet we all knew, and he and al-Zawahiri must have known, that the retaliation would be swift and substantial.

"But that, as it turned out, was exactly the point," wrote Lawrence Wright. "Bin Laden wanted to lure the United States into Afghanistan, which was already being called the graveyard of empires. The usual object of terror is to draw one's opponent into repressive blunders, and bin Laden caught America at a vulnerable and unfortunate moment in its history."

～

According to instruction manuals left behind, the 19 hijackers who attacked New York and Washington on 9/11 were exhorted to shave their body hair the night before. "Purify your head," it said. "Cleanse it from dross. . . . Be cheerful, for you have only moments between you and your eternity, after which a happy and satisfying life begins."

The manual is a chilling window into the extreme psychological state the 19 terrorists must have shared in the hours leading up to the worst terrorist act in U.S. history. "Keep a very open mind, keep a very open heart of what you are to face," the documents say. "You will be entering paradise. You will be entering the happiest life, everlasting life."

The day the twin towers fell, I had been living in Hanoi, Vietnam, for three years. Although it was obvious bin Laden was the mastermind and going after him in Afghanistan was a no-brainer, the saber rattling about Iraq and Saddam's weapons of mass destruction took hold, paving the way not just for an invasion of Iraq but also for wiretapping, expanded suspension of the writ of habeas corpus, the abrogation of the Geneva Convention on torture, and the USA Patriot Act. Within weeks, the global goodwill for the United States from the carnage of 9/11 had been extinguished. Fear seized the moment in America: gun, gas mask, and burglar alarm sales skyrocketed along with Disney World cancellations. Paraphrasing James Traub, Bush's "Freedom Agenda," the post-9/11 Bush doctrine, was the latest restatement of the idea that Providence had chosen America to ensure liberty for all. The vast majority of the country, including the media, followed Bush's lead like sheep. All told, as reported by the Center for Public Integrity, in the two years following September 11, President Bush and administration officials made 532 false statements about weapons of mass destruction in a campaign that successfully galvanized fear and, thus, American public opinion.

～

Almost four years later, in the summer of 2005, my wife and I moved back to the States. Joellen traveled ahead of me and began a new job in Boston, while I returned to the States by freighter. It was goodbye to my tropical togs of sandals and T-shirts and hello to L.L. Bean and a Red Sox hat. Rather than flying, I chose to take the slow boat, to take measure of every degree of longitude and latitude between Bangkok and Beantown. As with many returning expatriates, an inner voice had been playing a familiar message: "You can't go home again." Perhaps out of caution, which is not my first instinct when traveling or otherwise, I felt the need to acclimate, as one does when going to extreme altitudes. In my decade abroad, friends, family, politicians, and policies had been shuffled and reshuffled until so many of the familiar hole cards were turned upside down, reversed, or replaced by jokers. States were now divided among red and blue, foreign nations were either with us or against us, and many of those with us were leaning toward the latter.

After three-plus weeks on the freighter, which left from Port Kelang, Malaysia, with three stops in China, one in Taiwan, and another in South Korea, we entered the Santa Barbara Channel, a postcard visage of California sunshine, shimmering blue waters, and rugged islands. The baked-earth-colored Sierra Madre drew closer by the second. Gulls gathered in our wake, pelicans streamed by, and flocks of ducks lighted in the clear water of the Channel Island littorals; schooners and light craft tacked the cobalt sea, and the foghorns of working boats blew. Santa Barbara, where I had shared a house on Cota Street in 1972 with a couple of naval-academy-turned-anti-war guys and their girlfriends, came into view.

I never thought returning to America could feel so right, its familiar beauty slapping me silly, fond memories flushing through me like a numbing truth serum, and the warmth of its bosom welcoming me in. The German master came by barking about something, but even his surliness couldn't dash my good feelings. The channel felt like a processional way, and it seemed that all surrounding us was there for this one triumphal moment. Then, Los Angeles came into view, ringed in a rust-colored cloud; the city's linear shapes blurred in a sepia fade. The pilot boat arrived. My cell phone beeped; we were in range. The voices of family and friends, even their recordings, played in my head like a soaring melody.

In minutes my passport was stamped, bags were inspected, and I was gleefully sprinting down the gangway—the 10,000-mile sea journey and ten years abroad was over. A 40-something, blinged-out black guy with gold necklaces, bracelets, and earrings, who talked with my southern accent and said he was originally from New Orleans, gave me a golf cart ride to the gate. He dropped me beneath a lone streetlight to wait for a taxi and said, "Welcome home, man."

~

The Red Sox hat fit just fine, but sitting still during my first year in Boston struck me as an awful lot like being sent down to the minors during the World Series. While I kept hearing about the bounty of Bush's Freedom Agenda, my gut told me that as an expatriate and traveler I had learned more about America from foreign shores than ever I would have while living in the United States.

With every year spent overseas, the moorings of my Yankee egoism had loosened a few more links, until I became more than marginally conscious of the rest of the world. Among other things, that decade abroad revealed that Timothy McVeigh, Mohammed Atta, the end-timers, and the war wizards all too often, by projecting their fears and faith on the rest of us, set forth a black-and-white worldview, one that says you are either for or against us, kill or be killed, paradise or eternal hell. Given those false choices and the nightly streaming U.S. news videos of one-size-fits-all Muslims in an underdeveloped, war-torn region, I felt a welling sense of urgency to go and savor and suffer the living history and cultures of Arabs, Turks, Kurds, Jews, Persians, Armenians, Berbers, and Bedouins, to breathe their air and behold their sacred monuments and to take measure of America's footprint in a 21st-century Middle East.

PART I

~

WARS OF CHOICE

CHAPTER ONE

~

Be Nice to Americans

"You are not going to like this news," predicted my wife as she woke me before dawn. Israel had bombed the Beirut airport, a response to Hezbollah border attacks and the capture of two Israeli soldiers a few days before. My wife was right: I was scheduled to leave for Beirut in three days with a friend, Mark McDonald, a foreign correspondent, for a month-long pleasure trip to Lebanon and Syria.

For two months Mark and I had talked up the day when we would tramp through the crusader castles and classical ruins that overlay the fabled Phoenician cities of Byblos and Tyre. Exploring temples, shrines, mosques, churches, and belief systems then and now—how better to understand a country's people and attitudes than to look at the icons of their past? Maybe we would venture a mountain trek among the medieval monasteries of Bcharre, shadowed by the Holy Cedars of Lebanon, the timbers used to construct old Solomon's temple so long ago. Or we could wander about the rocky, Mediterranean beach enclaves of Beirut and the upscale shops and cafés of the rehabilitated Solidere district, where Maronite Christians and modernized Muslims promenade in peaceful coexistence. It was these fresh shoots of the Cedar Revolution—as Lebanon's fragile new democracy was heralded—that our imaginations had set upon to sense and apprehend.

Now it was stranger than fiction as I watched the live news accounts of Beirut's Rafik Hariri International Airport up in a ball of flames, missiles still thundering into its runway, and hundreds of thousands of refugees fleeing Israel's collective retribution. "This is World War III," proclaimed Newt Gingrich, while Condoleezza Rice called the bombing the "birth pangs of a better Middle East" and the White House proclaimed their desire for peace and a ceasefire as they expedited shipments of precision missiles to Israel.

In stark contrast were the urgent dispatches from David Holdridge, a friend from Hanoi now based in Beirut as the Middle East director of Mercy Corps, and others on the ground. Their first concerns were of impoverished Shia refugees flooding the Sunni and Christian neighborhoods of Beirut, while even greater waves of Shia fled to the mountains, in a predetermined evacuation plan. David was at those camps within days, providing food packages, hygiene kits, and mattresses. For this 34-day war, mercifully, it was these acts of charity, coupled with the forbearance of the many confessional groups of Lebanon, that helped avert another sectarian civil war.

Inexorably, our Middle East pleasure trip was being drawn as a fool's errand. If I had been optimistic about a revitalized, secure Lebanon, with 1.5 million foreign tourists expected in 2006, the pundits, politicians, and intelligence community, from Jerusalem to the Joint Chiefs, were asleep at the switch. With Iran and Syria seeding Hezbollah, the words of one Beirut observer from the '80s had become a Middle East dictum: whenever a cloud gathers in the Arab world, it rains in Beirut.

As the Israeli air-land-sea blockade of Lebanon took hold, Mark improvised and turned south to Mississippi to explore the Blues scene as an idea for a book. As he exited the Memphis airport, he rear-ended an eighteen-wheeler, totaled his rental car, and suffered a neck injury.

Reading the tea leaves, I rerouted to Istanbul, and made my way by bus to Syria, whose embassies in Sudan and Jordan had refused me visas in the late '90s simply because I was American. That was not my worry now. My passport was stamped.

∼

A week later, trundling down the tortuous roads of the Amanus Mountains—the Syrian Gates of Alexander the Great's time, Cilicia, giving way to the Orontes Valley—and with darkness sighing into dawn, my bus arrived in Antakya, the biblical city of Antioch. Thumping arabesque music, hissing brakes, grinding gears, foul smells, and shuffling bodies made for a restless ride that night. The modest elderly Muslim woman who sat next to me, soberly dressed in a traditional chador, alert and upright lest there be an inadvertent touch, was replaced by a twenty-something man sporting an evil eye T-shirt, who used my back as a pillow to bury his moist, bearded face. In this ancient holy land where God is feared more than anywhere, the evil eye talisman is common.

As my seatmate roused, embarrassed by his trespass, he introduced himself as Ruditz. The bus steward splashed us both with eau de cologne. Once fully woken, I recognized Ruditz from the day before at the bus station in Bodrum, a package-tour mecca for Europeans. He had been vacationing with his cheeky Muslim girlfriend. Her form-fitting miniskirt and navel ring had caught my attention.

Turkey was being mentioned as a key player in the much-discussed UN peacekeeping force in southern Lebanon, not least because they were moderate Muslims with diplomatic relations with Israel (becoming more outspokenly pro-Palestinian by the day). Not forgotten in this cultural calculus was the Armenian genocide in Turkey a century ago. Many of the survivors resettled in Lebanon and Syria. And in the Middle East, as we know, memories are like vast minefields, lying in wait, marking people's wrong steps.

After suggesting to Ruditz that he might be Lebanon-bound, out of earshot of his Muslim countrymen he confided, "I am a Christian. Maybe they won't take me." We both laughed, knowing that Christians, who are thinning out around here, are the first to go to the front lines in the Turkish army.

Streams of condensate rolled down the windows as I stepped out into the crisp air and swarm of morning arrivals and departures. While retrieving my rucksack from the heap in the baggage hold, a middle-aged stowaway came to life in a hasty yawn. Holding forth in the distance, a golden halo traced the ashen ridgelines of Mt. Staurin (Mountain of the Cross). It was here, they say, that almost 2,000 years ago a new cult, composed of Jews and pagans, congregated in a limestone grotto to listen to strangers, such as Peter and Paul, tell a miracle story. As the converts multiplied, Aramaic-speaking locals branded them "Christians," lineal ancestors to Ruditz.

∼

Antioch, a former Silk Road entrepôt on the banks of the fabled Orontes, has been a revolving door through which the world's great civilizations and invading armies have passed: Greek, Persian, Roman, Byzantine, Arab, crusader, Mamluk, Ottoman, French, and Syrian. Now, in the stifling summer heat, the river is a silent ribbon of sludge and refuse, with Sunnis on one side and Alawites on the other.

Yet in 1097, when the thundering hooves of the 50,000-strong army of the First Crusade arrived, Antioch was a teeming river port. Its ancient Church of St. Peter had been converted to a mosque, the Holy Sepulchre in Jerusalem was in Muslim hands, and Christian pilgrims were being harassed across the Holy Land. The crusaders were called to arms by Pope Urban and led to battle by Count Bohemund of Taranto. Their first clash was cultural, in Constantinople (Istanbul), where the crusaders were as dismayed by the Greek Byzantines' choice of diplomacy with the Muslim Turks as the Greeks were disgusted with the crusaders' clamor about the holiness of war.

Exhilarated by victory over the Muslim Turks at Nicaea, the crusaders' arrival on the outskirts of Antioch must have seemed auspicious. The crusaders' food supplies, however, were not to last the winter; their Cluniac vision of a pilgrimage, where rich succor the poor, became their worst nightmare. At least half the army starved to death, eating horses, camels, dogs, and rats before perishing. According to several accounts, the poorest fed on animal hides and grain seeds found in manure. The wealthy and powerful equestrian knights were reduced to riding donkeys, scavenging like the rest.

By the time this withered army of Frankish firebrands laid siege to Antioch, steeping the streets in Muslim corpses and chaos, their struggle with death and deprivation had transformed them. Wearing crosses boldly stitched across their tunics, they had become God's new chosen people. "Deus hoc vult!" (God wills it), they exulted, while marching on to Jerusalem, where they soaked the streets in the blood of 30,000 Jews and Muslims. "The Crusader's God was an idol; they had foisted their own fear and loathing of these rival faiths onto a deity they had created in their own likeness and thus given themselves a sacred seal of absolute approval," wrote Karen Armstrong in *The Case for God*. "Crusading made anti-Semitism an incurable disease in Europe and would indelibly scar relations between Islam and the West."

Time—as history along the Orontes tells us—moves on. Antioch became a Latin principality, which survived for almost two centuries. When the Ottoman Empire collapsed after World War I, like the Byzantines a millennium before, religious tolerance in its dominions fell in tandem, spurring an exodus of minorities, Muslim and non-Muslim. According to John Moschos, an itinerant monk of the late 6th century, Antioch the Great in Syria boasted a Christian population of over 100,000. Today, this medieval home of the great patriarchs has fewer than 200 Christian families.

∿

As the only passenger in the *dolmus*, a minibus taxi, I crossed the desiccated Orontes to the old town of Ottoman-era homes and mosques. Nearby is the covered Antioch bazaar, where Arabic is as common as Turkish. Beyond, overlooking the Syrian highway, the cool confines of St. Peter's Cave, the oldest of all churches, had sheltered me from the scorching heat the day before. Beneath a statue of St. Peter, placed there by crusaders eight centuries before, Christian and Muslim pilgrims shared the holy water dribbling from the cave walls.

Historical Antioch and its sun-bleached escarps, once forested with column-bound stylites, the rage of 6th-century Christian ascetics, were in the rearview mirror. We drove by green fields of cotton and corn, shielded by windbreaks of poplars and cedars. Timelessly, big-eared sheep grazed in the stubble of freshly cut wheat fields. Shepherd boys, wrapped like mummies, giving no flesh to the blistering sun or blasts of wind, rode atop donkeys. Soon this agrarian frontier turned to concertina-wired fences, forlorn guard towers, and from there a mile-long queue of trucks. We were at Bab el Hawa, Gate of the Wind.[1]

Falling in line amidst a fog of exhaust fumes, pastoral reverie gave way to anarchic pestering: truckers lashed out at us for our attempts to pass; money changers swarmed like flies; the odd pedestrian cadged cigarettes; and a robed young woman laid her ample breasts over my forearm, which was resting on the door window. Lizard swift, she scooped up my water bottle, gulped a drink, and thrust her calloused palms in my face for food and money—a prostitute for the truckers, perhaps.

Protestations and flurries of hand signals followed us as the *dolmus* driver throttled it in the narrow gap between trucks. He swept by the Turkish check-point, which we cleared as one exits a paid parking lot: a stamp and cheerio.

On the Syrian side, the driver and border police conferred aloud in Arabic, bandying "American" back and forth as if exchanging a radioactive glob. Or was it preferential treatment? There it may be one and the same as an introduction to the *mukhabarat*, the Syrian secret police. As it turns out, the Syrian officials were demanding baksheesh. With my American passport in their hands, like an ATM card signaling easy wherewithal, the driver was obliged to pay.

In the customs building, below a pious portrait of dictator Bashar al-Assad, a greeting sign read: "My Dear Traveller; If you face any trouble please contact the responsible officer . . . Welcome."

Bashar was a promising ophthalmologist in London before his brother Basil was killed in a high-speed, one-man car wreck, and their father, President Hafez al-Assad, whisked him away to command an anticorruption task force. Riding the officially proclaimed success of that call to service, upon his father's death, a grieving parliament rewrote the constitution to catapult Bashar, at age 34, to the presidency. As the president-in-waiting he married London friend Asma Arras, a British-born Sunni of Syrian descent and a rising star in mergers and acquisitions at JP Morgan.

The customs office portrait was a modest introduction to the Soviet-style hagiography adopted by Hafez al-Assad, who anointed himself with such honorifics as Father-Leader, Struggler, and Commander of the Nation. Father and son portraits would appear everywhere—billboards, taxi windows, shop fronts, and kitchen walls—often joined by images of deceased son Basil. Revered in

---

1. Beginning with the 2011 Arab Spring uprisings, thousands of Syrian refugees fled to the safety of Turkey through the Gate of the Wind.

Syria as a cultish, James Bond figure, he is often portrayed in aviator shades and a close-cropped beard—a symbol for coming generations. It is said that, if the secret police aren't watching, then the al-Assads are: the Father, Son, and Holy Ghost.

As for Bashar, he has been faithful to the legacy of his father, to his relatives who have built an empire from inside deals, to his country, and, ironically, to biblical history (from 1 Kings 11: "He was an adversary to Israel . . . and he abhorred Israel, and reigned over Syria"). Modern Syria is mirrored in the heavy-handed and inept policies of father and son.

～

The stony hills of Syria shimmered white like a bed of well-heated coals. Olive groves spread in a monochromatic blaze across the parched plains. Dusty fields were dotted with the burlap tents of the Bedu, the forbears of all things Arabic. These days, these ancient nomads are often a source of cheap migrant labor in the Middle East. They live in slum-like encampments that skirt rural villages in the way salt-of-the-earth Americans find themselves in trailer parks. The Bedu, a people once timelessly woven in a desert setting, have been diminished from the ideal of pastoral greatness.

In these hardscrabble villages, shop signs of Arabic curlicues replaced Latinized Turkish. Windswept huts were crowned with satellite dishes, informing the world's fellaheen (peasants) with real-time news. Bearded men in djellabas and keffiyehs and women in black chadors far outnumbered the secular dress of the Turks. A hazy skyline of modern buildings came into view. Apparent as this cultural transition was, in no time a chamber of commerce billboard greeted us with the news: "Welcome to Aleppo, the Capital of Islamic Culture."

In the midnineties, Mohammed Atta, the leader of the 19 hijackers on September 11, lived in Aleppo, working on his master's thesis in urban planning from a German university. He saw Aleppo as an example in the Middle East of modernity—from the new skyscrapers to Western culture—encroaching on the ancient Arab neighborhoods.

Fiendishly hot, teeming traffic, and dust upon dust was Aleppo at a glance. The taxi driver drew to a stop in front of the Baron Hotel, where a statutory 50-foot banner of President Bashar al-Assad was draped across the second-floor balcony. Next door men abandoned themselves among tables of chessboards, sipping Turkish coffee. The owner daubed the dust from his slice of the street using a liter bottle of water.

Nearby was a seedy complex of cinemas featuring American B movies, luring young men with promo posters of divas in thongs, stretching the strands of free speech in this country. Then again, one of the most popular TV shows in Syria and the Middle East is *Superstar*, a takeoff on *American Idol*, on which a Syrian woman recently won the title of runner-up.

Across the street from the cinema, a popular falafel and doner kebab restaurant prominently displayed placards of Sheikh Hassan Nasrallah, the chief Hezbollah mullah. That these placards appeared everywhere in a matter of days after Israel bombed Lebanon should not have been a surprise. It wasn't fundamentalism: Shias have no favored status in Syria, though their popularity is rapidly growing. This was political Islam.

"Welcome, welcome," said a table full of bearded men, who had assembled around the placards in a visage of patriarchal harmony. Filling the air of this Arab street were the smells of grilled meat and frying fava beans, the din of beeping taxis and men's shouting voices. Waving them off, I imagined here a fuzzy line between reason and folly.

~

The Mazloumian family owns the Baron Hotel. Their ancestors fled here during the Armenian genocide in Turkey. Hundreds of thousands of Armenians perished nearby in the Aleppo Desert. At the time, Aleppo, a melting pot of commerce and confessions, was also a jumping-off point for Edwardian travelers and their steamer trunks going east on the Orient Express. The Baron was their preferred resting place; it was away from the souk and Great Mosque, rural in ambiance, with surrounding gardens and canals. From its balconies hotel patrons are said to have shot down migrating ducks.

Agatha Christie wrote tracts of *Murder on the Orient Express* here, but T. E. Lawrence was their most famous parlor patron. Lawrence's unpaid bill, dated June 8, 1914, is encased in a glass shelf in the Baron's television room, from which the Qatar-based Al Jazeera channel now blares the message of a new Arab revolt, political Islam (not to be confused with extremism in the name of Islam). There were no subtitles, but with frequent mugs of enemy number one—Bush—the message of the Western-attired readers and reporters was understandable. A mere 20 years ago the vast majority of the developing world had no access to global news. Now, we live in the age of information, and America's actions, good or bad, are broadcast on the world stage literally within seconds of occurring—and without American spin.

Walid Malah, the Baron's in-house fixer, minder, and travel agent, sat hypnotized in front of the TV among ten empty, smallish marquetry thrones. Modernity aside, it was this feel of vacancy and melancholy about the Baron that enhanced the sense of being thrown back in time.

Hearing my footsteps, Walid startled to his feet, instantly effusive. His bulging red cheeks and brush moustache framed a broad, toothy smile. His overfed belly spilled through his open shirttail. He was hungry for business, deferential beyond cultural custom: "Welcome, welcome," he punctuated each sentence.

Off the pages of a Dostoevsky novel, behind the desk I found a gloomy, henna-haired woman of pugnacious temperament and looks. Barely tall enough to see over the counter, she fetched a stool to reach the wooden mail slots, once used in Lawrence's time for resident guests. As a uniform, or possibly a fashion statement, she wore a black dress and white blouse, matching her dark-edged eyes and spectral skin.

Next to her sat the Armenian proprietor, "corpulent and clean shaven, respectable like a city official," laboring over a desk full of two-inch-thick ledgers. He never looked up while she slavishly handled the desk, as she had for 40 years. Thumbing my passport, the diminutive desk clerk blurted, "We haven't seen any Americans lately. How many nights?"

"Depends on how much the room is."

"Go look at the rooms with the boy and come back," she said, while summoning the youngish man known as boy. "If you like it, it's 40 dollars."

Comfortably cheerless, Room 201 gave way to a balcony that overlooked the cacophonous street, Sharia al-Baron. Except for the mattresses and sheets, little had changed in the room since Mustafa Kemal Atatürk, the modernizing father of Turkey, roosted there 80 years ago. Remembrances of those days—black-and-white photos of Atatürk donning a fez, sitting atop a camel, and dressed in a tux with his new bride—stared down from the room's imposing walls of peeling plaster. That the adornments seemed to evoke an age of imperial innocence was a passing thought, given the historic bloodlettings between Turks and Armenians, and Ottomans and Arabs.

"Welcome, welcome," Walid greeted me in the downstairs bar, which was crowded with clubby leather chairs. The paint-chipped shutters were flung open to the street. Four Italians perched at the altar-like bar, jabbering above the street noise and drinking Al-Charks, an Aleppo-brewed beer. A Rube Goldberg air conditioner the size of a deep freeze teetered on a small bar table, blowing frosty air in our faces and on out the window.

Over tea and a bag of pistachios, Walid—with a cell phone, a son who drives, a friend who rents cars, and an address book of every guesthouse from here to Damascus—began negotiating the cost of my travels in Syria. The bar was his office. There would be no invoice, only cash and a handshake. All business, his expression betrayed nothing.

On more than one occasion during our parley, the "Syrian tongue"—as the ancient Egyptians characterized the indigenes' penchant for changing the deal—seemed also to be a modern truth. Once in some stage of agreement, Walid shifted the conversation to security issues.

"It is okay for Americans to travel in Syria. There is no problem. I take one last week to the Iraq border."

"So should I tell people I am from Canada?"

"If you like, but it's okay not to. It's that crazy Bush who is a problem. We are not a 'rogue nation,' as he says. Besides, the government tells everyone to welcome Americans."

I had heard of the Syrian government mandate to "be nice to Americans." A friend told me of a local bumper sticker: "Don't buy American goods but it's okay to talk to Americans."

⌒

Late that afternoon, near sunset prayer time (*maghrib*), Walid accompanied me to the Great Mosque. We had settled on the money so he was ecstatic as we approached the mosque that was constructed in 710 CE, only ten years after the fabled Ummayad Mosque in Damascus—both eloquent testament to the deep religiosity that long ago transformed the Arab world.

In school-of-fish unison, emerging from the street, braces of men holding hands or hooking arms entered the north gate of the Great Mosque. Clusters of women arrived separately, their heads cowled and bodies cassocked, absent as nuns among these men, avoiding too much worldly interaction; but a far cry from the hushed congregants gathering in the sanctuary of a church. The open architecture gave way to a hubbub of walking, talking, praying, tea and coffee drinking, fraternizing, and faith in delicate balance.

The sky-blue and beige-tiled courtyard still sizzled from the broiling heat. A steady stream of the prayerful padded barefoot to the ablutions fountains at one end. In the opposite direction, the 1,000-year-old minaret loomed like Damocles' sword in an earthquake-inflicted lean. Nearby, in the shaded colonnades, older men—dressed uniformly, in white cotton gowns and matching prayer caps—slouched in plastic chairs in their Sufi trances, drunk on the suras being chanted, like Tibetans entranced by the mantra of *mani padma om!*

"No matter how many times we hear the call, it still gives us the creeps," an Australian couple complained to me back in Ephesus, Turkey. The pub-crawling duo was naive, but they were not Muslim-haters. The sinister valence they describe comes from decades of Western news producers, when reporting violence in Muslim countries, setting up their stories with a shot of the mosque and a soundtrack of the call to prayer. The Aussies' revulsion was as subliminally inspired as the thirst for a Coca-Cola in the movies was once induced with an ad agent's subtle flash of the drink image on the screen.

We uninitiated, indeed, don't appreciate the tonal beauty of Arabic, a language with an impressive pre-Islamic poetic tradition. Like Hebrew, Arabic is a sacred language, God's own spoken words.

"The Koran was not meant for private perusal but for liturgical recitations," said religious scholar Karen Armstrong. "When Muslims hear a *sura* chanted in the mosque, they are reminded of all the central tenets of their faith." Such rituals of transcendence—"non-empirical realities" that give meaning to the faithful—are universal in religion.

Inside this ancient prayer hall, a scoreboard-sized digital clock told the prayer times; otherwise the place held a timeless ambiance. This great room of Italian marble columns and crystal chandeliers was devoid of furniture but patchworked in colorful carpets of every design, on which bearded Sufis prostrated in meditation. More men were scattered around the mihrab—the marble niche in the wall that indicates the direction of Mecca—touching their heads to the floor in prayer. Separately, women circled the glittering tomb of Zacharias, the father of John the Baptist, a holy figure to Muslims. In the 9th century, Muslims began collecting and enshrining the body parts of saints from here to India. They say only Zacharias's head is entombed here, but like many shrines in the Holy Land, this is surely more religious allegory than reality. It is of these not-so-animated shrines that Sunni revivalists and Wahabist influencers of al-Qaeda condemn the veneration. Meantime, pilgrims' cameras flashed, capturing these shrines-as-idolatrous-images for posterity. (The Jewish religion does not allow graven images in their synagogues either.)

Walid led me out of the sacred halls through an imposing wooden door, and a medieval passageway, into the free-for-all bustle of the Ottoman-era souk. The hive-like hum of shoppers and the assault of pungent smells drew me in like a floating cork in the crowd's slipstream. Soon the call to prayer sounded. The praises of Allah rang forth. The souk emptied, shops were abandoned, and there were no more whispers of "mister, mister." A religious neutron bomb had gone off. We departed.

～

That evening, a few blocks from the Baron, I found an ice cream and pastry shop filled with young couples, men in snappy civvies and women in colorful hijabs. The Internet café on the second floor was all men, mostly student age, and no foreigners. The computer I was assigned was still fresh with porno images.

By choice, I read the news of the war in Lebanon: Ambulance bombed by the Israelis, killing women and children. Bush and Blair were in week 2 of their alternate reality: peace soon, but not now, they chorused across the Atlantic.

Hoping to find Skype, I approached the cashier who didn't understand my patois of basso baby talk and hand gestures.

From across the room, a local man, who said he was living in Saudi Arabia, spoke up. "Where are you from?"

Again, hesitantly, I squeaked out, "America."

An uncomfortable silence followed. Then, head by head, the room full of men turned to apprehend the elephant in the room, giving me the hairy eye. Wars and sanctions aside, that Syria was being referred to by Washington as a "junior varsity axis of evil" was not going over well here, nor was Bush's irresponsible use of the term "crusade" to describe the War on Terror, perceived in the Middle East as a war on Muslims.

"We like Americans," the man said, smiling, "but not George Bush. He has caused us much hardship." His face was no longer friendly but twisted in revulsion.

"I know," I told him, "but I didn't vote for him."

He didn't respond, unfazed by the finer points of democracy. All Americans, by extension, were to blame for Bush.

The anonymity one enjoys in travel, shedding the stereotypes of one's own culture to learn another, was threatened here. So, rather than falling into the trap of being the American agent provocateur again, it was time to identify myself as Canadian. Unknowingly, I would be practicing the ancient Shia artifice of *taqiyya*—dissembling about my identity.

⌒

Friday morning, the Muslim holiday (Jumu'ah), when all men must congregate for prayer in the mosque, Walid's son Mohammed picked me up at the Baron. His ride was a 1980, two-toned Opel, royal blue, and trimmed out in rust. His belly, from which jolliness seemed to rise to his smiling, chubby face, pressed against the steering wheel.

Soon we were circling Aleppo's polestar, the citadel, which was clouded in the dust of a fleet of dozers, dredging the Byzantine moat. It looked like a working quarry, but as the air partly cleared, a dusty daguerreotype of crenellated ramparts, bridges, and apparitional figures in black robes came to life.

Legend has the prophet Abraham over 4,000 years ago stopping atop the citadel to milk his cows on his journey south to Canaan. By one account, poor villagers would gather at the foot of the citadel—near where I had taken respite in the Ottoman-era hammam (bathhouse) the day before to have the grit sanded and peeled from my body with steel brushes—and Abraham would distribute milk to them. In anticipation of this daily benevolence, the villagers would assemble and chant, "Ibrahim haleb" (Abraham has milked). Today, Haleb is the Arabic name for Aleppo.

Motoring on with Mohammed, we pushed north through New Aleppo—wide boulevards, palm trees, and prim tenement buildings. Condos were selling here for a pasha's ransom. It's where the moneyed Christian families live, mostly Armenian. Like the Jews, Armenians are of the ancient merchant class in the Middle East. Because Armenians lay no proprietary claim to the Holy Land, I was told, they are welcome in Syria.

We bucketed along the empty highway, twisting through limestone hills, where we stopped for brief tromps through the famous Dead Cities: pre-Islamic, late antiquity communities, with tumbled archways, Ionian columns, Roman tombs, Byzantine domes, and churches, all gone to seed but for the goatherds and Bedus encamped nearby. Over 600 of these cities can be found in northern Syria, with no hint of why they were abandoned. Water? Pestilence? War?

～

We soon arrived at Qala'at Samaan, the holy mountain where St. Simeon the Stylite (*stylos* means pillar in Greek) took refuge atop a limestone column from overly curious pilgrims. He did so for 37 years, they say, becoming the most famous man of his time.

Few visitors had arrived on this holy Friday. After all, with wars to the east in Iraq and west in Lebanon, tourism wasn't exactly flourishing. There was, however, a European man dressed as a Bedu. When I asked the gatekeeper about business, he averted his eyes and said, "I think you know."

"You mean Iraq and Lebanon?"

"Yes. Bush blames Syria for everything."

As we explored these ruins, my guide sketched out this storied and eccentric monk, St. Simeon. The son of a shepherd, he was born in Kalikya, Turkey, around 390 CE, a time when the ascetic movement was flowering and monks were retreating to the Syrian Desert to meditate on scriptural texts. At 17, he traveled to Teleda, a monastery near Antioch, where he described himself to the abbot as "low and wretched," in need of salvation. While there, due to his severe mode of life, his feats of endurance—fasting, sleeplessness, and baking in the sun—created bad blood (and jealousy) among his fellow monks.

Hence he moved to Telanissos, a monastery now known as Deir Samaan (Monastery of Simeon), at the foot of Qala'at Samaan, where he lived for three years on a diet of soaked lentils and water. His extreme ascetic lifestyle, his apostle-like conviction, attracted the attention of pilgrims, the forerunners of modern tourists, from "Britain to the Persian empire, Arabs, Romans, Greeks, Gauls, Spaniards, Ethiopians and Armenians."

While the pilgrims sought his blessing, he searched for more solitude. Like a cat scared up a tree, he built his first "pulpit atop a pillar." As the story goes, his celibacy turned him into a diehard misogynist who even disregarded his mother when she came to see him. (Technically his pillar was a monastery, in which women were not allowed.)

As the decades passed, St. Simeon felt the need for a taller pillar, one over 60 feet high. From this uncomfortable roost, where legend has him chained to a railing lest he fall in the night, he shouted exhortations down the column to pilgrims gathered round the two-tiered plinth; one can imagine him, in a Christlike imitation, or even like the Delphic oracle, up high and close to heaven, issuing the words of God.

Apocalyptic speculations, redemption, original sin, exorcising demons, healing the sick, and raising the dead must have been on their minds (as lightning and toilet habits were mine). According to Marius Kociejowski in his book *The Street Philosopher and the Holy Fool: A Syrian Journey*, St. Simeon's influence was catholic:

> [He] was involved in social work, spoke on behalf of slaves, in many instances securing their release, settled family disputes, sought refuge for orphans and widows, delivered the oppressed from their oppressors, had taxes remitted, unjust policies reversed and food distributed to the poor, engaged in delicate negotiations concerning ecclesiastical policy, and even took part in matters of foreign policy, mediating for example, between the Byzantine emperor and unruly Bedouin tribes.

He was both judge and jury. Today his once hallowed pillar is a nub, having been chipped away by pilgrims, those original tourists.

St. Simeon died on the spot in 459 CE. Yet amid intrigue to prevent armed Arab disciples from taking the ascetic's corpse to their own burial grounds, an army of 600 Gothic soldiers arrived with Martyius, the patriarch of Antioch. Five days later, thousands thronged the streets in mourning, sprinkling spices over those who escorted the saint. After a negotiation with Emperor Leo of Constantinople, St. Simeon was buried at the church of Constantine in Antioch the Great.

Beginning in the day of St. Simeon and reaching to modern times, every Christianized tribe, country, or empire, according to its fears or hopes, has perverted the theological teachings of the apostles and the peaceful and virtuous beliefs of the primitive Christians, with saints, miracles, monks, popes, martyrs, relics, ritualists, demons, spirits, angels, the whore of Babylon and a new Jerusalem. The paganism of the Romans and Greeks, all but destroyed by the time of St. Simeon's death, was replaced by a continuum of revelation, superstition, and sacrifice, which, in many respects, has added up to sainthood by the sword. Given this theological shift, today churches from Mexico to the

United States, Ireland to France, Serbia to Bulgaria, and Lebanon to Syria are one with canton or country. In *The History of the Decline and Fall of the Roman Empire*, Edward Gibbons writes that "the conduct of nations requires and deserves the celestial powers of the Gods or of the Genii."

And so the supernatural gifts of St. Simeon live on. With the patronage of Roman-Byzantine emperor Zeno, after 15 years of slave labor an audacious pilgrimage center, a cruciform church, laid out along the cardinal points and composed of four basilica buildings, each in its own right grandiose, was erected on the stub of St. Simeon's pillar.

For almost six centuries pilgrims flocked to the church, entering through the triumphal archway southwest of the baptistery. Bedouins brought their dromedaries and sheep, chanted and danced to the sound of drums, while ritually circling the iconic pillar. Greek, Roman, Byzantine, and Maltese crosses remain etched in the basilica lintels as imprimaturs to this heroic ascetic.

When the Islamic invasion of Syria occurred in the 8th century, the Byzantines entrenched, and the mountaintop church became known as it is today, Qala'at Samaan, or Fortress of Simeon. Last sacked by the Islamic Fatimids in 1017, Qala'at Samaan was never again used as a Christian worship site. Yet St. Simeon the Stylite remains a venerated figure in the Roman Catholic and Eastern Orthodox churches, commemorated with icons and an annual feast day on September 1.

~

From Qala'at Samaan, we drove up the Afrin to the top of Syria, on the Turkish border, home to the Kurds. Although some are now Christians, the vast majority of the 1.5 million Kurds living here are Muslim, with an attitude of independence toward Damascus. No love is lost from either direction. Kurds arrived in Syria from Turkey by the hundreds of thousands during the Kurdish uprisings of the '20s and '30s. From here, to the east and north, they occupy lands that overlap four nations: Syria, Turkey, Iraq, and Iran. It's a European-made jigsaw puzzle, with pieces that hardly fit for all the dysfunctional borders.

Ironically, it was Kurdish warriors Nureddin and Saladin who successfully led the Islamic campaigns against the crusaders, claiming territory from here through Damascus to Jerusalem and Cairo.

Near the east bank of the Afrin River, irrigation pumps thrummed above the whoosh of a breeze. Kurdish women wearing Gypsy scarves and colorful double skirts, ranging like baggy hoops, worked cotton, corn, and sunflower fields. Orchards of pomegranate, apples, and cherry flourished alongside autumn-hued vineyards, all tracing the course of the Afrin. Olive orchards braided the rolling hills, fencing the fecund valley. Olives are not just a food here but a symbol of abundance, of holiness, of that which anointed Christ and others.

I fell in with a herd of long-haired sheep on the chalky, winding trail up Ain Dara, an archaeological mound inhabited by Neanderthals over 50,000 years ago. Most famously, though, it was the Bronze-Iron Age neo-Hittites who settled here circa 1,000 BCE. Yet the accumulated remains of the large tell covers many historic periods, including the Muslim invasion almost two millennia after the Hittites.

Crowning the hilltop is the Aramaean temple (a kingdom that traded with Israel during David and Solomon's time), featuring a striking limestone and basalt plinth of lions and sphinxes, along with four giant footprints. These lion images are said to be symbols of Ishtar, the Semitic goddess of fertility.

As the human migration to cities took place (1,000 to 200 BCE), stepping up the urgency for martial skills and new expressions of religious belief, religions from Rome to Greece to India became more patriarchal and monotheistic. Heroic pagan goddesses such as Ishtar disappeared. This mirrored a decline in the standing of women.

The holy ones are always turning over—goddesses, rabbis, patriarchs, sheikhs, and ayatollahs—thus the constant ebb and flow of religious tensions and communities. Gone to seed are the ancient gathering places—the markets, the inns, and the Greek and Roman cities. The pagan worship sites have been recycled into churches, synagogues, or mosques, from which the ancient ideas of the holy ones are called forth to fire the hatreds of modern times.

CHAPTER TWO

∼

Refugees from Iraq and Lebanon Flee to Syria

Two days later I was having coffee with Abdullah, the madcap manager of a backpacker guesthouse in Hama, only a couple of hours south of Aleppo. Mohammed had dropped me off that morning after a sweep through Apamea, a colonnaded former Roman city.

Abdullah, dressed in jeans and a T-shirt, swept his hair back in a tousled pompadour and sported a well-groomed goatee. His British accent was as disarming as his chain smoking and cheeky opinions, often tendered in a Western idiom. When I inquired about his religion, he said, "Syria honors all religions," before calling out to his brother, "Are we Sunni?"

A muffled response came back in Arabic, which Abdullah translated as "I don't know what we are." (For reasons not so apparent to me, he keeps his faith on the down low.)

Sunnis represent 65 percent of the population here, just as Shias in Iraq account for the same ratio. And like the minority rule of Sunnis in Iraq before "liberation," Syria is ruled by Alawites, a nominally Muslim, minority sect from the coastal hills of Syria. The Alawite religion blends aspects of Shia Islam, Christianity, Zoroastrianism, and paganism, even believing in a peculiar brand of reincarnation. It is their practice of religious dissimulation, or *taqiyya*—disguising their beliefs in order to fit in (as I was doing by calling myself Canadian and Abdullah was doing by not knowing what he was)—that led one Sunni fundamentalist to mock their faith: "In short, their only invariable doctrine is to ensure plentiful supplies of food, drink, and sex." It was a fitting description for Abdullah.[1]

---

1. It should be noted that Osama bin Laden's mother, Alia, was an Alawite from Latakia, Syria. At age 14, she became Mohammed bin Laden's fourth wife. In keeping with tradition, Osama's first wife, Najawa Ghanem, was also 14, from his mother's village here in Syria.

President Hafez al-Assad, an Alawite, came to power in a coup d'état staged by a radical wing of the Ba'ath Party. It was 1970; the loss of the Golan Heights to Israel was a fresh wound to Syrian pride and to Arab honor, one from which Syria has yet to recover. A decade later, when sectarian violence erupted in Hama between Alawites and Sunnis, al-Assad responded with a bloodbath for the Muslim Brotherhood, the local version of the Sunni fundamentalist movement that brought us Fatah, Hamas, and al-Qaeda. By no surprise, they resented his minority rule. When the Syrian T-62 tanks and al-Assad's Alawite-controlled army withdrew from the banks of the fabled Orontes, as many as 20,000 Sunnis were dead.[2]

Abdullah was here during the massacre of '82 but saw its outcome as positive.

"Oh, yes. I had friends who were killed, but at that time people lived in fear. They [Sunnis] were bombing buses and public places. Now we don't have that. We can walk the streets at four in the morning. It's much better."

Sheikh Hassan Nasrallah, the secretary-general of Hezbollah, is a man of "God, guns, and government," wrote Robin Wright in *Dreams and Shadows*, "a cross between Iranian revolutionary leader Ayatollah Khomeini and Latin America's Che Guevara, a mix of charismatic Islamic populist and a wily guerilla tactician." Abdullah and I talked about how ubiquitous the Nasrallah posters were.

"Isn't the 'Arab Street' crazy? Those posters were never here, and now these people are into it. But foreigners compare Osama bin Laden to Nasrallah. We never heard of this bin Laden until September 11. We don't know him here. Nasrallah is not the same. Bin Laden is Sunni and hates Shias. They like Nasrallah because he stands up to Israel. It's not the '67 Six Day War. These guys are winning; it's two weeks now."

"Really? Tell me more."

"Think about it," he shouted, pointing his forefinger to his temple. "The elephant [America] is trying to step on the mouse, but the mouse keeps slipping through his feet. Then the elephant stomps randomly, hoping to get lucky." Stomp, stomp, stomp, he danced around the room in great fury, chasing the elusive yet triumphant mouse beneath the coffee table and couch.

"Bravo. Now I get it, more coffee."

The sun was falling. I could hear the street filling with people. Abdullah's star performance had faded into conspiracy theories about September 11, which are not uncommon here or in Europe: Hezbollah television station Al Manar said it was the work of Israeli agents, while in France, the bestselling

---

2. In the 2011 Syrian uprising, as thousands of demonstrators took to the streets, President Bashar al-Assad, like his father, dispatched tanks and soldiers for a weeklong assault on Hama. But, six months on, it is nearby Homs, with up to 9,000 civilians and military defectors killed so far, that has received the worst of the brutal crackdown and bombardment by the Syrian army.

L'effroyable imposture claimed White House complicity in the attacks on the World Trade Center. Though it sounds fantastically bizarre to most in the United States, including me, the fact that these theories are held up as truth should be a cautionary lesson about American credibility.

In talking to Abdullah it was clear as day that the Syrians' implacable hostility toward Israel gives them common purpose; otherwise, political and national unity here is a polite fiction, a means of survival.

~

That evening I walked the old town, which was rebuilt after the massacre of '82. The wooden houses that once overhung the Orontes River (first visited in Antioch) were destroyed. Yet its timeless waterwheels, *norias*, still churn the same crème de menthe water as they did in medieval times. Given the slow-moving rivers in Syria and most of the Near East, these wooden waterwheels were used for both irrigation and grinding grain for flour. Today, *norias* are more ornamental than industrial.

Dromedaries blanketed in wine-colored pads stood hobbled in the *norias'* shadow— photo ops for the evening's visitors. A bead salesman in a white turban worked out of a blue wooden cart, his stones displayed in bulging piles, a sparkling version of the mounds of purple pistachio and amber cashews being sold across the street.

A portable tea hawker wore a red fez, the black baggy pants of Kurdish men, and a bold brush mustache. Strapped around his waist was a customized silver belt with seven cupholders. Bandoliered across his back was a three-foot-high silver teapot. The spout was filled with white and red roses thrusting above his head in a cockade of petals. Sprinkled with fountains and flower gardens, this riverside medley seemed more like a *Mary Poppins* set than a massacre site.

Across the street, barking mongrels, the steady buzz of shoppers, and the cries of hawkers brought the open-air souk to a dinning pitch. The tasty smells of food stalls coupled with the musk odor of markets overwhelmed me while simultaneously drawing me in. It was one grand street buffet: here a lamb roll, there a falafel fresh from the frying pan, and next door some *bor'ma* (pistachios wrapped in fine noodles).

The view was circular. The Orontes sparkled, falling to the north, spinning the *norias* like gilded metronomes. The heat had risen to the stars, and the horizon faded from pumpkin yellow to darkness. The sounds and smells of the market guided me back to my guesthouse.

At breakfast an extraordinarily fat Frenchman wearing shorts joined me at a long table. Next to him, an attractive South Korean woman in ass-hugging cutoffs took a seat. The contrast was stark: she, cool, petite, and attractive at

90 pounds; he, 300 pounds, daubing his sweaty cheeks at seven in the morning. Over tea, toast, and eggs, it occurred to me that none of us were a neat fit here, where locals think of men in shorts as half dressed, of women as plain profane, and of Americans as immoral by nature. I mused at the myriad ways—clothes, touching, greeting, and tone—in which a non-Muslim can walk into a Muslim home and unconsciously offend somebody, whereas the opposite scenario is often a nonevent.

The Korean had been traveling for six months. She complained to me of harassment in Serbia, in Turkey by Kurds, and here by young men on the streets. Meanwhile, Abdullah took me aside to tell me she needed a ride to Palmyra.

"If she will put on a chador she can ride with me. Otherwise I'm carrying too much baggage [American] as is."

"Yeah, those Bedu will chew her up out in Palmyra. You better go it alone," Abdullah advised.

⁓

Shouldering my duffel bag, I hurried down the stairs. Abdul waited for me near the old clock tower. He was polishing his Tiffany jewel: a white, chromed-out 1952 Pontiac Eight, five in the floor. Under the hood, the original V-8 had been replaced by a 2,000 cc Nissan. He had it tricked out with automatic windows, a broken DVD player, a digital clock, a Kenwood stereo, and faux leather seats. The wire wheels sparkled like roundels of whirling silver.

Abdul took my duffel bag. In the same motion he opened the door with a remote, brandished with the drama of a conjurer pulling out a rabbit. He then assumed the driver's seat as a king would his throne, gloating all the while. He adjusted the wooden prayer beads swinging from the rearview before taking off.

As for traveling beneath the radar, I may as well have been the Korean girl in a miniskirt. I couldn't have stuck out more with an American flag wrapped around the antenna.

Abdul was 58, handsomely gray, lean, and ramrod straight, with a tendency to puff his chest, filling his short stature with confidence. He has owned the Pontiac Eight for 32 of the 40 years he has been driving.

We drove west into the mountains, toward the strategic divide known as Homs Gap, between the Anti-Lebanon Range in the south and Jebel Ansariyya in the north. In the plains we passed densely populated Sunni villages, more traditional than Aleppo or Damascus. Most of the men wore the red-and-white-checkered keffiyehs of Palestinian peasants; and women, black chadors. Sheep hides dried on the side of the road in the sweltering heat as villagers made their way on foot and by bus to a dusty, makeshift market. Compared to Hama, the standard of living was much lower and reflected in every way.

The scene shifted with unexpected swiftness. We turned off the Tarsus highway, ascending the Jebel Ansariyya foothills. The roadside was jauntily carpeted in purple and yellow wildflowers. Climbing higher, apple orchards sprawled next to tracts of wheat, all artfully terraced along the abrupt slopes. The curvy, threadlike road twisted through prim Christian villages, over 30 in the area. Stone and stucco houses were fresh with white or pastel paint; porches and shuttered windows were perked up with potted flowering plants. Women wore jeans; young girls dressed in shorts. It could have been a summer day in the Italian Alps.

As we arrived at St. George's monastery, coming into view through a dreamy haze was the fairy-tale-like promontory of Krak des Chevaliers, the famous crusader citadel that T. E. Lawrence once called "the finest castle in the world." I was met in the courtyard of the "new church" by a young man named George, who told me he was named for the saint, that immortal who mounts a white horse and protects Christian and Muslim travelers alike from their enemies, each faith taking away their own narrative of miracles. St. George is said to be of Palestinian origin, executed by Romans in the 3rd century for tearing up a decree forbidding Christianity. For Muslims, Khidr (St. George) is also alive and well, often found at the center of miracles.

A monastery was first built on this site in the 6th century. Inside the chapel, women were lighting candles, nuzzling the carved wood iconostasis, crossing themselves in prayer, and rubbing the icons—touching from the mundane adherent to the transcendental image and back. George and I took seats on the back row, where it was wine cellar cool.

We talked about the war and Hezbollah, the Party of God.

"I like Nasrallah and Hezbollah," he said. "Israel is bombing ambulances, killing women and children. When my father was in the army his best friend was a Muslim named Ali. Now my older brother is called Ali. We love Nasrallah and live as brothers with the Muslims."

"What about the Assads?"

"The father was a good man, but not good with people. Bashar likes getting out with the people, all kinds, Muslim and Christian. He has been here twice."

It was hard to tell if this was a true love affair with Hezbollah and the al-Assads or fear of the secret police. But George never blinked or offered a conspiratorial whisper. In 2006, al-Assad "won" another seven-year term, with a 97 percent majority. Although he was the only candidate, there is a quiet sentiment among Syrian Christians, who are 10 percent of the population, that the devil they know is better than some Iraq-style democracy that targets minorities and Christians.[3]

---

3. In the summer of 2011, when the armed resistance of the Free Syrian Army was formed, Christians and Alawites took the side of the government and al-Assad.

Before going downstairs to the "old church," George avowed that along with the ancient books, amphorae, crosses, and icons, there were original documents in the basement, written by an early caliph, which asserted that Mohammed forbade fighting among Christians and Muslims.

Unobtrusive as an intruder can be, I padded into the 800-year-old Greek Orthodox chapel. It was cavernous and crowded with men in suits and women dressed to the nines, in strapless tops with golden crosses hung like a coat of arms around their necks. In the center of the chapel, away from the ebony wood iconostasis, a priest in a gray habit was conducting a baptism. Other than the family's apparel, the clock was stuck in a 2,000-year-old Christian practice that, for an infant, depending on denomination, can signify anything from a means of grace and a covenant with Abraham (not unlike circumcision) to guaranteed salvation.

That I was a year old and have no recollection of my own baptism, that I left the church over 40 years ago, and that I would later give my kids a pass on baptism (though my daughter was recently baptized at age 30) left me curious enough to see what I had been missing.

On cue, the parents and godparents stripped the contented three-month-old of his striped pink gown and swathed him in a white linen sheet. The priest grabbed the baby as I would a sack of potatoes and dunked him three times while saying, "In the name of the Father, Amen. And of the Son, Amen. And of the Holy Spirit, Amen." And then everyone did what sounded like a war cry, but must have been a gung ho "Hallelujah!" Resurrected and cleansed, wrapped in the white linen, anointed with olive oil, blessed with confessions of faith and signs of the cross, the helpless infant was hysterical for the next ten minutes. A reception followed with gifts, wine, and food. Godspeed to the little critter, I said to myself, as I slipped away, pondering the inseparability of ritual and religion.

⌒

A prosperous Muslim enclave has sprung up next to the crusader castle, with hillside mansions built by oil barons from Bahrain, Qatar, United Arab Emirates, Kuwait, and Saudi Arabia. Yes, the times have changed. At the entry gate to Krak des Chevaliers, rather than images of the titans of the Crusades—Sultan Saladin; Prince Tancred, regent of Antioch; or Richard the Lionheart—there were rock-star-size posters of contemporary local legends, Sheikh Nasrallah and Hafez and Bashar al-Assad, set against a mural of St. George on his white horse. It was the incongruity of this fairy-tale place that transfixed me.

A reluctant, if not surly, guide shepherded me up the cobblestone horse ramp, through vaulted hallways and rooms of Gothic arched ceilings. We climbed the battlements to the many towers that hover above the moat, now a ribbon of pea-green sludge. The sweeping view of the Anti-Lebanon Range and the Bekaa Valley of Lebanon was painterly, but according to news reports, the Bekaa was still being heavily bombed. From this castle aerie, at the moment, I couldn't see or hear the F-16s.

At the time of the Crusades there were over 2,000 soldiers of the Knights Hospitallers, with stables for 400 horses, housed here. Stored in the armory were mounds of steel balls, once catapulted from the imposing 60-foot walls. It was during the early Crusades that European warriors first discovered that if gunpowder, invented by the Chinese a millennium before, was contained and directed, it could propel their steel balls to maim and kill.

Secret entrances, iron gates, hot oil vats, dungeons, and round tables for the knights all fed the intrigue. Everyday life at this castle was amply provided for: water wells, windmills, a commercial kitchen, wine vats, tandoori ovens, warehouses of food, and olive presses. There was even a chapel adorned with mosaics and frescos but later converted to a mosque, and a Turkish bath, now stagnating in a soup of slime.

"Where did the women stay?" I asked the guide.

"There were no women here."

"You're sure."

"Never."

"If you say so."

In the industrial-sized crusader kitchen, a Syrian-Canadian family overheard me speaking to the guide. In Arabic they asked him where I was from.

"Canada," the guide responded. (I had told him I was Canadian.)

"We're from Montreal," said the elder son, switching to unaccented English. "You don't sound like you are from Canada," he ventured, having picked up on my drawl.

"Southern Canada. Windsor," I shot back, with a vague smile, but wanting to ask if they had any extra maple leafs.

The conversation shifted, but as the Syrian-Canadian family walked away I heard them tell a snarl of youthful Muslims that I was American. From there, the youngsters shadowed me through the courtyard and the converted chapel, now a mosque, and up the command tower stairs, skunk-eying me and spoiling for a confrontation all the way.

"Welcome, welcome. We love America," said a woman in her mid-20s, wearing a chador and a mock grin, as we topped the castle ramparts. "Only an American would come to Syria now. A Syrian would never go to America." I had been caught out.

"That's not true," I said, once again admitting the obvious. "There are many Syrians and Lebanese living in America, and they travel back and forth."

She was from Tartus, on the Syrian coast, an hour's drive. With her were three women and men, all from Tripoli, refugees from the bombing.

"Roads, bridges, people are being bombed," weighed in the brown-haired, blue-eyed, freckle-faced woman from Lebanon. With those fair looks, in her blue jeans and pink blouse, she could have been from Kansas. Meantime, two of the men held up fists, and, in Arabic, hurled invectives at me that were surely meant to be fighting words.

"Are you followers of Nasrallah?" I asked the girls, faking nonchalance.

"We love him," the woman in jeans shouted back. "Do you love Israel? Do you love Jews? Do you like bombing ambulances and women and children?"

"I don't care for any war," I said, trying to quash the tension.

Of course, this was not the place or time for rational discourse. Their reaction to me was born out of emotion—and my take was pure imagination. Here, passion precedes everything, and the line between anti-Israel and anti-Semitic is a porous one, if existent at all. That genie is not going back in the bottle anytime soon.

⌇

What is known is that Jews coexisted here in peace under Muslim rule for 1,200 years, albeit as second-class citizens. Then 19th- and 20th-century pogroms of Europe and Russia, the ascendant nationalism of Middle Eastern countries, and the Jewish genocide by the Nazis shook the territorial status quo of Palestine. The anti-Semitism avowed by Hitler and the Nazis, while finding resonance in the Middle East (the Muslim Brotherhood distributed Arabic translations of *Mein Kampf* in the '30s), crossed a fault line of consciousness when Palestine became the State of Israel in 1948, commonly referred to as *al-nakba*, the "catastrophe."

Given that decolonization was occurring worldwide and that the Holocaust was still fresh, it was a unique moment of grace allowed to Israel.

Two decades later in the '67 Six Day War, given its name by Israel after the six days of creation but known by Palestinians as *an-naksab*, the "setback," the malignity swelled: 400 aircraft belonging to Egypt, Syria, Jordan, and Iraq were destroyed in one day; Egypt lost the Sinai Peninsula and Gaza Strip; Jordan gave up the West Bank and East Jerusalem; and Syria lost the Golan Heights. It was at this time that blind American support for Israel took hold, partly as a Cold War alliance, but today for no apparent moral or geostrategic purpose.

Honor lost, even as temporary as "setback" might imply, is a festering wound. It has occasioned many, particularly the youth, to return to their Islamic roots for answers and identity. And like the Nazis, Islamic militancy has been largely born out of the shame of these territorial defeats. That this was hardwired in the minds of these young refugees, played out on former crusader grounds, should have been no surprise: of peace, they have little consciousness.

～

Shortly, I found myself alone, tramping along the rampart walls, transported to another time. Then lightning swift, as if my reverie had willed it, an army of Mongolian horsemen rounded the castle's west wall. Muslim men in white cotton garments were fleeing. The horsemen wore furry headdresses and long black coats of ring mail. They were variously armed with swords and shields, bows and arrows, and axes and lances.

This reincarnate scene of terror was the film set of *Hulagu*, a joint venture between Egyptian, Jordanian, and Syrian production companies. The movie took its name from the Mongolian conqueror, grandson of Genghis Khan, who ravaged Baghdad, as well as Syria, in 1258.

In addition to the bloodletting he inflicted, Hulagu ordered all the books of the Abbasids' House of Wisdom thrown in the Diyala River, turning its waters black with ink. With the Crusades coming to an end, the Islamic world could not have anticipated this Pax Mongolica. Their conquest of Baghdad signaled the end of the Abbasid caliphate, the golden age of Islamic civilization, which was defined more by its words and ideas, its poetry and science, than Islamic jihad.

In 2003, when the American army arrived in Baghdad in their Bradley fighting vehicles, as the National Library burned, and as looters savaged the National Museum of Antiquities, Iraqis were reminded of the dark days of Hulagu. Libraries, after all, are an ancient Mesopotamia invention.

～

At the entrance gate, Abdul had caught wind of the dustup on the command tower. He was in a hurry to get on the road. As we turned in the direction of the desert, what Syrians call the Sahara, Abdul admonished me to work on the Canadian guise. Indeed, there was reason to suggest I was being cavalier: touring a crusader castle in the morning, on the edge of the Lebanese war; in the afternoon, racing in the Pontiac Eight down the "Baghdad Highway" to some Roman ruins.

Our destination for the night was Palmyra (City of the Palms), an oasis settlement deep in the harsh Syrian desert along the Baghdad Highway, the former caravan route between the Mediterranean seaboard and Mesopotamia. On occasion, every Sufi and saint, patriarch and prophet, has served monastic time in the Syrian Desert.[4]

---

4. Before turning to guerrilla warfare, Yasser Arafat, then a successful engineer, once tooled down these desert highways in a two-toned, pink Thunderbird.

Making tracks across a shining slash of asphalt at 90 miles per hour, Abdul fingered his prayer beads and polished a smudge on the chromed-out dash. He then reached beneath his bucket seat and came up with a newspaper wrap of sweet filo pastries. "These are only found in Hama [his home], not Aleppo, not Damascus," he avowed. We each took one. Sensing the absence of perfection, he puffed his chest, beamed, and proclaimed, "No problem. We can go faster." Vroom, vroom, faster we went, one hand on the wheel.

We were in Bedu country: whelmed by a minimalist tableau of white sand, white tents, white djellabas, and white heat. Windows down, although the desert wind washed over us like a blast furnace, we were feeling cool as kitty-cats there in our white, shiny Pontiac Eight—laying down asphalt, freewheeling, and heedless in our beltless bucket seats. Transported, *Cool Hand Luke*'s cover of "Plastic Jesus" played in my mind:

> Goin' ninety, I ain't scary,
> 'Cause I got the Virgin Mary,
> Assuring me that I won't go to Hell.

⌇

Three hours later we left the main highway. The bilingual blue road sign proclaimed Iraq 120 miles (or as the crow flies, Anbar Province 70 miles), close enough for this pilgrim's curiosity, especially with the recent revelation by Syrian officials that they have been attacked over 100 times by Islamic militants inside Iraq.

Traffic had been nonexistent but for military transports and the occasional overloaded bus of Iraqi refugees traveling west, from the nearby border. With 1.2 million Iraqis having fled the war to Syria, and a total of over 4 million displaced in Iraq or having fled to other countries, I expected an unending dust devil trail of convoyed refugees. After all, the reported influx in Syria alone at this time had swollen to 40,000 a month, straining the clinics, schools, potable water supplies, and emergency relief agencies' capacities to support.[5] We are not talking insurgents here—these are innocent bystanders who have fled for their lives. Over 70 percent of the refugees interviewed by UNHCR (United Nations High Commissioner for Refugees) have been eyewitnesses to a car bombing or know someone who has been killed.

For the Iraqis, who are mostly middle class, making ends meet in the crowded camps and dilapidated apartments in the poorest areas around Damascus has meant selling off their few transportable assets, spending their life savings.

---

5. As of February 2012, there are still over a million Iraqi refugees in Syria.

Many have reached the point of not being able to afford the basics: rent, heat, and food. With official work permits denied, the gap between their former lives grows wider by the day. Meantime, the unthinkable is happening in this proud Arabic culture: the prostitution of their daughters, "survival sex" it is called. "During the war we lost everything," said one teenage victim, reported by Reuters. "We even lost our honor."

For now, Syria keeps an open border for Iraqi refugees, but like Jordan, Egypt, and other countries, they may be forced to tighten immigration policies. On this slow refugee day, I couldn't help but wonder if the Iraqi refugees (a few thousand of whom happen to be Palestinian) will be in Syria six decades from now, as are the half a million Palestinians who fled to Syria in 1948. Will al-Qaeda and its look-alikes flourish in these camps as they now do in the Palestinian camps of Syria and Lebanon? Will Syria use the Iraqi refugees against Israel as they have the Palestinians and Hezbollah?

Since the 2003 invasion, a mere 466 Iraqis have been given asylum in the United States, as compared to the Vietnam War when President Ford accepted 130,000-plus refugees within months of the fall of Saigon. (Within seven years, 500,000 immigrated.) In contrast, Sweden, which is not a member of the coalition of the willing, admitted 25,000 Iraqis in 2006. Where is that President Ford spirit today?

⌁

Roman colonnades sprang up from the windy, woebegone valley of Palmyra, gladdened by a profusion of palms and orchards of pomegranates, dates, and olives. It was surely the underground springs, flowing from the mountains to the north and east, that attracted the first inhabitants here over 4,000 years ago. Assyrians, Persians, and Greeks (Seleucids) would occupy this Silk Road trading post, but it was Rome's expensive tastes for products of the East—spices, perfume, and silk—that occasioned prosperity in Palmyra.

Abdul dropped me in front of the Temple of Bel, said to be the most important religious edifice of the 1st century in the Middle East. The entrance is through a cyclopean defensive wall, off which locals built homes before the archaeologists arrived. Pagan rituals were first performed here over 4,000 years ago, but the provenance of Bel in the Palmyrene pantheon remains mysterious (perhaps a Babylonian adaptation of Zeus and Jupiter).

In a surreal commotion, the *cella* (central chamber) is bracketed by an ablutions fountain and sacrificial altar. Above is a stone niche where seven planetary divinities are carved, surrounded by the twelve signs of the zodiac. The animist, pagan faiths were not jealous ones, though. Flanked by a local solar and lunar god, the lintel has Bel manifested as an eagle—wings outspread, holding up the heavens.

In the tradition here of recycling religion, the temple became a Byzantine church 400 years later; after that, a mosque and Muslim fortress. Though the ruins present a nicely circumscribed cumulation of the region's religious history, it's more allegory than literal, more linear than ecumenical.

Inferentially, each stone-carved mutation must have been colossally punctuated by epic warfare that would have challenged the imaginative genius of Cecil B. DeMille.[6] Over the centuries, the derivative mana of this enchanted worship site, and countless others, nurtured and legitimized the next religious regime, until the water and warriors disappeared and the site was returned to dust. As such, here at the Temple of Bel, God had left the building. By and by, diggers, treasure hunters, and tourists arrived, completing a familiar circle.

---

6. Upon entering the gates of the Kaaba, the Prophet Mohammed and his army smashed all the pagan idols that Meccans had worshipped since time immemorial.

CHAPTER THREE

~

Holy Fools and the Red Crescent

A chorus of roosters crowed me awake. The Bedu stew of lamb from the night before lay like a football in my stomach. Three cups of tea, two white pills and one blue one, and all was better. Other than the shop that sold fake Seikos to the Japanese, Palmyra still slept, as was its nature these days. Abdul and I departed.

The Damascus highway was another shiny slash of asphalt through a vast emptiness of desert, a realm that has understandably addled minds and nurtured souls for all eternity. On this day, the solitude was splendid, except for a lone bus barreling down the road bullfighter-bravado style that careened to avoid us at the last nanosecond. "Head-on in the Syrian desert, victims vaporized, 72 virgins witness," I thought the obituary might read.

We stopped midway at a teahouse, with two Bedu beehive houses for rent across the highway. Outside was a broken-down ox cart covered in sand, with a sign poking out that read Baghdad Café 66. It was a takeoff on the American movie *Baghdad Café*, filmed on Route 66 in the Mojave Desert. Amid a cocoon of Persian carpets and stools of leather that were camel saddles, two men served us tea and pointed out the kitsch for sale that ranged from postcards to Bedu honey. Jack Palance, the Hollywood movie's costar, would have been proud of this cowboy watering hole.

An hour later we were in fabled Damascus, greeted by a crush of hurtling metal and Hezbollah adverts in taxi windows; Old Damascus is where we were pointed. Mark Twain, in *The Innocents Abroad*, waxed about this timeless place:

Go back as far as you will into the vague past, there was always a Damascus. In the writings of every century for more than four thousand years, its name has been mentioned and its praises sung. To Damascus, years are only moments, decades are only flitting trifles of time. She measures time, not by days and months and years, but by the empires she has seen rise, and prosper and crumble to ruin. She is a type of immortality.

In the 7th century, the Umayyad caliphate moved the capital of their swelling Islamic empire from Medina, a desert oasis, to Damascus, a city set strategically between the Mediterranean and the Fertile Crescent and thus able to support a growing world power. With this in mind, standing in the Al-Hamidiyya souk next to the Umayyad Mosque and watching the crowd flow by brought the Arab world to a geo-pinhead: there were bearded mullahs from Iran in black turbans and robes; Wahabist imams from Saudi Arabia in all-white *shalwars*, wearing great black beards; and tattoo-faced Bedu women in colorful headdresses from the northern desert of Jordan, pilgrims all.

Gold merchants fitted veiled women in bracelets and necklaces, while traders in silk, carpet, leather, and antiquities enticed foreigners with "mister, mister." Drawing me further in was the pleasing scent of potpourri and spices—deep purple sumac, amber cumin, yellow coriander seeds, black cardamom, and orange turmeric—artfully combed in colorful mounds. Less inviting were the pungent smells of fly-caked lamb carcasses and tubes of tripe.

In vain we searched for the famous storytellers of this ancient souk, known through history for their imaginative improvisations. Eventually, Abdul led me through a halal butcher shop and up three narrow flights of crumbling concrete stairs, emerging in a room of brass oil lamps, Persian red carpet from floor to ceiling, and the scent of steamy teapots rising like a balm from each table. A few men and packs of women adorned in gold circled around low-set tables that overlooked the Ummayad Mosque, the muezzin chanting in the background. The seductive Scheherazade must have been present under one of those veils, spinning modern versions of Aladdin or Ali Baba.

A middle-aged, fair-haired man in a pressed white shirt and black pants seated us by the sepia-stained window, in the corner.

"Where is he from?" the waiter asked Abdul in Arabic.

"Canada."

"Tell him welcome."

Soon the table was brimming over with platters of hummus, aubergine, cucumbers, tomatoes, lamb and chicken kebabs, flat bread, and brass pots of mint tea. For most, including the women, the lingering lunch was followed by a nargileh.

Abdul and I were back in the crowded souk when the call to prayer sounded. Once again that great sucking sound could be felt and heard—pressed and jostled by the noisy masses, and then empty silence, piety arising.

On the west wall of the mosque in a cozy garden was the tomb of heroic Saladin, who led the Muslim army against Richard the Lionheart at Acre in the Third Crusade. Dying in Damascus in 1193 after pushing the crusaders (but not the Christian civilians) out of Jerusalem, Saladin has since been lauded in literature by the great ones, for example, in Sir Walter Scott's novel *The Talisman*. Indeed, when his superior army laid siege to Jerusalem—rather than slaughtering the Christian survivors and desecrating the Church of the Holy Sepulchre, as had been done to Muslims and the Al-Aqsa Mosque a century before—Saladin permitted Christians to continue worshipping and residing in the holy city, while also inviting Jews to return. A period of relative peace ensued.

Joining me in this marble shrine to the crusaders' greatest adversary were three other infidels, French women dressed as soberly as nuns, in drab olive hoods issued at the mosque gate. Though we chatted briefly, these Frankish descendants of Tancred regarded me with wariness. As they departed the tomb of this mythical figure of chivalric romance, the oldest of the French threesome said, "You are very brave to be here." That the Crusades weren't over for Americans, that the energy of this sepulchral force field might zap me at any moment, was on her mind.

Inside the Roman-built walls of the great mosque, like some cosmic babushka doll, successive layers of sacred shrines were revealed. A Roman temple dedicated to Jupiter was grafted onto the site where the former pagan temples to Bel and Baal once stood, followed by the Byzantine St. John's Basilica that honored John the Baptist, and now, the Ummayad Mosque.

For 70 years after the Islamic conquest, Muslims shared the former Byzantine basilica with Christians, using part of the church for their communal prayers. In 706, the sixth Ummayad caliph, Klaled ibn al-Walid, reckoned the new Islamic capital of the world, Damascus, needed something more grandiose, like the Dome of the Rock in Jerusalem. He built the Ummayad Mosque, and its mosaic walls of a garden paradise, over the next ten years, employing 12,000 slave laborers, and costing all of Syria seven years of taxes. The caliph al-Walid was said to have burned the 18 camel loads of account books, saying, "We have done this for God, and need no accounting!"

There is something here at the Great Mosque for everyone, including body parts of the great ones. For Shias, the martyr Hussein's head is enshrined in a small room, brought here after his epic battle with the Ummayad dynasty that divided Shia from Sunni. The skull of John the Baptist, a minor prophet to Muslims, mentioned in the Koran four times, is interred in a marble-columned mausoleum in the middle of the prayer hall. The story of his miraculous birth by a barren mother and aging father draws Muslim women here to pray, in hopes of getting pregnant. It is even said that bone relics from Moses and the Queen of Sheba have found their way here.

This is only a prelude to the more cosmic narrative that a wider Damascus has to offer. Jesus, it is said, will descend from heaven on the southeast minaret on doomsday. Mohammed is believed to have journeyed from Mecca, looked down over Damascus from Mount Qasiyun, and declined to enter the city: he only wanted to enter paradise once. Then he died. Locals will tell you Mount Qasiyun is variously the Eden of Adam and Eve, the place where Cain slew Abel, and the birthplace of Abraham, the patriarch of Jews, Christians, and Muslims.

It's all beyond historical conjecture. Its pure poetry draws pilgrims of all faiths, many of whom wander these streets, wearing their rapturous expressions like an ill-fitted mask. It's not hard to spot the holy fools, talking to themselves, with the same disturbed visage of those ranting souls with Bluetooths on the streets of America.

We walked east of the mosque, through a Roman arch, down a street called Straight, mentioned in the Bible from Acts to St. Luke. Seventeenth-century Damascene homes, with wooden doors and brass knockers, Persian rugs and inner courtyards, were fronted by pergola-covered cafés, many with Christian men languishing around nargilehs, filling the air with their perfumed exhalations. Maronite, Armenian, Greek, and Syrian Orthodox churches crowded the street, basking in the "supernatural radiation" of this biblical landmark, not unlike the higgledy-piggledy crush of Jerusalem.

Abdul led me through a stone gate into a walled compound. A monkish African man swept the courtyard, tidying the area around two marble statues of a man half kneeling (Saul of Tarsus) while being blessed by another (Ananias). Fresh roses lay at their feet. This was the house of St. Ananias, a Jew, who biblical history tells us was summoned by the Lord to meet the Greek-speaking Jewish traveler Saul in the house of Judas "in the street called Straight." There, through the imposition of his divinely inspired hand, Saul was healed of his blindness. Ananias then baptized him in the nearby Barada River, now a mud waddle. Recast as Apostle Paul (Greek for Saul), he gave up harassing Christians and went forth to introduce to the world the Christian theology that the dead shall be raised.[1]

St. Ananias became the first bishop of Damascus but was later stoned to death outside the city walls. After a proselytizing campaign not seen since Emperor Ashoke introduced Buddhism to the world, and not to be seen again until Mohammed and the caliphs spread Islam, Paul was imprisoned in Jerusalem and died in Rome, a martyr.

The African, possibly a former Senegalese soldier brought here during the French Mandate, dutifully led me down the basaltic steps to the unprepossessing

---

1. Paul's letters to his converts are the earliest writings found in the New Testament. They demonstrate a "radically inventive exegesis of the Torah and the Prophets" that Jesus was the Jewish Messiah.

cave chapel, which, a few centuries after the death of St. Ananias, became the Roman-Byzantine Holy Cross Church. The African's humble countenance—slight physique, castaway clothes, and pious eyes—exuded more spiritual presence to me than the chapel icons depicting St. Paul's conversion. I made a donation in case the maxim is true: "God takes care of the one who takes care of the holy fool." He never spoke, just swept in shambling steps, entranced in his faith, in his menial tasks, and in the aura of a biblical miracle.

Abdul waved at me from a coffee shop, mystically inspired by a brilliant emerald 1953 Pontiac parked nearby. With a voyeur's eye for nuance, he pointed out that the contour of the chrome hood over the windscreen was different from his model. A voluptuous, cherry red 1959 Cadillac was parked next to it, and a black one next to it—a candy store of American vehicular déjà vu. We left the enchanted ground of the old city through the 3rd-century Roman Gate of the Sun, Bab Sharqi. Holy land icons aside, I was puzzled: in this former satellite of the Soviet Union, if they hate us so much, especially our consumerism, what's with the worship of our old cars?

～

We were late for my meeting at the Omayyad Hotel with Ghoussoon Arnouk, a volunteer with the Syrian Red Crescent. She was late, too, and upon her arrival, one could almost wonder if it was planned. She swept grandly through the lobby in a black stretch blouse and pants ensemble, cinched by a bold silver buckle slung sexily low on her waist, with "Kooka" scrolled in white across her chest. Her sunglasses matched her dark hennaed hair, which fell upon bare shoulders. At age 50 she was not only fashionable but also displayed uncommon moxie.

Ghoussoon cut to the chase, asking how an American got a visa to Syria. "I got it in the States two months ago," I said. "It was my third attempt."

I explained that I was here out of shame and embarrassment over the American bombs killing women and children in Lebanon and that I simply wanted to make a donation to the refugees. That was it.

"Then we should go right away to the Red Crescent," she said. Ghoussoon's new model black Renault was parked by the front door. The offices of the Red Crescent weren't far, but on the way she talked effusively, venting her spleen at times.

Ghoussoon has a doctorate in pharmacology and is the general manager for Perfect Diagnostics, a distributor of Dade Behring products, used for testing blood. Because of the U.S. and European sanctions against Syria of the last two years, she has been unemployed, with lots of time to volunteer for the Red Crescent. Even broader sanctions were imposed after the March 2005 assassination of former Lebanese prime minister Rafik Hariri. That Syria was accused of the murder has caused Ghoussoon's business to go kaput.[2]

Still, there are ways around the sanctions as evidenced by the fivefold increase in imports of U.S. products since the sanctions were imposed. Thanks to globalization, Americana is everywhere, from Ford cars imported from Europe to Gap, KFC, Betty Crocker, and Johnson & Johnson. The sanctions don't apply as long as the goods are manufactured outside the United States and consist of 10 percent or less of American products.

The Red Crescent office bustled with volunteers and freshly arrived mothers and children. Tellingly, there was a dearth of men. With understandable wariness, volunteers who wore red jumpsuits with embroidered Red Crescent patches greeted me. This was the first contact point for many refugees who had paid heavy sums—life savings in some cases—to taxi owners and bus drivers to escape the bombing of the Bekaa Valley and southern Lebanon. White sheets and flags hung from the side mirrors of taxis, signaling the Israeli air force of their civilian status.

"They must be staying in the shelter to get drugs or food," Ghoussoon said. "That is the test. Otherwise we give them nothing."

Back in the car, en route to one of the Red Crescent shelters, Ghoussoon was driving erratically, while explaining the willy-nilly traffic in this city of six million. She maneuvered, honked, cursed, gossiped, and drifted through her family history.

"I'm Christian. Long ago my family was from Jordan. King Hussein was a real man." Giving me a sidelong glance, apropos of nothing, she said, "You know Queen Noor's father is Syrian, from Aleppo?"

"I didn't know that."

"Now King Abdullah plays poker and likes women. What's new? He's a king."

She continued: "After Jordan my family moved to Latakia, where my father owned 85 hectares. During the Nasser regime [United Arab Republic] our land was expropriated. We were considered bourgeoisie for owning more than 50 hectares. Once we moved to Damascus, my father never again spoke of Latakia. It was too painful."

I asked her about siblings.

"One sister is married to a Muslim in Latakia. Another lives and works in Dubai. My brother moved to Chicago 30 years ago, but I have not talked to him in 20 years." After a long pause, she finished her thought: "Politics. He's American now and has forgotten us."

---

2. In 2011, a United Nations Special Tribunal fingered members of Hezbollah for the assassination.

My take was that Ghoussoon had become more radicalized, while her brother had moderated, becoming comfortable in middle-class America. Her brother was probably part of the brain drain here that, they say, has seen up to 50,000 doctors, and countless entrepreneurs, emigrate to Europe and America.

We parked the car in a Sunni neighborhood and walked from there to the refugee shelter, talking without cease. "Is Assad necessary?" I asked.

"Not like Saddam Hussein. We get along in Syria. There would not be a war. I am afraid though that the isolation will go on a long time. What can we do?"

Sighing deeply, she continued, "Before Assad we had choices. We need them again; we are safe now. It is okay for my daughter to come home at four in the morning."

Robin Wright, in her book *Dreams and Shadows*, addressed this same question of Syria without Assad: "Syria will be one of the two most difficult regimes to democratize. The other is Saudi Arabia. Their governments' hold on power is absolute. People have the fewest rights or avenues of action. The secret police—and public fear—are the most pervasive. The two regimes have spawned sufficient support networks through family and corruption and by playing on cultural traditions."

I asked Ghoussoon to tell me about Syria's relationship with Iran and Hezbollah.

"Syria is secular. The only thing we have in common with Hezbollah is that we are anti-Israel. Once this is over, it will be difficult to get rid of Hezbollah. It's a problem. We are not like Iran either. It's a theocracy, but we can get rid of Iran too." Looking despondent over the implications of her words, she groaned. "I am afraid it might take a long time."

I thought to myself that these were the kinds of differences that competent geostrategists might exploit. As they say, divide and rule.

We discussed the dire condition of the Syrian economy: unemployment is over 20 percent; gasoline and food are heavily subsidized; and after the Syrian army pullout from Lebanon in '05, not having control of Lebanese ports and commerce is taking its toll here.

"It's good that our army is no longer in Lebanon, yet I'm not sure it is over," Ghoussoon said. "Assad is liberalizing the economy, while the Ba'athists are still hanging onto socialism. It's all they know."

This, of course, is deep irony in a country known for a merchant class that predated the Silk Road.

∽

The refugee shelter was housed in a primary school adjoined by a mosque. Pre-adolescent kids played soccer on a concrete basketball court. Only three weeks before, they had been skylarking in their front yards and watching the World Cup on satellite TV. Sheikh Nasrallah posters adorned the doors above where weary-faced mothers sat in a line of plastic white chairs, watching the kids. Men were few.

The headmaster greeted me with a handshake and a welcome. A curious-minded group of uniformed volunteers gathered around me in his makeshift office. Their bemused expressions signaled their suspicions: why was this American here taking pictures, donating money?

In Arabic, the headmaster asked Ghoussoon if I was CIA.

"Yes. Maybe. I just met him. I don't know."

"If he is CIA, it's good to have them back. We haven't seen them since the end of the Cold War. Tell him welcome again." Ripples of laughter flowed around me.

Ghoussoon translated the conversation as we walked to the courtyard. We laughed together.

On the basketball court, a thirty-something man in a black shirt, jean shorts, and sandals, cultivating an Iranian-style, short-growth beard, introduced himself in fluent English: "Welcome. I'm Ali. When I lived in California they called me Mike." Ali had resided in Orange County, living with a cousin for five years.

I found in my travels this sort of connectedness to America pervasive. Middle Easterners talk about our music, movies, and science and technology, and often copy our fashions, but the Statue of Liberty is never mentioned. For them, America is financial salvation, but the rest is a necessary evil, like taking up with a modish but disturbed rich uncle. Otherwise emigration occurs because of hunger, disease, or war. By nature, though, people are sedentary.

We asked him where he was from and how he got to Damascus.

"Nabatieh [the Hezbollah heartland], in the south," he told me. "I paid a taxi all the money I had. I am a barber, so I don't make much." He paused before continuing. "We don't want money or help. We want to go home and back to work."

A fair-haired man in a blue baseball cap joined us, echoing Ali's ethos about returning to work. He had also been the victim of war profiteering by the taxis and freelancers, paying a thousand dollars for his family to get here from the Bekaa Valley, about 30 miles away. Like Ali's hometown of Nabatieh, the Bekaa was being heavily bombed. Israeli fighter planes had blown up the Liban Lait dairy farm that had employed over 300 people, near his home. It was alleged to be a Hezbollah militant hideout.

In a shaky voice, the fair-haired man told me about his next-door neighbor who had lost his mother and four children. "Until you have been in a war, you don't know what war is," he slurred, becoming inarticulate. The unstated was understood.

Hani, a French literature major, edged his way into our circle of four. He had been volunteering with the Red Crescent for three years. Two of those years were spent in the Sunni refugee camps on the Iraq border.

"Now we have 400,000 more refugees, this time from Lebanon," he grumbled. "Would Lebanon do the same for us? They had nowhere else to go. So we have put them up in schools across the country. What do we do in September when school starts back?"[3]

The kids not playing soccer marauded in packs, stressed by their displacement, by the whimsy and wickedness of war. At first they were wary of this American, in the way one distrusts the intentions of a strange animal, a stray dog on the street. Then they glommed onto me in a fury, breathless with interest, to touch an American, to see their clowning images on my camera. It's the beauty of the digital age: the images are now for them to see, not just for us to take home unseen.

Remembering my many photos of children from Rwanda taken in the year leading to the genocide there, as I scanned these images, then and now, fears arise: by way of birth lottery, will this cycle of human folly spawn the next generation of militants?

A study conducted by Mona Maksoud on the impact of children of Lebanon's civil war found that "90.3 percent of the sample had been exposed to shelling or combat; 68.4 percent had been displaced from their homes; 54.5 percent had experienced extreme poverty; 50.3 percent had witnessed violent acts such as the intimidation, injury, or death of someone close to them; 26 percent had lost someone close to them; and 21.3 percent had been separated from their families."

Some of those children Maksoud studied are now 20 to 30 years old, possibly the ones not present here, left behind to do the fighting today.

∼

Thirty minutes later Ghoussoon and I were in her black Renault, picking up where we left off: the Golan Heights. Then, out of the blue, she asked, "You're not Jewish, are you?"

"No, but why do you ask?"

With that, volcanically, her Syrian passion and prejudices rose to the surface: "We get along with all people but Jews. We will not have them. Who do they

---

3. Thankfully, the war ended after 34 days on August 14, before school was back in session, which may have been no coincidence—children's education being a common interest, if not a motivator for peace, of Hezbollah and Israel. And Hani's grousing about Lebanon not reciprocating became a reality five years later when Syrian refugees fleeing al-Assad's army to the Bekaa Valley were often detained or sent back by Lebanese security forces.

think they are? The chosen people. They have the right to land and we don't. What religion gives people the right to real estate?"

"Are there no Jews in Damascus?" I asked, with false candor.

"I promise you there are no Jews in Syria."

Biblical history tells us that Assyrian king Shalmaneser V deported the "ten tribes of Israel" to Mesopotamia (Syria and Iraq) over 2,700 years ago. In 1948, the Jewish quarters of Damascus and Aleppo were home to 30,000 Jews; today their synagogues are abandoned, and if any families remain, they are negligible.

I winced at the thought of how Ghoussoon would have reacted if I were Jewish. Yet when the anti-Semitic rant was over she seemed to be on the verge of weeping—sniffling, lower lip aquiver. That her beauty, passion, and intellect had charmed me made her sudden twist into that cruel rage all the more profound. Closer than two blinks of the eye, she had elegantly laid bare the innate duality of compassion and cruelty that, at some level, we all possess.

Like most Syrians, Ghoussoon has a popular, Zionist-centric narrative of history. Her hate is merely a failure of her own imagination. And the isolation has only hardened her seemingly intractable state of mind. Michael Ignatieff, who wrote *The Warrior's Honor: Ethnic War and the Modern Conscience*, must have had Ghoussoon in his crosshairs when he wrote of fear as a trigger for war:

> It is the fear that turns minor differences into major, that makes the gulf between ethnicities into a distinction between species, between human and inhuman. And not just fear, but guilt as well. For if you have shared a common life with another group and then suddenly begin to fear them, because they suddenly have power over you, you have to overcome the weight of happy memory; you have to project onto "them" the blame for destroying a common life.

Yet of all the conflicts in the region, this one between Israel and Syria should be the easiest to resolve, since it involves real estate rather than religion. It almost happened in 1994: Yitzhak Rabin, the colaureate of the Nobel Peace Prize that year, agreed in principle to give the Golan Heights back to Syria in return for normalized relations.

Since his assassination a year later by a right-wing Orthodox Jew, who was opposed to the Oslo peace process, Israel has backpedaled, piggy-backed by America. In response, Syria has ratcheted up their support for Hezbollah, Hamas, and Iran, while anti-American terrorism spread at an unprecedented rate.

It is true, though, that land here seems more valuable than life itself. Of the three impediments to a Palestinian state—the return of refugees, splitting Jerusalem, and West Bank settlements—it's the latter two that are the hardest to overcome.

CHAPTER FOUR

~

Made in America

On August 14, 2006, the United Nations brokered a peace agreement in the Israel-Lebanon War. Even so, it would be almost another month before Israel lifted their naval blockade. The disproportionate response by Israel (and the United States for not reining them in) to the Hezbollah "kidnapping" of two Israeli soldiers left over 1,200 dead and resulted in refugee camps, brimming with homeless; up to a million unexploded cluster bombs littering the countryside; and as much as ten billion dollars in public infrastructure degradation. In this 34-day war, the damage—the cost to rebuild—was greater than in Lebanon's 15-year civil war.

Moreover, Hezbollah, the Party of God, enhanced their political standing in Lebanon, if not their regional and international profile. The forces of anti-Americanism had found a champion in Sheikh Nasrallah, while Iran's regional influence looms larger.

A month after the naval blockade ended, Nadine Naffah sat next to me on the Air France flight from Paris to Beirut. As associate director of admissions at the American University in Beirut, she had been attending a college recruiters' seminar in Pittsburgh. Single, Nadine is unaware of glass ceilings among Beirut's upwardly mobile. At age 34, she is the product of an Armenian mother and Catholic father from Damascus yet Lebanese to the bone. As with the anti-American blowback from the Iraq War, she said that Lebanese, who are by nature atomized, agreed on one thing: America helped destroy their country.

As we taxied to the gate, we looked out at the blackened bomb craters. "Before the war there was not so much anti-American sentiment, but now it's everywhere," Nadine said. "It's not a good time for Americans to be here, especially in the south. If people want to express their political views, okay. But you shouldn't; they are nervous here."

My plan was to see all of Lebanon, so I remembered her words as I hailed a taxi at the terminal building of Rafik Hariri International Airport, which was spared the bombing that destroyed fuel depots and several runways. A chubby chatterbox of a man wearing a black derby, a Sunni from south Beirut, motioned me into his taxi. He had won the fare over several others who had overpriced their services. Once in traffic, he pointed to one of many billboards featuring the airport's namesake, assassinated prime minister Rafik Hariri. He blew him a kiss, while shaking his head and saying, "Syria is bad."[1]

A crush of white tenement buildings, with lines of laundry hanging off the balconies, sprang up from the roadway. Goggle-eyed as any first-time arrival, my snapshot of crowded Beirut on the sprint from the airport was as superficial as the communication with the cabbie. As he dropped me on the fashionable Rue Hamra, predictably, he demanded more. After paying him the fare we had agreed upon, plus a tip, he pursued me into the corner liquor store, where I was picking up a key to a friend's apartment. Samir, a Maronite Christian, owner of the liquor store, had no patience for the cab driver's surliness. According to bystanders, something was said about Samir's mother, so Samir cuffed the man. At that point I was more than ready to go—everyone in Beirut had guns, and there was no telling where the feud would end.

I hotfooted it to my friend's flat before the police arrived. The Sri Lankan maid showed me to the apartment. Minutes later the police called to say they wanted to talk to me but, thankfully, never showed up. I had been in Lebanon less than an hour.

David Holdridge arrived home around nine, his usual time to finish work, even on this Saturday evening. Annie, his wife, had arrived from Nabatieh in the Hezbollah south only minutes earlier. We all hugged and promptly plopped around the coffee table, centered with a bottle of Cuervo Gold tequila. David threw down a block of cheddar cheese, from which we manically chomped down chunks between cigarettes and tequila. Until late in the night, we spilled out stories.

This was my first time to meet Annie, but David and I had become friends while living in Hanoi. He first went to Vietnam in 1969 as an army lieutenant in the Americal Division. Three months later he was gutshot. Losing several feet of his intestines, it took him years to recover. He returned to Vietnam in 2001 as country director of the Vietnam Veterans of America Foundation (VVAF), which shared the Nobel Peace Prize in 1997 as partners in the International

---

1. The Syrian *mukhabarat*, or secret police, were initially accused of the assassination.

Campaign to Ban Landmines (ICBL). While in Hanoi, David successfully negotiated the first bilateral agreement between the U.S. Department of Defense and Vietnam's Ministry of Defense for a comprehensive survey of the remaining unexploded ordnance and landmines in Vietnam.

David, who exudes a reticent, yet confident kind of physical courage, is no stranger to crisis. In the 1980s, he directed emergency relief into civil wars and famines in Lebanon, Sierra Leone, Burkina Faso, Togo, Benin, Ethiopia, and Eritrea. In the 1990s, it was Kosovo, Bosnia, and Belgrade. Once the mission was accomplished in Vietnam in March of 2003, he followed American troops into Iraq with Mercy Corps, working outside of the Green Zone for the next three years.

In 2006, David moved to Beirut as director of Mercy Corps Middle East operations, which still gave him responsibility over Iraq, plus Gaza and Lebanon. A mere three weeks after he arrived in Beirut, the Israeli bombardment began. He was in his wheelhouse, so to speak.

Stuck in Amman, Jordan, with Annie in Beirut, David hired a taxi the morning of July 13, a day after the war began. That very day, Israel had bombarded the main roads and supply routes from Syria. This included the Mdeirij Bridge, which links Damascus with Beirut, its 230-foot columns an engineering showpiece in the Middle East. All 65 million dollars of it were destroyed. Though there were alternate routes, David's driver balked and left David in the mountains above the Bekaa Valley.

At four in the morning, one of David's coworkers in Beirut braved the fractured roads and drove into the mountains to retrieve him. Back in Beirut, he sent me a message saying he wouldn't recommend entering Lebanon that way. (I was en route to Syria, considering crossing into Lebanon.)

A day later, apart from Hezbollah relief workers, David was the first to meet with the Shia town council in Keyfoun, in the Chouf mountains above Beirut. In a predetermined evacuation plan, just as Maronite Christians do in their mountain villages north of Beirut, tens of thousands of Shia civilians living in south Beirut and southern Lebanon had fled to Keyfoun. They arrived in a gridlock of cars, buses, and taxis, all wrapped and hung with white flags and sheets, just as those I had seen arriving in Damascus. It was unlikely that Israel would bomb Keyfoun because Druze mountain villages surround it. An offshoot of the Egyptian Ismaili sect of Islam, the Druze are not necessarily unfriendly to Israel.

But when it came time to deliver the relief aid—food parcels, hygiene kits, and mattresses—17 of David's 20 staff were no-shows, staying in their homes. He grabbed volunteers off the street, co-opted Annie, and moved the aid into the mountains. In time, Mercy Corps ventured south of the Litani River with convoys of food, ahead of the UN and the International Committee of the Red Cross (ICRC). Once the peace agreement was signed, as refugees returned home, perhaps even those I had met in Damascus, they were welcomed with food packages. The "hearts and minds" surge had begun: cleaning up rubble, building and rebuilding schools and youth centers, creating connectivity with Microsoft computer training, providing seeds to farmers, and holding psychological-social events for the kids who now know what F-16s are about, all paid for by U.S. taxpayers.

"Still, you can't sell America like toothpaste, which is what Karen Hughes is running around trying to do," David said. "Arabs understand the difference between software and hardware, the substance of good and bad policy."

On Karen Hughes's first Middle East trip in 2005, after being named undersecretary of state for public diplomacy, she warmed to audiences by telling them, "My most important title is mom" and that Americans "greatly value many religious faiths." As a hyper-Bush loyalist, her phoniness was transparent, here and at home.

"Sure everyone in the Middle East has seen *Baywatch*, Tommy Frank's army, or Bono saving them," David said, "but they don't own it; it's not theirs. They've created nothing in the Middle East but war for 60 years. They need something to feel proud about, but not Karen Hughes."

We were almost out of cigarettes. If there was a worm, it tasted of tequila. It was then that David reminded me that more Lebanese live outside of Lebanon than in. They're voting with their feet and have become a diaspora of rugged mercantilists: motel owners and dry goods purveyors in Mali, grocers in Belize, and fabric traders in Brazil—where six million Lebanese now live, more than the current population of Lebanon. In the 1880s, it was the persecutions of the Ottomans that drove them, mostly Christians, out. With the civil war beginning in 1975 and the recent 34-day war, Lebanese immigration to the United States has swollen. As of 2008, over one million were living in the United States.

David understands the Arab connectedness to America better than most. "In the heart of every Lebanese (or Iraqi), they see their destiny in life as getting a piece of the American pie," he said. "An uncle or a cousin or a friend is there. They tell you about it, and you want it too. In the Shia south of Iraq, every time I posted a training position in the U.S., there were over 1,000 applications. They don't *hate* us, hate us. It's the spite of a spurned lover. Change our policy and they will be back. Give them hope! Dignity! We are one John Kennedy away from the world loving us again."

〜

It felt like Johnny Cash's Sunday morning coming down—unshaven, stumbling out into the incandescent light to meet the new day in Beirut. But for the

Filipino maids going to church, the silence of the sleeping city sidewalks was deafening. It was day 18 of Ramadan here in the Hamra and Ras Beirut, mixed Christian and Muslim neighborhoods. David slipped out to work early, and Annie and I walked to the Corniche to begin our day's tour of Beirut.

The Ferris wheel at Luna Park was not operating, but the lighthouse and its radar tracking devices were back in working order after the bombing. Missing were the fishermen, joggers, dog walkers, sidewalk vendors, nargileh cafés, and lovers who would normally be promenading along the headland, above the crashing waves of Pigeon Rocks. New Saudi-built, squarish, white high rises; Starbucks; Pizza Hut; Hardee's; KFC; and two bombed-out tenements from the civil war shadowed the park.

"Once the rightful owners get sorted out, they will go condo like the Saudi-owned high rises that rent for four to seven thousand dollars a month," Annie said. Agreement on ownership rights is tricky. In the case of a single lot near the old souk, there were 4,700 claimants. The Tapu Defteri, or Ottoman land registry, will have to be consulted on this property dispute.

We caught a lift in a beat-up Mercedes past the old American embassy to the Solidere, the French name for the downtown business district. Glassy new bank buildings and the sky-blue domes of Al-Omari Mosque (nee a crusader church) hung above as we made our way through the refurbished Ottoman- and French Mandate–era buildings. Flanking Martyrs' Square, stacked in competitive proximity, minarets of masonry yellow pierced the sky. Maronite and Armenian churches stood their medieval ground. Nearby, Roman ruins were being excavated next to horizontal cranes, hoisting this ancient phoenix into another uneasy modernity.

Beneath this mix of Dresden, of old and new architectural glories, boutiques sell shoes from the fashion houses of Milan and Paris for $1,000. Old world waiters in pressed black-and-white liveries serve up European haute cuisine among the colonnades of French colonial buildings. Richard Branson's Virgin Megastore, located in the former Beirut Opera House, competes with the drama of Martyrs' Square, where the Green Line, Rue de Damas, once separated Christian and Muslim Beirut, ground zero for 15 years of civil war in which 130,000 were killed; and 150,000, injured.

Living up to Beirut's reputation for conflict and militarization, Russian T-55 tanks, American-made M113 armored personnel carriers, and platoons of heavily armed soldiers patrolled streets and alleyways. Early that morning, about the time David and I called it a night, rocket-propelled grenade (RPG) rounds were fired into the Buddha Bar. A couple of nearby parked cars were targeted. No one claimed responsibility; it was another Rashomon situation.

Beirut is a country of minorities—Druze, Shia, Sunni, Armenian, Maronite, Palestinian, and Syrian—living here because of differences elsewhere, all believing in a loving, peaceful God but rarely a God who espouses turning the other cheek. Everyone here has two identities, Lebanese and confessional, which means sectarian in local parlance. Shias are making a power bid, but not by terrorizing civilians. Other Syrian sympathizers might be up to old tricks. Throw in the simple truth that every confessional shares three predictable defaults: weapons, a militia, and a hideout in the mountains. Ho-hum—twisted metal, broken glass—seemed to be the mood on this day.

～

A sprawling white funeral tent verges Martyrs' Square, in the former parking lot of the Virgin Megastore. It is a shrine to Prime Minister Rafik Hariri and the seven men killed with him on February 14, 2005. Several tons of explosives awaited them as their motorcade passed nearby in front of the upscale St. George Hotel, which suffered 10 million dollars in damage, leaving a crater in the road 30 feet wide and 6 feet deep.

We were greeted by a platoon of sentries in flak jackets, cradling their automatic weapons amid a tawdry wash of Astroturf. A mortuary hush pervaded. As if the funeral were yesterday, eight caskets are partly interred in Astroturf, buried in wreaths of white flowers. Favorite photos of his deceased men, mostly in sunglasses and sport shirts, introduce their gravesites. Hariri portraits have him tending to a flock of doe-eyed fellaheen or mantled in a white robe, emoting on stage like a television evangelist, or more commonly as mister-buttoned-down-businessman.

Rafik Hariri was from a modest Sunni family in Sidon. After college, in 1965, he went to Saudi Arabia as a 21-year-old schoolteacher. In a rags-to-riches tale, in a place where powerful clans, militia leaders, and political families rule, he returned to Lebanon 27 years later as a billionaire prime minister.

Early on, his entrepreneurial skills had caught the eye of Crown Prince Fahd, who later became King Fahd. Hariri amassed a fortune in construction, banking, real estate, media, and telecommunications. His wealth and Saudi influence wired him into Lebanese politics.

In 1989, in Taif, Saudi Arabia, he was a principal negotiator of the Taif Accords, a blueprint for reconciliation that ended Lebanon's civil war, a war he had had no part in and therefore was not tainted by its atrocities. During the 1990s and until his death, he dominated post–civil war Lebanon with his massive rebuilding projects as prime minister and real estate magnate. The World Bank, the Gulf States, the European Union, and the United States gave him plaudits. That local journalists wrote about Hariri-ism is testament to his cross-sectarian popularity.

That said, when the dust settled the country was saddled with massive public debt and huge budget deficits. His burgeoning fortunes, coupled with the declining fortunes of Lebanon and the Lebanese, raised suspicion.

Even so, martyrdom awaited him: 150,000, of all sects, turned out for his funeral. Stirred by Hariri's assassination, an increasing tide of anti-Syrian anger poured into the streets—Muslim, Christian, man, woman, young, and old. They demanded the withdrawal of the Syrian military, free National Assembly elections, freedom for political prisoners, and the return of exiles. In a rare and potent display of Lebanese solidarity, a month after Hariri's assassination up to a million protesters (or 25 percent of the population) gathered in Martyrs' Square. Shoulder to shoulder they stood, with fists slashing the air, their "Cedars of Lebanon" flags raised as one. The withdrawal of the Syrian army and the tenuous resolution of other political demands prompted a U.S. State Department analyst to describe this as the Cedar Revolution.

Next to Hariri's tented shrine, a red digital counter tracks the days since his death, the progress of the investigation to determine his assassins. "The Truth for the Sake of Lebanon," a banner read.

～

Except for the sapphire-hued shimmer of the Mediterranean, nothing moved in the harbor. Only a month before, in September, U.S. destroyers had stood by in the distance as emergency supply and rescue ships from around the world came and went at the pleasure of the Israeli military. With respect to Levantine history, from Homeric times to the Crusades to last month, I could have pulled a date from a hat and described a similar scene.

Sadly, as the 34-day war erupted, Beirut was named by *Travel and Leisure* magazine as one of 2006's top ten destination cities. Over a million and a half tourists were expected in '06. Other than Saudi sex tourists, I didn't recognize what might have been a single sightseer while in Lebanon.

Facing the harbor, we crossed the Rue de Damas (the former Green Line) near an Armenian church. From there we twisted through the cobble streets of Achrafiye, an affluent section of Christian east Beirut. In 1989, up to 5,000 shells a night had landed there. A few months before the recent war, when news of the infamous Danish cartoons hit the streets of Beirut, 20,000 Sunnis marauded through the gentrified precincts of Achrafiye, destroying cars and burning residences. The mob was set on burning down the Danish embassy but torched the wrong building. No one was injured. The tension dissolved in the flash that ignited it.

We took the church crowd's lead into the Entrecote, a chi-chi steak house, in a former Ottoman home. Families gathered around long tables, slathering their medium-rare-cooked steaks in Bernaise sauce. Bluestocking women smoked Gauloise cigarettes, and buttoned-down men in black puffed hand-rolled Havanas. We ate well and consumed exquisite wine. The fasting of Ramadan was 1,000 miles away. We tabbed out at $80.

A not-so-tony neighborhood awaited us.

In sparse Arabic, with a random cab driver, Annie negotiated a misery tour of the Haret Hreik quarter of south Beirut. The neighborhood is known in Arabic as *dahiya*, or suburb, in this case a maze of slums.

Soon a blown-up bridge greeted us. The blue and yellow charity boxes of the Hezbollah popped up on every street corner; Shias are obliged to donate 20 percent of their income to charitable causes. Marking territory, bigger-than-life Sheikh Nasrallah posters were accompanied by the yellow and green flags of Hezbollah.

Then we came upon the first of several blocks of bomb-ravaged buildings.

Yet, on our gallop through Haret Hreik, the resiliency of the residents stood in striking relief to the damage. Crowded streets teemed with commerce, amid dozers, dump trucks, and cleanup crews, Hezbollah's aptly named Jihad Construction Company at work, with petro dollars from Iran footing the bill. Percussion-shocked schools were under repair, although freshly bulldozed city blocks had the aura of planned urban renewal. This was Hezbollah's hearts and minds surge.

But for the massive destruction and crowded conditions, on the surface Haret Hreik is an ordinary neighborhood, a grid of dusty white tenements, dense traffic, markets, mosques, and schools. Some say that because of the evacuation warnings and the pinpoint accuracy of the bombing, the collateral human damage was minimal.

David is one of those. "In Vietnam, if a chicken moved the whole village got burned down," he said. "With the media watching every move of this war, attacks were carried out with precision."

Even so, when you see whole city blocks turned to blackened craters of rats and rubble, shredded clothes and chunks of concrete, and shattered toys amid twisted metal, it's easy to imagine carnage on the scale of Beirut in the '80s. Often walls and balconies were blown away, leaving an eight-story honeycomb of open living rooms. Clothes drying on the balconies were the only sign of life in these eviscerated tenements; otherwise, a funereal stillness lingered.

Anti-American banners draped the worst of the Dresden-style piles of debris: a ghoulish effigy of Condoleezza Rice captioned "The Middle Beast," or "Made in the U.S." and "Thank You American People," inscribed in English and Arabic. And if the blackened heap the cabbie pointed out as the former security headquarters of Hezbollah is indeed that, sleep should be better for the war wizards now that it's all pulverized.

Lawrence Wright, in *The Looming Tower*, cites this kind of war-ravaged tableau during the 1982 Israeli invasion of Lebanon as the tipping point for a youthful Osama bin Laden, who wrote, "As I looked at those demolished towers in Lebanon, it entered my mind that we should punish the oppressor in kind and that we should destroy towers in America in order that they taste some of what we tasted."

～

Soon Annie was directing the cabbie into the Palestinian camps of Saba and Shatila, where not even the Lebanese army dares to go. Established by the UNRWA (UN Relief and Works Agency) for Palestinian refugees in 1948, the year Israel became a state, these camps, which are only 2 of 12 still existing in Lebanon, hold over 400,000 refugees.

UNRWA defines refugees as those "living in Palestine" during the 1948 Arab-Israeli War and their descendants.[2] Plainly, the Palestinians who were babies at that time are now in their sixties. Three more generations have since been born into these camps from Gaza to Jordan to Syria, living in squalor, poverty, and lawlessness.

Their rights are limited, including not being able to own property in Lebanon. The social tensions of poverty, where few are prospering at the expense of others, are getting worse, not better. Here and across the Arab world, from Iraq to Morocco, 70 percent of the population is under 30 years old; a third of those are unemployed, and their only cultural outlet is the mosque.

Though a return to Palestine looms epic in these refugees' minds, their hopelessness and lack of more moderate options leaves them vulnerable to jihad ideologies. Former Israeli prime minister Ehud Barak said that, had he been born a Palestinian, he "would have joined a terrorist organization."

David, who also provides emergency relief in Gaza, where over a million Palestinians depend on food aid, says the Israelis treat them like "dogs in a pen." A more appropriate description for the camps of Saba and Shatila does not come to mind. These Palestinians continue to pay the price for European and American anti-Semitism as well as for the democratic election in Gaza that produced the wrong result.

Many here will tell you that Lebanon's multilayered problems of today, if not the Middle East, began in 1948, in these camps. In 1975, when fighting between the Christian militias and the PLO (Palestine Liberation Organization) set off Lebanon's civil war, the Lebanese army initially stayed away lest they crack

---

2. Immediately following the 1947 United Nations Resolution 181, which recommended the replacement of the British Mandate for Palestine with independent Arab and Jewish states, war broke out and the two-state solution is now a 65-year-old geopolitical failure.

along sectarian fault lines. Nevertheless, that eventually happened. A 15-year civil war ensued, alliances shifted, foreign powers intervened, and effective political control devolved to regions, provinces, and communities.

Half a century later, the edginess remains atmospheric in these camps, not unlike the combustible feel of Taliban villages I passed through in Pakistan. On this occasion, even the Sunni cabbie was spooked. "This is where al-Qaeda and other terrorists stay, sneaking in and out," he said.

Here, in September of 1982, the Maronite Christian Phalangist militia acted as mercenaries for the Israeli army—150 militiamen, commanded by Elie Hobeika—and massacred unarmed civilians in the Saba and Shatila camps. Israeli defense minister Ariel Sharon, known as the "godfather of settlements" for his success in resettling the West Bank, was chief strategist for the Israel Defense Forces (IDF). The IDF guarded the gates and turned a blind eye, while turning back those who attempted to flee.

Depending on whose account you read, the militia systematically murdered and often mutilated 800 to 2,000 Palestinian civilians. Witnesses reported bloated corpses everywhere: children, the elderly, and disemboweled pregnant women. Many others were raped before having their throats slit. Mass graves were found; others remain undiscovered. A la carte investigations were staged in Tel Aviv to appease local protestors. The international community was indignant, while Israel, a country of Holocaust survivors, played the moral-immunity card.

Three months after the massacre, the UN General Assembly condemned it as an act of genocide. Elie Hobeika went on to become a member of parliament, before being appointed to Rafik Hariri's cabinet as minister of social affairs and the disabled. He was assassinated by a car bomb in 2002. Ariel Sharon was dismissed as defense minister over the massacre, but as a resilient political infighter, in 2001, he became prime minister of Israel. A massive stroke ended his career in early 2006. The cautionary lesson is that education and political esteem are not antidotes to blind savagery.

Bam. Bam. Bam. Materializing out of nowhere, a bearded and stern-faced vigilante in his early thirties pounded the car. He waved his fist at my camera. We edged on cattle-like through a warren of streets where pedestrians outnumbered cars by, say, 500 to 1. Two octogenarians crept along with canes, probably young dandies when they arrived here. It felt like a camp, the crumbling stockade walls, razor wire, and rusted rubble, the anger palpable. We squeezed through the market, barely skirting the people and piles of fruits and vegetables. The ramshackle walls of the former headquarters of the PLO were plastered with posters of a younger Yasser Arafat, as if the PLO command had never departed. When we cleared the camps, I sighed out loud. Going there felt like something you do on a dare. An Orpheus glance back reminded me that, after food, water, and sleep, war has been these Palestinians' most enduring habit.

～

A fresh bottle of tequila awaited us this night. David was taking calls from Iraq every hour or so. In between, we talked about his three years of living outside the Green Zone, from the Shia south to the Kurdish north. Traveling between was predictably tricky. "I always took the same beat-up taxi," he said. "Sat in the back seat, wore a keffiyeh and sunglasses to hide the blue eyes, affected an old man's drool. My cabbie would drop me close to the Green Zone. The 100-yard walk from there to the marine guards at the gate petrified me."

In Vietnam, David volunteered to walk point. Courage aside, it was a means of gaining respect from his men, mostly blacks and southern whites. Otherwise they weren't fond of this prep school, Yankee second lieutenant. "But we weren't stealth back then; we were Barnum and Bailey."

"In Baghdad I would stay one night with a local contact and leave the next day. Move to another contact's house. Never over 45 minutes in a coffee shop, then skedaddle. Betrayal was always on my mind. Yet, the only way to build trust and community bonds was to be there. That's why the Green Zone is a joke: bowling alleys, hamburgers, and no one speaks Arabic. The only Iraqis you see are cleaning toilets or mowing lawns. I went there for donor meetings, often with congressional delegations. There would be six or seven presenters. They would allow us each half an hour, which meant that I had four or five minutes to explain our successes in the Shia south."

Given carte blanche, David directs resources to the most vulnerable populations, those marginalized by their own societies, which in Iraq and Lebanon are the Shia. "You can't have peace without justice," goes the relief worker's dictum. "For months after Baghdad fell, it wasn't uncommon for Shia mosques to display posters of George Bush the liberator," David said, before venting about the existential dilemma of democracy in sectarian Iraq (or anywhere). "He let the cat out of the bag on democracy. Of course they bit hard on the idea of one person, one vote. Why wouldn't they with 65 percent of the vote? Given that Iran had been funding the Shia parties forever, they loved it too."

Soon the "occupation" was confirmed with Resolution 1483, which gave the United States and Britain all rights over Iraq. "With that and no water or electricity, violence erupted," David said. "Saddam had also released the rabbles—the war-demented Shia psychopaths, cannon fodder against the U.S. and Iran—from prison, back into the streets. By the day, it became more obvious that de-Ba'athing was a big security screwup. Then the foreign uniforms arrived in the villages. It looked like what it was—an occupation, with a heavy American footprint. American soldiers became lightning rods for the escalating militia and insurgent attacks. Now it's a civil war."

In 2003, David was given an audience with Grand Ayatollah Sayyid Ali al-Sistani, the most influential political figure in Iraq, Iranian by birth and citizenship. "When I met with Sistani and others it was understood that there would be no boots on the ground in the villages where we had projects [schools, community centers, and leadership training centers]. That way our work wasn't politicized. Then we were able to give hope to impoverished Shia villagers. Something they hadn't seen in a long time." Al-Sistani was among those who greeted America as a liberator, but once the U.S. proconsul in Iraq Paul Bremer made it clear we were occupiers his support vanished. It was over foreign "boots on the ground" that in 1996 Osama bin Laden goaded fellow Muslims to "cause them [Americans] as much harm as can be possibly achieved."[3]

David never met Muqtada al-Sadr but said his enormous popularity was matched only by his ineptness at managing his followers and militias. "His support comes from poor, young nationalists who have learned to hate the imperial hegemon—America," he said.

Unlike the American military, David and Mercy Corps' approach, which incorporates the importance of subtlety in shaping Arab affairs, takes a page from T. E. Lawrence: "I could at least conceal my own, and pass among them without evident friction, neither a discord nor a critic but an unnoticed influence."

~

The next morning I accompanied David to the Mercy Corps offices, on John Kennedy Street, near the American University of Beirut. His office commands a sweeping view of the Mediterranean, but his curtains were pulled. As I pointed this out, he gasped in laughter, saying, "It's my al-Qaeda side that postpones fun and beauty until death."

Two fifty-something ladies representing a women's charity in Burj al-Barajneh, a poor Shia and Palestinian neighborhood in south Beirut, were waiting in the conference room. It's not always the case, but often women, who can be emblematic of their families' suffering, fill the role of facilitators for unity and peace. "Warlords focus on dividers," said David, "but aid workers look for common ground."

Aly Harakeh, Microsoft's license compliance manager in the region, joined them in the conference room. Hearts and minds money was flowing at high

---

3. After studying terrorist activities that took place from 1980 to 2004, Robert Pape of the University of Chicago makes the case that "overwhelmingly suicide-terrorist attacks are not driven by religion as much as they are by a clear strategic objective: to compel modern democracies to withdraw military forces from the territory that the terrorists view as their homeland. From Lebanon to Sri Lanka to Chechnya to Kashmir to the West Bank, every major suicide-terrorist campaign—over 95 percent of all the incidents—has had as its central objective to compel a democratic state to withdraw."

tide from USAID (United States Agency for International Development), the Gates Foundation, and others. As David put it, "A cloud of 4,000 computers is getting ready to rain down on south Beirut and southern Lebanon." At the same time he groused about the "branding" USAID does, targeting only our allies with development projects, while OFDA (Office of U.S. Foreign Disaster Assistance) has few strings attached, and funds go to the most needy in an emergency context.

Created by President John Kennedy on November 3, 1961, USAID has its roots in the Marshall Plan, created to rebuild Europe, with a secular goal of winning hearts and minds around the world through long-range economic and social development assistance. Although this legislation was intended to separate military and nonmilitary assistance, USAID has from time to time operated as a front for the CIA, such as in Vietnam and during the 1980s in Afghanistan.

This is the norm now. The Bush administration has transformed USAID from its more independent roots of combating poverty, disease, and malnutrition to a minor mechanism of our State and Defense Departments' "War on Terror." We now have the three pillars of foreign policy: defense, diplomacy, and development. The clever alliteration might suggest an equable distribution of resources, but not so.

David believes this to be an improvement, referring to the "daffy liberals promoting socialism" who once ran USAID. "They did their own thing but didn't represent the political status quo of the U.S." Now he says they have accountability (maybe even too much), as well as a disciplined, multisector agenda: health, education, human rights, economic assistance, responsible, democratic governance, and the building of a civil society. "Poland's Solidarity Movement was never helped by USAID, but now it would be," he said.

This reorganization, the end to liberal internationalism, has also trampled on rules meant to ensure separation of church and state. Under Clinton, 10 percent of the total USAID assistance went to faith-based NGOs. Under Bush, that benchmark exceeded 25 percent, with evangelicals taking the lion's share. A state religion aside, the fear is that prospective recipients will turn down assistance because they are of a different faith. It is no longer uncommon, particularly in Africa, for American aid organizations to have a Bible lesson before administering vaccines or other health interventions. Neither David, who is staunchly secular, nor Mercy Corps would sanction this, but he is less troubled than I am by the idea. "Hey, we are a Christian country. We were founded by Christians," he said. "Ninety percent of the country believes in God, mostly a Christian one. Why shouldn't *that* be reflected in our foreign policy?"

David and I joined two Mercy Corps staff members and volunteers from Burj al-Barajneh in the conference room. Mercy Corps needed a local implementing partner, preferably one who had performed relief work during the recent war. The aid money was changing character from emergency relief (OFDA) to development (USAID). Before the meeting got under way, David confided to me that the Western concept of conflict of interest was hard to get across here, that it was a real ethical dilemma to Mercy Corps' partners in the Middle East. "Family is everything here, giving a relative a job is what you do," he told me.

David began the meeting by asking questions intended to confirm their community bonds, which didn't take long to firm up. "The Harakeh family has lived in Burj al-Barajneh for 800 years," Aly stated.

In his usual casual attire this morning—soft-top baseball cap, faded blue windbreaker, collared shirt, Levi jeans, and well-worn jogging shoes—David worked the chalkboard with the calculated cadence of a math professor scrawling out his formulas. Matrixes of objectives materialized: connectivity, impoverished youth focus, gender equality programs, and games for six- to eleven-year-olds. Budget grids took shape: rent, refurbishing cost, equipment, Internet service, Microsoft trainers, and center managers. Rat-a-tat-tat, the meeting went. Aly and the Burj al-Barajneh team would return in two days with a proposal for the initial half a million dollars in funding. The first youth center would open in a matter of weeks (which it did with a spectacular turnout). In the world of emergency relief, of hearts and minds response, dollars have to flow fast to stanch the ever-rising tide of anti-Americanism.

～

A short walk down the shop-lined Rue Bliss, among a forest of mature cedars, pine, and banyans, is the American University of Beirut (AUB). The campus quad sprawls handsomely along a hillside before dropping gently, estate-like, to the Mediterranean. Reverend Daniel Bliss, an American missionary, founded the school in 1866, at the height of the Victorian missionary movement, the beginning of international charity. "They were exporting their culture, like tennis and soccer," David says. "They believed charity was the white man's burden, and if we can't convert them here in the Middle East, we will educate them and then they will see the light."

Long considered the best university in the Middle East, the school boasts an alumni list of prominent scientists, CEOs, recognized authors and journalists, presidents and prime ministers of Lebanon, and the former U.S. ambassador to Iraq, Zalmay Khalilzad. In 1945, at the inaugural event of the United Nations, 19 of the delegates were graduates of AUB. Beirut's heritage as a hub of scholarship has its roots in late Roman times when it was the leading center for the study of law.

A guard stopped me at the main gate, not for a search but to help me find my way. Nadine Naffah, whom I had met on a flight from Paris to Beirut, was expecting me in the admissions office. It was between classes, and the campus was abuzz, with cats as plentiful as feeding birds. With the exception of a minority of girls in Muslim dress, students were uniformly attired in blue jeans. As I was being vetted by two receptionists, Nadine arrived. "Welcome," she said. "You look more rested today." Students and staff circulated through her office on her first day to work since returning from the States. Generously, she gave me a quick but officious orientation.

"We have over 7,000 students, 80 percent of whom are Lebanese. The majority of our faculty and staff are Christian, but that is changing. All classes are in English," she said while handing me a catalogue with tuition rates. They were impressive: ten to fourteen thousand dollars a year for an undergraduate, and over twenty-five thousand for a med student. Room and board was not included but could be for an additional six to nine thousand dollars a year.

With over 28 percent of Lebanese, mostly Shia, falling below the poverty line, I asked, with tongue in cheek, "Who can afford these prices?"

"Many people have money in Lebanon," she said. "We also have financial aid, scholarships, and charities who help the poor."

We talked about the school's story of daring and survival.

"This is west Beirut, which is still predominantly Muslim. School was disrupted, but during the civil war it stayed open, more or less." She raised and lowered her open hands in a gesture of balancing. "In our branch in Christian east Beirut, many of our faculty got fed up and left. There was brain drain all over Lebanon. Now we are rebuilding." In the interest of being upbeat, Nadine had skipped over the darker details.

In the three decades leading up to 9/11, there were over 100 anti-American terror attacks in 40-plus countries, from Guatemala to Kenya to Lebanon. They included killings, kidnappings, hijackings, and the bombing of embassies and other symbols of America. With the backing in many cases of Iran's Revolutionary Guards, Beirut was the scene of over 20 such incidents: the bombing of the marine barracks and the U.S. embassy, the kidnapping of journalist Terry Anderson, and the torture and execution of CIA station chief William Buckley come to mind first. Hezbollah, or Islamic Jihad, a fledgling terrorist militia at the time, took responsibility for these anti-American attacks. Yet the most recurring bull's eye over those three decades was AUB.

David Dodge, acting president of AUB, was kidnapped in 1982 on Rue Bliss and was released a year later. Malcolm Kerr, president of AUB, was killed outside his office in 1984. Frank Reed, director of the AUB, accused of being a CIA agent, was kidnapped and released 44 months later. Joseph Cicippio, comptroller of AUB, was kidnapped and released five years later in 1991. That same year the uneasy peace that followed the civil war was broken when a 200-pound car bomb destroyed the administration building of AUB, killing one and injuring twelve. The list goes on.

Laura, a 19-year-old business major, with a sunny disposition, arrived to give me a brief campus tour. Blond from a bottle, wearing painfully tight blue jeans, her skin was Nordic white. She is a Christian from a small village in the south, "near Palestine," she says. Her summers are spent in Detroit with her grand-mother, and like many of the educated class, she speaks English, French, and Arabic. Although she said her friends and family in Lebanon are important, it was clear that the security and economic opportunities available in the States had become her aspiration.

We circled College Hall. Blown to smithereens in the 1991 car bombing, it had been rebuilt in the same 19th-century concrete-block style as before. From there we walked to Medical Gate, where Laura said goodbye, in a rush to make her next class. During the civil war, AUB built a tunnel at the Medical Gate so that doctors and med students could avoid sniper fire as they crossed to the AUB Medical Center.

The hospital is now home to the Children's Cancer Center of Lebanon, an affiliate of St. Jude Children's Research Hospital in Memphis, founded by the late entertainer Danny Thomas, a Lebanese emigrant. During the recent war, over 1,000 doctors, staff members, and students, many in their blue scrubs and white coats, marched down Rue Bliss, where the tunnel crosses. They were protesting an Israeli air strike on a bomb shelter in Qana that killed 60 people, 37 of them children.

Due to the 34-day war's sea blockade, the hospital was within days of run-ning out of fuel, which meant lights out for the critically ill. Dr. Nadim Cortas, dean of the medical faculty, addressed the march that spontaneously became a sit-in: "We urge the international community, and especially the United States, to press Israel to a cease-fire and to lift this oppressive blockade which does not serve any purpose other than causing a humanitarian crisis." In fact, Israel escalated the bombing in the lead up to the peace agreement, while the United States Congress gave Israel an overwhelming vote of confidence.

CHAPTER FIVE

~

Warlords and a Lebanese Prophet

The next morning, Farid Chrabieh awaited me in front of David and Annie's. Farid is a law student at La Sagesse, a French university in Beirut. He had been recruited by his sister, Gilda, the chief financial officer at Mercy Corps, to help during the recent emergency. At David's suggestion, he became my dragoman for a week.

An extroverted dynamo, Farid aspires to run for parliament once he finishes law school, an ambition born from his experiences in student government, coupled with a quiet sense of rebellion that tells him he and his generation are different. Blackly comical, I told him it sounded like he preferred assassination to growing old.

Before law school, Farid had been in Montreal for graduate school, where his twin sister Lydie is now studying. He's a Christian, his mother a Syrian Catholic and his father Maronite. And of course he has a relative in the United States. In the granddaddy of ironies, his Uncle Roger is a U.S. Air Force pilot and trainer.

We circled Martyrs' Square and pointed north toward the ancient city of Byblos, up the coastal highway. Traffic slowed our pace by the modern buildings of Jounieh, a city built by Christians during and after the civil war as a quick escape from Beirut. Above Jounieh Bay is Casino du Liban, looming with the immensity of a crusader castle. Farid's father has been the controller there for over 40 years. The approach to the casino is a Vegas-like strip of bars and "super" nightclubs. Russian and Eastern European hookers populate this playground for spendthrift Gulf Arabs, mostly Saudis, who, since 9/11, are more comfortable debauching here than in the West. These are the keepers of the faith, of the holy cities of Mecca and Medina, airing out their stock portfolios. Although

Saudis account for a mere 1 percent of the worldwide Muslim population, they pony up 90 percent of the bucks to build the venerable madrassas (religious schools) around the world. Thus, the spiritual hypocrisy of their carousing—high rolling at the gaming tables, anteing up $500 to $1,000 for a circus romp with these fair-skinned blondes—doesn't wash back home with Wahabist fundamentalists, or even a few miles south of here in the Palestinian camps and destitute Shia enclaves. Worse, it betrays their "American" influence.[1]

This then has been Lebanon's tightrope for centuries, mixing East and West, Islam and Christianity, and decadence and piety.

∼

Traffic on the new coastal highway was diverted below the casino. Two bridges bombed during the war remained impassable. In my wanderings around Lebanon, I would see few bridges in operation. Even so, the Lebanese were able to find humor with the Israeli obsession for pummeling overpasses and bridges. Fairouz, a national idol and Lebanon's wartime answer to France's Edith Piaf, sings a popular lament about an imaginary bridge (Laouzi). During the war, Israeli prime minister Ehud Olmert, as the joke goes, called Fairouz in a panic, saying, "Where is that damn bridge?"

Moored fishing boats bobbed timelessly in the photogenic marina of Byblos, caressed by epochal layers of classical antiquity and ramparts of recycled stone. Seven thousand years ago Neolithic fishermen called this rocky littoral home. Amid Roman ruins, a crusader castle, and the six-thousand-year-old pagan temple of Baalat Gebal, their limestone floors and Stone Age tools have been excavated.

A seafaring culture, then known as Canaanites, colonized the coastline from here to Israel in the third millennia BCE. After 1,200 BCE, Greeks called them *phoinikes*, which became Phoenicians, the "red people," named after a purplish, red cloth they exported. As inventors of an alphabet that would become Roman, the Phoenicians imported so much papyrus from Egypt that Greeks named the port city Byblos, referring to the ancient paper. Bible, or "the book," takes its name from Byblos (as does *bibliotheque*).

We detoured from the four-lane highway at the Batroun Bridge. It was cratered. A canary yellow billboard rose above it with a black silhouetted image of an inebriated man staggering across a set of broken spans. The sponsor was Johnnie Walker Scotch.

---

1. Before modernity was ever an issue with Islamic extremists, Osama bin Laden was obsessed with Saudi royals behaving like American lackeys.

⁓

A rough demographic sketch of Lebanon would have Shias occupying the south, the Druze in the Chouf, the Sunnis prevailing in Sidon and Tripoli, and the Christians in the mountains north of Beirut, with the Bekaa Valley and Beirut a mosaic. Here on the coastal highway, St. Charbel, a 19th-century monk and healer of Maronites, was writ large on billboards and in alabaster statues up the coastal mountains. In a country the size of Connecticut, though, the next precinct is never far away.

Just when I thought I was getting a handle on Lebanese politics and demographics, Farid avowed that slain prime minister Rafik Hariri not only had stolen $20 billion but also was a Syrian agent. So they really didn't sing "Kumbaya" back there in Martyrs' Square?

We stopped briefly for directions along Tripoli's palm-lined cornice. This was Al-Mina, the modern port area, where fishing boats unloaded fresh crabs beneath the gaze of glassy office buildings. From this harbor, Yasser Arafat retreated to Tunisia aboard the Greek ship *Odysseus*, for the long fight to get home. The Islamic green flag of Saudi Arabia, the keepers of the faith, fluttered above a mosque and madrassa along the waterfront.

"Tripoli is a city with the best and worst of Muslims," Farid said, as he pointed out the bad guys in brown robes. Their heads and upper lips were shaved, with untended beards. Arafat left Palestinian guerrillas behind when he sailed for Tunisia. "These Sunni extremists and the Palestinians are the terrorists in Lebanon now, not the Hezbollah," Farid assured me. "During the civil war they rode horses down Tripoli's main street proclaiming the return of the caliphate [the rule of Islamic clerics]." Indeed, they were stern faced and riveted in purpose, but it was Ramadan; everyone was hungry, I thought.

These rowdy guys, "friends of al-Qaeda," as Farid described them, were *takfiris*, or Sunni nihilists. They were everywhere, gripping their Korans like a weapon and snarling like wild dogs. As fearless, rootless young Sunni Arabs, they are trapped in a jihad worldview, with no plan for the future other than returning to the past. Evolution ended with Mohammed—and the crusades are full on for them. They use their Korans to pose as thinkers, but their scholarship ends with an IED (improvised explosive device) in the market and a Koranic verse: "Fight against them until idolatry is no more and Allah's religion reigns supreme." They, of course, ignore opposing decrees for tolerance, in the same way crackpot Christians advocate Old Testament justice over Sermon-on-the-Mount benevolence. Radical Sunnis, they say, are undisciplined because they don't have a pope like the Shias who are led by grand ayatollahs.

⌒

Farid had been eerily prescient about these Islamic militants. Six months after my visit, they became known to the wider world as Fatah al-Islam, as they engaged the Lebanese army in fierce battle in Tripoli. Their leader is Shakir al-Abssi, a former associate of Abu Musab al-Zarqawi, the assassinated leader of al-Qaeda in Iraq. Both al-Abssi and al-Zarqawi were sentenced to death in absentia for the killing of an American diplomat in Jordan. Al-Abssi, a former Palestinian refugee, was recently released from prison in Syria. He is thought by many to be taking his cues from the pro-Syrian Fatah Uprising, but apportioning blame in this region is never easy.

Though they number fewer than 300, not unlike al-Qaeda before September 11, Fatah al-Islam has been a formidable opponent for the Lebanese army. Fighting erupted after a bank robbery in a Christian village, spurring police to raid several Fatah al-Islam hideouts in Tripoli. From there, armed clashes spread to the nearby Palestinian refugee camp Nahr el-Bared, yet another hatchery for al-Qaeda-inspired groups. As the Lebanese army pounded the militants with tank fire, Fatah al-Islam pushed back with antiaircraft guns, mortars, rocket-propelled grenades, and Kalashnikovs (Soviet rifles), martial skills they honed in Iraq.

In three days of fighting, over 60 were killed from both sides. Among the dead were Sunni jihadists from Saudi Arabia, Algeria, Yemen, Tunisia, and, of course, Palestinians. These foreign terrorists were surely holed up in Lebanon because their militancy at home has left them without a country; they thrive on a good sectarian split, to which more than anywhere Lebanon is vulnerable. The hope is that the Lebanese armed forces will hold together, becoming the only functioning nonsectarian institution in Lebanon.[2]

As 30,000 Palestinian refugees fled their refugee camp, *double refugees now*, David Holdridge and Mercy Corps moved in emergency relief. At the same time, Hezbollah and the United States each announced their support for the fragile Lebanese army. In the microcosm of Lebanese politics, this is a rare aligning of stars. Paradoxically, the United States expedited arms shipments, this time to the Lebanese army, when a mere nine months before they were doing the same for Israel to bomb the bejesus out of Hezbollah and the rest of Lebanon!

---

2. Brigadier General François al-Hajj, who led the Lebanese forces, was car bombed by terrorists six months later near Beirut.

～

We parked near the Nahr Abu Ali River, a dull jade ribbon bordering the old town on the east. Vintage '70s Mercedes taxis beeped their way down the crowded, dust-laden streets. Pushcart vendors, selling fruits and vegetables, were wedged into the jumble. A willy-nilly crush of breezeblock dwellings retreated vertiginously up a hillside near the municipal clock tower. The colorful flutter of clothes on the balconies and political posters on their half-painted walls gave this concrete blight an aspect of Havana's cluttered charm. Oppositely, the rock solid footings of the surrounding Mamluk and Ottoman khans, mosques, hammams, and souks stood in stark contrast, a stone hive of living history.

The souk was shaded and cool, sandwiched between the medieval stone-block buildings of the Mamluks. Paint-chipped shutters and wrought-iron balconies hung above rusted awnings that covered the cobbled alleyways. Dusty shafts of sunlight pierced the gaps, washing over the gold shops with a dazzling sheen. Shoppers were variously dressed in prayer caps of white, brown, and green mixed with black scarves, gossamer veils of lavender, and amber. The pungent and intoxicating smells drew us in near an alley of colorful mounds of spices. Nearby, for the nightly Ramadan feast, halal butchers hung split carcasses of lamb, while delivery trucks decanted mounds of crab on ice.

Posters of a handsome, mustachioed Rashid Karami, the assassinated Sunni leader of Tripoli, hung on market walls as a saint's image would in a church. In 1987, Karami was killed in a midair explosion of his helicopter. Christian warlord Samir Geagea was convicted of the assassination; he spent 11 years in prison and was released in the "conciliatory mood" of the Cedar Revolution. "If we were to judge everyone, the whole country would be a prison," wrote one observer.

Karami was from a Sunni power clan in Tripoli; his father was prime minister for one term, while Rashid served eight terms in that role. Since his assassination, his brother has served two terms. "The prime minister is always Sunni," Farid said before explaining the National Covenant. Brokered by France in 1940, based on a 1932 census that gave Christians a slight majority, the gentlemen's agreement among Lebanese is that the president is a Christian Maronite, the prime minister is Sunni, and the speaker of the national assembly is Shia.

For all that, demographics made an epochal change in the 1980s. While Karami was prime minister, Muslims overtook Christians as the majority population. Consequently, Karami pressed for true democracy, while Lebanese Christians and their Western supporters opposed this on shaky grounds: Muslims (Shia, Sunni, Alawite, and Druze) have 59 percent of the population, but their economic input is far less. The fear is that true democracy might open the door for Lebanon to become an Islamic state.

As in Iraq with the Shias, Lebanese Muslims are crowing over one-person, one-vote democracy. The Christian minority members, who are increasingly voting with their feet, want it the way it has always been. By no surprise, Hezbollah's recent war with Israel was as much about their rights to representation in Lebanon as about gaining political capital with Israel by "kidnapping" the two Israeli soldiers. Karami's legacy of inclusive democracy will not go away.

⁓

Above the market, a steep hardtop leads to the Citadel of Raymond de Saint Gilles. Crusaders arrived near here in 1099, coming from Antioch en route to Jerusalem. It was Easter; they had been traveling through hostile territory and were glad to have the "brotherly affection" of the Maronites, who flocked down from Mt. Lebanon. The Maronites advised them to keep to the coastal road for safe passage. The pope would later recognize their assistance, which was the first evidence of Maronite contact with Rome.

For the first two years of the civil war Sunni fundamentalist militias used this 12th-century crusader castle as their headquarters. Robert Fisk wrote about this in *Pity the Nation*: "Along the great escarpments that form the spine of modern-day Lebanon, above the rivers that vein their way across the country, the crusader castles that once formed the outposts of Christendom are still part of a front line, albeit with roles of their defenders historically reversed."

From here, villages scrolled by like a ticker tape of tribalism—Maronite, Shia, Syrian Orthodox, Druze, and Sunni—their ideological separatism often driven by clan loyalties, warlords, and militias. But for Farid providing a running commentary, I would have been blithely unaware of the organic delicacies of these sleepy, mostly provincial villages. Accordingly, it was clear to this first-time arrival that Lebanon's stone-etched divisions made the polarization of American red and blue states, Democrats and Republicans, seem like a family tempest in a Neil Simon play.

By turns, each village would consecrate, with signs and statues, their living leaders and fallen heroes, religious icons and political grandees, in a permanent campaign of cultural identity and revelation. Past injustices, Farid said, provide an ample basis for present and future wars. That religion and politics are inseparable here prompted a Druze warlord to mock Maronite churches who raised money for the Phalangists during the civil war: "The tonsured heads of Lebanese monks give off a golden halo."

As a rule, Christian villages are more prosperous than Muslim ones, and Druze are better off than Sunnis. Shias are at the bottom of the food chain, with the biggest militia and the largest families—born to suffer, one could say. The picturesque, three-day drive from here to the Bekaa and to the Israeli border, a mere 120 miles, the east-west axis of Connecticut, would expose a sequence of parallel universes, where they intermingle out of necessity but are loathe to intermix.

⌣

Now, we were in the foothill village of Zghorta, a pristine Christian enclave. The modernist cityscape of Tripoli was still in view, but culturally it seemed a planet away, like moving from the slums of Algiers to the gardens of Provence. Those rowdy guys we'd seen earlier, at least the ones who didn't dress like me, were not to be seen again until the Bekaa Valley. We were in the Mt. Lebanon homeland of the Maronites, a proud and profoundly Christian sect founded in the early 5th century by St. Maron, a Syriac monk who broke with St. Peter's church of Antioch at the time of the Monophysite schism, the debate over the divinity and humanity of Christ. The Maronite psyche has been shaped, if not disfigured, by 1,600 years of struggle—invasion, repression, and internecine fighting.

We drew up to a patisserie on Zghorta's picturesque main street, taking a table in a shady spot on the drowsy sidewalk. Famous for his desserts, the pastry chef, white toque and all, concocted a paste of sugar, flour, and peaches, topped with whipped cream and cashews. On this occasion, the fresh mountain air was as soothing as the dessert was sweet. Locals dawdled by in familiar Western finery, their dispositions sunny but their double glances giving away a hint of suspicion. If verbalized in Americana, those glances might say, "Hey stranger, what brings you to Dodge?" The main square in this Maronite village recalled another time, as torpid and tangled as some of those southern Gothic towns that I came of age in, where in William Faulkner's words, "The past is not dead. In fact, it's not even past."

Banners adorned the light poles along the main intersection of Zghorta, proclaiming the local grandees, Suleiman (Arabic for Solomon) and his son Tony Frangieh. Their glossy mugs, which looked as if they were photographed yesterday, could have been that of the mayor of any old town in America: well dressed, narcissistic, and solemn but strong. Of course, Suleiman and Tony have been dead for years. But their deeds, uncivilized as they were, remain as symbols of faith and justice here.

In William Dalrymple's book *From the Holy Mountain*, Suleiman Frangieh is said to have had a Muslim a month killed in Tripoli just to remind locals that he was feudal lord in northern Lebanon. He even boasted of having personally killed over 700 Muslims. What finally brought the heat down on Suleiman Frangieh and the family militia was a blood feud with a rival Maronite clan, the Douaihy family—that played out at a funeral held near Zghorta. Again, apportioning blame is never easy, but based on eyewitness testimony a massacre took place at the church, the Christian version of Hamas and Fatah going at it. With over 50 of the Frangieh militiamen indicted, Sulieman Frangieh fled to the Alawi Mountains in Syria; there he was befriended by Hafez al-Assad, then a young air force officer. Following a decade in hiding and a pardon, Sulieman Frangieh became president of Lebanon.

⟋

Mt. Lebanon rose before us in a cascade of shaded, lion-colored folds. The winding road was soon fringed in olive orchards that gave way to a garden pathway of roses, ripe pomegranates, autumnal-hued trellises of grapes, and the much ballyhooed Bsharre apples. Sprouting in profusion from these fields of plenty, closing the gap between eternal heaven and mundane earth, were crosses and iconic images of St. Rafka, who, after a life as a blind, paralytic nun, regained her health and vision; of St. Hardini, a priest who was devoted to the Eucharist and the blessed Virgin Mary; and of St. Charben, the 19th-century monk who performed many life-saving miracles. Colossal alabaster statues of the Virgin Mary and Jesus crowned two peaks overlooking Ehden, an enchanting mountain fastness, where Christian piety is matched only by tribal terrorism.

A Lebanese army roadblock, manned by Maronites, greeted us on the outskirts of Ehden. In Arabic, Farid mentioned "tourist," and they waved us through like diplomats. Around the next bend, we turned into the empty parking lot of the Church of St. George. Older women, their heads wrapped babushka style in scarves, tottered through a side entrance to the red brick and cut-stone church for afternoon prayer, drinking in the sweet piety for their men folk, too.

Farid and I made our way to the garden lookout behind the church. Red-tiled roofs and sunny church steeples fenced the horizon, but in the time we stood there, the afternoon shadow recast the town in a soft twilight. Beneath two 50-foot fir trees, a bronze statue of a man on a horse seemed poised to gallop off the garden precipice. A marble plate on the monument's stone plinth was carved in Arabic and English, with the rider's name, Joseph (Youssef) Karam.

Joseph Karam was born in Ehden in 1823, the son of Sheikh Boutros Karam, lord of Ehden. The Karams were fervent Maronites, as well as legendary Lebanese nationalists who often took up arms against the Ottoman occupiers. So successful was Joseph Karam in defeating the Ottomans that, by 1867, Napoleon III sent orders to remove him from Lebanon. A national hero, he agreed to be exiled in return for the safety of his people and a promise that his political demands, especially the removal of the Ottomans, would be met. That was not to be in his lifetime. He never returned to Lebanon, dying of natural causes in 1889 in Napoli, Italy. His last words had a familiar ring: "God . . . Lebanon." Six months later his body was returned to Ehden, to the Church of St. George.

Reverently, I slid unnoticed into the chapel. A priest was conducting a service beneath a Bosch-like mural of St. George, who wielded a lance from his white horse, protecting these Maronites. As he followed me to Joseph Karam's glass sarcophagus, Farid was expounding in a tone that would wake the dead. Attired in a faded red fez and embroidered green tunic, Karam's mummified body was taut and blackened, his fingernails long, his mouth stuffed with cotton, and his eyes as peaceful as any old death mask. An ornamental sword was slung across the wall above the corpse, set as gracefully as a Madonna in a Pietà, the scent of blood on both. Given the equestrian bronze outside, Karam has been cast as St. George's spiritual twin.

"For the Maronites, the church existed to lead the community from the very beginning and serve as a repository for its historical experience," wrote Kamal Salibi in A House of Many Mansions. As with the Cold War Communists, embalming was done to pay homage to the dead and, as a demonstration of power to the living, to mold a martyr and to evoke patriotic emotions.

∼

Ehden and Bsharre have been in a blood feud for almost two centuries. The Frangieh clan controlled Ehden, while Christian warlord Samir Geagea, the convicted assassin of Sunni prime minister Rashid Karami, is from Bsharre. During the civil war a power struggle pitted Geagea's Phalangists against Frangieh's Marada Militia. Geagea wanted to partition Lebanon and Frangieh didn't. Apple orchards spread from the twisting road to Bsharre. Giant posters on every street advertised Samir Geagea. In Bsharre there is an acceptance of God and the devil, whereas in America we are Calvinist inspired and think we can do away with the devil. Upon arrival, like passing from one country to the next, Bsharre and every village we would travel through afterward would be bookended by the Lebanese army or militia roadblocks, bristling with weapons.

Hotel Chbat overlooks Bsharre and the holy Qadisha Valley, a UNESCO (United Nations Educational, Scientific and Cultural Organization) World Heritage site of dramatic cliffs falling precipitously into a bucolic valley of rock-hewn monasteries and churches. The hotel, catering to skiers and trekkers, has been here since 1955. On this day it seemed abandoned, closed for the season. "Hello, hello, hello," Farid called out, as we circled outside before tunneling through a breezeway and out into a dining hall, a showplace of pine and oak handiwork: floor-to-ceiling paneled walls, wide-slat floors, and locally crafted tables and chairs. The room's dark-stained walls offered a gallery of exceptional outdoor photographs. I was especially taken with one of a 60-foot snowbank near the Cedars of Lebanon, two miles up the road. The more I took in, the more the Hotel Chbat reminded me of an old New England home or lodge—idiosyncratic, homey, dowdy, charming, patched, and ever evolving.

Mr. Chbat, the innkeeper, boomed a "welcome" from across the dining room. He and his mother, an eighty-something widow, had been off in the half-lit kitchen. She stayed in the shadows, ill dressed for meeting people. He was in his midfifties and had a close-cropped beard, a chubby face, and dark-set eyes. His demeanor was pleasant, even solicitous, with courtly manners. Preceded by a barrel chest, Mr. Chbat was outfitted in hunter brown—field hat, shooting vest, and canvas pants—as if fresh from a pheasant kill.

He waved at us to sit at the dining room table, where he told me that I was the first guest in his 50-room lodge since the war began. Three months before, like the rest of Lebanon, he was ramping up for his slice of 1.5 million tourists. "We were 65 to 80 percent booked from June to November," he said. For a moment, a look of despair crossed his face. "With this war, business is dead. It's a bad dream. The bookings were all Europeans, no Lebanese, Gulf States, or Saudis."

"You mean the Saudis don't come here to ski or trek?"

Grinning now, he said, "Let me put it this way. At 11 when the Europeans are going to bed, the Saudis are going out to the clubs in Jounieh."

He hefted himself out of his seat, took my American passport, which, even in the busiest of times, would be an unusual sight here. Once upon a time, being an American guest conferred prestige upon a place, but not on this day. Mr. Chbat didn't remark about my home country, nor did he mention America when he groused about the war. Sometimes silence says more. He was a gentleman and an innkeeper.

It was after dark. A Filipino "waitress" arrived at the table. She also cleaned rooms and cooked, but with no tourists, at $130 a month, relatively speaking, she was making off like a bandit. She was one of 30 living in the village, brought here to help with the heavy tourist traffic. As she waited, Mr. Chbat preemptively recommended the mezze plate, which featured *tapen*, a local smoked fish, and for a main course the usual spread of lamb and chicken kebabs. He disappeared into the moonlight-darkened kitchen. The plaintive strains of an oud played on CD. As one of the best meals I would have in Lebanon, it seemed wasted in this lonesome dining hall. In saying goodnight, Mr. Chbat asked about my shower time; with 48 empty rooms, there was no need to keep the hot water heater on all night.

The next morning, Mr. Chbat appeared in the dining room early, impeccably dressed in a black suit. His shiny pate, barrel chest, and likeable manner made him a dead ringer for Tony Soprano. He led his mother, also in her best finery, across the room to say goodbye. They were on their way to a funeral in Tripoli.

"This happens all too often these days," he said in a tone of dreamy fatalism. "It's an old family friend."

⌒

Farid and I corkscrewed down into the Qadisha Valley, through apple orchards and grape vineyards and fallow terraces of wheat, used to make flat bread. Stacked rock fences like those found in the Cotswolds of England to contain small flocks of sheep encircled the modest estates. Monkish care had been given over decades to cultivating and cobbling these farms into a postcard visage. Oppositely, the craggy walls of the valley were splotched with cedar, oak, and pine and pocked with caves, one used by Maronite hero Joseph Karam while holing up from the Ottoman army.

Velocity driven (caffeine), Farid was smoking, talking, and honking at boys herding sheep down the middle of the road, while taking hairpin curves at a dangerous clip. I had him pull over for a call of nature. Standing above a copse of mulberry trees, we could hear the echo of braying donkeys, rushing water, and ringing bell towers, the quietude of a hermit city. Tracing the serpentine coil of asphalt to its end, the rampart walls and red-tiled roof of the Monastery of St. Anthony of Qozhaya sprang from the valley floor with the presence of a medieval castle but laid low like a box canyon hideout.

The monastery and hermitage are commingled with the Cave of Qozhaya, first inhabited by Syriac monks in the early 4th century, predating St. Maron's rise to notoriety. With communal facilities for up to 200 monks, hermit priests still burrow up here, including Father Dario Escobar from Colombia, a doctor in psychology and theology, whom we glimpsed as he finished a prayer service upon our arrival. Regrettably, he disappeared as we turned off to inspect a printing press, the oldest in the Middle East, first used to print the Psalter in 1585. Among the ancient Syria manuscripts was a scepter from Louis IX of France, the patron nation of the Maronites, as Britain is to the Druze, Russia to the Orthodox, and Iran to the Shias. Every confessional relies on a foreign patron, a coreligionist.

Christian and Muslim pilgrims alike come here not only to pray and worship in a serene setting but also to be cured of their diseases. The Cave of Qozhaya narrows and forms a mystic passage into the mountain, some say all the way to Ehden. It has been known for 1,600 years, across Lebanon and the Middle East, as a treatment venue for the mentally ill. This interested me, because I have often thought a narrow line divided these willfully self-deprived cave dwellers, especially today, and those in society whom we deem unbalanced or insane.

As with most spelunking settings, the cave had the musty whiff of dirty laundry. Buckets were placed around the earthen floor to contain the dripping. A short distance inside was a house-sized boulder, fronted by a slab of rock the measure of a queen bed. Beneath a portrait of St. Anthony, the father of monks and monasticism, hung chains and shackles that pooled into a junk heap of iron on the rock slab. An altar, with burning candles and a smaller portrait of St. Anthony, was to the side. This was the chamber, if you will, where the mentally ill were treated. They say it hasn't been so long since the shackles and chains were retired.

St. Anthony was born in the 3rd century in Egypt to a wealthy Christian family. The sudden death of his parents, in late adolescence, occasioned him to renounce his worldly possessions and to take up the monastic life in the Egyptian desert. In time, he reckoned that torturing the body would build resistance to physical and spiritual sickness. Fasting, not sleeping, and being isolated, he became terrorized by demons that took the form of wild beasts: hissing snakes, roaring lions, ferocious wolves, and an ornery pig. This menagerie, as the story goes, was Satan disguised, testing St. Anthony's faith in Christ. Once the demons were defeated (exorcised even), St. Anthony heard the Word of God:

"Lord, where was Thou when these sufferings and tribulations came upon me? Why didst Thou not help me?" He heard a voice.

"I was here, Anthony, but I wanted to witness your combat. Having seen that you withstood your adversary without retreating, I shall from now on be your Helper and shall make your name celebrated far and wide as my faithful servant."

This fateful revelation began the Maronite practice at the Cave of Qozhaya of St. Anthony conquering demons (of curing the mentally disabled). Before returning to Bsharre, Farid felt the need to assure me, more than once, that the chains and shackles were no longer in use.

⁓

Bsharre's most famous son was not a Maronite saint or heroic slayer of Muslims but the mystic Prophet of the Beats, of the '60s counterculture and New Agers, Kahlil Gibran. Through his poetry or paintings, he took on themes such as unity of being, the continuity of life, the beauty of nature, marriage and love, reason and passion, and the conflict between East and West. Though his critics are many and suspicious, his audience remains monolithic and faithful. *The Prophet* is a book of the ages, translated into over 30 languages, having sold nine million copies in the United States alone. Wordsmiths from John Kennedy ("Ask not what your country . . .") to John Lennon ("Julia") have borrowed from his gnomic writings. Even today, academic researchers worldwide parse his poetry to better understand the conflicts between us.

Gibran died at age 48 of tuberculosis and cirrhosis in New York's St. Vincent's Hospital. When his body was returned to Bsharre, Mary Haskell and devoted sister Mariana fulfilled his wishes to purchase St. Joseph's Monastery and a 7th-century hermitage, now his tomb and the Gibran Museum.

The oak forest of St. Sarkis surrounds the monastery. Farid and I were the only visitors that day, which I suppose is every tourist's dream. Yet it was hard not to imagine something sinister in the air when greeted by a snarl of middle-aged men, three or four staring at camera monitors, another selling tickets, and another taking tickets. Security aside, it looked like an employment relief act, with winners take all.

Before dying, Gibran donated the royalties from *The Prophet* to the village of Bsharre. Rather than accepting his largesse in the charitable spirit in which it was intended, rival Maronite clans turned the streets of Bsharre into a virtual civil war. The government had to intervene to restore order. Surely these gate-keepers were the heirs to that greed.

A treasure trove of manuscripts, his personal library, the modest furnishings of his New York apartment (51 West Tenth Street), over 400 original paintings, and his wine-cellar-like tomb have transformed this ancient monastery into an exquisitely faceted memorial to Gibran.

The alchemy of his many nudes gamboling in nature, set in clouds that wash over craggy mountaintops, was surely inspired by the ethereal landscape of Bsharre. It is said that, as a child, when a storm arrived in Bsharre, he would run disrobed into the downpour in a fit of euphoric abandon. Drawing on his life, Gibran's paintings here conflate this cosmic but conflicted beauty of Bsharre, with the sexually charged artistic freedoms of Paris, and the existential immersion of a poet in New York, liberating the imagination all.

Although he was a poetic disciple of Christ the exemplar, steeped in the revelations of the Bible, Gibran's religious curiosity was extraordinarily catholic. He envisioned a more mystical, Sufi-inspired God of all (Unity of Being), which was, inferentially, a solution to sectarian conflict. His introspective bias and abstract sensibility were, if nothing else, not matter-of-course Maronite. That a Gibran museum is here in this zone of conflict, proud as the Bsharre residents must be, seemed no less out of place than a Strawberry Fields memorial in Baghdad's Green Zone. In Gibran's poem "Pity the Nation," he takes aim at Lebanon and the ones who now manage his legacy:

> Pity the nation that is full of beliefs and empty of religion. . . .
> Pity the nation that acclaims the bully as hero, and that deems
> the glittering conqueror bountiful.

~

"Ask the Muslims," Farid said. "They think we screwed up everything, even the trees." He was on to something, as we picnicked the next day on a stone wall at the north end of the Qadisha Valley beneath the Cedars of Lebanon, devouring *kawarmas*: fatty lamb seasoned in olive oil and sesame seeds, wrapped in thin, handmade tandoori bread.

The moonscaped ridge of Mt. Makmel, at almost 10,000 feet, the highest peak in the Middle East, hovered above this venerable, but paltry, cathedral of towering cedars. These cedars that built old Solomon's temple had seen better days.

Good hardwood has long been a scarce natural resource in the arid Middle East. Going back almost 5,000 years, over two millennia before the stories of Solomon or Isaiah were written, the *Epic of Gilgamesh* tells us the "forest of cedar" of Mount Lebanon was coveted by kings for their palaces. When the semimythical King Gilgamesh and his faithful companion Enkidu arrived here on a military-like expedition, "they saw the mountain of cedar, seat of gods and goddesses throne." Then Gilgamesh faced off with Humbaba and the seven auras, and they "slew the ogre, the forest's guardian, at whose yell were sundered the peaks of Sirion and Lebanon."

Zigzagging up the mountain, in the direction of Baalbek, we were soon upon "Gibran's ski slope," but it was closed until December. At the village of Ainata al Arz, Farid pointed out Samir Geagea's home, a nondescript stucco house standing alone but with an air of fortresslike impregnability. Roadside, in front of his house, an arched white sign emblazoned with an American flag read "US-AID, Ainata Potable Water Project." Another 100 yards, we halted at a militia roadblock. Glancing back, the Cedars of Lebanon were a flyspeck, a tuft of sage on a bereft landscape.

CHAPTER SIX

~

Poppy Fields, McDonald's, Armageddon, and the Loire Valley

If the spectacularly beautiful Qadisha Valley is a grotto-filled, Maronite hide-out, the Bekaa plains, a name with a magical resonance, are a scenic checker-board of commercial and family farms and sprawling vineyards, cantonized by every confessional from Syria to Israel and the Mediterranean to Iraq. For now, precision-guided munitions had turned large tracks of hardtop into earthen mounds, 20 feet wide and half as deep. Farid Chrabieh found this to be an occa-sion to smoke with one hand and talk on his cell phone with the other, dodging debris and drop-offs in between. (And I was trying to take notes.)

Thirty minutes later we were in the farming village of Deir al-Ahmar, known widely, if not infamously, for its produce: potatoes, opium, and hash, the latter two historic staples of the Levant. Yes, the famous blond Lebanese hash, found in the Amsterdam coffee shops of the early 1970s, was cultivated beneath my feet. Decades on, those sweet, potent vapors remain fixed in my memory as a first kiss, yet I can't recall a single word from one of the relevant books of the time, *The Prophet*. Today, however, it felt like a reunion of mind and spirits no less moving than a pilgrimage to the Tennessee home of Jack Daniels.

The Maronite village of Deir al-Ahmar, home to eight historical churches, has long been beyond the pale of law, a no man's land where money sprouted on trees: cannabis, which produces hashish, and opium poppies, from which heroin is refined, have long been the currency here. Before and during the civil war, one-third of the arable land in the Bekaa Valley was cultivated with opium or cannabis.

Providing the beeswax for 10,000 families, the Syrian military-controlled drug trade here financed arms purchases and militias. To sidestep sanctions for being on America's drug trafficker list, by the late 1990s both Lebanon and Syria publicly supported eradication efforts.

As an alternative income, USAID (United States Agency for International Development) brought in American Holstein cows. Because Lebanon imports much of their meat and dairy products, this was intended to reduce the cost of imports and provide food and money to the farmers, or so the theory went. At the time, however, an awareness of cattle-borne diseases was sweeping the world, spurring Hezbollah to put the word out that the American cows were a wee bit skinny, sickly even.

Doeng, the mythical Cold War communist in *The Ugly American*, likewise responded to the introduction of American milk cows: "If it succeeded, the Sarkhanese would believe that America was their savior."

In a counter to the U.S. move, Hezbollah, with bucks from Iran, provided their own dairy cows. Predictably in this hearts and minds enterprise, Hezbollah's milk cows cost the farmer $1,000 less than they were paying for the American Holsteins.

With a kilo of hash selling for $300, the farmer is working more and bringing home less. "In the days of hashish we were so happy," said one farmer to a *New York Times* reporter, adding, "I once owned a car, but now, thanks be to God, I have a cow." Many farmers have returned to cultivating garden plots of the drugs, staying below the radar of America's drug trafficking list.

~

During the civil war, Robert Fisk described Deir al-Ahmar as "a village of chickens, puddles and concrete bungalows—Syrian tanks dug into the fields, a bunch of dirty-fleeced sheep leaning elegiacally against their gun muzzles."

On this day, a poppy field bloomed smack in the center of this low-roofed, somnolent village. Plastic-covered gardens of marijuana grew along the dirt tracks that radiated from the highway. A line of Mercedes-Benzes nosed up against a restaurant near the luxuriant pink poppies. At two in the afternoon, a table of ten or more men convened beneath a pergola of grape vines, eating mezze plates and drinking arak. They didn't wear overalls, nor did they have manure or clods of dirt on their shiny street shoes. If a firecracker had gone off, I could imagine an arsenal of weapons blazing forth that would shock Scarface.

Beyond the militia roadblock, attendant to each village as trailer parks are to American small towns, was an up-and-coming Bedu camp. This one boasted satellite dishes, two old Mercedes, barrel-sized plastic water containers, and layers of burlap battened with used tires. Dusty green tobacco fields, littered in the plastic-bag rubbish of the Bedu, gave way to the Anti-Lebanon Range, which is the border of Syria and the source of these migrants, Farid says. Cheap labor aside, they are outcasts, nonentities, as Gypsies are from Mesopotamia to Europe. That is changing, however. With one person, one vote (and one gun), Lebanese Sunnis are taking advantage of the Bedu's political value—as fellow Sunnis—and signing them up at the polls.

⌒

Historical Baalbek slaps you in the face like a Palestinian camp writ large. These are Shias, the Hezbollah, or the Party of God, whose message of hope resonates with the disaffected here in the same way evangelical churches do in America. The faces of modern-day martyrs competed with the imaginary painted images of the Prophet's grandson, Hussein, the original Shia martyr. Here again, even though Hezbollah set the standard in the early '80s for suicide bombers and extremist tactics now used by al-Qaeda and others, Farid reminded me that they will terrorize the dickens out of Israel but not fellow Lebanese. "Hezbollah is disciplined, not a bunch of anarchic suicide bombers anymore," he told me.[1]

Indeed, alliances are not easy to unravel here: In the 1980s, Israel and Iran's Revolutionary Guard engaged in a proxy war in Baalbek and in the south of Lebanon. At the same time, Israel found common cause with Iran in the Iran-Iraq War and shipped them arms (leading to the Iran-Contra Affair).

"Baalbek Welcomes Whoever Feels the Pain of the People," a greeting sign read.

Dusty and poor, the old Roman capital bustled with beat-up cars and beat-down people. Scattered among the concrete box homes were militant Islamic banners of Iran's Ayatollahs Khomeini and Khamenei and Hezbollah's Sheikh Hassan Nasrallah, who takes his spiritual and political cues from Iran's supreme leader. Their super-sized black spectacles matching their exalted robes and black *imamas* (turbans) border on self-parody.

Along the parklike median of Resistance and Liberation Street, where a municipal clock tower might have stood, a Russian-made Syrian battle tank was mounted on a 20-foot quarry-stone pedestal. To the extent cities take on brands, just as Alma, Arkansas, is the Spinach Capital of the World, Baalbek, seemed to purposely promote a martial image.

It went on. Streetlight poles were hung with Hezbollah flags and the mugs of suicide bombers and Kalashnikov-toting martyrs, or *shahid*, in Arabic. Even Sheikh Nasrallah's son is a *shahid*, killed by Israelis in 1997. Their militant but

---

1. The exception, we would not learn for five more years, was the 2005 assassination of Prime Minister Rafik Hariri.

youthful visages, often set against the clouds of paradise, were more tumultuous than graveyard silent.

Though suicide is prohibited in the Koran, many of today's clerics refuse to declare it haram, or forbidden. It's too effective against the West in the holy war, or modern jihad, which literally means struggle. Over the course of history, jihad has covered everything from defending Islam against attack to cleansing the soul with charitable deeds and the struggle to be a better person. The latter is on the rise among young Arabs and progressive clerics such as Sheikh Yusuf al-Qaradawi of Egypt and Mohammed Tahir ul Qadri of Pakistan who play a constructive role in Islamic society and reject suicide bombers and extremists.

Tannoy speakers blasted a live Nasrallah oration, rebuking Israel, America, and Maronites. Only in this country of contradictions could this rock-star cleric's militant sermonizing, also widely viewed on Hezbollah TV across the Middle East, compete for audience share with *Superstar*, Lebanon's answer to *American Idol*.

Farid delivered a blow by blow, laughing at times at Nasrallah's redundant use of *karameh* (dignity), trotted out to rally the masses against the Great Satans, Israel and America, who are denying them their dignity. These Ramadan-fasting faithful of Baalbek weren't hard to stir: the recent Israeli bombardment had provided the fire in the belly. As with many Bekaa villages, this had been a ghost town a mere two months ago.

We drew up to the Palmyra Hotel, like the Baron in Aleppo, another faded grande dame of the Middle East. Its French colonial facade was now a mangy buff yellow, the shutters chipped green, overlaid in the dust of 20th-century dynasties. Inside, lights were out, and no attendants seemed to be in. Spread with threadbare Persian-style rugs, the dim corridors signaled our footfalls not unlike the squeaking nightingale floors of ancient Japan. Period posters of 19th-century French stage actress Sarah Bernhardt and of Kaiser Wilhelm II, perhaps a remembrance of the German occupation of the hotel during World War I, adorned the otherwise spartan walls of what must have been a sitting room. There was no furniture.

Then, quieter than silence, a corpse-like silhouette appeared: rheumy pools of blackness set deep into the pallid face of the caretaker. His slept-in clothes hung loose as a potato sack from his frame of frail bones. In slow motion, his lips parted, showing two gnarled incisors, tobacco black. "Do you want a room?" he murmured. His twisted expression led me to think that speaking gave his mouth a bad taste.

Farid was uninspired but agreed to look at an upstairs room. I unlocked the door with an antique cast iron key. As I flung open the shutter doors, giving onto a balcony, roaches scattered in the sudden sunlight. The shuttered doorway framed the Roman ruins of Baalbek, the famous six Corinthian columns of the Jupiter temple thrusting to the heavens.

On the mundane grounds of Rome's lyrical architecture, epoch composed on top of epoch, the transcendence of god on earth had taken place: from the mystery of the skies to Phoenicians and biblical Semites performing bloody sacrifices to a fertility god (Baal); from Greeks worshipping the sun (Helios) and Romans their orgiastic goddess (Aphrodite) to Yahweh the Jewish creator and Jesus the more anthropomorphic Son of God, or Mohammed the Prophet. Whether animist, polytheistic, or monotheistic, here within the walls of Baalbek, the gods have all died like the people who conceived them.

Fronting ancient Baalbek was an emergency relief tent sponsored by Iran's Revolutionary Guard and Hezbollah. A temporary road encircled it, the old one now a bomb crater. Near the Grand Mosque around the corner, built by the Ummayad caliphs, three concrete buildings and the souk had been reduced to mounds of glass and gravel, the Iranian-built hospital riddled in bullet holes. The sky was smoky blue, the air acrid, as if the bombing had occurred yesterday. Below, street vendors were listless, immobilized from the aftershock and staring with vague interest at all that moved. The Roman air of civilization was lost upon us.

We stood at the window talking. "I am never afraid of Israel's bombs," Farid said. "They are very precise. It's the Syrians I worry about. Israel drops leaflets, and even calls, leaving a recording: 'This is the State of Israel. We are getting ready to bomb you.'"

"I don't believe that."

"It's true. Once my mother answered the phone in the middle of the night, and, without waiting for a voice, told them to call back in the morning." Mockingly, he added, "It's a recording, Mother!"

Turning to go downstairs, Farid confided that the hotel attendant reminded him of an ax murderer. My thoughts had turned to sanitation, the kitchen. Was Mr. Addams Family the cook, too?

"Let's get out of here," Farid urged. "I know a man who is head of the Baalbek Tourist Bureau whose cousin has a guesthouse nearby."

Abdullah was pacing in front of his restaurant, where he displayed rotisserie chicken browning in the sun. There would be no takers on day 25 of Ramadan until after sunset. During the fasting hours, even the Christians in Baalbek are polite about not eating in public. Abdullah, however, appeared never to have missed a meal. He engaged me in the same shifty but directed manner of a pimp scouting johns: "Hello, you are from America, where you stay?" He had learned his English in the '70s at the University of Houston; however, when I tried to talk up Texas, he was a blank slate.

Whatever Texas was then, it represented something different to him now. It wasn't modernity he was shy about; he owned the Internet Café next door, filled with youngsters playing games and sullenly awaiting the arrival of *iftar*, the postfast feast held each evening after sunset prayer.

We walked together up a windy hillock to the guesthouse, talking awkwardly about Baalbek lodging prices, as if it were the end-all to my visit here. His "cousin" wanted twice what Abdullah had promised us. Fortuitously, three Mercy Corps staff arrived as we did at the guesthouse and we piggybacked their rate. Disappointed, as head of the Baalbek Tourist Bureau, Abdullah waddled back down the hill, searching for stragglers.

Farid and I had dinner at the Sinbad Restaurant among a platoon of Lebanese Armed Forces, after which we watched the garish afterglow of sunset across the Bekaa plains. Magur, an engineer from Romania, now working for Mercy Corps, joined us. Tall, dark, handsome, full of bravado, smart, and smartly dressed, Magur was in Darfur before frustration set in with the politics of development there. "We build schools and in Darfur we had four people doing the work of 14," he said. "You can only do that for so long. I stayed two years. Most people I worked with left, too."

In Baalbek he is supervising the construction of ten schools, while in Lebanon's south another 25 were destroyed during the 34-day war. That good and bad can happen in the same place keeps Magur employed. Darkness fell like a curtain; locals burrowed in for the night. In all directions, minarets cried out the last call to prayer for this day: there is but one God and his Prophet is Mohammed.

⁓

Next morning, Farid and I enjoyed a hearty bowl of *fuul*, a pasty mix of fava beans, chickpeas, and olive oil. Soon we found ourselves among the flowering shrubs of orange pyracantha at the entry gate of Baalbek's fabulous Roman ruins. Along with the unemployed guides, we were the only ones there.

Inside the great court, surveying this eerie vacancy reminded me of what Nairobi friends had described about Queen Hapshepsut's temple near Luxor, Egypt, two days after the Islamic Group massacre on November 18, 1997. Baalbek was suffering the fate of Luxor, occasioned not by paradise-bound terrorists but at the pleasure of Israeli pilots flying fighter jets and firing rockets, made in America all.

The year before, Farid had attended the Baalbek International Festival, first launched in the midfifties, suspended during the civil war, and resumed in 1997. Among the well-preserved and dramatically backlit temples of Bacchus and Jupiter, the festival has hosted the Chinese Circus, Miles Davis, Ella

Fitzgerald, the Dizzy Gillespie All-Star Band, Placido Domingo, the Buena Vista Social Club, Sting, and Andrew Lloyd Webber's *Cats*. It is the Lebanese folk music, though, that Farid and friends revel in, singing their heads off and dancing the rhythmic, stomping steps of the *dabke*, in the way grapes were once mashed into wine.

Given that this global gathering, that even Bacchus, objectified in carvings of grapes and poppies in the pagan temple, is antipathetic to Hezbollah's message of Islamic rigidity, the friction between Baalbek's past and present is separated by a mere fortress wall built at the time of the Muslim conquest.

In this city of dead emperors and obsolete gods, we gave up the calm vacancy that had set upon the ancient glories of Rome, returning to the heaving, chaotic streets of Baalbek. As we drove away, a bannered double archway with photos of black-turbaned descendants of Mohammed, two of whom had been assassinated by Israelis, hung above the road, exhorting all passers: "The Martyrs are the Ones Who Preserve Your Dignity." By nightfall we would be in Nabatieh, the Hezbollah stronghold in south Lebanon.

～

Farid soon directed my attention to a field of twisted metal and glass, the remains of the Liban Lait dairy farm, the largest producer of milk and dairy products in Lebanon. The dairy farm employed some 300 locals before a barrage of precision munitions destroyed it. This unchallenged bombardment occurred in the early morning hours on the fifth day of the war. Curiously, hangars next door, which could have stored Hezbollah rockets, were not targeted, while supermarkets and food storage facilities were all over the south and the Bekaa. One of the refugees I met in Damascus was from here. His neighbor had lost his mother and four children.[2]

"This village is where drug dealers and car thieves come from," Farid said, gesturing toward a loose assemblage of militia roadblocks, bunkered houses, Bedu camps, and potato fields that marched purposely to the foothills. That this rather typical-looking Bekaa village didn't reek of common gangsterism provided the cover for all manner of lawlessness.

Britel, a wide spot in the road, is home to renegade Hezbollah leader Sheikh Sobhi Toufaili, who coordinated the 1982 terrorist bombings of the marine barracks and American embassy in Beirut. American hostages, such as Terry Anderson, may have been held captive hereabouts in the 1980s. Over 10,000 victims were kidnapped and killed during the civil war, many of whom must

---

2. Not to inappropriately insert levity here, but I wondered if they had also bombed the American Holsteins or just the Hezbollah milk cows.

have died here. Today, Toufaili is an enemy to the central Hezbollah command, but Britel still thrives on the "hot" car business.

"Local thugs steal cars in Beirut and bring them here," Farid said. "Then they call the owner and offer to sell it back for, say, $2,000. It doesn't help to call the police. They will not come to Britel. So you pay for your car twice, the second time at a discount."

When the 34-day war erupted, Farid was working a summer job near Britel on a college friend's potato farm. One morning, while in the field, three precision-guided missiles ripped through the sky. Nanoseconds later the missiles thundered into a nearby heliport and the storage tanks at a gas station, the one we were now passing.

Across Lebanon, 20 fuel depots and 25 gas stations were destroyed, under the rationale that if it's fuel (or food), then terrorists must be consuming it, too. Adjacent to the Seminary College of St. Anne, the cinder-block station was whole but for the blown-out windows and glass doors. The metal-lined storage tanks, after exploding into a fireball, were now black-singed craters.

We were now in Rayak, only a few miles from the Syrian frontier, where Palestinians remain holed up in the stony escarps of the Anti-Lebanon Range; the escarps were visible with the naked eye. Farid said that in the '80s the Palestinians trained everyone from the PKK (Kurdistan Workers' Party) and Nicaraguan Sandinistas to Saudis and Iranians in those mountain camps, teaching Marxist-Leninist doctrine and guerrilla warfare. The Syrian hillside resembled a giant dirt dauber's nest—perhaps nature imitating life.

"During the civil war massacres of Christians occurred throughout the Bekaa but not here in Rayak," Farid said. "Christians reside on one side of the Ottoman-era high street and Muslims on the other." They live together, coexist harmoniously, an evolutionary adaptation that defies local laws of natural selection. On both sides, their tin-roofed, brightly painted homes and fastidious shops bespoke Bekaa middle class. "Some are even crossing the street and mixing!" Farid avowed. We agreed to not talk about this antitribal blasphemy.

The road came to a T-junction at the crossroads village of Chtaura, left to Damascus or right to Beirut. Thinking better of a stop at McDonald's, we pushed on through the West Bekaa, weaving through steepled villages that retreated up Mt. Lebanon, tall and green with cedars topped by a crisp blue sky. Vegetable and watermelon vendors skirted the road in the shadow of terraced, autumn-hued vineyards, dynamited from nothing out of Mt. Lebanon's stony foothills. Guarded by bunker-filled militia and Syrian tanks, we turned into Chateau Kefraya.

Together, Michel de Bustrus, an aristocratic Christian from a Beirut family, and Walid Jumblatt, the principal grandee of the Druze, who lives in a palace in the nearby Chouf region, own the winery.

I felt as if I were being repeatedly drawn in, and then tossed out of, a time warp, if not just a grand schizophrenic episode: poppy fields, McDonald's, Armageddon, and the Loire Valley?

In the modern tasting room, surrounded by racks of wine, commemorative hats, T-shirts, and corkscrews, with well-trained hostesses plying us with miniature glasses of white, red, and blush, we selected a $50 bottle of Chateau for lunch at Le Relais Dionysos. The waiters, liveried in starchy black and white, decorously seated us by a terrace window. We faced a rose garden tended by a vineyard keeper sporting a derby, raking, pruning, and mowing. Farid paused briefly to exchange pleasantries with a smartly dressed man who had waved him over to his table. He was the brother of Amin Assouad, a Christian martyr, who was killed at age 17, while fighting Palestinians in the Beirut souk.

The lingering lunch was of black olive tapenade, followed by a mezze plate with *kebbes* (meatballs), an entrée of almond trout, a digestive and mango sorbet, and then Turkish coffee. All the while, the jazzy sounds of a better angel, Diana Krall, wafted across the terraced atrium.

⌢

Clouds had gathered as we breasted Mt. Lebanon on a rain-slick and artillery-rutted road. The craters were to the side of the narrow hardtop, a strategy they say the Israelis employed to impede lorries more so than family cars. Two abandoned Syrian army bunkers stood like hapless Sphinxes at the head of the pass. Beyond was Maaser el-Chouf, a cloud-shrouded cedar reserve, more bountiful but less regarded than Bsharre's famous Cedars of Lebanon. From here, the scenic descent into Moukhtara and the Chouf precinct recalled the pristine care and pride of Swiss alpine villages. The Chouf is better known as the medieval homeland to a mystical offshoot of the Egyptian Ismaili sect of Islam, the Druze.

A thousand years ago, Druze preachers arrived in the Chouf to spread the word to local Arab tribes. Within decades the preaching stopped, and the doors were closed; Druze are not interested in converts. Their sacred books are guarded by centuries of secrecy, but their traditions do not include the Muslim pillars of prayer, fasting, or a pilgrimage to Mecca. They don't have mosques or imams but rather "holy men" who are more social and political than religious. Plato and Pythagoras are prophets just as are Abraham, Moses, Jesus, and Mohammed. Their holiest shrine, located in Tiberius, Israel, is the tomb of Jethro, who assisted the Jews during the Exodus. And like the Alawites, they believe in reincarnation, and the practice of *taqiyya*, obscuring their faith when under threat.

Outside the Chouf, Druze settlements are found in Jordan, Syria, and Israel. Other than in the Golan Heights, their assimilation into modern Israel is so complete that the all-Druze Herev (Sword) Battalion of the Israel Defense Forces, drawing from their knowledge of the south Lebanon terrain, took no casualties in the recent 34-day war, while reportedly killing 22 Hezbollah militants. They continue to patrol the border as a decorated, elite unit of the Israel Defense Forces.

Solidarity, though, is a moving target among Druze communities in the Middle East. Here in the Chouf, feudal warlord Walid Jumblatt, co-owner of Chateau Kefraya, head of the PSP (Progressive Socialist Party), and member of parliament, is rabidly anti-Semitic, even championing the crash of the space shuttle *Columbia* because there was an Israeli astronaut on board. If nothing else, Jumblatt is a political survivor, working both sides of an issue, switching loyalties faster than most of us throw away our socks. His political intrigues would have impressed the Medicis, former trading partners of the Chouf. During the civil war, he and his father, who was assassinated in 1977, were staunch allies of Syria and the Palestinians. And after peacefully coexisting with Christians for over a century, as commander of the Druze militia, responding to an attack by Samir Geagea and the Christian Phalangists, he massacred Maronites across the Chouf, sealing his absolute, if not centuries-old, authority in what was coined the "War of the Mountains."

Today, Jumblatt is anti-Syrian and against an expanded Hezbollah presence but allied with them in protecting their representation in Parliament. He reluctantly recognizes Israel and favors Palestinian statehood. As an act of rapprochement, he has resettled Maronites to their medieval villages in the Chouf but has also been instrumental in reducing their influence in parliament. As one who knows more intimately than most the red, toothy nature of human folly, it's no surprise that Jumblatt describes George Bush as, among other epithets, the "mad emperor."

CHAPTER SEVEN

~

Hezbollah and U.S. Cluster Bombs

It was late afternoon when we dropped out of the cool, mist-shrouded Chouf to the tropical swelter of the coast. In a split screen of timeless beauty and human folly, sunny banana orchards traced the chromatic turquoise waters of the Mediterranean, while degrees away was the bleak and bombed-out coastal highway south of Beirut.

From here to Nabatieh, every bridge, culvert, revetment, and overpass had been crippled. Like terrorists, Israel had concentrated their bombing on that which links people together—infrastructure, markets, and petrol stations. Yet life went on among the charred cadavers of old cars, the neighborhoods of rubble, the military checkpoints, and the fallen bridge spans that flashed by faster than I could count them. Chrabieh Farid lightened the moment in this desolate theater, quipping, "Israelis just don't like bridges."

Fresh out of a spell of amnesia, a quick survey might suggest that a natural disaster—a massive earthquake, a hurricane, or a tsunami—had swept through here. Or picture the postapocalyptic movie set of the film *Blade Runner*. What separates humans from their technology? Was this wasteland the handiwork of the "replicants" or the humans?

The cold reality that this dystopia was as man-made as the militant nations, the fierce religions, and the fanatical sectarian strife behind it was more unsettling than the contrived pathos of any Hollywood flick. Had America's planes and precision ordnance won this war? No. Did U.S. actions deliver justice, or better said, raise anyone's standard of living? No. Was it the end of something, or maybe the beginning? The weight of such senseless actions lay before us like the aftermath of a drunken brawl.

American policy analyst Walter Russell Mead defines Jacksonians as American populist, nationalist voters who supported this war and urge for a large military while opposing international organizations and humanitarian relief.

> [Jacksonians] believe that overwhelming and total retaliation against such tactics [as terrorism] can deter the attackers from striking again. This is how the American frontiersmen handled the Native Americans, how the Union general William Sherman "educated" the Confederacy, and how General Douglas MacArthur and Truman repaid the Japanese for Pearl Harbor. Jacksonians genuinely cannot understand why the world criticizes Israel for exercising what they see as its inalienable right of self-defense—for doing exactly what they would do in Israel's place.

These populists have conveniently forgotten that, but for our minutemen, who were 18th-century terrorists (noble as we hold them), America might still be a colony.

Meantime, traffic coursed around debris before pooling along makeshift pontoon bridges. It was a topsy-turvy circulation—a thousand bruised and banged-up cars, each navigating a different route, rushing by in all directions. It felt like being a real-life character in a video game that had short-circuited and gone amok.

We were in a bottleneck, traversing a French-built pontoon bridge. Frustration was high but nothing like during the civil war when motorists took shots at each other to break up traffic jams. One man raged beside his clapped-out white Mercedes, having just received a ticket from a motorcycle cop. The irate driver shouted and gestured at no one in particular: "I hope they destroy it all! Let the Israelis have it!" To have gotten a ticket in this traffic free-for-all, he must have insulted the cop's mother.

As we turned inland, a white banner fell across a bridge under repair: "The blood shed in Lebanon covers the faces of Bush, Rumsfeld and Cheney." Carbon-spewing dump trucks full of twisted rebar, en route to the recycling plant, groaned their way ahead of us. After seeing more craters, more bridges out, and more Bedu camps, the sun faded. "Thanks to Iran for reconstructing Nabatieh," the sign announced as we wearily drew to a stop in front of Kentucky Fried Chicken.

It was in Nabatieh on October 16, 1983, that Israeli soldiers killed two celebrants of Ashura, the day that commemorates the death of Imam Hussein in Karbala 1,400 years ago. "Eighteen years of unforgiving war followed, until the Israelis finally pulled out of Lebanon in May 2000," wrote Robert Baer in *The Devil We Know*. "The Middle East suddenly discovered Hezbollah, which emerged stronger than ever, both politically and militarily. For many Arabs, Nabatieh was Hezbollah's Boston Tea Party; Israel's forced departure from Lebanon its Waterloo."

～

Annie Holdridge, David's wife, arrived with two other women, Kaya Wislin-ska and Nancy Vernon, both in their early 30s, carrying bags of groceries. As Western women in Nabateah, they rarely go out for dinner, while abiding by a Mercy Corps security protocol that mandates a nine o'clock curfew. Farid and I were staying in a vacant Mercy Corps apartment, a floor above where Annie and Kaya hunkered down at night, in the aging tenement next door to the KFC. Iranian aid tents distributing medical supplies sprawled across the parking lot from the building's entrance. It's a constant here: Arab culture has always been dependent on the charity of tribal leaders, in this case from Persian ayatollahs, those same ones who stood up to America three decades ago, ushering in the modern era of Islamic fundamentalism.

Kaya Wislinska was a child of the Solidarity movement in Poland; its success opened doors for her not available to her parents. As a university student, she left Poland for the first time for the refugee camps in Chechnya. The experience captivated her body and soul on emergency relief and development work. She then found herself in Kosovo and Albania, where her Slavic accent made her a target as a suspected Serb.

From there she followed David and Mercy Corps into Kurdish Iraq, living in the northeast cities of Suleimaniyah and Khanaqin. Since Poland was a willing member of the coalition forces, once again she was looked upon with suspicion. Yet, given that over 50 percent of Mercy Corps' new arrivals in Iraq get freaked out and go home within three weeks, staying around for two years was heroic. "I'd give anything to have more like her," Annie and David assured me in sepa-rate conversations.

Kaya would like to go back to Iraq. She is frustrated here in her job manag-ing the flow of paperwork and money, often delivered in crates of greenbacks to ungrateful political leaders. "Burn rates, spend it or lose it, is the way we talk now," she complained. "In Iraq they have commitment, we gave them hope. They never asked for extra, but always gave their time. In Lebanon they say give me more money, give me more vacation, give me this, give me that," she mocked, and then added, "The rewards here, for me, are not as great." Blond and blue-eyed, her fair skin was splotched in red welts from stress.

Nancy Vernon wore a cleavage-revealing blouse and a knee-length skirt. She had never been to Nabatieh and had only arrived in Lebanon two weeks before. She turned up for dinner after a visit across the hall, a local policeman's apart-ment adorned with a prominent poster of Nasrallah. In two months of living there, Kaya and Annie had never met their neighbors, keeping to themselves after work as much as possible.

In an awkward display of her American sociability, Nancy had engaged the policeman's young kids in a noisy, drawn-out hallway soccer game. Meantime, the extended family courteously awaited their postfast feast before giving up and inviting Nancy. It all seemed equable and transcending for a moment, but by no surprise, Nancy was uncomfortable in this setting, speaking no Arabic, and being served strange cuts of meat as a vegetarian. She could only smile and gesture like an autistic kid, a child among children, beneath the imposing glare of Nasrallah. After a few minutes, she excused herself.

Nancy is ethnically Thai but was adopted as an infant by a San Francisco–based American Presbyterian minister and his wife. From them she got her call to social activism, having been raised doing community-based charity. After university she worked with the homeless for two years in the ghettos of Boston's Roxbury neighborhood. Voluntary social work in America is much different, though, than postconflict emergency relief efforts in the Middle East. She is a nice person intent on doing some good in the world for the wrong reason: to make herself feel better. She has a lot to learn to shake her American feet of clay, and, with the best of intentions, she was one of those to go home early.

~

Nabatieh's mood was celebrative as *iftar*, the evening feast, got under way: shouting, honking, backfiring, fireworks, and the crack of playful gunfire all spasmodically rang in the night air. It was probably no more than common rowdiness, yet indeed I had never heard or seen so much reveling that was largely unaccompanied by alcohol. Not for us—at the only spirits store in town, tucked away like a bootlegger's hideout, Annie had bought a couple of bottles of red Bekaa wine.

Kaya and Annie are in Nabatieh every week from Monday morning until Saturday afternoon, when they return to Beirut. Nancy was here for the night. Annie oversaw the evening with the care of a house mother in charge of a dorm, as we shared salad, cold cuts, homemade pizza, and wine. Although the night had a sense of occasion—visitors and vino—everyone was exhausted. Conversation drifted from their psychosocial projects to rebuilding schools and Hezbollah politics, punctuated every few minutes by a celebrative blast from the streets. Before Farid and I retired upstairs, Kaya and Annie passed along contact information for someone I wanted to see the next morning.

Our empty flat was steeped in the musty scent of disuse, an airless odor. Single light bulbs dangled from the ceiling, chipped concrete and rodent droppings peppered the floor, mattresses were stained and uncovered, and dust-laden curtains were rigged like cyclone-twisted sails to black out the windows. Most importantly, the aging toilet flushed. Otherwise, it felt like a Hezbollah safe house (my preconceptions running wild).

Sleep deprived, when the muezzin's call to prayer stirred me before sunrise, it felt like the muddled climax to a long dream. I figured my evening here to be as close as this pilgrim would ever come to being a Hezbollah martyr. There were plenty of authentic ones awaiting us on the streets, which by eight o'clock were filling with parade revelers, a psychosocial event coordinated by Hezbollah and paid for by the Iranian Committee to Reconstruct Lebanon.

Stopping at the small grocery on the ground floor, Farid ordered us coffees with milk. Two women arrived without veils, to which Farid remarked, "It may be the Hezbollah capital, but it is still Lebanon." The grocer, Hassan, was married to a Czech and had spent almost 20 years in Switzerland. His store was a prototype for Lebanese merchants around the world: sparsely supplied with cooking oil, soap, tin goods, and coffee. In good English, he said as he added the cream, "If you want milk then why don't you quit bombing our milk factories? I don't hate Americans. I just want you to go tell America what we say. You won't because Jews control everything." Flashing a knowing smile, he handed us our coffees.

Showing the order and discipline for which the Iranian-built, Hezbollah martyrs' school here is known, strongmen sporting mafioso starter kits herded around the streets kids garbed in Boy Scout–like uniforms, wearing red headbands inscribed with Koranic verses. Slick, black hair matched up with black T-shirts, black suits, and black, mirrored sunglasses. For crowd control they wore earpieces wired under the shirt to a mouthpiece on the wrist.

These stock characters were no fresh-faced initiates; they were heroes of the recent war. "To be known but not to be known," Farid began explaining this amorphous militia. "It's not a military uniform, and they never show their weapons, but everyone knows they are Hezbollah militia." In an asymmetrical conflict, as they call this 34-day war (and Iraq), these guys were able to blend in as Israel (America) can't.

Amputees in wheelchairs scooted around, parked on the sidewalk viewing the crowd. Signs proclaiming the dignity of martyrs popped up with the frequency of Coke ads in Atlanta, along with banners praising Iran. "To all aid agencies it's like a dog pissing on his territory," said one State Department official. The billboard of heavily armed militiamen, inscribed with "We Are Coming," with the Dome of the Rock in Jerusalem in the foreground, seemed to threaten a modern-day Crusade, the jihadist face of Hezbollah.

Charity boxes sat on every corner, signaled by fluttering Hezbollah flags with green markings on a yellow background, inscribed in red with the Koranic verse "Verily the party of God shall be victorious." The bracing green imagery is of an arm thrusting a Kalashnikov assault rifle into the air, with a globe to its side, insinuating that Hezbollah and Islam are on a global conquest.

Less prominently displayed, in front of one rebuilt school, was a sign commemorating USAID. Yet in this cold war of emergency aid here in Nabatieh, Iran, Hezbollah, and Amal (the rival Shia party) were winning the battle. And with oil prices at historical highs, Iran has many more carrots for their Shia coreligionists in Lebanon. As we know, depending on who, what, when, and where, aid can legitimize either war or peace.[1]

Hezbollah in particular thrives on its reputation, deserved or not, for *dawa*, which literally means "call." *Dawa*, the humanitarian face of Hezbollah, has to do with creating a social safety net for Shias, getting the hygiene kits and food out there first. That is not all—before the first week passed after the ceasefire Hezbollah was doling out $12,000 per household, in American bills, for all those who lost their homes. Even a low estimate would suggest this largesse alone had cost Iran 150 million dollars.

America has not fared as well in the public square of the Middle East, clinging to its bomb-happy foreign policy and blind hubris, which has only multiplied the terrorists that we sought to destroy. Farid imagines an alternative. "Don't fight Hezbollah with guns," he said. "Attack their children by connecting them to the world." He sees it as a war of influence, of information, and of creating a sustainable society, that is, as classic counterinsurgency.

∼

Farid and I circled the neighborhood twice before spotting MAG's (Mines Advisory Group) red-and-white logo of skull and crossbones atop an office villa. The 34-day war had ended over two months before, but people were still being killed or maimed every day by landmines and unexploded ordnance. MAG, a colaureate of the 1997 Nobel Peace Prize, has been in Lebanon since the civil war, reinforced with more sweepers once the recent peace was signed.

Past the wrought-iron gate the courtyard was littered with freshly defused rockets and missiles, products of arms makers mostly from America but also from Israel, Iran, Russia, Britain, France, and China—the UN Security Council fully represented, plus two. The house was a maze of rooms stocked floor to ceiling with shelves of landmines and submunitions (or bomblets) of cluster bombs.

We found Andrew Gleeson, program manager for MAG, in a makeshift corner office, its plaster walls papered over in topography maps. With an estimated

---

1. In the poorest countries it is estimated that 40 percent of aid money winds up in the hands of the military.

800,000 unexploded bomblets in southern Lebanon, Andrew was coordinating cleanup grids, which would require 50 clearance teams, 25 of which will come from MAG. This cleanup, as opposed to the ongoing one from the civil war, would take almost two years to make the conflict area habitable again.

In his early 50s, British, and businesslike but courteous, Andrew has vast landmine and explosive-removal experience, from Lebanon to Iran and Iraq, where America armed both sides in that ten-year conflict. Andrew started our informal meeting by showing me a defused U.S.-manufactured BLU 63-B cluster bomb. Its serial number and loading date were stenciled in white: 9-73, a Vietnam-era unit. I had seen these in ordnance heaps still being amassed in Laos and Vietnam, but why now in Lebanon?

Crisp and direct, Andrew fired off the facts like a human Gatling gun: "The Department of Defense contract with Israel says that they have to expend and not stockpile this ordnance before they can receive more. Israel wanted the newer M-26 multilaunch rockets, which contain 644 bomblets, each about the size of a D battery, and are both antipersonnel and antivehicular. The Vietnam-era clusters are only antipersonnel but have approximately the same number of bomblets. So the IDF [Israel Defense Forces] got rid of the old, some would say gratuitously, to bring in the new." He added, "In the last 72 hours Katyushas were fired by Hezbollah at noncombatants in Israel, and Israel fired CBU-58-Bs at noncombatants in Lebanon. There are no innocents here."

I was curious about the dud rate of those Vietnam-era cluster bombs.

"Ten percent for new unexploded ordnance [bombs, mortars, grenades, and missiles]. For just the new submunitions it is 25 percent, with CBU-58-Bs [Vietnam era] up to 90 percent." Shaking the numbers in his head, he then said, "So it is fair to say that an overall dud rate of 30 percent applies."

It also came up that many of those Vietnam-era cluster bomb units had expired warranties.

Farid asked about the minefields along the Blue Line.

"They have been there since the civil war, but both sides know that, so it's not a barrier," Andrew said, shaking his head doggedly. "The IDF drove right through 375,000 mines during the war, and with these maps"—he held up a pile of grid maps with increasingly concentrated red dots—"I could do the same, as I have done in Iran. Lebanon and Israel want the minefield to remain. It's their border."

To the extent candidness allows, Andrew avoided anti-American politics, as his NGO (nongovernmental organization) relies on donations. Given the nature of the subject, however, America kept coming up. The Blue Line provides a no man's land not unlike the two largest minefields in the world: between the Brigada Fronteriza in Cuba and the American base at Guantanamo Bay, and on the 38th parallel, dividing North and South Korea. Because of these Cold War conflict areas, and a loathing for any global agreements, always couched in a sovereignty polemic, America refuses to be a party to the International Campaign to Ban Landmines, signed by 153 countries. For much the same reasons, the United States, along with Russia, China, India, Israel, and Pakistan, were no-shows at a recent landmark signing, attended by 111 nations, to ban cluster bombs.

In the 34-day war, the Israeli Air Force launched 7,000 air attacks, while the navy conducted some 2,500 bombardments. At the peak of the American blitzkrieg in Vietnam and along Laos' Ho Chi Minh Trail, 10,000 sorties a month were conducted. Though it seemed like overkill then and now, American pilots were bombing an area at least 25 times greater than the entire country of Lebanon, with almost two million combatants on both sides. (According to Andrew, Hezbollah has a reported fighting force of some 3,000 militiamen.)

Here in southern Lebanon over 700 strike areas remain contaminated. Villages, wheat fields, and olive orchards are littered with unexploded bomblets. Andrew surmised the Israeli strategy to have been twofold: "to inflict maximum damage and to prevent the return of the 650,000 displaced people living in the south by leaving behind at least one unexploded bomblet for every man, woman, and child."

In the 1980s, the Reagan administration banned the sale of cluster bombs to Israel for six years after the IDF deployed them in civilian areas. At the close of this war, the Israeli newspaper *Haaretz* reported one top IDF commander's reflections: "What we did was insane and monstrous; we covered entire towns in cluster bombs."

Half a century ago, when President Eisenhower exhorted America to beware of the emerging influence of the military industrial complex (the Pentagon and captains of industry), he had the Cold War on his mind. What would he have said today about its hydra-headed successor—the all-embracing War on Terror, oil, Israel and its powerful American lobby AIPAC (American Israel Public Affairs Committee), Christian Zionists, and neoconservatives? AIPAC, Christian Zionists, and neoconservatives are not part of a conspiracy or a cabal; rather, they are just an odd confluence of legal, well-funded special interests, with a Congress that withers at the existential threat of being labeled unpatriotic or anti-Semitic if they oppose weapons funding in the Middle East—strategic interests, morality, and facts be damned.

In the midst of the Lebanon War, former State Department official Aaron Miller observed, "There is a danger in a policy in which there is no daylight whatsoever between the government of Israel and the government of the United States." During Eisenhower's Cold War we viewed the world through Moscow; now it's Tel Aviv.

As it has happened, weapons sold and shipped from the United States to the developing world today exceed 45 percent of the global total, with Russia—even with a Kalashnikov in most developing world homes—coming in a distant second at 15 percent and Britain next with 13 percent. China is fourth, but moving up fast, while Israel is the eighth-largest arms dealer in the world. In 2005 alone, the United States transferred weapons to 18 of the 25 conflict zones in the world.[2] "Whose hands will those be in five years from now?" Andrew asked, after a more general discussion of global arms dealing.

From the fall of the Berlin wall in 1989 to the Trade Center and Pentagon attacks of September 11, 2001, according to Robert Kagan, "the United States intervened with force in foreign lands more frequently than at any other time in its history—an average of one significant new military action every sixteen months—and far more than any other power in the same stretch of time."

As such, Andrew says, "the devil is in the details." American weaponry—Stinger missiles, tanks, fighter jets, and more—have made it into the hands of thugs from central casting such as Osama bin Laden and the Taliban, Ayatollah Khomeini, Saddam Hussein, Kim Jong Il, Augusto Pinochet, Manuel Noriega, Mobutu Sese Seko, Nicolae Ceausescu, Mohammed Suharto, Slobodan Milosevic, Ferdinand Marcos, Pol Pot, Samir Geagea, and the Christian Phalangists in Lebanon.

As reckless as the U.S. past comes off, it remains a tactical option to arm both sides of a conflict: India and Pakistan, Iraq and Iran, Turkey and Iraq (Kurdish), and Israel and Lebanon. Even more shocking is the arming of Pakistan's Baluchi Sunni fundamentalists against the Shia regime of Tehran. Baluchis are known to have cut off the heads of nonbelievers (Daniel Pearl), and at least two of their people, Ramzi Yousef and Khalid Sheikh Mohammed, were the masterminds behind the 1993 World Trade Center bombing and September 11!

Beyond absurd is that Israel is now China's second-largest provider of weapons (behind Russia) and that China sells rockets to Iran, which then gives them to Hezbollah to bombard Israel. Something makes me think it's time to talk, that the arms dealer's doctrine of "sell to anyone who can pay" may not be working. "Blowback," a term coined by the CIA to describe the boomerang effect of discrete covert actions, has surged into a global crossfire. As it stands, the United States provides military aid to up to 60 countries. While America and others pretend to be securing the world, in fact they are impelling the internal factions of recipient countries and neighboring states into an arms race. It is this vicious cycle that is draining Third World resources that could otherwise be used to build hospitals, schools, and roads.

Written at the time Eisenhower exhorted us, perhaps we should take heed of the warning on the last page of The Ugly American: "We are offering the wrong kind of help. We have lost sight of our own past that we are trying to sell guns

---

2. On average two civil wars start every year.

and money alone, instead of remembering that it was the quest for the dignity of freedom that was responsible for our own way of life."

Andrew toured us through the defused-explosives inventory room, and then out into the yard littered in olive drab casings from America, Iran, and China, where we thanked him for his time and shoved off for the Shebaa frontier and the Blue Line, the Israeli border.

〜

Soon we were tracing the Litani River, glimpsing armored personnel carriers of the Lebanese army that had not been this far south in over three decades. Traversing the stony foothills of Mt. Herman, tufted in a cedar green scrub, wispy clouds wrapped the biblical peak like a threadbare turban. The wadis were deep and dramatic, dry but for the pissing rain that glistened off the hardtop, which was eerily empty of traffic. Ghost towns popped up with uncommon frequency, but Farid and I were more dumbstruck by the Hezbollah hidey-holes, the rocky tucks in the hillsides, turned to pinpoints of scorched earth. Israeli thermal cameras had picked up heat flashes from these remote launch sites, before vectoring in rockets and cluster bombs. Just as Andrew had explained less than an hour before, these barren biblical hills starkly revealed the technological modernity of the IDF versus the cave-dwelling, rocket-toting, Hezbollah guerrillas.

Once again Farid was caffeined up, stoking a cigarette, and holding forth about the emergency relief he had assisted with nearby. In a fit of excitement, he pointed his cigarette to the bomblet-pocked hairpin curve we were approaching but didn't slow down. Suddenly, we were doing a 360 on the rain-slick road, coming to a stop on the edge of a drop-off, nothing but scorched earth below. We each took a deep breath, and then laughed aloud.

The United Nations Interim Force in Lebanon's (UNIFIL) blue hats and the green cedar tree flag of the Lebanese army greeted us on the outskirts of El Khiam, three miles from the Israel border. Drawing up to a guard shack brimming with firepower, a roadblock of old tires, red metal, and X-shaped barriers traced in razor wire, we were beckoned to stop. Commanding this, a barrel-chested burly sergeant charged over and ordered us to turn around. His abruptness was understandable: two guys rubbernecking in a clapped-out car.

It was a Christiane–Amanpour–ground zero landscape, infernos and killing fields. The entire village was cordoned as though it were a massive crime scene, one that was still being sifted through. The victims, those who had lived through the apocalypse that swept through, were sheltered in an apron of white UNHCR (United Nations High Commissioner for Refugees) tents. It could have been a Bedu camp but for its sterile linearity. All this devastation and displacement is a world Americans, including me, refuse to come to terms with.

On the other hand, current events, our economy (oil), our tax dollars, and our largely Judeo-Christian heritage should make it the center of our universe.

During the civil war and Israeli occupation between 1982 and 2000, El Khiam was famous for its prison. There the IDF indefinitely detained and tortured Lebanese civilians. As Guantanamo Naval Base is to America, El Khiam prison wasn't on Israeli soil, which provided IDF interrogators the lawless latitude they sought. After the civil war the prison was converted to a museum, a sort of Lebanese holocaust memorial, Farid said. Now the Israelis had reduced it to rubble, a flattened hilltop overlooking El Khiam. Lebanon would never again have an authentic, living history museum to remember their torture victims. That was Israel's mission: to destroy an important piece of the Lebanese identity.

Back traversing the deserted, hilly landscape, a humongous billboard sprang up in a barren wadi, awaiting the infrequent passersby: UNIFIL troops, an NGO worker, or a straggling tourist, perhaps. Across the top of this Hezbollah "wanted" poster, two black-and-white mugs were framed in a row of prison bars. The caption read, "The Great Capture Operation: 2 'Israeli' Soldiers in the Clutches of Hezbollah." The 34-day war, the sixth and longest ever fought by Israel, got its start a few miles from here with the abduction of the bodies of the pictured Israeli soldiers, sergeants Ehud Goldwasser, 31, and Eldad Regev, 26, both reservists on their last day of duty. They are now "war prisoners," Farid says, not to be confused with hostages.

But the price paid is staggering: across Lebanon, especially in Hezbollah enclaves and villages, 8,475 homes were destroyed and another 46,143 seriously damaged; 5,000 civilians were either maimed or killed and hundreds of thousands displaced; 149 schools, mostly Shia, were destroyed; 131 clinics and hospitals are either partially functioning or not operational at all; the country's roads are a broken mess; and the bridge infrastructure was wiped out. Yet Hezbollah is unbowed. Indeed, they seem to be chest beating over capturing the bodies of two Israeli soldiers, who will no doubt some day be bargaining chips in a prisoner or body swap.[3]

The deductive mechanisms that drive revenge—such as cause and effect, the biblical injunction of an eye for an eye, or the civilizing mandate that says crime begets punishment—more often than not make perfect sense, until American and Israeli overreach disguised as moral virtue tilts the scales of justice. Through the eyes of victims, there is no chicken-or-the-egg mystery. Common sense tells us that without social and economic justice there is no peace, that the David and Goliath history of the Shias versus the Sunnis, going back to their martyr Hussein, makes them genetically coded to fight the long fight. The potent mix

---

3. Two years later, the bodies of the abducted soldiers were exchanged for four Hezbollah prisoners.

of poverty and piety precedes all, which makes the primal argument for revenge a circular one and never ending, with atrocity canceling out atrocity. "The experience of war," wrote Mary B. Anderson in *Do No Harm*, "increasingly becomes the root cause that leads to future wars."

Vietnam proved that bombed-out villages and body counts, as metrics for military success, were meaningless without political support. In his last dispatch, the late David Halberstam, Vietnam journalist and historian, offers up a cautionary tale of the colonial war in Vietnam: "When a French patrol went through a village, the Vietminh would on occasion kill a single French soldier, knowing that the French in a fury would retaliate by wiping out half the village—in effect the Vietminh were baiting the trap for collateral killing."

In Lebanon, before the 34-day war, Nasrallah's political popularity was a paltry 20 percent; now, some say, it has leapt to 50 percent. Fellow Arabs voted him the most popular leader in the Middle East, a modern-day version of the heroic Muslim crusader Saladin.

~

The road rose steadily but circuitously through Chouaia, a picturesque Druze village. White-capped holy men and women in nunlike habits flashed in and out of the shadows among the prim, stone homes, untouched by the bombing. Phantom eyes scoped us as we stopped for photos. We were indifferent, as it seemed we were on top of the world: below was the southern leg of the Bekaa Valley, its cornrows of olive orchards and stubbled wheat fields, left fallow by the war, sprawling to infinity.

A lone donkey and a goatherd seized the tarmac on the outskirts of Shebaa. The village's whitewashed concrete homes appeared to defy gravity, hanging on the abrupt slopes of Mt. Herman, the western shoulder of the Golan Heights. The valley, among the dun-colored lines of agricultural toil, was an unremarkable 30 square miles known as Shebaa Farms but as contentious a slice of plain old dirt as the planet holds.

Israel annexed Shebaa Farms along with the Golan Heights in the 1967 Six Day War, in which Lebanon did not participate. Deeds, tax receipts, and residents' testimony all leave it unclear whether Shebaa Farms was within the borders of Lebanon or Syria. There is no evidence that suggests Israel had any legal claim to this property (other than those who assert biblical eminent domain).

Its annexation and that of the larger area of the Golan Heights have given Israel a more secure border, but at the same time this has radicalized Palestinians, Hezbollah, and Syrians. Since Hezbollah followers occupy most of the border area in Lebanon, they allege ownership rights on behalf of Lebanon (and only recently did Syria give up its claim). These "rights" are often asserted by cross-border paramilitary action, which, of course, ignited the recent war and gives a pretext for more conflict.

It's a given that Israel needs strong border security. It is surrounded by Arab nations brimming with jihadists who often threaten it; neighborly friends are scarce. Yet conflagrations are sapping the Israeli military, their economy, and morale over unnecessary border wars, while not addressing the real problem: Palestinians.

In my five years of living in Hanoi, I met many young Israeli backpackers, fresh from their mandatory military service, on a six- to twelve-month *wander-jhar* through Southeast Asia. They came in droves, sticking together as a tribe, not a lost one but often keeping to themselves. Restaurants cater to them with menus in Hebrew, advertising Israeli salads as a specialty.

In my frequent encounters with these vets-cum-intrepid-travelers, they were bemused by my questions about Palestinian statehood, replying mantra-like, "It will happen when the U.S. wants it to happen." In contrast, in the United States, as journalist Michael Kinsley wrote, "the lack of public discussion about Israel . . . is the proverbial elephant in the room: Everybody sees it, no one mentions it."

～

Motoring through Shebaa, Farid and I had Israel in our sights at all angles south. We weren't far from the Blue Line. A Sunni holy man stepped out of the mosque, ignoring our approach to cross in front of us. The playful screeches of children kicking a soccer ball echoed down the donkey-path-like streets. Farid warned all-comers, honking and hollering, as we cautiously squeezed our way around corners and to the outskirts of Shebaa, where the hardtop road turned to a muddy, washboard track. A four-wheel-drive would have served us better than the clapped-out Datsun.

Thirty minutes later, sliding and groaning our way up the valley rim, graphite-gray clouds fell over us, not a car or a goatherd since Shebaa. We stopped to listen and look. A rush of wind broke the otherwise thunderous silence. Suddenly, a blue-hatted UNIFIL soldier popped into view and just as quickly vanished among boulders in a house-size outcropping. A loosely coiled razor-wire fence lay beyond a 15-foot warning track. Powder blue markers formed a tenuous boundary, the Blue Line.

A string of rope stretched to the warning track, where it disappeared near a crudely constructed wooden box, a listening device, maybe. Surely there's not a rabbit trap here? Beyond the razor wire, 40 yards away, was a stony hillock with gnarly trees sprouting between the rocks, a suitable and likely watch post for the IDF (the same youngsters who would hopefully be on the beaches of Thailand in a few months, smoking dope and drinking Singhai beer). On this day, they were not showing themselves.

We stopped and got out, surveying the emptiness, but we were both spooked by the combustible aura, by the specter of Grendel the bloodthirsty boundary walker. For along the Blue Lines of the world, whether the 17th parallel in Vietnam, the 38th in Korea, or downtown Baghdad, it's not a question of if there will be a primal conflagration, only when.

A half-hour later, in the Christian-Muslim market town of Marjaayoun, we passed on the Big Boom Pub in favor of the Roadrunner Restaurant. Two jeep loads of French and Spanish UNIFIL troops, all wearing the blue beret, joined us at outdoor tables. We all ordered what the Roadrunner offered: beer, hot dogs, hamburgers, and French fries. The Christian proprietors catered to these UNIFIL and NGO workers; most locals couldn't afford the prices even if they liked the transplanted fare.

The fifty-something red-haired wife wore a big, fat, gold cross around her neck, hung low to her aging but ample cleavage. She was nervous, not sexy. Her frown lines were heavy, addressing us in a whispering, conspiratorial voice: "We hear the Israelis have been crossing the border. Their planes roar by every day. We are afraid this is not over."

She seemed trapped, a hostage to the existential angst of border residency. While she talked, Farid and I watched a steady stream of UN white SUVs and flagged jeeps race by.

As it turned out, her suspicions weren't just paranoid thoughts conjured by a worried mind: there would be more discord and opportunistic violence than in any period since the civil war. Al-Qaeda and the Palestinians battled the Lebanese army in Tripoli for months; seven anti-Syrian politicians were murdered, and an American embassy SUV was bombed in Beirut, killing three; and six months later, 800,000 followers of Hezbollah and Michel Aoun (former prime minister and Christian populist leader) occupied Martyrs' Square, the Green Line, protesting the American-backed government of Prime Minister Fouad Siniora.

Here in Marjaayoun, a month after my trip, the first al-Qaeda-style IED (improvised explosive device) in Lebanon exploded beneath two UN vehicles, killing six Spanish UNIFIL troops. Civil war and al-Qaeda are always on people's minds here.

Blithely, America marched on. Congress approved the largest arms sale in history to Israel and Saudi Arabia, a country, given their excesses, that gets the least respect of any from their neighbors in the Middle East. Israel continues to maintain their "qualitative military advantage," while both countries received "satellite-guided bombs, upgrades to its fighters and new naval vessels." Saudi Arabia and the neighboring Gulf States also received a $20 million package as a counterweight to the growing power of Iran. One senior administration official justified at least part of Israel's $30 billion arms package as necessary "to replace equipment expended in its war against Hezbollah."

Allegiances to America, as with treaties in the Middle East, are predicated on all parties getting American weapons, and in most cases, billions of dollars for a signing bonus. Why else would anyone talk to us?

As with Vietnam and the Nixon White House, the Middle East arms race is being characterized as "a long-term investment in peace." In fact, the war wizards talk about peace in an abstract sense, not as a viable instrument of everyday diplomacy (said Martin Luther King Jr.). The absurdity of which brings to mind my favorite Vietnam-era bumper sticker: "Fighting for peace is like fucking for virginity!"

CHAPTER EIGHT

~

Istanbul

Ground Zero in the Clash of Civilizations

Americans and Europeans often think of the Middle East as being monolithic. The truth is that the Arabic oil-rich monarchies of the Emirates, Qatar, or Saudi Arabia are as different from the Islamic state of Persian-speaking Iran as are the constitutional monarchies of Morocco, Jordan, and Kuwait. The autocracies of Tunisia, Egypt, Syria, Yemen, and Libya (at least until the recent Arab Spring uprisings) have enjoyed much more stability than the secular democracies of Lebanon and now Iraq.

Then there is the Kurdistan Regional Government (KRG), in the Republic of Iraq, where David Holdridge offered to have Mercy Corps staff host me. The KRG, the illusory country of Kurdistan—squeezed between Iran, Turkey, Syria, and, until recently, Saddam's Iraq—has been relentlessly exploited by colonial rulers, Cold War rivals, neighbors, and America. "No friends but the mountains," goes the Kurdish saying.

In 1973, Mullah Mustafa Barzani, the Iraqi Kurdish leader of the time, famously proposed providing the United States with oil if Iraqi Kurdistan could only become America's 51st state. President Richard Nixon declined, but the door has been left open, again and still.

New York Times columnist Thomas Friedman called the KRG "a decent democratizing example" for the region. Indeed, the KRG has tasted the raw elixir of democratic values, of a civil society and secular governance, fledgling and corrupt as it is. The self-possessed Kurds are inviting the West, particularly America, to seize the moment, to be their partner in progress (which they also did to no avail with the British when their Mandate drew to a close in 1932).

The map on the KRG website depicts a region in north-central Iraq, boldly labeled Kurdistan, overshadowing the surrounding country names, including

103

Iraq. If the map were to scale, Kurdistan's southern boundaries would include Mosul and oil-rich Kirkuk, if not Baghdad. So, there is much to be settled in all directions, not least being the escalating tension between Turkey and the terrorist group PKK (Kurdistan Workers' Party), whose guerrilla army has tunneled into the Qandil Mountains of northern Iraq, the KRG.

Since 1984, when the PKK armed struggle began, they are blamed for the deaths of 40,000 Turks but no Americans. Yet, most Turks, with the exception of Kurdish separatists, resent the United States for not providing "actionable intelligence" on PKK movements, for allying with KRG president Massoud Barzani, who rather than expelling the terrorists, which is easier said than done, allows them a safe haven, if not a base from which to recruit. Many outside the region would say that the United States is not assisting Turkey with the PKK because Turkey refused to be used as an infantry staging area for the invasion of Iraq. History may soon reveal this to be a turning point in U.S.-Turkey relations, as our Cold War ally strengthens commerce between Europe, Iran, and Iraq, while America is consumed by its military adventures.

In the weeks leading up to my KRG trip, several ambush killings and kidnappings of Turkish soldiers occurred along the border, the one I would soon be crossing in, what else, a Turkish taxi. In response to those cross-border attacks, protestors took to the streets across Turkey, and the military mobilized tank divisions and 100,000 troops to the border, while American-financed F-16s and attack helicopters patrolled the skies. Meantime, in a flurry of "drive-by" diplomacy, Turkish prime minister Recep Tayyip Erdogan was called to Washington to discuss the wider, destabilizing possibilities of a Turkish invasion of Iraq.

This transoceanic tension didn't happen in a news flash; the Beltway, once again, failed to see the storm gathering across the Atlantic. After all, not so many years ago it was reported that less than half of the U.S. Congress held a valid passport, which to that august body of nontravelers, at best, makes the wider world an abstraction.

That the American airbase at Incirlik, Turkey, was transshipping 70 percent of the war materiel for Iraq; that Turkey had been our NATO ally for decades in the Cold War and fought alongside us in Korea, Kosovo, and Afghanistan; and that today they support us against the Salafi Jihadis (Sunni revivalists) didn't seem to faze the navel-gazing U.S. Congress as they attempted to pass a resolution damning our ally for the Armenian genocide a century before.

With that, the Turkish ambassador was withdrawn to Ankara. Under article 305 of the Turkish penal code, the mere utterance of genocide in the same sentence with the Armenian "accidents of war," is grounds for a 15-year prison sentence. Anti-American, nationalistic street demonstrations escalated. "All Turks are born to be soldiers!" protestors chanted.

As I prepared to depart, public opinion in Turkey, convinced that America is no longer a friend and ally, had reached an all-time low: only 9 percent of Turks held a favorable view of America, the lowest of 46 countries surveyed by the Pew Foundation in October 2007 (but close to average for the Middle East).

Turkey's most popular movie, *Valley of the Wolves*, and best-selling book, *Metal Storm*, portray the armies of Ankara and Washington pitted in wars to end all, with Turks as victors. That the *Valley of the Wolves* occurs in northern Iraq against an American army—depicted as barbarous—mirrors Turkey's frustration, if not the regional perspective, with our foolhardy incursion into Iraq.

Amid the political faux pas, the street protests, the cinematic drama of anti-Americanism in Turkey, and the existential media drum roll to a destabilizing border war, I was also being contacted by friends and family (especially my kids), who cast me as unstable, as well by a hex-minded former colleague who told me of a dream she had where I was a headless corpse.

Delivered with the ringing tones of certainty, the sheer fury of their collective fear gave me pause, if not bewilderment: I was not going there to die; I travel to live! I kept reminding myself that not a single American had been killed in northern Iraq, much less eastern Turkey—which made it understandable when Mercy Corps representatives in Iraq were taken aback at my suggestion of postponing the trip. Their message was matter of fact: everything here is hunky dory in peaceful KRG; forget the worrisome weather and would-be wars (and these guys and gals aren't inclined to cowboy behavior). Thus, I trusted the shepherds with soil on their shoes. So it was that I set out to witness pro-Americanism, to harvest it, and to honor it, in Iraq. But to get there by land I needed to travel through Turkey.

⌒

Twenty-four hours after that message from Mercy Corps, I piled into a yellow taxi at Atatürk International. We were off, at race car velocity, along John F. Kennedy Boulevard (Caddesi), a 12-mile stretch of modern asphalt that rims the Sea of Marmara, ending at the Golden Horn, near Istanbul's historic district. Billboards of provocative panty and bra ads flashed by—incongruously set against a landscape of minarets and Ottoman walls (Turkey is one of the world's largest lingerie manufacturers). The driver spoke cabbie English but understood me when I asked him why the boulevard was named for Kennedy.

Shrugging, he pointed to the Sea of Marmara, and said, "It [the road] was like that [covered in water] before, so Kennedy built this nice road for us. He was a great man."

Throughout Istanbul, I asked a cross-section of Turks about Kennedy and the namesake boulevard and got a different answer every time: he stopped the

Vietnam War, he fought the Russians, or he came to Turkey and liked it, but mostly the response was something like, "I don't know, but he was a great man, a friend of Turkey." Current events aside, the inherent goodwill and promise of the Kennedy legacy seemed to be an unquestioned truth in Istanbul, if not Turkey generally.[1]

Drinking Turkish coffee in the Pudding Shop, the iconic hangout of the '60s and '70s hippie crowd, I was joined by Pilder Suleyman, better known in the day as Sammy. We met over three decades ago when I stayed next door in the Gungor for three weeks, at two dollars a day. On this afternoon, the coffee gave way to milky glasses of raki, the anise-flavored aperitif that is Turkey's national drink. Loosened up, Sammy got around to offering up his sidewalk slant on America: "They poke their nose in things, then stall around and sell more guns. They do it everywhere: in Nicaragua, South Africa, Iraq, you name it. That's how they make money."

Sammy's flourishing niche with Westerners disappeared with the demise of the Hippy Trail, the ancient Silk Road, which, for all of recorded history, had been a trade route to barter goods between East and West, to exchange ideas and technology, to propagate the world's great religions, and to bring cultures together through commerce. And, of course, out of this ferment, the Silk Road provided a surreal, if not Odyssean adventure for the '60's Magic Bus crowd flocking to India, epiphany-like, tripping through Afghanistan's Khyber Pass—which in the day was nature's toll gate for time travel, the Ginsberg-and-Beatle transcendental light awaiting.

All that ended in 1979: the shah of Iran was overthrown in favor of Ayatollah Khomeini, founder of the Islamic Republic of Iran. From afar this was a sea change, if not an "Arabian Nights" abstraction, but inside Iran it was the culmination of 26 years of simmering anti-Americanism, midwifed by the 1953 CIA-backed overthrow of the democratically elected Mohammed Mossadegh, who had sought to roll back oil concessions to foreigners. On Christmas day of the same year (1979), the Soviet Union invaded Afghanistan, hurling that country into a circle of conflicts that produced an emboldened Osama bin Laden and the Taliban, whom America famously armed to the teeth in the Taliban's Islamic jihad against the Soviets. Afghanistan, and 50 years of conflict and confrontational diplomacy, from Vietnam to the moon, brought the Cold War to a close.

While Washington celebrated the downfall of the Soviet Union and communism, a mere tick on the ancient clock of civilization, a new era of global conflict with roots almost deeper than time raised its ugly head: jihadi terrorism,

---

1. In the Kennedy era we did enjoy good relations with Turkey, who allowed our missiles there, pointed at the Soviet Union, an old enemy of Turks and the Ottoman Empire.

East against West, and modernity versus tradition. Afghanistan and Pakistan were the incubators, breeding grounds for the university of jihad. Meantime, further sealing the fate of the Hippy Trail, Saddam Hussein, a secularist who had risen to power in Iraq in the late 1970s, invaded Iran to start a war that would last eight years and kill over a million people. So it goes.

⌢

My sepia-stained recollection of the Sultanahmet neighborhood at that time was of bleak winter and quaint minarets that fenced the globular grandeur of Byzantine and Ottoman monuments. Black chadors and gray apartment buildings, austere tea shops crowded with noisy but somber-faced men, stray dogs sniffing the sidewalks, and boat funnels spewing black smoke from the Bosphorous near the Galata Bridge were common urban vignettes. An Ottoman prison, with crumbling walls but still with inmates, breasted the south side of the hilltop square, near Topkapi Palace and Aya Sofia.

Even then modernity and neo-pashas could be found across the Golden Horn at the Hilton, where we would splurge for a five-dollar hamburger, our daily budget, while frequenting the fashionable shops and bars around Taksim. On a few nights Sammy would gather the Pudding Shop crowd and we would bus over to the "Hydromel," a forerunner of the disco—glass dance floor, cheesy music, and chic people. (It's still there but is now full of "Natashas," or Russian prostitutes.) Orhan Pamuk, Turkey's Nobel laureate, characterized Istanbul in those days in terms of *huzun*, imbued with a malaise of lost empire, "alienated from the East and mortified by the West."

Today, the atmospherics of Istanbul have changed. Now, almost in your face, Turkish flags fly everywhere as if every day is a nationalist celebration of the conquest of Constantinople, of Gallipoli. The former historic-district prison is now a Four Seasons Hotel. The Hippodrome, where all the VW vans, London double-deckers, and Magic Buses once collected India-bound passengers, is encircled by a Technicolor beehive of pastel bars, al fresco restaurants, and Kurdish carpet shops. It's hard to distinguish locals from tourists, with the trappings of modernity everywhere: mobile phones, Lacoste shirts, navel rings, and silk-sheen blond hair. "We have to change [women] to get in the European Union," Sammy posited. He was tapping into something here: the provocative dress of women as a fundamental indicator of liberal democracy, of Westernization.

A year before, in Bodrum, the Aegean resort south of Istanbul, I spent an afternoon on the public beach. Well-to-do, educated Turkish women settled in around me, sunbathing topless. It's an amazing sight, in this country of contradictions, where since the days of Atatürk it has been illegal to wear the fez, but now women are free to go topless on the beach! In Bodrum their liberation was as self-consciously undertaken as the bra burners of the 1960s was in America—both some sort of pent-up antidote to the past.

On this trip to Istanbul, over and again, each time I mentioned the radical cultural changes I had witnessed in my 37 years of traveling to Turkey, the response was of a voice: the secular, wealthy, West-looking Turks have become more liberal, while conservative Muslims, those often less fortunate, are turning east to Iran, becoming more Islamic by the day. The gap between the two is ever yawning.

Samuel Huntington addressed this dilemma in a warning to Turkey's NATO allies, in his 1998 book *The Clash of Civilizations*: "At some point Turkey could be ready to give up its frustrating and humiliating role as a beggar pleading for membership in the West and to resume its much more impressive and elevated historical role as the principal Islamic interlocutor and antagonist of the West." Indeed, in a span of only a few years, Turkish support for joining the European Union has dropped from 70 to 50 percent.[2]

⌒

Aya Sofia (Sancta Sophia in Latin, Hagia Sophia in Greek), Justinian's 6th-century architectural glory and Istanbul's most famous monument, if not the greatest church in Christendom for 1,000 years, faces the Blue Mosque, a stone's throw from where Sammy and I were dawdling. For my part, it felt like being at the Byzantine and Ottoman threshold, its historical gravitas conjuring up the spirit of 1,500 years of opulence, conflict, and intrigue.

Upon entering Aya Sofia for the first time, Justinian proclaimed, "Glory to God that I have been judged worthy of such a work. Oh Solomon! I have outdone you!"[3]

While fending off Kurdish carpet hawkers, I joined Mustafa Oktar in front of the Aya Sofia. Like Sammy, Mustafa is an iconic old hustler in the historic district, giving tours of Aya Sofia for over 50 years. Now in his mid-70s, Mustafa has a leathery face generously marked with the blemishes of age. Slightly stooped and flirtatious with the ladies, he casts a sly smile with his rascally sense of humor. A baseball cap, sneakers, and windbreaker are his trademark

---

2. On January 15, 2012, Soner Cagaptay, a senior fellow at the Washington Institute for Near East Policy, wrote in the *New York Times*, "Of the 33 new Turkish diplomatic missions opened in the past decade, 18 are in Muslim and African countries. This has resulted in new commercial and political ties, often at the expense of Turkey's ties with Europe. In 1999, the European Union accounted for over 56 percent of Turkish trade; in 2011, it was just 41 percent. Over the same period, Islamic countries' share of Turkish trade climbed to 20 percent from 12 percent."

3. It is no surprise that the Blue Mosque was built by Sultan Ahmet, the namesake of the historical precinct, over a 1,000 years later as an attempt to outdo the glory of Aya Sofia.

duds, giving the effect of a tout at Churchill Downs more than a tour guide at a Turkish museum (and he still spits when he talks).

On this afternoon, Mustafa's spiel, laying out the broad outlines of history, began outside, around the foundation stones of the first two Aya Sofias, both destroyed by fire. He proceeded to 1453, when Mehmet the Conqueror besieged Istanbul, ending the Byzantine Empire and inaugurating the 500-year reign of the Ottoman Empire.

As the story goes, after the conquest Aya Sofia was converted to a mosque: minarets sprang up from the four corners, a mihrab replaced the Christian altar, and crosses gave way to crescent moons, church bells to the muezzin's call to prayer, and Christian iconography to calligraphic Koranic verses. The church's rich, posticonoclastic mosaics were plastered over, readorned with eight moon-sized, black wooden discs, each inscribed in Arabic with flourishes of gold.

In 1935, Mustafa Kemal Atatürk, the secularist George Washington of the Republic of Turkey, in a goodwill gesture to Christians and Muslims, to East and West, proclaimed Aya Sofia a museum. Now sponsored by UNESCO (United Nations Educational, Scientific and Cultural Organization), its rehabilitation is ongoing.

As Romans had done with the great Greek monuments, the Byzantines and Ottomans did with Aya Sofia: recycled antiquity's best. The library walls next to us were squared in the same blue ceramic tiles found in the Blue Mosque. Mustafa says they were carted here from Nicaea, home to Constantine's Council, which adopted the ecumenical statement of Christian faith, the Nicene Creed, in the comforting shadow of these swirly blue tiles.

Eight ornamental, red granite Corinthian columns from the Temple of Artemis (Diana) at Ephesus, one of the Seven Wonders of the World, stood regally across from the library. And near the imperial entryway were two seven-foot-tall ablution urns, quarried from single blocks of marble from the pagan Greek city of Pergammon. It's the central nave encircled by the massive dome—wide as the sky and tall as the heavens—and rimmed by 40 arched windows that truly proclaims Aya Sofia's architectural grandeur, if not a Saturn-like aspect of a floating, ringed planet, of cosmic weightlessness. The use of the dome, in lieu of columns, was an engineering triumph, designed so that Aya Sofia could double the congregational capacity to 20,000.

For Christians, it's easy to say that the damage done by the Ottomans in converting Aya Sofia to a mosque has rendered it spiritually extinct. In a perfect world, true, but looking forward, in the living history museum context, the mixed iconography is a powerful metaphor of peace and reconciliation.

Upstairs was the floor crypt of Henrico Dandolo, doge of Venice, commander of the Fourth Crusade. Rather than conquering Cairo and the Abuyyids as planned, and heading to Muslim-occupied Jerusalem, the doge's crusaders redirected to Constantinople. These Venetian and Frankish firebrands had marks of silver and settling old debts on their minds.

Greek historian Speros Vryonis, in his book *Byzantium and Europe*, gives a chilling backstory of the crusaders' barbaric behavior in Constantinople. What Vryonis describes was decidedly the last straw in the schism between the Roman Catholic and Eastern Orthodox Churches:

> The Latin soldiery subjected the greatest city in Europe to an indescribable sack. For three days they murdered, raped, looted and destroyed on a scale which even the ancient Vandals and Goths would have found unbelievable. Constantinople had become a veritable museum of ancient and Byzantine art, an emporium of such incredible wealth that the Latins were astounded at the riches they found. Though the Venetians had an appreciation for the art which they discovered (they were themselves semi-Byzantines) and saved much of it, the French and others destroyed indiscriminately, halting to refresh themselves with wine, violation of nuns, and murder of Orthodox clerics. The crusaders vented their hatred for the Greeks most spectacularly in the desecration of the greatest Church in Christendom. They smashed the silver iconostasis, the icons and the holy book of Hagia Sophia, and seated upon the patriarchal throne a whore who sang coarse songs as they drank wine from the Church's holy vessels. The estrangement of East and West, which had proceeded over the centuries, culminated in the horrible massacre that accompanied the conquest of Constantinople. The Greeks were convinced that even the Turks, had they taken the city, would not have been as cruel as the Latin Christians. The defeat of Byzantium, already in a state of decline, accelerated political degeneration so that the Byzantines eventually became as easy prey to the Turks. The Crusading movement thus resulted, ultimately, in the victory of Islam, a result which was of course the exact opposite of its original intention.

This Christian-on-Christian warring between the Catholic Church of Rome and the Eastern Orthodox did not melt into the night: Pope John Paul's 1999 visit to the Orthodox East was the first by a Catholic head in almost 1,000 years. And, as we know, the Latins didn't come to Constantinople to convert souls; they were here for the "riches." Similarly, the carnage and cultural degradation visited upon the Middle East and Europe by the Ottomans can't be blamed on religion alone. Rather like the Christians, Jews, Chinese, pagans, pharaohs, Greeks, Persians, Romans, Kurds, Arabs, Hindus, Bantus, Mongols, Mayans, and others before, these cultures of conflict arose out of greed for territory, for power, for trade, for women, for influence, for ethnic dominance, and for revenge (Saddam Hussein was a secular nationalist).

Religion is the convenient shroud the wicked and wiser hide behind, invoking fear as a precursor to hope. It's that same piety that fundamentalist heads of state and stateless terrorists, posing as "thinkers," draw out like a weapon, to fire ancient racial hatreds, to bleed the poor and vulnerable. And today it's those vulnerable ones who renounce modernity, not because they are inherently Islamic terrorists, but because they were born poor and have since been left behind. Their profile—two sides of the same coin that romanticizes violence yet seeks to impose order—is not altogether different from the chivalrous and heroic gang banger in L.A., or the crime-prone dropout who joins the American army. (After several arrests, a judge ordered me into service.)

It's no surprise to see what the unintended consequences of conflict repeatedly turn up, as the historian's account of the Fourth Crusade throws into relief—a country (Iraq) is weakened by war, and another (Iran) fills the vacuum, repeated with biological rhythm. A monument to reconciliation, Aya Sofia is also a testament to the limits of the human imagination. As with art, the mixed iconography of Aya Sophia brings together seemingly paradoxical ideas, holding them in an uneasy balance, creating an orderly illusion, but not one with full resolution.

⌒

By tram, the next day I crossed the Golden Horn (Khaleej) on the Galata Bridge, constructed in 1845. In a letter to Sultan Beyazid II in 1502, Leonardo da Vinci was the first to imagine the building of the Galata Bridge. These were the waning days of a 500-year stretch of cultural exchange between Islamic intellectuals and early Renaissance scholars. Had the sultan acted on da Vinci's innovative design, it would have been the first parabolic bridge ever built. The 13th-century Genoese tower, now known as Galata (or Pera), loomed north of the bridge like a phallic mystery, puncturing the sky in the middle of the former Genoese neighborhood.

Near the tower I was meeting Nilay Ornek, an editor and columnist at the national Turkish newspaper *Milliyet*. We got together at the Litera Café atop the Goethe Institute, where the headland of historic Istanbul's Seraglio Point fell before us in a gilded sprawl to the Sea of Marmara.

Nilay, in her early 30s, was urban hip, in girlish bangs and ponytail. She wore a jean skirt, below-the-knee black boots, and dangling silver earrings. Her midriff was slightly exposed. On her wrist she wore a silver band with an evil eye amulet, there to cast off the bad luck that had recently befallen her in not obtaining a journalist visa to Britain.

Even working six days a week, she finds time on Friday nights to deejay at a nearby club, shunning the vibrant Turkish pop scene for Kurt Cobain's grunge rock tunes. Only three months before, Nilay had returned from a journalism fellowship in the States. A friend of mine was her advisor while there. Over the years, she had often been to events at the Goethe Institute. In countries around the world, the Goethe Institute is to Germany what Alliance Français is to France, and what the Confucian Institute is to China, a low-key instrument for exporting culture—music, food, festivals, art exhibits, language lessons, and educational exchange. McDonald's aside, today the United States has no such equivalent, yet during the Cold War cross-cultural diplomacy, if not propaganda, was first employed by Eisenhower through the United States Information Agency (USIA), which owned radio and TV stations and magazines around the world. "The agency devoted half its very large budget in West Germany to cultural centers and libraries known as *Amerika Hauser*," reported the *New York Times*.[4]

Though our foreign missions still strongly push American commerce, even USAID (United States Agency for International Development), our best diplomatic face, has walled up in the hermetic world of those embassies. We know that the quick fix, public relations strategy of dispatching a clueless Karen Hughes to the Middle East—as David Holdridge put it, "selling America the way you do toothpaste"—does not work. Neither does hunkering down in willful isolation behind crash walls, doing a mole run to and from work, without meaningful cultural exchange. It sends a message of fear, of withdrawal, and of separateness.

"Europe is boosting its common diplomatic corps, while China is deploying retired civil servants, prison laborers and Chinese teachers—all are what the historian Arnold Toynbee called marchmen, the foot-soldiers of empire spreading values and winning loyalty," wrote Parag Khanna. "There are currently more musicians in U.S. military marching bands than there are Foreign Service officers, a fact not helped by Congress's decision to effectively freeze growth in diplomatic postings. . . . We need a Peace Corps 10 times its present size, plus student exchanges, English-teaching programs and hands-on job training overseas—with corporate sponsorship."

Given that the United States has over 700 military bases abroad, and a defense budget of over 700 billion dollars, Secretary of Defense Robert Gates agreed that our foreign service needed to expand. He pointed out that the entire American diplomatic corps of 6,500 is less than the staffing of one U.S. aircraft carrier. "It simply does not have the built-in, domestic constituency of defense programs," he said. "As an example, the F-22 aircraft is produced by companies in 44 states; that's 88 senators." It's not just about pushing American values but also about creating reasons for East and West to come together. We need to rebuild the U.S. information services.

Among other reasons, Nilay is a fan of America because of the educational opportunities extended to her. She first went to the States for English-language training at Rutgers University, where her boyfriend, Ceyhun, a Turkish com-

---

4. While living in Hanoi between 1998 and 2003, I saw the 1950s remnants of these centers.

puter engineer now working in New York, also attended. He will soon receive his American citizenship, at which time he will return to Turkey. "If you have a different passport life is easier," Nilay said, explaining why many Turks are doing as her boyfriend has done. "You have a choice for the future. It's easier for your children to get a better education in another country. Plus, these days with the AKP [Islamist] government, if need be, you can abandon this country if anti-secular opinions get too bad." Ceyhun had bought an insurance policy.

While at Rutgers, Nilay made many American friends, telling them of fashionable and progressive Istanbul. "It was important for me to portray a positive image of Turkey while I was in America. Then another Turkish woman, wearing a hijab, and chaperoned by her brother, arrived," she said. "The woman couldn't go to Istanbul University and wear the hijab, so her parents, who have plenty of money, sent her to America!"

We both paused to laugh and think about that before Nilay finished her story: "All my American friends thought I had deceived them. I was very upset with this woman, but eventually we became friends. I bet you in three years she will dress Western. The problem is that she is the image that America will keep of Turkey. And now the prime minister's wife is wearing a scarf, too," Nilay concluded, throwing her hands in the air in frustration.[5]

⌇

Nilay told me about her American "road trips." Topping her favorite destinations were San Diego, Boston, New York, and Key West. She had seen more of America than most Americans. "Everywhere in America is different in some way, but most Americans only know about their neighborhood," she said. "They are lazy about understanding the rest of the world. Turks read newspapers or talk in the coffee shops every day. They know what is going on in America. Some people even call us 'little America.'"

We talked about the proposed Armenian genocide resolution the U.S. Congress had recently proposed. "My family has been friendly forever with our Armenian neighbors, but since this has been dredged up, things are tense between us. I wish it had not occurred. Even my mother has put a flag out. Why? I don't know. Besides, what would America think if Turkey passed a resolution denouncing the American genocide of Indians?"

I told her about recently attending a book reading by Orhan Pamuk, Turkey's Nobel laureate, at the Memorial Church at Harvard. The event occurred on the same day that the Turkish ambassador was recalled to Ankara. When asked about the genocide resolution, in so many words, Pamuk said, "I was expecting the

---

5. Two months later, the Turkish parliament would vote with an 80 percent majority to lift the ban on headscarves in universities. Prime Minister Erdogan would champion it as a "triumph of democracy and justice," while secularists, like Nilay, would see it as a giant step back for women.

question, and I know how to get out of it," tacitly acknowledging the indictment he had been under—"insulting Turkishness" under article 301 of the Turkish criminal code—over his own public comments about the genocide.

"International arm twisting of this sort does not work in Turkey," Pamuk said. "It is a moral issue, a Turkish problem with freedom of speech, which we do not have like in America. Our right to free speech is limited, so this kind of foreign intervention will only set that back."[6]

Similarly to other places I visited in Turkey, it seemed that for every cultural bridge there was a bias, a historic memory. When I asked Nilay about Sulukule, the Gypsy (Roma) slum known for its music, belly dancing, and protests against urban renewal—recommended to me by a Greek journalist who had written about their plight—she was dismissive: "We see the Romas every day, so that is not of interest. And the Greeks don't like Turks, so I don't like them," she said, flatly.[7]

As we walked out to Istaklal Caddesi (Independence Street), a pedestrian mall running from the Galata Tower to Taksim Square, Nilay stopped to say hello to a couple of friends on their way to the Goethe Institute. Istaklal can be as fashionable as Fifth Avenue, while the larger Pera neighborhood—Galata, Taksim, and Cihangir—is a cobbled rabbit's warren of confectioners, jazz clubs, restaurants, fish markets, mosques, kebab stalls, appliance dealers, tattoo and piercing parlors, curio stores, churches, and street-side coffee shops. Cihangir is the bohemian haunt of artists, movie directors, academicians, writers (Orhan Pamuk has a flat here), transvestites, and Anatolian villagers. Even the homeless are bohemian, dwelling in a locale with the grandeur of Ottoman-era mosques. Throughout history, the Western-minded denizens of Pera have been accused of currying favor with the enemies of Istanbul.

It is compelling to witness the public exuberance for free speech here on Istaklal, or Independence Street. Organized protests occur every day, "like Hyde Park," Nilay said. As the 19th-century tram—fire engine red and trimmed in white—inched by with kids hanging off the running boards, two groups of protestors marched in its wake: doctors over 65, in their white jackets, carried placards and clamored about work benefits beyond the statutory retirement age. A phalanx of women in robes and Western dress, with signs protesting the conflict with the Kurds, were minded by a formation of embarrassed policemen in riot gear—guns and cudgels relaxed—ready to scatter, at the first signal, like restless boys in a choir.

Nilay walked me through the Bahar restaurant, next to the fish market, where I would return for dinner that evening. Before its newest incarnation as

---

6. Under pressure from the European Union [EU], the law has now been appealed.
7. After 49 years, only recently did a Greek prime minister pay an official visit to Turkey.

a fish restaurant, the Ottoman-era palace was once a harem, a military school, and a flower emporium. Women patrons smoked as much as men, and all had glasses of beer and white wine along with Marmara white fish. That evening, after I told the waiter I was American, he quickly confessed to being a Bush hater, because of Iraq, of course. He then made disparaging remarks about Arabs: "They eat with their hands," he said, making a hideous face.[8] His facility with language—he spoke four—and his reflexive racism, were only exceeded by his duplicity in dual pricing my dinner, grossly overcharging me.

People watching with Nilay was fascinating. Men and women trended flashy and fastidious. "Mac," the high-end cosmetic store, was a caricature of this urban strain of fashion. Through the smoked glass, their invitation-only party, where black was the dress and silk was the color of women's hair, appeared to be a convention of those people-as-petrified-primps, goggled out in feline Pradas one sees through the glass at Harry Winston's in New York. Here the fashion was more filled with irony.

A block further, a modelesque woman sashayed by in black fishnet stockings—her eyes rimmed black in kohl, wearing a silky, lavender hijab, tightly fitting around her face. Another in a black scarf and robe stood in front of her lingerie shop whose merchandise would make Victoria's Secret customers blush. "These women who cover themselves are not always so pure," Nilay said. "Trust me: many are wearing G-strings under those robes."

Modernity comes at a price, though, just as in Madrid, London, and New York. We were walking near the British consulate, walled like a fortress after the 2003 al-Qaeda-inspired bombing that killed 27 people.[9] Across Turkey, for over four decades, terrorist attacks have targeted Americans, Jews, and secularist Turks, all symbols of modernity. The tension never completely goes away, with Islamism braying at the gates: in the roiling shantytowns, known as *gecekondu*, that encircle Istanbul, or in the nearby fundamentalist neighborhood of Carsamba. There the men's shaved scalps, skullcaps, bushy beards, foreheads calloused with prayer marks (or *zebidah*), and animal-faced anger at least superficially resembles the Taliban more than modern Turkey. Religion alone is not to blame for these parallel worlds: income inequality in Turkey is one of the highest in the world.

Before we descended the San Francisco–steep hillside, Nilay took me to Cihangir mosque, designed by architect Mimar Sinan, the Christopher Wren of early Ottoman Istanbul. It was probably the Renaissance creations of Michelangelo that influenced Sinan in his 50-year reign of throwing up one

---

8. It is not uncommon for Turks to view desert Arabs as backward, if not unworthy as founders of Islam.

9. Nearby was the American consulate, which al-Qaeda gunmen attacked on July 9, 2008; three terrorists and three guards were killed.

masterpiece after another. (Michelangelo and da Vinci were definitely known at the time in Istanbul.)

"You are very lucky today," Nilay said, arriving as the call to prayer sounded. Beyond, an infinite blue sky melded with the shimmering waters of the Golden Horn and Sea of Marmara, a hive of maritime commerce. Prayerful ones in caps and veils arrived. We sat in the leafy courtyard, praising the historical panorama, Seraglio Point and the Prince's Islands to one side, the Bosphorous and Black Sea to the other.

⁓

In the throes of the Enlightenment—born out of resistance to religion in favor of human rights and individual freedoms—the 18th-century Ottomans recognized that cultural change and technology were linked. Thus, the sultans of the time adopted Western architecture, music, literature, and clothing. They soon embraced, if not contributed to, the innovations of the emerging industrial revolution. A century later, with the Republic of Turkey freshly inaugurated, Atatürk abolished the Ottoman monarchy, the 400-year-old Istanbul caliphate, the biblical practice of polygamy, the traditional veil, and the signature headdress of all Ottoman men, the fez. At the same time, he adopted the Italian penal code and Swiss legal system, and the Latin alphabet replaced Arabic. A multiparty democracy took hold, while women got the vote (only a few years after they did in the United States), and the Friday Muslim holiday was replaced by the Christian Sunday, the weekend of the West. It seemed that Turkey was forever changed.

Yet since Atatürk's early death in 1938 of alcoholism at age 57—though secularists, including the elite, bureaucratically entrenched military, hold his reforms sacred—Islamists have chipped away at Turkey's liberal democracy, which is often seen as an American imitation. For Turkey, as well as the larger Middle East, this dissonance has become the conflict of the ages.

⁓

Nilay flashed her press pass at the ticket window of the Istanbul Art Fest, held in a godown-cum-gallery on the Golden Horn, next door to the Istanbul Modern Art Museum. Sweeping into the exhibit with flair, Nilay was quickly drawn to Turkan Soray, the Elizabeth Taylor of Turkish cinema, who was featured by several artists in decorous air-brushed portraits and film noir collages.

She then turned to what I was trying to get my mind around—having just left the mosque—an oil painting of a monkey pulling up a pantyless woman's dress. "Isn't Bedri Baykam outrageous?" Nilay said, joining me. Of course she knew his work. He was famous for provocative nudes, which were almost a genre here. His was great work but at this exhibit gratuitous in number (and slightly uncomfortable for me to discuss with a Muslim-raised, though avowedly secular, woman I had just met who is my daughter's age).

The physical immodesty got better: there was an entire wall of takeoffs on 19th-century French realist Gustave Courbet's *L'origine du monde* (Origin of the World). Portrayed with the same explicit pubic and labia definition, they were each set upon clouded crimson backdrops. Even these progressive, Istanbullah art lovers tended to self-consciously view the "Origin of the World" from afar.

An upstairs wing, in an annual competition among well-known Turkish artists, displayed subversive, modern renditions of Leonardo da Vinci's *Last Supper*. One portrayed the "Supper" as an EU meeting of relentless infighting over Turkey's admission, while another depicted a private orgy of modern, debauching Turkish politicians, being entertained by a belly dancer—as drawn by da Vinci but with Christ giving a bone white finger to the world. Nilay and I said goodbye, cheek kissing and jumping in separate taxis. A curtain of darkness had fallen. As we twisted down through Pera toward the Galata Bridge, where the reformer Atatürk's cortege had traveled 70 years before, a luminous crescent moon hung above the Golden Horn. It flickered like a kaleidoscope switching scenes between East and West, between tradition and modernity.

CHAPTER NINE

~

Bombs Away on the PKK

Since the great Atatürk's time, Kurdish identity has been muted, their language and history banned and their cities and villages renamed in Turkish. They were forced to live under the slogan "Happy Is He Who Calls Himself a Turk" but without the same political and economic opportunities. Out of this systematic marginalization, after decades of separatist rebellion, the PKK (Kurdistan Workers' Party)—a Marxist-Leninist-inspired terrorist organization—was founded in 1978 by student-turned-revolutionary Abdullah Ocalan. The group was officially inaugurated in Fis, a village outside of Diyarbakir.

Unlike those of many iconic revolutionaries of the 20th century, Ocalan's bio is unremarkable. Given to tirades about Marx and his own village-boy greatness, his chance arrest at a student protest and subsequent imprisonment did not foretell his dictatorial, bloodthirsty propensity. Overseeing the PKK from training camps in the Bekaa Valley and after from his villas in Damascus and Aleppo, he usually appeared in khaki trousers and loose-fitting sports shirts. He bragged of being a guerrilla war mastermind but never lived in the bush or fired a gun.

After 19 years of living in Syria, the government expelled him under threat of invasion from Turkey. Caught by surprise, with no alternate plan, his farcical frenzy to find asylum took him to Greece, Russia, Italy, Tajikistan, Russia, Greece, Belarus, Greece, and Kenya. Apparently he never considered hightailing it to the PKK mountain redoubts with his comrades.

In the end, he was lured unceremoniously into a plane in Nairobi, with the promise of yet another sympathetic country awaiting his arrival; instead, he was handcuffed, blindfolded, and drugged, bound for Turkey. Once the blindfold came off, according to his captors, an agent said, "Abdullah Ocalan, welcome home."

No one ever accused Ocalan of being Che, his facade of revolutionary mastermind shattered like a fragile China doll upon his capture in 1999. To the chagrin of his followers and the families of those who fought and died, he renounced violence, promoted peace, and praised Atatürk and the Turkish state—his life more important than the PKK. Even so, he never gave up his hold on the PKK; as a prisoner-for-life, the organization and its members are his only purchase on power. In 2004, after his death sentence was commuted, yet realizing the finality of his incarceration and that peace and reconciliation were not talking points for the Turks, he ordered the armed rebellion resurrected. Perfidy aside, today his captivity is symbolic of the larger Kurdish struggle for political and cultural relevance, if not autonomy.

That his vision of an independent state achieved by armed struggle—which included killing fellow Kurds, often innocent women, children, and school-teachers, and assassinating hundreds of cadre-in-arms over paranoid delusions of betrayal—would be blindly accepted by ordinary and even well-educated Kurds was jarring to the outsider. Prudent people don't behave like this, it seemed from afar.

Lawyer-turned-PKK rebel Zeki Ozturk explained: "People chose armed struggle as a last resort, it wasn't the first choice. In Europe or the United States, it seems like a strange choice, but for someone from the Middle East, the conditions are different, the evaluations different. There was no democratic opening in Turkey." One man's terrorist, he was saying, is another man's freedom fighter.

The PKK filled a power vacuum of Kurdish nationalism created when the United States and the shah of Iran abandoned Mullah Mustafa Barzani and the Kurdish independence movement in northern Iraq in 1975. The shah and then vice president Saddam Hussein struck a deal at the OPEC (Organization of Petroleum Exporting Countries) summit in Algiers on the Iraq and Iran border in the south, where the Tigris and Euphrates come together south of Basra, to form the Shatt al-Arab. Saddam conceded that the thalweg, the deepest channel in the middle of the river, would be the border.

In exchange, the shah agreed to cease his support of the Kurdish rebellion in Iraq, which was largely sponsored by American weapons given to the shah by President Richard Nixon and Secretary of State Henry Kissinger in a secret pact that included Barzani and covert CIA assistance. This would be the first time the Iraqi Kurds tied their faith, if not actions, to the goodness of America. The shah's close friend Kissinger famously dismissed the abandonment: "Covert action should not be confused with missionary work."

As a postscript, amid the world's relative silence, Saddam gassed over 5,000 Halabja Kurds during the Anfal campaign, while killing another 177,000 in other ways, and eradicating as many as 4,000 Kurdish villages. Across the border in Turkey, over 40,000 have been killed in PKK-Kurdish struggle, mostly innocent civilians. The Turkish army has retaliated by terrorizing tens of thousands of villagers, forcing them to live in city slums. There are no innocents in this Maoist-fought war (nee missionary work).

By the early 1990s, the rebel group had galvanized a mass movement of Kurdish politicians, university students, early adolescent village boys, and high school–aged girls wanting to break out of traditional roles. They even branched into legal, nonviolent political organizing, publishing, and cultural events, such as Noruz, the Kurdish national day of celebration that falls on March 21, the ancient Zoroastrian first day of spring. The PKK used the occasion of Noruz to launch their guerrilla war in 1984, and though in 2006 the Diyarbakir festival turned into a riot, in any given year, among the food, fireworks, music, and line dancing, PKK volunteers work the crowds, inspiring Kurdish pride. The trajectory of the PKK struggle has come to resemble a popular uprising, if not the only act in town pushing for Kurdish rights.

⌒

Eight F-16s cracked the sky as I stepped off a Turkish Air flight in Diyarbakir, the unofficial capital of Turkish Kurdistan and stronghold of the PKK. The fighter equipment had changed, but the sonic screeching was familiar from my last time here. In 1974, this was a Cold War listening post where the United States siloed missiles while Phantoms patrolled the skies, both awaiting a wrong move by the Soviet Union. This time, northern Iraq and the separatist, terrorist group PKK, organically grown here in Diyarbakir, are in the crosshairs of those fighter jets.

It was November 5, 2007, and Prime Minister Recep Tayyip Erdogan and President George Bush were meeting at the White House. Given that I had planned this trip two months before, it seemed that a more tumultuous time could not have been scripted. Or was the epic border showdown all media hype, another Turkish feint for money and weapons? Hard to know the inside, but I was certain of this: the PKK had been conducting cross-border attacks from northern Iraq since August of 1984, the Turkish army and air force had pursued them into Iraq since 1986, and the two sides don't talk. That would not end with a one-day meeting.

As I collected my bag, a Turkish journalist I met on the flight vented about America: "We think the U.S. is playing with us, that they are imperialists, first in Iraq, and now they talk about Iran. Barzani and the PKK are in bed with the Americans." They think, therefore it is, said the philosopher (in so many words).

"You go to Iraq; I take you," said one cabbie after another. "Iraq, Iraq, Iraq!" The pitch followed me like a shrill echo as I shouldered my rucksack past a long line of taxis. My innocence would be offered up soon enough to this braying bunch. As for now, a ride to the Kervansaray (Caravanserai) Hotel, which was nearby, would do me.

We drove along the distantly familiar Roman-era walls of black basalt. Much had been modernized outside the ancient ramparts—malls, hospitals, schools, and tenements. The *gecekondu*, the roiling squatter neighborhoods of Kurdish migrants, who fled here in the midnineties as the Turkish army decimated villages sympathetic to the PKK, gave way to dun-colored plains. The mass removal of villagers to the city struck me as a page from the American "Vietnamization" plan decades before (or as Saddam did a decade later with Kurds in Iraq). For sure there was no parade day of Turkish flags here as in Istanbul, not even appearing above the tired old train station, the same one I had arrived at over three decades before from Ankara, on the ten-dollar hard seats, with no charge for the 36 hours of hissing cylinders.

As we puttered through traffic, I was reminded of a story a reporter friend had told me when he was here in early 2003 in the lead-up to the Iraq invasion. With the hype of weapons of mass destruction, based on nothing concrete other than Saddam having gassed Kurds in Halabja 15 years before, many here put plastic sheeting over their windows, secured with duct tape, which they called "Saddam."

The basalt ramparts encircle this ancient city in the shape of a fish. At six miles long, locals like to say it is second only in size to the Great Wall. Across the street from the southern parapet, which rose above the lush banks of the Tigris River, was the Ottoman-era caravan inn, eerily empty of travelers but for me. Silk Road traders had gathered for 500 years in the cobbled courtyard, centered with a fountain, and embowered by pines and pomegranates along the arcade of rooms. They must have arrived here from faraway places like Baghdad, Erbil, Aleppo, Nineveh, Herat, Istanbul, Damascus, Beirut, and Bokhara, and shared nargilehs and samovars of tea, swapping their wares of Silk Road exotica and spinning fanciful yarns of plundering pashas and plots of derring-do. The plaintive tones of a Kurdish *saz* (lute) might have drifted in the brisk night air. Livestock—camels, sheep, and donkeys—were fed and boarded in the tunneled stalls below, now the location of an unfrequented restaurant feeding only me on this night.

A young man showed me to one of the cave-like rooms giving off the courtyard. The room's arched stone doorways suggested an era when men were not so tall. I tossed my bags into the chilly cavern before falling into the street with a nostalgic zeal, memories flushing through me.

The streets were heaving, but as I ascended the fortress walls ringing the historic district of Sur, near the Mardin Gate I found myself alone on the basalt bastion, buffeted by an Anatolian wind and facing the emerald bend in the

Tigris as it sluiced through the Roman-built Ten-Eye Bridge. Onward was the Silvan Highway, which coiled east up a bleak and brown mesa, trailing off into the rolling Anatolian plains toward the former Armenian city of Silvan.

Missing from this picture were the Gypsies (or Qurags in Kurdish), who once spread makeshift tents beneath the Ten-Eye Bridge. Along the fecund littoral, still carpeted in pepper, eggplant, and tomato plots and Diyarbakir's famous watermelons, Gypsies encamped seasonally, raiding the fields of their crops. In the 1970s, I stayed for several months with my brother at a Halliburton encampment in Diyarbakir. Tracing glorified goat trails to remote drilling sites, we often crossed the Ten-Eye Bridge in 80,000-pound Halliburton trucks. Once in the mountains near Batman it was not uncommon to be assaulted by rock throwing Kurdish villagers. They were understandably angered over American and European companies extracting their oil, but more so we were seen as complicit with the repressive Turkish government, American lackeys. Oh yes, those were the rock-throwing days. The few Kurds I knew at the time were employed in the oilfield, and though there was plenty of anti-Turk and anti-American rhetoric, life was good and we were treated as family.

Midnight Express, a Hollywood movie Turks find offensive even today, was about those times. We were guilty as portrayed, fugitives by nature. But given that we had Turkish army guards patrolling our barbed-wire compound, we felt secure, as if a cordon sanitaire protected us. We spent many evenings, when not lumbering down those dark trailways in clunky Halliburton pump trucks, engaged in a Mesopotamian version of "white mischief," drinking thimbles of raki and Turkish coffee, smoking local tobacco laced with opiated hashish, with Kurdish friends. Years later when I saw the movie, I thought better of all that.

My memories, ambivalent as they are, were the only acquaintance I now had in this Mesopotamian time warp. Yet that didn't keep me from peering into the eyes of the older men along Gazi Caddesi, looking for a familiar glint. Although some were spiffily dressed, most wore the dusty Kurdish ensemble of shabby coats, baggy "Allah" pants, cummerbunds, and long-toed shoes. Some wore skullcaps, others flat caps, and most fingered their amber worry beads in one hand while smoking with the other. Could that be Gurip? Or that one Shevik? In this city of over a million, I had a needle-in-a-haystack chance of finding long-lost friends.

For these older ones the muezzin's call to prayer marked linear time. Of course, the Ulu Camii Mosque stood as it had for a thousand years in the center of the Sur district; the Assyrian Church has been there since the 5th century, and the Roman sundial next to the ablutions fountain was there before that, all sharpening the focus on one's own insignificance in the grander scheme of things.

The former Turkish military outpost near the Yenikapi Gate (East), nestled into the castle-like ramparts of the Roman wall, was being renovated into a museum and cultural center. The prison there once housed thieves, druggies ("yikes"), and PKK women, who were often tortured. Below, the Tigris moved silently like a giant brown snake, slithering south, impervious to that without gravitas.

On September 12, 1980, a military junta ascended to power in Turkey, with a mission to quash the political violence leftover from the '70s. That date has become to Kurds what September 11 is to Americans—an iconic moment of barbarism. Over the course of a few years, the Turkish military rounded up and imprisoned over 2,000 PKK rebels and sympathizers. Without a shred of due process, most were sent out of sight and sound of the Sur district, to the infamous Diyarbakir Military Prison, more isolated near the outer edge of the city.

Over the four years that Turkey was ruled by the MGK (National Security Council), a military assembly of five generals, killings and torture of Kurdish dissidents became the norm. "Prisoners were sodomized with batons, dunked into vats filled with excrement, left in rat-infected cells, terrorized by a dog, given water mixed with detergent to drink, and forced to lie in the snow in their underwear," wrote Aliza Marcus in her book *Blood and Belief.*

Although few inmates were broken and dozens were murdered, the torture and killings broadened the PKK base of support exponentially, not unlike what happened in Iraq to the United States after the news of torture at Abu Ghraib was made public and al-Qaeda popularity surged. Civil government returned to Turkey after democratic elections in late 1983, but the generals, according to Marcus, had fashioned a different Turkey for Kurds: "Cultural, linguistic, and political identity were eradicated by law. The simplest expression of cultural identity—giving children Kurdish names, singing Kurdish songs, and certainly, speaking Kurdish in state offices—was seen as a separatist act." For the moment, the Kurdish minority of 15 million in Turkey was considered legally extinct. Like the Viet Cong against the Americans, the guerrilla war was on the ascendant: the Turkish army would rule by day while the PKK owned the night.

Walking back to the Ulu Camii Mosque, atmospherics were unchanged from the 1970s. Kurdish merchants still sold carpets and handwoven saddlebags, for camels and donkeys. Next door, the arched hallways of the old medina housed a frenzy of gold shops, a Kurdish woman's obsession. Throughout Diyarbakir, more women dress in Western fashion, though the black chador was still ubiquitous. The Kurdish costumes could be extremely variable. Men in lilac scarves and pantaloons, and women in all black or nun white, dresses either sequined or filigreed in gold, blousy double skirts, and scarves of all colors, often gauzy or silk, were but a few looks. Yet clothing is more than style here; its nuances symbolize the Kurdish clan, marital, economic, and social status, each swatch a piece of living history. For my part I couldn't tell merchant from mullah, and without the benefit of common language, I was blissfully romantic about it all.

Pushcarts, hauling everything from fresh grapes, olives, fish, and eggs to mattresses and refrigerators, trundled the narrow cobbled lanes of the market. Confectioners organized their candied dates, apricots, and squash in perfect symmetry; filo pastries were generously adorned with native pistachio. Dried fruits and vegetables, aubergines, and peppers hung in picturesque, pendulous bunches, preserved for winter. Carefully groomed mounds of chili paste, cardamom, and cinnamon perfumed the air. On another lane, villagers sold striplings and branch wood that lay in heaping pyramids, for cooking and heating. All the while, the heavy hammers of blacksmiths banged out ax handles and scythes, ringing up another era.

As recent as a century and a half ago, 50 percent of Sur was made up of Armenians and other Christian faiths. It was a microcosm of the multiculturalism that the Ottomans held together: tenuous as it might have been. Next to the market, the four-legged Arabic minaret rose above the basalt walls of the Chaldean Church, the surrounding neighborhood still known as the infidel quarter. Uniformed schoolchildren walked through the legs of the minaret in hopes of a wish coming true. The church still has a few dozen congregants, but next door, at the abandoned Armenian chapel with its roof toppled, the worshippers are long gone.[1] In the early 1990s, Hezbollah, a right-wing, Islamist group unrelated to the Hezbollah of Lebanon, terrorized many Christians of Diyarbakir into fleeing, after their ancestors had most likely lived here since Constantine's time.

On the surface much had improved since those turbulent days. Demet Gural, a doctor and nongovernmental organization (NGO) executive I met in Istanbul, bragged to me of the Kurdish universities, of the intellectual class in Diyarbakir, and the building boom and signs of modernity that had set upon this traditional Kurdish city. Because of the absurd ban on speaking their own language, she was guardedly optimistic about conciliatory attitudes here.

Demet had recently been in Diyarbakir and enjoyed the animated film *Persepolis* at the multiplex cinema in the new Galleria Shopping Mall. Turkey and Iran share a common border, a language overlay between Kurdish and Persian, the violent upheavals of both countries, and a diaspora of Kurds to Europe. Thus the animated film had "resonance" here. It is a heartbreaking true story of modernity clashing with tradition, of a spirited and sky-is-the-limit girl named Marjane Satrapi, who is sucked in by the ferment of Iran's recent history, spin-

---

1. Kurds are said to have acted as proxies in the genocide here almost a century ago.

cycled by its havoc, and then centrifuged out as a cultural fugitive in Paris. The mall was within walking distance from the Kervansaray, but I took a pass on evening forays, as I was leaving before daylight the next morning.

Modernity and a passing military bus as their target, six weeks after I left Diyarbakir PKK members exploded a car bomb that killed 5 students and injured 60 in front of the upscale Galleria Shopping Mall, where *Persepolis* had been showing.

∽

It was five in the morning, the first prayer call sounded. The faithful in the streets were few as we passed through the Mardin Gate, pointed south to the Iraq border. The cabbie, Efrem Aykut, was smoking, and proceeding at a moderate speed, a mutant condition among Turkish taxi drivers. We soon hit the wide-open stretches of the highways and crossroads of Anatolia and Mesopotamia but without any extra throttle. Silence was golden: Efrem and I shared only a few words, mostly pleasantries, which were exhausted moments after he picked me up.

At the first flush of daylight, on the outskirts of Mardin, known for its vineyards, we drew up to a dirt-fronted row of concrete-block buildings, all with closed shops. Soon two shiftless men stumbled themselves awake from behind the mangled metal door of a storefront with no sign. Efrem barked a few words, and the men disappeared back into the shop, returning in a few minutes with two black market jerry cans of gasoline. Suspiciously, we had passed several open stations—Petrol Ofisi, BPet, MOil, and Nargaz. With 100-plus miles to go, Efrem bought what amounted to a quarter of a tank.

Three weeks before Turkey had canceled all flights into KRG (Kurdistan Regional Government) due to the recent PKK ambushes. This led me to think there ought to be more traffic on this morning, yet with the exception of the occasional spindly legged donkey, with its cargo of firewood bulging over like a hay wagon, and accompanied at a distance by a solitary woman, the road was empty. Villages were hidden in the shadowed folds of the undulating hills. Outside Midyat at a Petrol Ofisi station Efrem stopped for breakfast, coffee, cigarettes, and conversation, rituals that are never postponed. An hour later, we crossed the highway from the Petrol Ofisi to purchase another partial jerry can from a black marketer.

Towers and tanks and Turkish flags screamed forth from a small refinery with a military installation fronting it. From there it was bottomland of corn and cotton. Shepherd boys atop donkeys watched Kurdish long-eared sheep grazing in fallow barley fields. Cairns of rocks marked plot lines and paths. Here we rejoined the Tigris River, widening and falling in white riffles, bending toward

Mosul, 50 miles downriver, where Alexander the Great had defeated the for-midable Persian army.

More Turkish-flagged guard towers appeared. Faces hidden in a web of cam-ouflaged and sandbagged concrete bunkers studded the Tigris's banks. Leopard tanks faced the highway. Abruptly we faced a roadblock: three men in civilian clothes checked my passport. One who spoke perfect English asked me why I was going to Iraq. "There are problems there, you know," he said, not mention-ing by name the PKK.

"I'm going there for humanitarian reasons," I told him, which was what I was cautioned to say, along with not referring to northern Iraq as Kurdistan.

Laughter followed until the English speaker said, "Welcome to Turkey."

"You mean Kurdistan," I imagined saying.

Teashops and an urban-sized fleet of yellow taxis, border shuttles, lined the main street of the uninspiring concrete-block village of Silopi, the last before the border. Everything was shuttered at this hour of the morning. We pressed on, carried by mere fumes. Rusted tanker carcasses propped on small boulders became a frequent scene. These 18-wheelers once hauled crude oil from Iraq to Turkey for refining, and then back to Iraq to be unloaded on the black market, all of course in contravention of the UN Oil-for-Food Programme. As we now know, this was how Saddam gamed the system. Similarly, petty war profiteers (and insurgents) have benefited from the handiwork of saboteurs, which, begin-ning with the Iraq civil war and until recently, resulted in the unreliable flow of the Kirkuk-Ceyhan pipeline here.

Outside Silopi, trucks progressed like inchworms in both directions. This convoy of mostly tankers, but also a motley procession of flatbeds, dump trucks, and wood-paneled trailers, went for miles, as one sees every day at the Laredo, Texas, border with Mexico. But no "made in America" here: mostly Swedish-built Scanias for the Iraqis, which were tagged with yellow plates, with Arabic swirls, while the Turks (Kurds) preferred German-made Volvos and Mercedes (and a few decrepit Otosans), bearing white tags and Latin letters. The gumbo of screeching brakes, of diesel horns booming, of gears grinding, and of exhaust plumes rising all sounded and smelled like another gritty truck stop, a mirage of shoulders-against-the-wheel just the same.

KRG businesses want all they can get of Turkish consumers' goods (including electricity from GAP, the massive Tigris hydroelectric projects). An industry of petty retailers has blossomed around the unending line of truck traffic: black marketers, tire changers, and dozens of boys on three-wheeled bicycles sold jerry cans of gasoline, kebabs, candy, and cigarettes.

The long lines gave plenty of time for getting out of the cab to stretch, cadge a cigarette, jabber, and angst. Many of the drivers have hocked the farm to buy a truck, making up to 15 trips a month into Iraq, investing in loads of everything from kebab skewers to produce to alcohol. A profit of $300 a trip is not uncommon for these rugged entrepreneurs.

Scores of tarp-covered trailers brimmed over with potatoes. Feeding the building boom in the KRG, countless flatbeds of rebar also formed a double line behind the produce haulers. If anything has provided a shot of economic relief to Anatolia, it's this border trade. Since the KRG was granted semi-state status in 2005 by the Iraqi constitution, solidarity between Turkish Kurds and the KRG has flourished, not least due to commerce. And the thought of a monolithic Kurdistan, where Iraqis, Turks, and Syrian and Iranian Kurds coalesce into a single state, gives Ankara the hives.

While Turkish Kurds remain politically informed by the PKK, the rebel group is no longer the dominant force that it was in the early 1990s when it readily commandeered this highway and controlled the border: the usual traffic of 500 trucks a day slowed to less than a dozen. Today, given that the poor and powerless of Anatolia are benefiting from the cross-border trade, and that Turkish businesses are heavily invested in the KRG, to shut the border for an invasion would be an economic disaster for everyone (as it was when sanctions were imposed on Iraq after the first Gulf War). Even so, drivers were worried, gnawed at by a sixth sense of inevitability.[2]

Meantime, I tried to picture the bleak specter of some half a million starving refugees, who were refused official sanctuary by Turkey, crossing the mountainous border after the first Gulf War. Though the meaning of the first President Bush's casual remarks remain controversial, it is clear that he admonished Kurds and Shias to "take matters into their own hands." They both did as encouraged but fully expecting American support. Yet when Saddam loosed on them the full force of the Iraqi army and Revolutionary Guards, only marginally diminished by the Gulf War, he brutally quashed the uprising: 20,000 Shia were killed and two million Kurdish refugees fled (over a million were welcomed in Iran). The silence from across the Atlantic was deafening. This was the second time Iraqi Kurds had put their faith in America.

Only after Turkey's diplomats agitated Washington to act on the mounting Kurdish refugee crisis did Secretary of State James Baker pay a routine visit here. When Baker saw the Kurdish suffering with his own eyes, with an estimated 1,000 refugees blighted a day, many freezing and starving to death, he swiftly responded with compassion and conveyed to Washington our moral imperative: "We can't let this go on. We've got to do something, and we've got to do it now."

---

2. Three months later, Turkey closed the border while 10,000 Turkish troops, ferried by armored personnel carriers, crossed into Iraq.

In days, Operation Provide Comfort was launched, with 21,000 U.S.-led NATO troops pushing the Iraq army back, while relief camps were set up. Along the 36th parallel, separating the KRG from the rest of Iraq, the Green Line was drawn, protected to the north from Saddam by daily NATO flyovers. Baker's leadership saved the day. The humanitarian intervention was a proud-to-be-American success: genocide was averted, the refugees were returned home from the border frontier (Operation Safe Haven), and de facto statehood followed, with historical elections a year later. After that, there were many hurdles to cross, not least the nasty civil war in the mid-1990s between the rival parties of Massoud Barzani's Kurdistan Democratic Party (KDP) and Jalal Talabani's Patriotic Union of Kurdistan (PUK). Even so, those two million refugees who tapped into Baker's humanity are today likely to be pro-American—and helping to build the KRG's nascent democracy.

Human events are really in the eye of the beholder. Paul Wolfowitz, another Washington policy maker, also witnessed the refugee crisis at the border. Yet General Anthony Zinni, who was chief of staff of Provide Comfort, says Wolfowitz was moved more by the walkover success of the military campaign than he was by the life-saving moral intervention. Watching the multidisciplined forces—army, marines, and air force—come together and push Saddam's army back was a watershed moment for Wolfowitz. Cross-pollinated by family Holocaust experiences and an academic smugness, the seeds of Wolfowitz's anticontainment idée fixe sprouted. In another decade it would mushroom into the Iraq War (raising the costs from 1 billion dollars to over 200 billion dollars a year).

Difficult as it was, I tried to imagine "what if" Wolfowitz's new obsession had been to sell the moral-high-ground diplomacy to Washington, to fine-tune those elite, multilateral forces for more limited, objective, pragmatic, humanitarian interventions. Would Rwanda have happened? Would genocide be occurring in Darfur? Would 200 billion dollars a year spent on disease, poverty, and hunger give us fewer terrorists? Would America be the world's envy instead of its goat?[3]

An expensive three-hour drive had taken five hours, but finally we drew up to the Habur frontier gate, the only official crossing between Turkey and Iraq. The KRG civil war broke out after Talabani accused Barzani's KDP of pocketing all the custom revenues at the Habur crossing. Given the simultaneous UN sanctions on Iraq and Saddam's embargo of the KRG, the border tariffs counted for tens of millions. I expected the worst, to pay dearly.

---

3. Samantha Power, an advisor to President Obama and winner of a Pulitzer Prize for her book *A Problem from Hell*—a historical look at the U.S. response to genocide—envisioned Operation Provide Comfort as a model for military, humanitarian intervention. Almost 20 years later, when civil war broke out in Libya, with the support of the Arab League, she pressured President Obama to form the NATO air alliance that prevented a Gaddafi massacre of his own people.

Dozens of tankers of crude oil chugged in the other direction, coming from oil-rich Kirkuk. Depending on the lines at the border, they would return in days or weeks with tanks of gasoline to feed the black market of Iraq, now ranked third in corruption in the world. After all, smuggling is a timeless tradition here. Additionally, the KRG and Iraq are cash economies: credit cards and international banking transfers are not business as usual.

Below, the Habur River, a tributary of the Tigris, purled southward in sheets of rippled jade along a wide littoral of gravel bars. For all the serene surroundings, it seemed we had arrived at a massive tollgate, a well-fortified one, and Kurdish taxis had the EZ-PASS. We zipped past the endless queues of trucks, the only taxi crossing on this morning. The gauge was below empty.

"Welcome to the Kurdish Region of Iraq," read the border greeting. The tricolor Kurdish flag—red, white, and green with an emblem of the sun in the middle—flapped prominently above the river like the masthead of the Dreadnought. I didn't have a visa, only an introductory letter from Mercy Corps written in Arabic. I had no clue what it said. Two middle-aged *peshmerga* (meaning "those who face death"), the Kurdish armed forces, motioned me into the customs building, where they obligingly served me the traditional small glass of hot tea with an inch of sugar sediment. A truck driver plopped down beside me and pinched my tea when I wasn't looking before turning to chat it up with other arriving teamsters. Thirty minutes later, after four officials vetted the letter, tracked me on the computer, and made a phone call, an officious, smartly attired bureaucrat approached me, gave me a rote handshake, and handed me my stamped passport. He then tapped on his heart with a soft fist. I returned the customary greeting. "Welcome," he said. "No fee for the visa."

A short distance beyond, a wall mural advertising Silav and Bekhal Resorts, depicting tumbling waterfalls and Edenic lush, washed over the front wall of the drab customs house like a window to paradise. Though the KRG is hopeful that tourists will find their way here soon, the mountain resorts are, for now, favorite weekend getaways for Kurds. Portraits of Mullah Mustafa Barzani, the Kurdish independence fighter, first president of the KDP, in dramatic three-quarter profiles, flanked the mural.

Attired in Kurdish warrior fashion—turbaned, cummerbund, and baggy pants, crossed with a sword and cinched with a cartridge belt—Barzani seemed to be the prototype for several middle-aged peshmerga gathered at the guard station. Efrem motioned me out of the taxi to join a snarl of soldiers who packed .45s and assault rifles (but no swords), while he drove behind the wall, leaving me to wonder about his mysterious affairs. The peshmerga offered me cigarettes and assured me of their love of Americans with a thumbs-up. Efrem returned 15 minutes later, pointing in gleeful pride to his fuel gauge—full.

It all clicked into focus: Efrem held out for the Iraqi rationed gas, subsidized by the United States at 200 dinars ($.17) a liter and sold on the black market at 900 dinars ($.70) by KRG officials, a tidy 400-plus percent profit. Back in Diyarbakir, petrol went for $1.23 a liter, 40 percent more than the bargain basement black market gas here. It was nothing if not savvy entrepreneurship. By ten in the morning, Efrem had made a nice fare from me, while saving the better part of a 20-dollar bill on petrol.

CHAPTER TEN

~

The Peshmerga and Mercy Corps

In a parking lot full of yellow taxis, Amar Galaly, the procurement officer at the Mercy Corps office in Suleimaniyah, was leaning against a faded maroon Mitsubishi, a cigarette appended to his lip. His youthful head of hair shined with gel, eyes puffy and face amiable, and round, an easy demeanor. At age 28, Amar speaks impeccable English, plus his speech has the languor of an American southerner. That I liked. I threw my rucksack on board and shook hands with the driver, Bakhtyar Nuri. We were off for the eight-hour drive to Suleimaniyah.

Amar purchases the hygiene kits and "livelihood assets" for IDPs (internally displaced person) for whom Mercy Corps provides emergency relief. Most of those products are bought in Turkey, the KRG's biggest supplier and investor. Amar had made this run before. As had Bakhtyar, who is 40, graying, and shy about speaking English. He listened intently while Amar and I talked, nodding his head in agreement on occasion.

Zakho was the first village after the border, with over 100,000 people, situated on the Habur River. The first refugee camp was established here during Operation Safe Haven. Bookended by two *peshmerga* checkpoints, Zakho's a border-town clone of Silopi—streets of unpainted concrete and commerce on the fly, a metering station for the Kirkuk-Ceyhan pipeline. The nearby Qandil Mountains, their remote ridges and precipices visible to the north, are home to the PKK (Kurdistan Workers' Party) redoubts that Turkish F-16s had been pummeling.

About this time, in one of those naive, doesn't-everyone-look-the-same kind of questions, I asked Amar how the peshmerga and their checkpoints were able to keep the bad guys away.

"It's not the peshmerga; it's the people who make it safe," he said. "If someone is suspicious, the people call in on their cell phone. There are hundreds of calls a day. Most of them don't mean anything. But they all get followed up on," he concluded proudly.

Unlike American Homeland Security, where some intelligence bureaucrat may or may not issue a blue or yellow or red alert, the citizenry here does not trust those channels, taking matters into their own hands in a de facto national neighborhood watch. There are, however, shortcomings to having too much volunteerism, especially when it's ethnic based.

After passing through more checkpoints, and seeing a few cars being taken apart and searched (reminding me of I-35 crossing Texas from Mexico), Amar continued.

"The peshmerga looks at the license plate first. If you are from Mosul, Kirkuk, Baghdad, they will want to talk. Or if your skin is dark, like the Arabs from Baghdad and south, or your accent is not local, then they will check you out even more. The PKK is not a problem; they stay in the mountains and don't have cars," he explained. Paraphrasing Mao, there is no friendly sea of people here for bad guys to swim in.

I was already feeling safer careening down the roads of Iraq in an SUV, signs for Mosul and Kirkuk whizzing by, ever vigilant for dark-skinned guys. It was almost noon as we turned off the four-lane Highway 2 for lunch at Dohuk, which along with Erbil and Suleimaniyah make up the three "official" provincial capitals of the KRG. Modern by any standards, Dohuk has a decided flair for yellow, Barzani's KDP (Kurdistan Democratic Party) colors. On every street corner vendors peddled petrol in five-gallon plastic containers, the contents varying in hue. This Rosetta Stone of fuel marketing had been puzzling me since leaving the border. Soon Amar deciphered the color-coded mystery of Iraq's black market petrol for me.

"Dark brown is diesel from Iran and Iraq. The red is gasoline from Iran, amber from Turkey, green is Kuwait, and Iraq is clear white," he said as casually as if we were discussing M&Ms. "The most expensive and best gasoline is the red from Iran. It costs 1,200 dinars (one dollar) a liter but gets the best mileage. The worst is from Iraq," he finished, with a self-deprecating laugh.

Based on the market and how much local and ministry officials, insurgents, gangs, al-Qaeda, police, and council members demand for a cut, prices fluctuate across Iraq. In fact, corruption is so widespread it is estimated that, from the Baiji refinery (north of Baghdad) alone, 500 tanker trucks a day are loaded, at a street value of 10 million dollars. Yet up to 70 percent of the petrol is sold on the black market. "It's the money pit of the insurgency," Captain Joe Da Silva, who commands several platoons of guards at the refinery, told the *New York Times*.

We passed a knockoff set of golden arches, then an entire neighborhood of mechanic shops advertised by rusted chassis and beat-up car bodies on their rooftops, before drawing up to a well-guarded restaurant. Two nuns in white habits rushed by. As we circled the restaurant's blast barricades, Amar said the nuns had fled here from Baghdad in the last few years.

Lunch was traditional Kurdish, with shish kebab and salads, but Amar and Bakhtyar were without appetite, feeling puny from drinking until three in the morning in a local bar. To shorten the journey today, they had stayed in Dohuk the night before, drinking raki in a local bar until the early morning hours. Nursing their hangovers with a robust breakfast a couple of hours before meeting me, they were now smoking cigarettes and rearranging the salad plates as I ate. The restaurant filled with a mishmash of Western-dressed men and women and traditionally attired older Kurdish men, a dozen of which took the tables next to us. With all the sidearms and assault rifles they carried, this relaxed, older crowd struck me as the local police force. Amar said they were just friends and family having lunch.

My guess is these old fellows from Dohuk had never had a day in their adult lives without a weapon nearby. This place has a history: in August 1988, Saddam dispatched helicopters and fixed-wing aircraft to drop bombs of poisonous gas over villages in Dohuk Governorate. The death count was never clear, but according to Peter Galbraith, who interviewed several of the 65,000 refugees along the Turkish border as the gassings were occurring, Secretary of State George Schultz's failure to respond was not because he didn't believe genocide was happening but because humanitarian intervention went against our vital interests: Saddam was the biggest importer of rice from Arkansas and Louisiana farmers.

We talked about family, and Amar told me he was married to his cousin and has two kids. "About 50 percent of Kurds still marry their cousins. Thirty years ago it was closer to 90 percent," he said, not defensively, but with an awareness of Westerners' attitudes. Yet Kurds thrive on being different—costume, food, song, language, customs, habits, superstitions, and cultural lives—which is why Damocles's sword has forever hung over them.

Kurds should never be put in a basket: their nuances are as numerous as their many dialects, their clan-based history of 800 tribes, and the residual traces of foreign influences. Of Indo-European origins, they are more ethnically and linguistically Persian than Turk or Arab, although Saddam and many before (Greeks, Romans, Persians, Mongols, and Ottomans) have attempted to Arabize or assimilate them. The Kurdish golden years of the Media Empire occurred in the 9th century BCE, about the time Homer was composing the *Iliad* and the *Odyssey*. Noruz, the annual March 21 celebration, conjures up their pre-Islamic, Zoroastrian roots. Some say, but certainly not Arabs, that the Kurds' ancient fire worshipping began in oil-rich Kirkuk, where seeps of hydrocarbons once flamed in an eternal desert inferno. Due to casual borderlines drawn by Britain and France, and upheld by America, Kurds are neither fish nor foul in this Middle East neighborhood.

Amar is a moderate Muslim, as are many Kurds, but he votes outside the mainstream KDP and PUK (Patriotic Union of Kurdistan) parties. Westward looking by nature, he has a master's degree in linguistics from Suleimaniyah University and has been with Mercy Corps for four years. The latter has given the United States a good friend: "Americans are the warmest of all the people I have worked with, including Europeans, Asians, and Africans," Amar said. "They are also the most moral. I'm not just saying that, either." Refreshing to hear, but before I had fully absorbed the good vibrations, not having heard anything so heartfelt about Americans in some time, he then politely added, "There was a promise when the U.S. came into Kurdistan [2003 invasion] that they would assist in making it independent, and now they are doing nothing." It's far from over, but this was the third time the KRG had put their faith in the goodness of America.[1]

For sure, Amar not only appreciates Americans but also relishes Americana. He spends Friday evenings with his pals at the bowling alley in Suleimaniyah, drinking beer and being a guy. On Thursday nights—with Friday and Saturday as the weekend here—Amar stays home, watching movies until two or three in the morning. He has a pirated DVD collection of 200 Hollywood-made flicks. Along with most young Kurdish men, Amar prefers action flicks; Bruce Willis and Nicolas Cage are his faves. For comedy, laughing out loud while saying his name, Eddie Murphy trumps all.

Since 2003, almost everyone here has a satellite dish, even the occupants of the mud huts in the moonscaped mountains, where villagers look more like denizens of the Iron Age. The youth rage is American reality shows and sitcoms, not least being *Prison Break*, which has started a fad of tattooing. Amar tunes into MBC (Middle East Broadcasting Centre), a pan-Arab news and entertainment network now based in Dubai City. With an audience of 300,000 million, broadcasting in English and Arabic, they are known as the "CNN of the Arab world." MBC's multiple channels feature everything from sports and soap operas to science and current events.

～

From Dohuk we crossed a great plain of wheat fields, dirt daubered in mud-hutted villages. Shepherds with assault rifles slung across their backs tended their

---

1. Behind the United States, the 80,000-strong peshmerga were the second-largest coalition force in the 2003 invasion.

flocks alongside roadside plots of tobacco, a major export here. Only since the recent onset of winter had they returned from summering in the high mountain pastures, as they have done for centuries, guerrillas by birth. Tracing the highway to the north were the Safin Mountains, a forbidding rampart of natural protection. Over and again, we stopped at peshmerga checkpoints, at least as often as entering and exiting each village.

I asked Amar about security and changes since the invasion.

"Before you leave you will have a picture of the KRG and all its parts," Amar said. "All they [Americans] did was take Saddam out; everything else here is the same. Since 1991, we haven't had Saddam, so people like me did not have the same experience as my parents. The older generation likes George Bush, but younger ones don't care."

Smoking with one hand, wrestling the steering wheel around hairpin curves with the other, while talking to me in the backseat, Amar had taken over the driving. Winding up the narrow-lane hills of the village of Shaqlawa, we whizzed by an Assyrian church.

"The village is 50 percent Christian," he said. "It's quiet and cool here. People from Baghdad and Iran come in the summer to escape the heat." Amar powered on, leaving the confectioners, colorful fruit stands, and vineyards in our dust.

We skirted Erbil 20 miles to the north before crossing a relic iron bridge from the days of the British occupation. Flowing furiously from Iran through the Dukan Gorge—narrowed to a long gash of granite escarp above the iron relic—the phosphorous-smelling waters of the Greater Zab River poured by. Cars stopped and took advantage of the view, the river frothing from crème de menthe to white water, treeless and limitless in its meander south. The sun was low, washing the harsh landscape of mountains a fresh sheen of gold, lending the landscape a pastoral and hermetically protected feeling.

Two hours later, near the international airport, through the haze of the daily sandstorm blown up from the south, the dingy lights of a colossal concrete factory introduced Suleimaniyah. "It was once the largest in the Middle East," Amar said, "but if Saddam could have taken all the rocks south, he would have."

On the opposite side of the road, the ultra-modern dorms and red brick classroom buildings of the new campus of the American University came into view. "They just opened. Tuition there is $17,000, but I heard there are only 50 students. They teach business, maybe with a graduate degree, too," Amar pointed out, with a shrug of disbelief that amplified my reaction. Given that per capita income in the KRG is less than $300 a month, it was hard not to be taken aback.[2]

---

2. Later, I would learn that Paul Wolfowitz and the Johns Hopkins School of Advanced International Studies were behind the American University, the soft diplomacy of an American hawk.

Like Erbil, Suleimaniyah is a boomtown: gas lines, congested traffic, four-lane byways and interchanges, telecom towers, and construction cranes taller than mosques. Cell phones and the World Wide Web were here before their Arabic countrymen ever had the chance to dial and download the same. Foreign guest workers from the Philippines, Bangladesh, Ethiopia, Indonesia, and Somalia have arrived: maids, construction workers, street cleaners, and waitresses in bars—jobs Kurdish women are forbidden to take. We passed a water park, a new theater complex that could have been Lincoln Center, and a high-rise with condos going for $250,000. There were the golden arches of Matbox (which Amar sniffed at), Internet cafés, several liquor stores, and an open produce market, with Toyota Land Cruisers parked in front. Given the size of these SUVs—plump and wide—they are known locally as "Monicas," after a former White House intern.

A handful of Suleimaniyah institutions confer on the city a liberal, if not independent, temperament: the progressive Suleimaniyah University, the secular, communist influence of the PUK, which is headquartered here, and the international NGOs who have partnered with local organizations in support of education, gender equity, and other human rights. Their influence is ubiquitous, seen in the high value placed on voting, Western dress, English training, computer skills, and a college education (especially in America). Suleimaniyah is also home to the famous poets of Kurdistan, just as Shiraz is in nearby Iran.

"Baghdad is the capital of a deranged foreign country," said one KRG resident. The Iraqi flag is banned here (and throughout the KRG), and Arabic is rarely spoken on the streets, ignored completely by young people. The KRG imposes its own taxes, has its own army of 80,000 strong, and cuts its own oil deals.

Veils and robes are around in Suleimaniyah, as is tribalism and fundamentalism, but many Kurds see Islam as an "Arabic" religion, as the beginning of Arab imperialism. They are moderately conservative believers, partly, some say, because Mohammed wasn't a Kurd. Young women in tight jeans, holding hands and canoodling with boyfriends, is not uncommon, but in Erbil that immodesty would bring down the wrath of family and community. The gritty earth that rises every day here in a sandstorm from the south and rubs observable reality on the facades of the glassy, new skyscrapers seemed to reflect this tension between old and new.

Guardhouses were as common as mailboxes; peshmerga and assault rifles outnumbered pedestrians five to one. And that was great by me, as we drew to a stop on the quiet, relatively affluent neighborhood street of 1990s-built, zero-lot-line houses, walled and gated all, where Mercy Corps has its office and residence, for expatriates and "hot beds" for visitors.

The NGO's security protocol does not allow armed guards or personal weapons: payment of guards feeds into the military economy; it's also symbolic of power, which by nature politicizes relief missions. But with the PUK headquarters and their arsenal of guns and guards at the end of the block, who needed more fancy firepower? "Every family in the KRG has at least one assault rifle, and many have grenade launchers," Amar said with confidence, having a laugh at the wide-eyed attention I gave to the weapons.

⌒

For every humanitarian aid and development success there are probably ten failures, the headless heart at work. For example, I was in Sri Lanka a few months after the 2004 tsunami when I ran into an American woman from Austin, Texas, who donated a hundred thousand dollars to rebuild a small village that was wiped out. She was full of compassion and ideas and wanted the construction performed democratically, with a village council overseeing it. But she decided to put a Christian in charge because she didn't trust the Buddhists, who made up 98 percent of the village. She was considering giving the rehabilitated village her name, Bettyburg or something. The story ends there, but there are more.

That told, the aid and development industry is not just about headless hearts. And certainly Mercy Corps doesn't fall in that category. Who is Mercy Corps? I am often asked. By all accounts the NGO is the brainchild of social entrepreneurs Dan O'Neill and Ells Culver, who met at an evangelical forum for aid relief organizations. Dan O'Neill founded the Save the Refugees Fund in 1979, which provided emergency aid to thousands of Cambodians fleeing the genocide of the Khmer Rouge. After O'Neill and his wife, Cherry Boone, oldest daughter of singer-evangelist Pat Boone, made a conversion to Roman Catholicism in 1982, the Save the Refugees Fund was renamed Mercy Corps.

Since then, often as a first responder, Mercy Corps has sought to alleviate suffering, poverty, and oppression in all the major disaster and conflict zones around the world, from Katrina to Kosovo. David Holdridge describes the organization as a group of social entrepreneurs who believe that passion drives what you do. Anyone with a good idea who can mobilize the resources can make things happen. The organizational structure is flat, not hierarchal, a belief that good things can come out of chaos.

Though Mercy Corps has a cross-section of congregational donors, their partners also range from Microsoft to the European Community, and their competitors range from Save the Children to the Red Cross. And given that 40 percent of Mercy Corps' funding is from USAID, which is now interwoven with Defense, at least in Iraq and Lebanon, there is an element of counterinsurgency to their mission, fighting the frontline American battle for hearts and minds. Within limits, that's a good thing. As I did as a board member and donor of

World Neighbors, Mercy Corps advocates letting people set their own development and civil society goals and agendas, so that hope and dignity will follow. Plus they appear to follow the NGO maxim that what Americans want for others is not always consistent with what others want for themselves.

Given Boone and O'Neill's evangelical, charismatic past, I was a skeptic long before I drank the Mercy Corps Kool-Aid. Are they not peddling religion, converting souls, too? Yet as an organization, their deeds tell me they are indubitably secular, no Bible lessons on the way to the aid tent like so many faith-based NGOs. In fact, several of Mercy Corps' Muslim program officers have told me that they have never seen or heard so much as a "God bless you" come out of headquarters. Having it otherwise, of course, would be counterproductive. My theological or metaphysical differences with the founders have no impact on our like-minded ethical and altruistic beliefs in the power of hope and human dignity (the elixir in the Kool-Aid). My only lament here in Iraq, and Lebanon before, was that it was America that caused most of the human catastrophe.

⌒

Sean Collins, a sleek, soft-spoken former Canadian army officer of five years, greeted me on the front porch of the squarish, stucco two-story, the yard cats feeding on the rubbish heap of scraps below. Sean, at age 27, originally from Toronto, arrived a month before, having worked most recently in post-tsunami emergency relief in Aceh, Indonesia. Before that he spent six months in the refugee camps of southern Sudan and northern Kenya. He is now the operations manager and head of the Suleimaniyah office.

Appearing a few minutes later was Drakoulis Bekakos, from Athens, Greece, who had been in Iraq since 2003. Drakoulis, or Drak as Sean calls him, has a stocky build and gelled coal-black hair. He is instinctively gracious and hardworking. His ambivalent wide smile signals not agreement or dissent but rather an aptitude for listening, of guilelessness. At 35, Drakoulis was a marketing manager in Athens before going to work for the International Orthodox Christian Charities (IOCC). He was with IOCC a year before joining up with Mercy Corps in Iraq. He is now IDP (internally displaced persons) emergency response program manager.

The three of us convened around the kitchen table. Since I had just arrived from the border, the subject of the Turkish army showdown with the PKK came up. Though they didn't believe the KRG government or peshmerga were complicit with the PKK, Drakoulis did say, "I don't think it's any secret around here that young Iraqi Kurds are fighting with the PKK." Sean, as a newcomer, nodded his head in tentative agreement.

We shifted the conversation to IDPs. According to the most recent IOM (International Organization for Migration) data, only 3 percent have returned to their homes, mostly in Baghdad and Diyala. Given that the majority of IDPs have said they fled because of direct threats to life; that 86 percent said this was due to their sectarian identity; and that many of their homes have been occupied or destroyed, incentives offered by the Iraqi government (or U.S. taxpayers) of $800 per family to return have been broadly declined. And even though the displacement rates have slowed to a trickle, there are still well over two million who have not returned plus at least two more million refugees who have not repatriated from Syria and Jordan. Indeed, based on IOM interviews and estimates, slightly less than half of the IDPs ever plan to reoccupy their former residences. To the extent funds allow, Mercy Corps is responding to security, shelter, food, and health needs, reaching a total of 757,349 Iraqis, of which 223,218 are IDPs.[3]

Amar had mentioned "livelihood assets," but I asked Drakoulis to explain what they included.

"It varies, but usually clothes, kerosene, stoves, heaters, mattresses, and blankets. We also provide education kits, pencils, erasers, copy books." He added that Mercy Corps was ramping up for a food distribution launch that would target 232,000 IDPs in six governorates, two in the north central region and four in the south.

Mercy Corps' emergency relief focuses on families displaced post–February 23, 2006, after the bombing of the golden-domed al-Askari shrine of the Shias in Samarra, when wholesale sectarian violence erupted. Some would say that date was an Iraqi version of 9/11.

Drakoulis assessed the makeup of those IDPs.

"In our area of responsibility 80 percent are Arab Sunnis, 10 to 12 percent are Arab Shias, the rest Kurds, Turkmen, Chaldeans, and Assyrians." He paused briefly before summing up where the IDPs find shelter. "Statistics are different for each area, but nationally 59 percent are paying rent; 22 percent are in collectives [abandoned buildings, makeshift shelters, or mud huts]; 18 percent are with host families or relatives; and only 1 percent are in camps."

Amar picked us up around eight for a reception dinner to honor my arrival. The informal gathering was held at Astera, a Turkish restaurant, beneath an open pavilion in Azady (Freedom) Park. A former Iraqi army base, the park has a speaker's corner like Hyde Park in London, with a memorial to Kurds tortured and executed there by the pre-Saddam, Ba'athist regime. Victims would turn up in shallow graves, as a Ferris wheel, roller rink, open-air theater, and swimming

---

3. As of August 2011, the aggregate number of IDPs and refugees had only decreased slightly.

pool replaced the former army base. The park is surrounded by modern homes, many of which were built by exiles who have returned to the KRG. With the closing of the base in 1991, Freedom Park has become a symbol, particularly for Kurds, of all the possibilities of a new Iraq.

Ten to twelve of the Kurdish staff arrived for dinner, including drivers and watchmen. The usual Kurdish fare of lamb and chicken shish kebabs, salad with lemon and oil, hummus, yoghurt dressings, and Kurdish naan bread were ordered. There were no Hyde Park speeches or toasts (no alcohol in the park), but I rounded the tables and introduced myself to everyone. All spoke some English, most with a high level of fluency, and women were all secular in appearance. A few, such as Shapol Abdullah, deputy of the Mercy Corps office—who was breathless in her enthusiasm for the gender equality interventions she was implementing—I would get to know better in the coming days. She and others made it a point to tell me not to believe anything the media says about security in the KRG (prompted by all the PKK and invasion news).

CHAPTER ELEVEN

~

Refugees, Water, Schools, Clinics, and Wheelchairs

Shwan Amin, a driver, was waiting by the guard shack at eight the next morning. The sky was already clouded in particles of sand, stinging to the eyes and gathering like soot in the nose. With few words exchanged, we drove southeast from Sule before pivoting more southerly onto Highway 4 at the Halabja crossroads, the first checkpoint on the road to Kalar and Khanaqin, in upper Diyala Province. The next four days would be spent touring Mercy Corps projects there.

After 30 minutes Shwan radioed ahead. Soon we passed through a mountain tunnel on the shores of Lake Darbandikhan, where a city of the same name sprawled along the hillsides in jumbled tracts of unpainted concrete. A few miles beyond, near the village of Awbar, Shwan pulled off on an empty stretch of road in front of a sand-colored, shuttered roadside food stand. Though I was unaware that I was being shuttled, A'la Hussein was waiting there for me in a white Toyota SUV.

A'la was dressed Panamanian style in all white. He was swarthy skinned, with movie star good looks. He learned his conversational English in one year while driving at Mercy Corps. We talked for the next two hours, tracing the Diyala River, while often hitting the flat stretches at 80 miles an hour.

Kurdish and born in northern Iraq, A'la lived in central Baghdad for 35 years. He fled to Khanaqin two years ago with his Sunni Arab wife and their ten-year-old son (they are IDPs [internally displaced persons]). He and his wife both have fine arts degrees from Baghdad University. Like many unemployed men in Baghdad in 2003, he was forced to drive a taxi. Then, almost inevitably, in 2005 Muqtada al-Sadr's militiamen came to his residence and ordered his family to go. "This is my home for ten years," A'la protested.

"Go or you are dead," he was told.

"Before there were many Kurds in Baghdad, but if you stay you are dead," he said, sounding a popping noise and gesturing with thumb up and index extended, the expression of a pistol firing. "My wife's mother and brother are dead. I will never go back to Baghdad." He shook his head resolutely.

We were speeding alongside the beautiful Diyala River valley—the water a deep blue at the dam but turning forest green as it snaked through crags and chasms and biscuit-hued defiles. The Diyala rises out of the Zagros Mountains in Iran. From there it flows south and forms 20 miles of natural border with Iraq, an important trade area, overlooked by the Shamshir Heights of Iran. Near the town of Darbandikhan, the hydroelectric project provides drinking and irrigation water for locals, and power for the region and for Baghdad (at least a few hours a day). The river eventually flows into the Tigris south of Baghdad.

Villages we came upon all had the look of frontier outposts, with a simple mosque and two minarets; a police station with the Kurdish tricolors above; mud huts; and unpainted concrete houses fronted by rust-colored iron gates, all one robust windstorm shy of being buried in sand. PUK (Patriotic Union of Kurdistan) slogans and murals of Jalal Talabani appeared as permanent campaign signs. Often referred to by fellow Kurds as Mam (uncle), Talabani is the founder of the left-wing party and the current Iraqi president, an opportunist in the mold of Mullah Mustafa Barzani (at times allied with the PKK [Kurdistan Workers' Party], the Soviet Union, Turkey, Iran, France, the United States, and the UK).

Beyond these outposts, billboards would appear among a sea of dunes with a modern-dressed woman advertising cell phones; a herd of sheep might then be blocking the road; and a solitary man shielded from the sun might appear beneath a *palapa* (a frame of four striplings and a thatched roof) with a single half-pound Diyala perch on a rope stringer for sale. The sighting of green, a line of willows or blue gum, or buffalo in the shade, signaled the approach to another village, another *peshmerga* checkpoint, a dusty market full of produce and wary glances, another iteration of the same, in this harsh land with a harsh history.

Before Saddam Hussein's Anfal campaigns, overseen by cousin "Chemical Ali" (Ali Hassan al-Majid), beginning in the 1970s but reaching critical mass in the late 1980s, there were up to 4,000 more of these villages. Through the tracts of empty desert we might see a solitary hilltop with a dozer, four SUVs, and men surveying maps, pointing directions, and digging here and there. Were they mass grave sites from the Anfal days? Or just as likely, might they have been former Kurdish villages the Iraqi army purged of anti-Saddam sympathizers, before razing? Once their homes were laid to waste, survivors, who included few husbands, were moved to collective government settlements (*mujamma'at*). Tens of thousands of IDPs remain in those Saddam-era settlements (which were not included in Drakoulis's statistics). It's common among those Saddam-era IDPs to still hold out hope of finding missing relatives.

Kalar's market was bristling with traders spraying water on their fruits and vegetables, and donkeys and cars begrudging turf. In front of a police station, a crowd gathered, flowing out of the market. At least two dozen peshmerga and police in Kevlar vests, assault rifles in firing position, emptied a bus of 20-plus men. "Fresh IDPs from Baquba and Baghdad; they have no money," A'la said.

⌒

Near the crowd stood a bronze statue of a soldier with one leg blown off at the knee, a reminder of the tens of thousands maimed and killed by antipersonnel landmines and UXO (unexploded ordnance). Millions of landmines and UXO were left behind from the Iran-Iraq War, from Saddam's tactical minefields along the Green Line that separates the KRG and the rest of Iraq, and along the Turkish border. There are still hundreds of casualties each year, with over 2,000 communities contaminated. Much of this is concentrated in the three KRG governorates.

Since 2004, minesweepers such as MAG (Mines Advisory Group), which I called on while in Lebanon, have found security inadequate for clearing these contaminated areas. If security were to improve, MAG estimates that it will take between 35 and 75 years to make Iraq safe. And the added tally of un-exploded ordnance left behind by American forces, with 27,500 takeoffs and landings every month at Balad Air Base, is mounting. Arab Jabour, a farming community south of Baghdad, received a 100,000-pound barrage of American explosives (more than all of Guernica), but there has been no cleanup there.

⌒

A'la radioed in our whereabouts as we drove through Khanaqin, a 30-minute ride from Kalar. There have been several recent IED (improvised explosive device) attacks in the Khanaqin area of a tribal nature—better, they say, that it's not insurgents. Soon we drew up to a guard shack at the Mercy Corps office, next door to a Shia mosque fronted by blast walls. A'la said the mosque had been bombed two years ago. The Mercy Corps guard frisked us after we cleared the metal detector. Everyone gets checked. It's a Mercy Corps protocol that democratizes trust.

Terry Dowey greeted me in the courtyard and walked me straight to his office, whose walls were covered in quadrant maps, like the work abode of a military logistics officer. In some ways it was, and in many ways Terry is: now in his late 50s, after 25 years in the British army, he retired as a lieutenant colonel; his last assignment was commanding a specialist unit in Northern Ireland. Beginning in the mid-1990s Terry supervised emergency relief across former Yugoslavia. My take was that sectarian conflict was his stock in trade.

Though his parents are Irish, Terry's accent is high English, with the diction of a public school boy. When not in Iraq, he maintains a "base" outside Edinburgh, Scotland. He grew up a military brat, his father a general in the British army; home was Africa, the Middle East, the Far East, Europe, and America. As the only expatriate for dozens of miles, Terry leapt off the pages of Kipling's Raj.

Sundrenched and togged out in desert boots, cargo khakis, and a red-and-white checkered shirt, Terry briefed me on project sites we would visit (including pauses for some barracks humor). With maps as visual aids, he pointed out our location in upper Diyala, which, under Saddam, he said, was administered from Baquba. Since 2003, the Suleimaniyah governorate has overseen the area. "Some day this will have to be resolved," Terry posited, giving a wry, when-hell-freezes-over smile.

Given the Kurdish predominance here, during Saddam's time Khanaqin and Kalar were marginalized, made even worse by Chemical Ali's reign of terror in the late 1980s. To avoid Kurdish reprisal, most of the transplanted Arabs made tracks in 2003—as had the IDPs, or returnees, decades before, when many fled to Iran during the "Arabization" campaigns of the 1970s that lasted through the 1990s. After 2003, they began returning.

Shamil Ahmed joined us, proudly sporting a white Mercy Corps T-shirt. Angular from head to toe, with several days' growth on his sparse beard, Shamil was full of irony. He has a master's degree in "Road and Airport Engineering" from Baghdad University. "But my textbooks came from the University of Texas," he said, in an accent that coincidentally reminded me of a Texas twang.

Over an Ottoman-era bridge we crossed the torpid Alwand River. As we did, Shamil told me of his recent first journey to the States, where he attended several Mercy Corps training conferences. One was held in Cambridge. Shamil couldn't say enough about his visit to Harvard, about meeting author Roger Fisher, who conducted a seminar about conflict resolution. He drank the Kool-Aid and felt lucky to be one of the applicants chosen. Plus, as an Iraqi passport holder, the collateral benefit of having a U.S. visa stamp gave him a leg up for future travel to Western countries, if not regional NGO work opportunities (a downside to capacity building when skill sets outpace available employment options). The U.S. sojourn seemed a win-win.

Shamil is from a high-born, local family that once owned the date palm plantations in Khanaqin, which were systematically destroyed by the Northern Bureau chief Chemical Ali and Saddam. In its day, Khanaqin was famous from Baghdad to Beirut for its date palms. Beginning in the 1940s, it was a rail terminus for trains arriving from Kut in the south. Once off-loaded, and, if necessary, cleared through customs, from Khanaqin the cargo would often cross by road into Iran and on to Tabriz.

Shamil's ancestors were civic leaders, part of the merchant class, interacting with all sects and religions. Thousands of Iranian pilgrims stopped over here, en route to the Shia holy places of Najaf and Karbala. And like in most of the region, Jews were a piece of the ethnic melting pot. "They were here in my grandfather's time. They ran the businesses until they moved to Israel after 1948," Shamil said. "They left on their own but are welcome to come back anytime. My family has pictures of old rabbis. There were many Chaldeans here, too."

Informed by family stories and those black-and-white photos of cultural diversity, Shamil's words struck me as nostalgic but not hollow. Kurdish uniqueness aside, with the 1948 expulsion of 750,000 Palestinians from Israel, nationalist anti-Zionist-inspired violence throughout the Arab Middle East caught fire, driving 500,000 Jews to leave their Arabic lands of origin for Israel. The 100,000 plus who made the exodus from Iraq at that time, often assisted by Zionist organizers, did so under the code name Operation Ezra and Nehemiah, after the biblical Jewish leaders who returned their people "back to Jerusalem from exile in Babylon beginning in 597 B.C."

We parked next to the new Bakhtiyari Health Center, at Camp Malik Shah. The sprawl of 30-year-old UNHCR tents, patched and sewn, and soiled darker than mud, retreated toward the mountains. The camp hosts some 600 returnee (Iran) and IDP families, with an average size of six.

Before the camp were two new baize and red brick school buildings, shielded by six-foot concrete blast walls. A water tower, with the paint barely dry, stood tallest, like the holy calabash, the source of all sustenance, and was protected with a razor-wire fence. Mingled with some 60-odd tents were cinder-block latrines, each with a water tank perched on top.

As Terry explained in company parlance, "They comply with all the hygiene and sanitation standards, which should prevent the spread of disease." To my fresh eyes it was all desert bleak, austere as a Siberian gulag. I had not seen the IDP's primitive circumstances before, without shelter, sanitation, healthcare, water, or food.

Fatima Hussein Rahman's family, who fled here from the violence of Baghdad, might be a typical IDP story: "[My husband, three children, and I] have lived in the tent for three years now. And as long as my husband is unable to find a job, we don't have enough money to build a house, or sometimes even to buy food and water. We are happy to have this food and water that we can get from the network now. And we hope we will have a nice house in the future and that Iraq lives in peace."

Utilizing the ready backs of local and IDP laborers, with decisions made by resident leaders, Mercy Corps makes it clear that credit for these projects goes to local partners (though Terry says he often reminds partners that U.S. taxpayers are paying for these grants). "Aren't we all proud of what you accomplished working together?" goes the praise to the community, without posting sponsor signs as they do in Lebanon—"Potable Water Project . . . The People of the United States through a grant from USAID." All these bricks-and-mortar community enterprises were built under a cash-for-work program, intended to infuse money into the local economy, with a multiplier effect in each family. At 12 dollars a day per laborer, it puts food on the table and clothes on their backs but not much more. Still there is a local "buy-in," which is crucial to success.

A row of one-bedroom, concrete-block houses, each with a kitchen and latrine, spread away from Camp Malik Shah. Permission to build on the land was not easy for Mercy Corps to obtain: "The mayor was corrupt to the end of his eyebrows," Terry said. "He wanted MC to give something to the PUK. We wouldn't do it. We went over his head to Sule." This is the kind of endemic corruption Mercy Corps faces here every day.

"Who picked out the paint?" I asked.

"The color of some wife's knickers, I suppose," Terry said, with a laugh.

He pointed out a few of the dusty, pinkish homes with fresh paint, saying, "They are starting to take pride in what they have, joining the community, a garden here, a shop there."

In many ways it felt that Iraq had reverted to the 14th century, in a continual state of "civil war, plague, and ignorance." Yet one role model, Mother Teresa, once said it all counts: "What we do is but a drop in the ocean, but that ocean would be less without that drop."

She was right, while standing next to the school, I recalled the words from Sir Edmund Hillary, repeated in a recent book I was reading, *Three Cups of Tea*: "I have enjoyed great satisfaction from my climb of Everest. But my most worthwhile things have been the building of schools and medical clinics. That has given me more satisfaction than a footprint on a mountain."

The demonstrative influence of role models is important to forging cross-cultural bonds of trust. Hillary was performing charity for Buddhists in Nepal, while the heroic humanitarian in *Three Cups of Tea*, Greg Mortenson, an American, was building secular schools for Muslims, especially for girls (remember: educated mothers restrain their sons), in the impoverished and sometimes hostile fastnesses of northern Pakistan. The outcome, whether intended or not, has been to blunt the anti-American extremism being taught in the madrassas. Given that no one believed an American was capable of such feats of compassion for Muslims, locals thought of him as *hamdard*, or a saint, one who shares the pain of others.[1]

---

1. In April 2011, Mortenson was accused of taking too much literary license in *Three Cups of Tea* and of lacking financial transparency with regard to his charity, the Central Asia Institute. Whether or

School kids in a mishmash of backpacks, white shirts, and blouses, but many without any semblance of uniform, broke from classes for the day, one of four shifts (Mercy Corps also provides school uniforms and supplies to orphans here). "Teachers are easy to recruit; there are plenty who are unemployed. But we need buildings," Shamil said. Terry pitched in: "While many buildings in Iraq are being blown up, we are actually building them."

The school has two computer labs, where students learn to play games and to connect with an increasingly interdependent world. One Mercy Corps pilot program, "Fostering a Sense of Global Citizenship," focuses on providing Internet exchanges between the youth of Khanaqin and Portland, Oregon, home of Mercy Corps. This exercise is meant to improve creative thinking, communication and negotiation skills, and cultural sensitivity among youth. One IDP mother of three had this to say: "We have suffered a lot, but the fact that my children go to school now has made me forget all my grief."

Electricity is spotty: a generator sporadically powers the school. At shift change, between one of the three abridged sessions held each day, it was not uncommon to see 13-year-olds leaving classes with eight-year-olds, lost years of education being made up. It's estimated that 58 percent of the IDPs are less than 12 years of age, while over 30 percent are not in school, in a country that founded modern mathematics and invented writing.

For my part, while in Iraq, it was hard for my thoughts to ever escape the Manichean reality inherent in Mercy Corps' relief and development work: world making in the middle of world destroying. In the Qandil Mountains to the north, as Drakoulis noted, the PKK are recruiting young adolescent Kurdish boys, while in Baquba, less than 40 miles downriver, al-Qaeda is poisoning the next generation of Arab boys with terrorist training. It's a "conveyor belt," said one analyst: the number of suicide bombings in Iraq (which are increasingly being carried out by war widows) doubled to 18 a month in 2008.[2]

Yet school-builder-in-Muslim-Pakistan-and-Afghanistan Greg Mortenson tells us, with more authority than most, that these kids don't simply decide to hate America or become terrorists but that they have been denied secular educational opportunities: "If we truly want a legacy of peace for our children, we need to understand that this is a war that will ultimately be won with books, not with bombs."

"Given the poverty and violence, what are the other problems that kids deal with here?" I asked Terry.

---

not the allegations are true, his reputation has been diminished, but the values his charity promotes are intact, and the message of *Three Cups* remains compelling.

2. As of the end of 2010, suicide bombers were responsible for killing more than 12,000 Iraqi civilians and wounding another 30,000 in over 1,000 attacks.

"Drugs come from Iran, mostly hash and glue," he said. "You form a habit, you got to pay for it. So girls go into prostitution and boys into petty crime. With local partners, we try to stop that by getting them in school and creating sports and work opportunities."

As an example of one of Mercy Corps' psychosocial interventions, Terry told me of a football competition: "They chose their own uniforms, stripes or whatever, that say 'I Am Drug Free.' There are trophies for winners, who will then be given youth leadership roles in the community. The Iraqi national team, made up of Kurds, Sunnis, and Shias, will present the trophies at the competition. It's a unifying sport," he vouched.

Terry talked more about the young girls who resort to prostitution, to "survival sex." "We try to give them [prostitutes] alternatives. Mercy Corps started a clothes factory for disadvantaged women and put them to work there. That gets them off the street. They have money to buy food and clothes, which is what their families expect of them. All they need is oxygen, to breathe some life in."

UNICEF (United Nations Children's Fund) estimates that less than 30 percent of Iraqi children have access to safe drinking water. Until recently, tanker trucks arrived at Camp Malik Shah daily, hauling in chancy loads of river water. That was before the deep-water well was dug, before the heavy pumps and treatment plant were installed, and before the water tower was erected and two permanent maintenance men were employed.

"When we held the dedication for the water tank," Terry said, pointing up to the tower, "it was a carnival out here. The whole village turned up. At first they all said it was 'black water.' But then Paul and I took a drink [harrumphing], 'See here!' With that, they held up their empty cups, still standing, as if in a barroom drinking contest. Once that was done, the IDPs asked for electricity."

There is a colloquial Arabic phrase, *jildah madboogh*, which refers to someone who has endured too much pain and hardship. Its literal meaning is "his skin is tanned or is no longer alive." Fitting that description, three haggard women in black chadors, with two children in tow, came out of their one-room tent, where they have only a mat to sleep on.

The vast majority of IDPs across Iraq are women (no surprise with 740,000 war widows) and children, who have a chronic malnutrition rate of 23 percent. Even in the KRG, among the poor, rural cultures of the region, there is an irrational cultural bias against women working outside of the home. As we stood next to their tent, the oldest of the women asked about a new clothes factory, or when a cash-for-attendance training in weaving might occur, all of a piece here in the competition for scarce resources. Insistent, if not pushy, Shamil assured them something would come up soon, waving women and children off so we could talk.

"Civil war is development in reverse," wrote Paul Collier in *The Bottom Billion*. And like most NGOs in conflict zones, the potential success of Mercy Corps' development work in Iraq is by nature finite: *$20 million* a year for their share of the U.S. hearts and minds money compared to, let's say, up to *$200 billion* a year being spent on the war (or 0.0001 percent). The entire U.S. budget for IDPs and refugees is $197 million a year, half the daily cost of combat operations.

Indeed, a cost-benefit analysis would be frightening. And proportionality aside, credibility is also always an issue when there is a nexus between aid and a bellicose U.S. government. In the minds of aid organizations, the world is a "moral universe organized around sin and expiation." The hawks get their wars while the do-gooders are tossed a bone.

The sufferings of nameless refugees and IDPs are rarely the glossy-donor-brochure portraits of a food line to a happy ending (for the same reasons there are not pictures of soldiers in body bags or of their flag-draped caskets). The life of the dislocated is a long-term challenge, a dog-eat-dog daily grind, until, *Inshallah* (God willing), self-empowering, holistic development occurs and dignity is restored. Mercy Corps knows this better than anyone, while the war wizards of Operation Iraqi Freedom (OIF), the military term for the invasion, remain silent, with an indifference that suggests racism toward Iraq's IDPs and refugees. America's relative inaction will be felt here for decades.

⌒

A'la drove us through some of the old city—brick two-stories with upper balconies railed in ornamental iron and inner courtyards shaded with pomegranate trees, which are the homes of merchants, some of whom were Jewish. There was even a Jewish cemetery, where a few crumbled, tilted headstones were etched with the familiar Star of David. We pulled into a restaurant across from an abandoned Chaldean church; its fieldstone belfry peeked over the date palms at the nearby mosque, its dome shiny and turquoise. The days of Iraq as a Middle East melting pot are all but over. Tellingly, IDPs occupy the unused church, and the Jewish cemetery had the look of an excavation site.

The PUK headquarters next door seemed to empty into the restaurant as we arrived. It was yet another lunch of excellent Kurdish fare in surroundings of unmistakable civility, with everyone armed to the teeth. The armory smell of fresh-oiled metal loomed heavier in the air than the waft of cooking kebabs.

The legacy of conflict is that AK-47s are cheap, or even free if one were lucky enough to come upon one of the 110,000 rifles and 80,000 pistols, bought and delivered by Uncle Sam, that went missing in 2006 from Iraqi security forces. Even that doesn't compare to the "million metric tons," estimated by one American intelligence officer, of conventional weapons—mortar shells, rocket-propelled grenades (RPGs), rifle ammunition, and explosives—found in bunkers across Iraq when American troops first arrived. At the time, the search for weapons of mass destruction took priority (which leaves the "million metric tons" of conventional weapons in the hands of insurgents).

After dropping Shamil at the office, we parked in front of the Khanaqin Center for the PWD (People with Disabilities). The building was an attractive single-level brick, with reflecting glass windows, each covered by painted iron grates. The PWD center was built by cash-for-work laborers, a boon for the largely unemployed families here. For most people with disabilities in Khanaqin, many of whom have lost limbs from landmine accidents, this PWD center is their first glimmer of an opportunity to come together as a group, as a nascent civil society to organize for inclusive education, job training, and way down the desert highway, accessibility. Galvanized by Mercy Corps, 30 organizations in Iraq representing 150,000 people with a variety of disabilities recently formed an alliance to fight for PWD rights.

⌒

When I first met David Holdridge, he was working with a mutual friend, John Lancaster. John was critically wounded in Vietnam during Tet of 1968, becoming a paraplegic. After returning to the States, following a joyless interval of adapting to the harsh realities of his new life, John finished law school and began a career of advocating for people with disabilities. He came to grips with his fate and mastered its issues, which is why he was appointed by President Clinton to be executive director of the Committee to Employ the Disabled, the implementing agency of the Americans with Disabilities Act.

Always restless to reconcile and give something back to Vietnam, when Clinton's presidency ended John returned to live and work in Hanoi. What he found there among PWDs was appalling: 25 years after the war few had job skills, 35 percent were illiterate, and a majority never left home. For one, they had no wheelchairs. Relatives fed and clothed them, their dignity long lost in the war. Thanks in many ways to John, that situation is rapidly changing in Vietnam.

While I was in Lebanon, David confessed to having stolen a page from John in Vietnam, referring to when he persuaded Mercy Corps to begin funding PWD centers in Iraq. "From the north to the south we have joined our voices together to advocate for all of our people in the new Iraq," said Moaffak T. Hashim, the newly appointed director of the alliance.

With the usual budget constraints, Mercy Corps is now providing wheelchairs, which most PWDs around Khanaqin have never been able to afford. Ten-year-old Emad Atwan Alae's story is one not of war but of birth defect. "I was paralyzed since I was born, and the doctors assured me that I'll stay paralyzed for the rest of my life," Emad said, at a ceremony upon receiving a wheelchair from Mercy Corps in Mendali. "Having this nice wheelchair will definitely help me to move freely without annoying my siblings by asking them to carry me. I will move outside the house and play with my friends. Also I can do whatever I want. I feel I'm free and this really makes me joyous."

〜

Next door to the PWD center was the Institute of Fine Arts Khanaqin, also funded by Mercy Corps, and likewise owned by the community. Across the front of the building was a banner painted in blood red, which said in Arabic and English, "USA, you have responsibility for [Turkey's] aggression."

Terry saw it first. He was embarrassed, if not angry. "USAID built these buildings for them, and this is how they show their appreciation," he said. When Terry later informed Shamil of the banner, of course he had it removed, after which he tried to explain that there was something lost in translation. "They meant to say the U.S. should protect us," a truly embarrassed Shamil said.

As Paul Butler later told me, "Shamil is so pro-American he loves Bush. If he lived in the U.S. he would be a Republican." It seemed to me that until told otherwise, the fine arts institute's employees were exercising their right to freedom of speech (as had most KRG officials with a similar tone).

What Shamil said, though, is also true: Kurds want the United States to protect them. And why wouldn't Shamil's personal experiences make him a fan of President Bush? He comes from a Kurdish family that owned date palm plantations destroyed by Saddam. Bush had Saddam eliminated.

From our vantage point, Khanaqin spread like an oasis of feathery date palms: roads as angular as the river; a bland, low-slung skyline; and ragged on the edges with all the destroyed empty fields where date palm plantations once flourished. In the opposite direction, five miles to the east was the Muntheriya border crossing to Iran, where I imagined that I was hearing the fundamentalists' chants of "Death to America."

The border fortifications were visible only as monochromatic quadrangles in the sand, American and Iraqi soldiers and leftover minefields as motes in a mirage. The once well-traveled highway appeared as a forlorn slither turning to a black ribbon of heat haze.

〜

The western border of Iran has been in place since the Treaty of Qasr-i-Shirin, negotiated in 1639 between the Ottomans and Persians. It forms a neat boundary between Arab and Persian, Shia and Sunni. It was not one without traffic and commerce. Before the Iran-Iraq War, thousands of Shia pilgrims from Iran transited through daily, en route to Iraqi holy sites such as Karbala and Narjaf. Kurds also moved freely to cross-border communities, when not being ping-ponged as refugees from violence in Iraq or Iran. Today tanker trucks filled with unrefined Iraqi oil are almost as numerous as Iranian pilgrims traveling in the opposite direction.

The "curse of oil" has played a pivotal historical role in the hydrocarbon-rich valley we overlooked. In 1916, at the height of fighting in World War I, when the war wasn't going so well for Britain and France, Sir Mark Sykes and Georges Picot came together to forge a secret agreement on the division of the Ottoman Empire (Russia was a party until the Bolsheviks pulled out). Sykes and Picot were both Catholic aristocrats slicing up a Muslim, Arab world for oil, which British geologists discovered in Iran in 1908.

Arab outrage at the perfidy aside, the result of this backroom, cartographic conniving was the Sykes-Picot Agreement. It gave Britain the mandates for Palestine and oil-rich Iraq, and France the mandate for Lebanon and Syria. At war's end, the allies and the Ottomans formalized the Sykes-Picot Agreement with the Treaty of Sevres. To give Iraq an Arab face, Faisal bin Al Hussein, a member of the Hashemite dynasty of Saudi Arabia, and a descendant of Mohammed, was crowned king of Iraq.

In the same hour of history, President Woodrow Wilson made Kurdish independence one of his Fourteen Points. But as we know, Wilson's proposals and the League of Nations were snubbed back home in America. Tellingly, of the borders drawn at this time—the Soviet Union, Yugoslavia, Czechoslovakia, and Iraq—all of which artificially combined disparate cultures, Iraq is the only one that still exists.

Across the Atlantic, as a cabinet minister when the treaty was negotiated and signed, Winston Churchill would live to regret the forced incorporation of the Kurds in Arabic Iraq as one of his biggest mistakes. Making matters worse, after the Turkish war of independence, the Treaty of Sevres was abrogated in favor of the Treaty of Lausanne, which separated Greeks and Turks. The Treaty of Lausanne set a precedent for ethnic transfers and "ethnonationalism," politically correct or not, that continues worldwide until today. So far, this is of no avail for the Kurds, an ethnic group with a 3,000-year history as a stateless people. And not surprisingly, before the ink was dry on the treaty, British Petroleum (BP) discovered the first commercial oil reserves in Kurdish Iraq, smack dab in Khanaqin. By 1926, BP had created a new subsidiary, Khanaqin Oil Company.[3]

In our middle view, still looking toward Iran, was the rusted cadaver of a former BP refinery, known as Masfa Alwand. It was built along the Alwand River,

---

3. BP had a much larger stake in the Turkish Petroleum Company, later named the Iraqi Oil Company (IOC). Before the 1961 nationalization of the IOC, French, American, Dutch, and British companies shared ownership. Plus "Mr. Five Percenter," Armenian businessman Calouste Gulbenkian, took his standard cut.

a tributary of the Diyala, during the British Mandate in the 1920s. The concrete ramparts of several bunkers that protected the refinery can still be seen. "The Iranians bombed the refinery during the war, and then Saddam destroyed the rest," Terry said.

The Iranian bombing had only partly destroyed the refinery, but once "Arabization" began in the 1970s, Kurdish workers were removed by force and replaced by Arabs. The Kurds were relocated to the north in Sule, Erbil, and Dohuk and in the south to Nasriyah and Basra, while the Arab ratio here in Khanaqin went up. In the 1980s, Saddam cannibalized the refinery for spare parts and built another one in Arab-controlled Bayji, just north of Baghdad (where as of 2008 up to 70 percent of its throughput goes to the black market and insurgency). In doing so, his army destroyed the company village, schools, clinics, shops, a cinema, homes, and the Polish and British First World War–era cemetery.

"Except for the Islamic [fundamentalists], we Kurdish are pro-American because [the] USA helped us remove the tyrant Saddam and his government," wrote Ali Alwandy, who lived at Masfa Alwand when his family was uprooted and moved to Sule. Ali is now a 54-year-old civil engineer who lives in Erbil. After 25 years' absence, Ali recently returned to Masfa Alwand to commune with the memories of his youth. After that trip, he established a website to help locate former members of the community:

> When I arrived to the area I could only see ruins. The whole area was demolished and did not exist any more. I neither found the place of our house nor my primary school. Saddam's regime had apparently destroyed the area during the Iraq-Iran War in the '80s because he feared that the area would fall into Iranian hands. What a cruelty. In fact even cruelty has its limitations.
>
> When I stood there I remembered my school, the bell, and the first reading lesson: "dar, daran and dor," which in Arabic means "House, two houses and houses." I considered "dar" as our house, "daran" as the houses of our neighbors, Moshe and Isa, and "dor" as all other houses. And now not a single one of them exists.
>
> I couldn't help but wondering where everybody was. Where were my teachers and my childhood friends? No trees and no signs of life were there. Even the birds could not stand the atrocity and have left. I remembered the all-glass balls we played with. We hid them from our parents when we came home so that they would think we cared more about our homework than playing games. I saw as a child the beauty of the whole world in those beautiful glass balls.
>
> Suddenly I felt lonely and tried in vain to keep my tears jailed in. My children were astonished of course, so much emotion for the ruins. How could they understand? Everything was big in Masfa Alwand in my childhood. The Alwand River was an ocean in my eyes; the hills looked like mountains and the trees were tall. It does not exist anymore but my love for it is stronger than ever.

CHAPTER TWELVE

~

It's the Oil, Habibi, the Oil

It was early afternoon as we made the half-hour drive to Kalar, south of the 36th parallel, where Mercy Corps has an office that also serves as a residence for Terry Anderson, Ammar Zakri, and occasional visitors. We drove by an Iraqi army post (Fifth Division), and for the first time I saw the tricolored national flag—red, white, and black, with "Allahu akbar" (God is great) inscribed in Kufic between three green stars. By agreement, the Iraqi army stays south of the 36th parallel and the *peshmerga* protects the KRG.

Once in Kalar, we drove through what might be an industrial zone with grain silos, concrete plants, and an ice factory, a departure from the medieval aspect of Sherwana Castle. Along the main street was the modern headquarters of the local Communist Party, now a second-tier power in KRG politics. Russian jeeps, brought here during the Iran-Iraq War, plied the roads as taxis, now tricked out with chrome bumpers and regal blue paint jobs. Water buffalo gathered along the river.

A Wal-Mart-sized parking lot sprawled in front of the Mercy Corps office. Terry says Kalar city officials are thinking of putting a mosque up. Next to the Mercy Corps office is the Patriotic Union of Kurdistan (PUK) local headquarters, its balconies and front fence fortified with an army of guards. The Mercy Corps staff—four women, two in scarves, and three men—greeted me warmly on the front porch, beyond the metal detector.

Out of this familial-like reception came a blood-curdling yelp from Terry's two-year-old dog, Jack (maybe short for Union Jack). Jack had tripped down the steps. Terry's dramatic rush to rescue him suggested that Jack's fall was life-threatening. The concerned looks of the staff and guards turned to half-titters. Ammar Zakri leaned over, whispering in my ear, "The dog is clumsy; this happens all the time." That English blokes are truly mad about their dogs was well known here.

⁓

Ammar Zakri, the deputy head of the Kalar office, was waiting for us. Thirty-one years old, Ammar was wearing faded blue jeans and bulging at the beltline. He had a sophisticated Baghdadi air about him, but he was not aloof. He graduated from Baghdad University in linguistics, as did his wife, who has a doctorate and now teaches at Suleimaniyah University.

Ammar is a Sunni Arab from the April 7 neighborhood of eastern Baghdad, named after the 1947 inaugural date of the pan-Arabist Ba'ath Party, founded by an Arab of Greek Orthodox faith.[1] "The Ba'athists were originally communist," Ammar explained. "The 1970s were the golden era, with folk songs celebrating the homeland, the harvest, and the people. Then in 1979 Saddam Hussein began cleansing the party of communists."

Ammar's father was a low-level accountant at Iraq's Central Bank, living in a mixed neighborhood of Shias, Sunnis, and Christians. "He made peanuts in 32 years working," Ammar said. "During the sanctions of the 1990s, he had to drive a taxi at night to send us to school."

The Zakris' modest affairs, with no Ba'athist affiliation, put them below the terrorist radar as Baghdad exploded in sectarian violence. The Zakris' neighborhood was first composed of affluent higher-ups in Iraq's Central Bank. "After 1991 though everyone began selling out, trading up or emigrating," Ammar said. The demographics changed to lower-income people. Now the April 7 neighborhood is all Shia, "who are the same ones who looted Baghdad and now have money."

In 2003, David Holdridge hired Ammar to manage Mercy Corps' Baghdad office when Mercy Corps first arrived in Iraq. By early 2005, as attacks soared in Baghdad, Ammar had a choice with Mercy Corps of moving to Amman, Jordan, or Sule. "I chose Sule because it is still Iraq. I could be close to my family," he told me.

Ammar saw the violence in Baghdad take out cousins and friends but so far no close family members. His father is deceased, but his mother and two sisters still live in Baghdad. His brother-in-law emigrated to Sweden and hopes to soon have permissions for Ammar's sister and two children to go there as well. Ammar's younger brother Ishan, age 27, with whom I have corresponded, has also made the move to Sweden. Working with Americans in logistics and

---

1. Oddly enough it would be April 7, 2003, that Americans would fight their way into Baghdad and occupy a presidential palace on the banks of the Tigris, the beginning of de-Ba'athification here.

procurement at Orascom Telecom, Ishan was threatened daily by terrorists, both verbally and with "leave or die" notes. Though the Zakris are not affluent, they are well educated, which gives them options.

Ishan's life in Sweden is picking up, but when I first heard from him, he laid out his reasons for leaving Baghdad: "I had to make frequent visits to the Baghdad Airport to clear shipments through customs. Sometimes I was going twice a week, carrying lots of cash and traveling in a convoy. In the beginning it was not that big a deal. Later because I was carrying all the cash, and working with the Americans, the risk got worse. There were threats. I wished not to wake up some days to do this mission. I wanted to quit, but there were no other work opportunities. Then I got the chance to move to Sweden."

"Why Sweden?" I asked, anticipating the answer.

"The chances to get to America are almost impossible. Maybe with a Fulbright, but that is temporary. I was aiming for something more permanent since I don't know how long this mess in Iraq will go on," he said. "When I started searching for chances to escape, Sweden was one of the few countries that were open to Iraqis. I was lucky to find a job with a [mobile phone] company that does games. It pays well and they needed someone who speaks English and Arabic [for their business] in the Middle East."

At this point, repatriating is off the table. "I am not able now to think of when I could return, but maybe I will as a visitor," Ishan said. "I don't feel I belong there anymore. The shape of everything has been changed. [Everyone] is full of hate. Now I have no feelings for my country, only to my family and friends."

Brother Ammar feels deracinated just living in the KRG, where even speaking Arabic is something he does quietly. As an Arab from Baghdad, technically he is an internally displaced person (IDP). Special permissions were required for Ammar to live and work in Sule, no less than an immigrant from Uzbekistan. He and his wife must carry resident identification cards and register with immigration every three months, with a Kurdish sponsor to vouch for them. In spite of his employment at Mercy Corps and his wife's professorship at Suleimaniyah University, as Arabs they are treated with suspicion. They are not allowed to travel inside the KRG without sponsorship and the resident IDs.

Though the KRG officially espouses a policy of diversity, Kurds give it back as good as they've gotten from the Arabs. For most Arabs, even if they were granted permission to live in the KRG, often inflation and rents are too high, opportunities few, and the vibes, if not deeds, are less than hospitable. Ammar sees his dislocation as a challenge: "I want to show [Kurds] through my work the real me and what the difference is [between] the good and bad Arab."

He talked about the censorship of Saddam's Anfal campaigns. "Until I moved to Sule three years ago, I had never heard of Anfal," he said. "It was not taught to us in school in Baghdad, and we didn't see it on the local news. We didn't have satellite TV then. Occasionally, we jammed the BBC Arabic channel but heard nothing like this. So how would we know?" Like many Arabs, Ammar only knew of Kurds as allegedly being troublemakers.

Like Shamil, Ammar met Roger Fisher, author of *Getting to Yes*, in Cambridge (Massachusetts) on a Mercy Corps–sponsored trip to the States. "He changed my life," Ammar said. The author and the book inspired him to approach life and his humanitarian work with a fresh credo: "Separate people from the problem; focus on solutions not interests; work together to create options that will satisfy both parties; negotiate successfully with people who are more powerful; and do not resort to dirty tricks."

⌒

Terry stayed behind while Ammar and I tooled around Kalar. Soon we came to a stop in front of a monstrosity of a new library recently thrown up. "They build these all over the KRG with central government money. There is no electricity, no water, no modern books, no digital indexing system, and no coordination with universities," he said, with a blend of disgust and acceptance. "Built with shoddy materials, they are there to satisfy the [burn rates] expected from Baghdad. Local politicians take their share."

In the context of a poor village, it was plain weird to see six brand new HVAC units hooked up to an empty, modernly designed library with no electricity, and no chance of it arriving in the next few years.

"Transformative" was an adjective that Ammar, along with Terry and Shamil, had repeated like a mantra to describe their youth and gender interventions, the key to systemic change in Iraq. It seemed to me that, in this land of Abraham, Hammurabi, and Sharia, "transformative" was a big word, full of Yankee can-do optimism (if not counterinsurgency).

Even so, since April of 2007 Mercy Corps has gone from providing just bricks-and-mortar assistance to a laser focus on educating and empowering women and youth. This includes, among other strategies, health training, psychosocial activities, computer lessons, entrepreneurial endeavors, and promoting and funding leadership workshops (grassroots democracy). By promoting civil society through NGO partnerships, they are teaching locals to stand against bullying politicians and misguided policies, a tricky proposition given that USAID is in the country at the pleasure of the rulers. Borrowing a phrase from Tolstoy, Mercy Corps would like to merely take the vulnerable by the scruff of their necks and make them enjoy life again.

⁓

That evening we gathered about a long kitchen table, smoking Dunhills, while Ammar and I downed a half-dozen 16-ounce Tuborg beers. In the obligatory Arabic tradition of hospitality, Ammar was also tasked with preparing a pot roast dinner, cooked with potatoes, carrots, and turnips. Absent inquiry, I was fairly certain Terry had taught Ammar how to cook this bland British fare, pot roast not being a Middle East specialty. After nine months of this nightly routine, Terry and Ammar have become close friends, age and culture notwithstanding. "If it weren't for going to Sule every few weeks and having dinner with Ammar and his wife, I would be bonkers here, drinking and shagging the maid," Terry confessed.

"What do you do when you return to Scotland on R&R?" I asked.

"I start with a big juicy steak, rent a Jaguar, grab a bottle of gin, and do some whoring, what else," he said. "No, that's a joke, not any more, anyway. Seriously, I go see my kids and friends, my horses and dogs."

Terry told a story of a recent trip home, of a Scottish evangelical who attempted to shame him into more tithing and church attendance. "'That ain't me,' I told him. 'Bells, smells, iconography, and the Eucharist. . . . I believe in Jesus Christ; that's my faith. I don't have religion,'" he said. "The guy never hit me up again."

Changing the predinner discussion to Iraq, we talked about the mood in Baghdad before the war.

"In the two to three months leading up to the March invasion, hundreds of foreign extremists arrived in Baghdad," Ammar said. "They wore beards." Ammar held his hands at a distance from his face, projecting the reach of a full beard, while Terry got up to check on Jack. "Their body language and message gave them away. I saw and heard these people on the streets."

"Al-Qaeda and foreign terrorists were a small piece," Ammar continued. "During the Iran-Iraq War, and even before that, the Shias had been used by Saddam to fight but were not paid anything. So they were poor. Two hundred thousand Shias were in prison when Saddam opened the gates as the Americans arrived. Two months later, after de-Ba'athification, a half a million former Sunni police and military were unemployed. When the militias started organizing, there were plenty of people for hire."

As the evening progressed, Ammar recounted a November 2003 meeting with Senator Hillary Clinton in the Green Zone, that four-square-mile bunker of "bars, bowling alleys, and Babylonian palaces." It even has a 914 Westchester County area code, Ammar said.

Along with seven others from the CPA (Coalition Provisional Authority), Ammar, Paul Butler, and David Holdridge attended the 30-minute gathering with Senator Clinton. The bloody Ramadan offensive was raging beyond the tall blast walls of the Green Zone. Iraqi confidence in the U.S. mission in Iraq had only recently fallen to less than a majority. David and Paul were given three minutes each to convey seven months of witnessing through partners and clients and watching the insurgency unfold in Shia and Sunni villages across Iraq. Ammar, who has a casual charisma about him and is a native Baghdadi, was granted extra time, six or seven minutes.

"I told her that [Americans] needed to secure the borders, that terrorists were driving in from Jordan, Syria, Iran, and Saudi Arabia, coming from places like Sudan and Egypt and Libya. The border police were not being paid much, so they were taking bribes. She just listened and didn't say much. I don't know what to think of her," he said, checking the pot roast, while shaking his head in consternation.

Prewar planning at the Pentagon had nixed an added infantry division to secure the borders. Meantime, Ba'athists, flush with arms and money, used border sanctuaries in Syria to regroup while foreign jihadists crossed into Iraq from all compass points but the KRG. "Yet about a year [from the date of the March invasion] would pass before the U.S. military launched a serious effort to gain control of Iraq's borders—a step that is a prerequisite to mounting an effective counterinsurgency campaign," wrote Thomas Ricks in *Fiasco*.

By then, average Iraqis—who had no electricity and who watched in darkness from across the river as the secure and well-lighted Green Zone thrived—had lost faith in America's ability to protect them. The peace had been lost. Even still, 14 months after Ammar met with Senator Clinton, she declared much of Iraq "functioning quite well." (To be fair, she was only one voice in the junket-inspired congressional chorus.)

As Ammar's story ended, Jack gave out one of his yelps, which caused Terry to dive for the door. For a moment, it occurred to me we might be under attack. "It's okay," Ammar assured me, cutting into the pot roast. "Jack's fallen again. He does this all the time." Terry returned wondering if maybe Jack's diarrhea was caused by his diet of nothing but corned beef.

～

Hawer Ali Hussein, a project engineer, was waiting for me the next morning in his downstairs office. We were soon on our way to visit the Kurdistan Women Union office (KWU) 20 miles away in Kifri, home to a majority of Kurds, with a few Turkmen still around.

Hawer is 28, pudgy but stocky, with a high forehead and thinning hair. Bookish looking with thick glasses, he is enthusiastic about his work, and a friend of the Yanks. "In the south they see America as occupiers; in the KRG we see

America as our friends," he said. "We are under threat from Iran, Turkey, Syria, and Baghdad. We have no problem with America being here."

Hawer's uncle and four kids disappeared during the Anfal campaigns. "We celebrated for three days when Saddam was captured," he told me, with a look of tepid satisfaction.

That every Iraqi I would meet on this trip had a family story of woe recalled my five years in Hanoi, where the elemental nature of war—the dead and missing, the blind and limbless, and the heroic warriors and fatherless survivors—was revealed every day, 20 years after the war ended. Yet here, when wars end, it's more like a ceasefire, to be continued.

～

We made our way down an empty highway but for a couple of clusters of mud huts and small villages. Throughout this emptiness there was no surface water; the disked fields of wheat that surrounded us were dependent on rain. There is oil, though, Hawer said, "from here to Kirkuk."

Indeed, a half-mile from the road was a line of low-slung prefabs, a Canadian oil field camp thrown up a couple of months before. Two triple derricks pierced the sky to the north, "makin' hole," as they say, in the oil patch. The drilling rigs were owned and operated by Western Zagros Limited, a subsidiary of Western Oil Sands, a Canadian company. Hawer was unaware of any drilling in the area by American oil companies, although "they are around," he told me.

Iraq's proven reserves top 110 billion barrels, while potential recoverable reserves may be another 100 billion barrels. At current prices, if explored and developed, Iraq's pro forma revenue stream is nine trillion dollars.

Although the potential is great, it's no secret that Saddam's mismanagement of the oil, gas, refining, and electricity sectors across Iraq brought technological progress to a standstill in 1978: drilling equipment is now archaic, pipelines are corrosive and constantly leak, and 30-year-old Russian-built refineries have no spare parts. Power plants lack the capacity to give Iraqis a quarter of the demand. After the first Gulf War, 60 percent of the National Oil Company's facilities were degraded; since the invasion there have been over 400 attacks on Iraq's oil infrastructure.

Out-of-date methods like water flooding have been used to keep up monthly revenues. Given the security problems, no attention has been paid to modern methods of maximizing long-term production rates. Natural gas is flared as waste instead of consumed. Daily oil throughput is down 40 percent, below 2 million barrels, from a high of 3.5 million barrels before the first Gulf War. In short, Iraq has the lowest reserve-to-production ratio of any major oil-producing country.

Historically the most contested spot in the Middle East, the Dome of the Rock and Temple Mount in Jerusalem. It is believed that here Abraham went to sacrifice Isaac, the temple of Solomon and Herod stood, the Holiest of Holies housed the Ten Commandments, and Mohammed prayed with Jesus and the patriarchs before ascending, with the angel Gabriel, on his night journey to the seven heavens.

A snake charmer performs in Djemma el-Fna, Marrakech's main square and medieval theater.

At Qala'at Samaan in northern Syria, tourists pass by the ruins of St. Simeon the Stylite's 60-foot limestone column. The extreme ascetic roosted atop the pillar for 37 years in the 5th century, becoming the most famous man of his time.

For the first 70 years of the Ummayad dynasty, both Christians and Muslims prayed in Damascus's Ummayad Mosque, built over St. John's Basilica.

A tenement building eviscerated by the 2006 Israeli bombardment of south Beirut's Haret Hreik quarter.

Near Mt. Lebanon, the Maronite Monastery of St. Anthony of Qozhaya, a former cleric-run medieval mental asylum that boasts of the first printing press in the Middle East in 1585.

A 63-B antipersonnel cluster bomb from the Vietnam–American War era, employed, some say gratuitously, by Israel Defense Forces (IDF) in the 2006 war in Lebanon. According to a representative from MAG (Mines Advisory Group), the IDF strategy was to deplete their older cluster bomb stockpiles in order to receive expedited shipments from the United States of the superior M-26 antipersonnel, antivehicular cluster bombs.

Near the Blue Line on Lebanon's border with Israel, an Amal Movement martyr billboard declares in Arabic, "The martyrs are the Princes of Paradise" and "Amal's men are the commandos of this sacred land."

Justinian's 6th-century Aya Sofia, photographed during Friday prayer from the Blue Mosque, which was built in the 17th century by Sultan Ahmet in a grand attempt to outshine the Christian emperor.

In Diyarbakir, Turkey, Kurdish market boys working near the Four Footed Minaret that bestows good luck on all who walk beneath it. Beyond the minaret is the entrance to the infidel quarter, the site of the tumbledown remains of Chaldean and Armenian churches.

Iraqi Kurds display a protest banner at the USAID-built Institute of Fine Arts in Khanaqin, Iraq.

From atop a synagogue abandoned in 1948, the author takes in the dawdling pace of the old city of Kifri, Iraq.

مقام معظم رهبری :

بسیج سرمایه ملی کشور است

Eminet Leader of the islamic Revolution:
Basij is national asset of our country

بسیج قوه قضائیه و وزارت دادگستری

Near Tehran's Grand Bazaar, the Supreme Leader Ayatollah Ali Khamenei promotes the Basij, the vigilante, volunteer paramilitary of young Iranians who are best known for policing morals and quashing dissent.

An imposing Tehran skyscraper displays the imperious portraits of Ayatollahs Ruhollah Khomeini and Ali Khamenei. Some claim to have seen a light pass between the two Supreme Leaders of Iran upon Khomeini's death in 1989.

A statue of Reza Shah Pahlavi, cut off at the knees after the 1979 revolution and moved from in front of the Tehran train station, greets visitors to the Mellat Palace, now a museum.

In Yazd, Iran, the winged deity of Mazda Ahura gazes from above the doorway to the Zoroastrian fire temple, Atash Behram. Only 20,000 practicing Zoroastrians remain in Yazd, once the center of Zoroastrianism. Over the centuries, tens of thousands fled Iran in the face of religious suppression.

Twenty-three thousand shahids, or martyrs, from Iran's eight-year war with Iraq, are buried in this cemetery in Esfahan, Iran. Many of these fallen heroes were given a plastic key, a ticket to paradise, to wear around their necks, before charging Saddam's army in human waves.

The Jewish cemetery in the Mellah of Fez, Morocco, is the burial place of many saints who refused to convert to Islam.

Women shopping at a Marrakech street market near the old city gate, Bab Keshish.

In Tunis, Tunisia, on Avenue Habib Bourguiba where concertina wire, tanks, soldiers, and police are a constant presence since the Jasmine Revolution, the spark plug that ignited the Arab Spring.

Food preparation in a World Food Program (WFP) tent at Shousha refugee camp, near the Libyan border station Ras Jdir.

Eritrean refugees, who fled civil war and a brutal dictatorship at home to work menial jobs in Libya, catch some shade at the Shousha refugee camp.

At Shousha camp, Sudanese refugees, used essentially as slave labor in Libya, return to their tents with WFP-distributed food and water.

On Avenue Habib Bourguiba, the Tunisian Army band plays the national anthem, "Humat al-Hima," or "Defenders of the Homeland." Only moments before, tanks, soldiers, and police engaged Salafist thugs here.

Rome didn't go anywhere unless there was an economic advantage. At first blush, oil as a motive for war in Iraq is a safe rationale. Aside from Dick Cheney—Halliburton's former chief and major shareholder who is highly suspect—oil is America's most strategic interest in the Middle East. Remember the triumphant U.S. entry into Baghdad: protecting the oil ministry was more important to American commanders than 10,000 years of antiquities, Iraq's precious history.

In some minds, there may, however, always be doubt and uncertainty about why the war wizards chose to invade Iraq: Bush's family grievance against Saddam for the assassination attempt on his father; Paul Wolfowitz and Douglas Feith's personal Holocaust fixation; and Donald Rumsfeld's restlessness to show off his modern army (to "shoot polar bears in the Arctic" if necessary) all have individual, if not collective, resonance as conceivable motives. Yet, with similar plausibility, the loftier, less cynical rationales of weapons of mass destruction (WMDs) and nuclear war, spreading freedom and democracy in the Middle East, protecting Israel, or stopping an imaginary al-Qaeda in Iraq are within the bounds of possibility.

That said, "it's the oil, *habibi*, the oil," a phrase coined by Juan Cole, a professor at the University of Michigan and a Middle East expert. No country or global energy corporation is immune from the geopolitics of oil; it's always percolating beneath the surface, abhorring a vacuum and driving liberators, landowners, leaders, and lunatics to do anything for its prize. All American petro-addicts are part of this invisible conspiracy that underpins U.S. foreign policy that says Rwanda is not in our vital national interest. We are doing all this to ourselves, too: it's the U.S. dependency on oil that rewards the world's worst behavior, Iraq's terrorism, Iran's belligerence, and the Saudi's extravagance—willful self-destruction, they call it.

"I am saddened that it is politically inconvenient to acknowledge what everyone knows: the Iraq war is largely about oil," wrote former Federal Reserve chairman Alan Greenspan in his book *The Age of Turbulence*. "Thus, projections of world oil supply and demand that do not note the highly precarious environment of the Middle East are avoiding the eight-hundred-pound gorilla that could bring world economic growth to a halt."

Once security improves, and as Iraq comes to grips with the necessary network rehabilitation costs, it will have no choice but to look to the West for drilling and development expertise. Wolfowitz's wild prediction that oil money would lickety-split pay for reconstruction was a fairy tale worthy of Scheherazade.

On behalf of Prime Minister Nouri al-Maliki, General David Petraeus called on "large Western corporations" to invest in Iraq's energy sector. While at the same time, Omar Fatah, deputy prime minister of the KRG, in a speech given at the American Peace Institute, pleaded for all major American oil companies to invest in the KRG: "They will make a profit if they come."

Smaller national and independent oil companies, from Turkey, Canada, Norway, the UK, Switzerland, South Korea, China, Vietnam, Russia, and others have signed contracts with the KRG. Some are already conducting seismic tests and drilling test wells. The family-held Hunt Oil of Dallas, Texas (Ray Hunt, the president, is a Bush ally), was the first American company to strike such an agreement with the KRG. With security as it is, this is all pure wildcatting.

Although the Hunt oil contract calls for revenue sharing in the ratio of 83 to 17 stipulated by the central government, the U.S. State Department has publicly criticized the deal as being at "cross purposes" with the Baghdad regime. While privately encouraging the deal, even providing suggestions for additional drilling opportunities in southern Iraq, in truth, the United States sneezes at any whiff of self-determination on the part of Kurds, favoring instead a ham-fisted policy of forced unity, an American-style melting pot in tribal Iraq.

Once the central government's "hydrocarbon laws" are clarified, once a referendum on control of oil-rich Kirkuk is determined, and once security is improved, Mr. Fatah will no longer have to plead to the majors. Even so, woolly as those oil issues remain, in Baghdad the former owners of the Iraq Petroleum Company (Exxon, Shell, BP, and Total), along with other international opportunists, are gathering like moths to the flame. Chevron, ConocoPhilllips, ExxonMobil, Total of France, Royal Dutch Shell, Russian-giant Lukoil, British Petroleum, ONGC (India Oil and Natural Gas Corp), and the China National Petroleum Company are the headliners, competing for the opportunity to develop "supergiant" fields across Iraq.

In the meantime, given the Turkman population in Kirkuk, which by any count is a small minority, Turkey threatens invasion if the impending referendum gives Kurds the rights to Kirkuk oil.

⁓

Now, pulling into Kifri, officially part of the oil-rich Kirkuk governorate, Hawer came to a stop on the rutted road coursing through old town. The sharp elbows of oil prospectors were less apparent here than the wary glances of turbaned traders. With the potholes filled with fresh rain, and with makeshift tin roofs bent at their brims like a well-broken-in cow poker's hat, there was a frontier, Klondike feel to Kifri. Even so, at times here in old town it was difficult to distinguish between the natural ruinations of time and the denatured aftermath of war.

As the American invasion took place, Kifri was the target of heavy mortaring by Saddam's army, leaving behind dozens of casualties. Defended by peshmerga, and eventually American special ops forces, the ancient city is separated by a no man's land of booby traps and landmines. And it was here that hundreds of Baghdadi Kurds fled as American military arrived.

Hawer bought a few pieces of hard candy from two young traders, who also sold crates of eggs piled six high and three new water heaters parked on the road's edge. With origins in the remote past, there were no women merchandising or mingling in the market. Next door, four older men sat in a circle like pillars of patriarchy, talking over tea. Filling up their cozy space were woven baskets heaping with onions; roundels of peppers; burlaps of mint; a set of wood-framed scales, mounted on each end with empty tins; and 50-pound, white, food-aid bags of rice, with markings from Thailand. Until 1948, and from then back through the mists of the Ottoman Empire, if not to the hoary days of Babylon, this was the old Jewish quarter.

Hawer and I moseyed into the catacombed, antique medina, greeted by cheap textiles from China hanging from its arched, fieldstone roof. A bevy of clipped ducks and a small herd of sheep led us through the arched passageway, where the Jewish merchants once boarded their livestock for safekeeping. Cave-like stalls that today looked more like a barnyard habitat were where incense and myrrh, cinnamon and cinnabar, dates and apricots, and gold and grains were once bartered, a vignette of biblical days.

Two weather-beaten men in wooly but threadbare prayer caps, redolent of the industrious merchants of those times, sat off in an abandoned, dank nook. I felt as though the clock had stopped long ago, and I was the first to arrive as it began ticking again. Reeking of newly harvested wool, one man rolled and pressed a crudely matted carpet on a dirt floor thinly covered in strips of bamboo. The other rug maker hung a freshly dyed wool rug on the bare rock wall. That was it for inventory. They couldn't be producing more than two of these a week, at a local price of $10 a piece.

Like Shamil, Hawer's grandparents remembered fondly the Jewish community here: "They all worked hard and were prosperous. They left by choice after Israel was [established]. Massoud Barzani had a friendship with the Jews, but the Arabs always held it against him."

Tolerance and living together, or *convivencia*, as it was called in the golden age of Moorish Spain, was once a way of life here. Baghdad in the 1920s was said to be one-third Jewish, over 130,000 living there. From Persia to Vienna, the Ottomans relied on Greeks, Armenians, and Jews for mercantilism. It was neither Utopian nor classless, but before the surge of ethnic-based nationalism in the 20th century, it was an accommodation that nevertheless worked for 3,000 years. Today, there are said to be eight Jews still living in Iraq, two shy of a minyan quorum.

Further along, Hawer, who grew up near the market, led me into a room of high-arched ceilings forming multiple domes. Through a gaping fracture in the roof, an unintended skylight perhaps, date palms swayed against a wedge of clouded sky. The dirt floor was piled three feet high in fallen rock and rubbish. We were in a former synagogue.

Hawer pointed out the recession in the wall at one end where a few stones of the Ark remain, west in the direction of Jerusalem. On the south side, in the day, a minyan of skullcapped men would have sat for prayer; separately but behind me would have been women in babushka-style scarves. An oil-burning menorah might have been where Hawer stood; a rabbi or cantor reading from the Torah in ancient Hebrew would have placed himself about where I was perched atop the fallen rock. Incense might have sated the air in place of the decomposing stench of rubbish rising beneath my feet. The "eternal light" seemed to have dimmed here indefinitely. The last synagogue in Baghdad closed its doors after the 2003 invasion.

Through a gaping breach in the east wall, I billy-goated my way to the top of the medina's earthen ramparts. The market passageway and rock domes of the synagogue were behind me. Below, the narrow streets of the old city were walled in ancient stone, which in relief recalled fossilized barnacles. A field-rock minaret and medieval dome of a mosque, of the same era as the synagogue, modest and miniature by today's standards, peeked above the barnacled walls, honeycombed in shops and homes. Two women swooshed by, one in a black chador, the other with a scarf cinched babushka-style around the chin, like spectral figures in a time warp. Terry was right: someday Kifri's old city ought to be rehabilitated as a UNESCO World Heritage site.

⁓

Runak Abu Bakir, of the KWU (Kurdistan Women Union), was waiting for us in front of their nicely rehabbed, two-story headquarters. With national movements like the KWU, the cause of women has achieved enhanced legitimacy in the eyes of society here. After extending her hand for a shake, Runak walked us to her office, where her daughter Sara shyly joined us. Mother and daughter each painted their eyes in thick lines of kohl and were blinged out in gold bracelets, necklaces, and earrings that flashed like flickers of fire against their dark features.

Sara served us tea, as the obligatory threshold of pleasantries gave way to a parley about what KWU does through its clinic: awareness courses for pregnant women and child survival interventions and trainings to combat violence against women. The KWU also acts as a community center for women to interact, to share their experiences, often with the goal of breaking taboos of their ancient patriarchal culture.

To facilitate the social interplay, KWU has recently added a small gym, with workout equipment. The idea of treadmills and stationary bicycles struck me as out of place, a mirage of modernity and all its obsessions. Runak explained: "Our goals are to get the women out of the home to have a healthy, socializing experience. It is [especially] good for them to exercise when they are pregnant. They get to talk about problems at home, about economic matters, violence, and divorce."[2]

Due to the secular nature of the former Ba'ath Party (and of the KRG government), Iraqi women are said to have had more rights—voting, education, representation in parliament, and professional opportunities—than most in Arab Mashriq (eastern Arab world). Others would say, however, that with several hundred thousand war widows in Iraq, some of whom are now being employed as suicide bombers, their cause is going in the wrong direction.

Given the patriarchal nature of Sharia, and the Kurdish and Iraqi social cosmology that holds "honor" above life, domestic violence occurs frequently. Men are duty bound to exact retribution when honor is threatened, which is often whimsically invoked as a matter of control. And as we know, the most restrictive law in the world is the law of the family. In Kurdish Iraq alone, in the first half of 2007, the UN estimates that 255 women died in honor killings, usually burned to death with petrol or paraffin.

Runak told me that changes in the legal code are the key to women owning their own issues: the recent liberalization of gender laws in the KRG have made honor killings—in which the usual victims are mothers, daughters, aunts, and sisters—a crime punishable by 25 years in prison or death.

Enforcement is a different story. In 2004, a teenage boy recorded sex with a 17-year-old girl on his cell phone. The video was circulated in Erbil, the Kurdish capital. Within days, they were both killed by their families. The issue in that case was also the misuse of a cell phone, an ongoing clash in Iraq with the extremes of modernity, which has caused a dramatic rise in honor killings. Unlike the Erbil case, retribution is almost always exacted against the woman and not the man. Payment of blood money is the common solution, while the woman's family has no other recourse.

Although Runak wouldn't talk directly about the subject of female genital mutilation, Mercy Corps staff had told me that 60 percent of Kurdish women in Iraq have been circumcised. According to tradition, this controls a woman's sexual desire while cleansing the soul so that others can be safe eating meals she has prepared. "I would not eat food from the hands of someone who did

---

2. According to the KRG ministry of health, in 2007 some 600 women committed suicide to get out of miserable marriages.

not have the procedure," said 91-year-old Hurment Kitab (reported by the *Washington Post*). Dispensing with this ancient ritual, as I had learned in Sudan where my wife shepherded a project to reduce female genital mutilation, means debunking beliefs that some attribute to Mohammed.

Runak did talk about arranged marriages, age minimums for brides, multiple wives, the *talaq* divorce (a man says three times "I divorce you"), lack of contraception, abortion and healthcare, and high illiteracy rates, all issues being addressed in parliament and by human rights organizations in the KRG, not least being Mercy Corps and the Kurdistan Women Union.

She talked more about the improvements the clinic has made on women's healthcare.

"The greatest difference is in nutrition, hygiene, genital awareness, and acceptance of the services we offer. Mothers are having their children vaccinated. They are taking vitamins [during pregnancy]. They didn't do this before. They are also seeing doctors and going to the hospital. Before their husbands wouldn't allow this," she said, giving a shrug that seemed to acknowledge reality.

As such, unless challenged, women are trapped in a remote time past, reproducing and raising children, with no tolerance for mixing of sexes, even with a doctor.

Tricky as it is to talk about here, she touched briefly on the union's role in domestic violence.

"The people that work here have been trained in counseling for women who [report] violence. We also do training that addresses these issues and are trying to change behavior and the laws."

As we were leaving, two doctors and 30-plus women were arriving for breastfeeding training. The clinic is fortunate to have the services of doctors and nurses, as they are rarer than hen's teeth in Iraq. As part of the overall brain drain, over half of the 40,000 physicians in Iraq have been killed or have fled, most for more secure, lucrative opportunities abroad.

For the women clients, transformation comes in baby steps, and for feedback loops to take hold and the self-amplifying behavior of local leaders to resonate, it takes time and economic development. But I did leave with the feeling that Runak and others, at some level, saw themselves as a piece of a larger human renaissance, or *izdihar* as it is called in Arabic.

CHAPTER THIRTEEN

~

The Sunshine Peddler's Parlor Game

It was November 9, as I checked e-mails and news at Mercy Corps' office. With great interest I learned that the surge had succeeded, the 30,000-man force was going home. "American forces have routed al-Qaeda in Mesopotamia, the Iraqi militant network, from every neighborhood of Baghdad, a top American general said today, allowing American troops involved in the surge to depart as planned," reported the *New York Times*. Ammar Zakri walked in as I printed out the story. "Check this out: the surge worked; Baghdad is safe again," I said, handing him the article, aware that his mother and two sisters still live in Baghdad, all of whom he talks to daily.

He put down the files he was working on, pulled up a chair beside me, and slowly read the article. Ten minutes later he looked up and said, "That's good if it is true. So they [America and Baghdad government] need to build on that. Since the different political groups and militias didn't sign an agreement, where are the insurgents? Are they sleepers? Is the Mahdi army finished? Might they return when the surge troops leave?" Other than the editorial pages back in the States, the Beltway had no answers to these very obvious concerns.

After Ammar pointed out that the ebb in violence was a Baghdad phenomenon, he talked about postsurge life on the city's streets.

"The demographics have changed since I left," he said. "Each neighborhood is like a mini Green Zone, with blast walls and militias protecting it. Before the war, Baghdad was 65 percent Shia, and 25 percent Sunni, with the rest being Kurds and others. Today it is almost 85 percent Shia, 10 percent Sunni, and the Kurds are gone," he said matter-of-factly.

Hopes of a change of circumstances for Ammar and his family are bombarded by reality, not by what the press or politicians might say on any given day.

167

"I would love to return to Baghdad," he said. "But it will be at least ten years before I think it will be possible for my children to live there." Sighing deeply, he continued, "You see, Baghdad was famous through the Middle East for its nightlife. We would go out walking at night, visiting relatives and friends in the streets and shops and restaurants, until two in the morning. Now that is gone. That is what I miss about Baghdad."

Three months later, according to Ammar and his mother, not one Sunni IDP or refugee has returned to his neighborhood. And though it is difficult to admit, in spite of surges and ceasefires, as long as the sectarian hatred exists, it is not desirable to return. For now, the Shias won the battle of Baghdad, but with 28 separate militias in Iraq, it is predictable that the communal violence will start once again.[1]

"Americans don't understand the war in the context of their own lives, especially the massive displacement of Iraqis from their homes," says Leila Fadel, McClatchy's 25-year-old Baghdad bureau chief. "Imagine it happening here, living in the U.S., and finding you are no longer welcome in your own hometown. Americans forget the very human element of this war." Indeed, the Iraqi displacement is the relative equivalent of the entire populations of the states of Texas and New York disappearing.

⌣

Bush's proclaimed strategy for the surge was to move Iraqis to reconciliation. As Ammar pointed out, that hasn't happened. But for the first time in Baghdad, surge commander General David Petraeus attempted to make the people the prize, delivering security and safety to them. In four years, this had never been done, protecting the Iraqis we came to save. "The battlespace is psychological, not physical," said one civil affairs officer.

To make a bad situation better, Petraeus redirected American troops from the insulated, giant bases into smaller patrol outposts in and around Baghdad. Risky as these counterinsurgent tactics are, in the long term it is the only way to build trust between the civilians, the Iraqi security forces, and the Americans. Petraeus and U.S. troops could not have had better timing. As the surge strategy was being employed, by coincidence, the Sunni "awakening" against al-Qaeda took hold.[2]

For a moment let's forget the surge and suppose we are playing a parlor game with the following clues: It's 2008, a presidential election year in the United

---

1. As of March of 2009, the U.S. Army reported that 16 percent of Sunni displaced families had returned to Baghdad.

2. Looking back, the Sunni "awakening" was the beginning of an anti-jihad movement that would take on many incarnations, including the Arab Spring.

States. Americans have already spent 600 billion dollars—which is being financed not by Americans buying war bonds but rather by selling U.S. Treasury securities to China, Japan, oil-exporting nations, and others—on a failed state in the Middle East. So far over 4,000 American soldiers have died and 58,000 veterans have returned to the States critically wounded—blinded, limbless, or with brain trauma and spinal injuries (to hopefully be cared for forever). The military is stretched beyond its effective capacity—500,000 troops served two tours (now raised to 15 months), and 20,000 served four tours, many without body armor. One candidate promises another hundred years there, if necessary, while a Nobel Prize–winning economist estimates the war cost would reach three trillion dollars, much of which, if paid, would be for long-term veteran care (250,000 have already applied for disability). The three trillion, of course, is the tip of the iceberg for (American) human cost and lost opportunities.

The failed state is war ravaged, with terrorist attacks every day and over 100,000 people (some say 600,000), mostly civilians (aka collateral damage), from opposing religious and ethnic sects who have been killed in the failed state over a four-year period. The blood is still fresh.

Further, this country now has four million IDPs and refugees while 80 percent of the population has turned decidedly anti-American, and well over 50 percent condone terrorist attacks on American soldiers. A vacuum of security and political leadership in the failed state has galvanized a fledgling, on-the-run terrorist organization into a worldwide, American-hating movement.

The social, political, and economic failures of that state include potable water, reliable electricity, proper nutrition, primary and secondary education, a functioning health-care system, gender equality, safeguards against corruption, and curbing ethnic cleansing and sectarian violence. All of the failed state's urban center neighborhoods, many of which had no ethnic identity before, have become concrete-walled, tribal ghettoes, which are ethnically cleansed, like going from one country to the next, a little Lebanon of fiefdoms, all with their own flags![3]

Though this is a parlor game, these are not trick questions. If a tactical military operation had recently suppressed insurgent violence in that failed state's capital city for several months, while at the same time ceding large blocks of power to the region's biggest threat (Iran) in order to reduce violence, as president of the United States, would you characterize that as "kicking ass"? Or as a

---

3. In December 2011, Middle East expert Juan Cole provided an update on the social realities of Iraq going forward: 187 Iraqis were killed in November 2011; 17 percent of Iraqis lived in slums before the invasion versus 50 percent today; one-fourth of Iraqis live below the poverty line; there are 4.5 million orphans in Iraq, and 600,000 live in the streets; 2 million women, mainly widows, are now the primary breadwinners; since 2008, only one-eighth of the IDPs have returned home; and on the Corruption Index, Iraq ranks 175th out of 182 countries.

congressman who traveled to a market in the failed state's capital, with a presidential candidate, would you describe that military-escorted tour as a normal outdoor market in Indiana in the summertime? Finally, did the earth continue to revolve around the sun after Galileo was forced by threat of execution to recant? (If you answered yes to all, you won the Sunshine Peddler's Parlor Game.)

～

The next morning, around the kitchen table, I sipped tea and coffee with Paul Butler, Mercy Corps' country director for Iraq. He had returned the night before from Gaza. "Israel has a ghetto mentality of walling in, but they do have much more analysis of their politics than the U.S. does," he said, in response to my holding my nose at the mention of Gaza.

Paul has lived in Iraq for the last four years. At age 43, he was about to get married for the first time. With that, he hinted that his new bride—who is Spanish and living in Madrid—might want him to live closer to home and start a family.

Paul is the product of a Mexican mother from Guadalajara and an American military father who retired as an artillery master sergeant (but died of a heart attack 20 years ago). Paul was raised, for the most part, in the border town of El Paso, Texas, near Fort Bliss, home to U.S. Patriot missile batteries and training ground for U.S. Army Air Defense Artillery Brigades. Through osmosis, a respect for his father's profession, and boyish curiosity, he learned about army life and weaponry. None of that background would suggest that he would grow up to become an Arabist. Yet he has: after graduating high school in El Paso, Paul earned degrees in international relations from Georgetown and Harvard's Kennedy school, with a specialty in the Middle East. While at Georgetown he took a year abroad in Cairo to study Arabic, which he now speaks fluently.

Paul confirmed what, in my short visit, had become obvious: "Kurds love Americans like no place I've ever been." As a Middle East policy wonk, he had a lot more to say about Iraq and the region: "All of the Middle East has a sense of lost empire. Just when they think they are getting ahead, they slide further back. Even sub-Saharan African countries such as Ghana are showing more positive economic growth. And Spain, after a long civil war, and a 40-year dictatorship, if you don't include oil, today they export more than all of the Middle East, from Iran to Morocco."

The setbacks may not be over. Paul raised concerns about the Iraq civil war igniting a regional conflict. Mercy Corps national staff members in Kut, located near the Iranian border in the Shia south, have been telling Paul for two years that Iranians are not only coming across the border for trade but also opening shops and populating. As Farsi speakers they stand out in the Arab south.

Although Paul sees paying and arming 91,000 members of the Sunni "awakening councils" in Anbar as long overdue, he fears that the Shias and Sunnis may again lapse into civil war. "And the Saudis, who are bristling with American weapons, would love nothing more than to come across the border in a holy war against the Shias in Iraq and Iran," he said.

On the other hand, we discussed why Tehran has no reason to want to overthrow the first Shia government in Iraq. Thanks to the toppling of Saddam, an arc of Shia dominoes now runs from Iran to Lebanon.[4]

The clerical connections between Tehran and the new Baghdad are profound: the Grand Ayatollah Sayyid Ali al-Sistani, Iraq's most powerful political leader, is Iranian, and the founder of Iran's Islamic revolution, Ayatollah Khomeini, took refuge in Iraq for 12 years from Iran's pro-American shah regime. Even Iraq's Prime Minister Nouri al-Maliki spent 20 years in exile in Syria and Iran.

Paul said Tehran had recently agreed to fund a new airport at Najaf for the millions of Iranian pilgrims who will go there when security improves. The boon to the Iraqi economy could be in the billions. Is this just neighborly largesse, or all told, a play for the establishment of an Islamic state? Either way, we discussed, Iran will expand its influence in Iraq, not with an invading army (as Cyrus the Great did 2,500 years ago) but rather with clerical ties and binding economic relations.

~

Amar Galaly, who met me at the Turkish border, promised a visit to Suleimaniyah University upon my return from Kalar. Security guards at the school's iron-gated entrance recognized Amar. They waved us on, into a gathering of multistoried, blond-brick buildings, as shifts were changing: day students drifted away and night students lingered in the twilight. About the common, adorned with a folly of human-sized pencils, young men enjoyed a last smoke, and women jabbered on cell phones.

Meanwhile, four twenty-something girls awaited us in front of the College of Languages. As if in uniform, they all wore skin-tight blue jeans and bosom-stretched blouses, and hoisted laptops and designer purses. As night students, they each pay tuition of $600 a year but live at home, not in the dormitory. Their girlish enthusiasm was only exceeded by their taste for dark-shadowed eyes that they flashed like beacons (not for me; there were young men around).

Suad, Shaz, Hawraz, and Dashnay had reinvented themselves American. With their English skills on the ascendant, possibly as a memory tool, they all

---

4. "Geography is the most important factor in foreign policy because it is the most permanent," says one analyst.

gushed in a stream-of-consciousness manner, stringing together tidbits of Americana that appeared to be based on name association. Suddenly, I was Dr. Phil.

"Dr. Phil, we love you," Suad said, before being interrupted by Dashnay.

"I want to be like Oprah, Dr. Phil. She is my model. God helps her help people. She gives away houses. When I watch her, I cry."

Suad, who had a striking mane of hennaed hair, elbowed back in, "Dr. Phil, Dr. Phil," drawing my attention as one might with a teacher. "Elvis Presley, Michael Jackson, and Richard Gere are my favorites. Did I say George Clooney? Someday I want to go to Las Vegas and gamble."

A young man walked up and stuck his head into our circle. "We are only suffering here from not enough nightclubs." He then darted off.

"It doesn't matter; we can't go out at night," Shaz said in a wishful tone, her neck dripping in rings of colorful beads.

Dashnay was almost hyperventilating to be heard. "I'm very romantic. I cried when Ben and J.Lo broke up. I love *Inside Edition*; I watch it 24–7," she announced theatrically.

After my brief audience with these girls, the Kurdish (and Arab) living room struck me as a complicated place to go each night. It must be like an incubator that both hatches and inoculates cultures, where robed mullahs on Arabic satellite compete with disrobed dancers on American MTV. Dizzying as it was listening to these girls, America's pop culture—Hollywood, the music industry, blue jeans, and snappy jargon—had harvested some goodwill and, on occasion, provided humor.

But what did these college girls really think of Americans? I wondered.

"Americans are nice, fantastic even, but your president and Congress want to occupy oil," Suad said. Like the rest of the world, Suad had seen American soldiers on television, who were ordered, as a first act of security, to cordon off the ministry of oil.

Shaz, who was more reserved than the others, said, "American people are nice, but they always chase money." (She has a new GMC SUV and had to leave early to go shopping for jeans.)

Hawraz was more expansive: "I want to go live in America or England some day. But America does not need to bring all the soldiers to Afghanistan and Iraq. All of the explosions are made by the United States, Israel, and Britain. If it's al-Qaeda [doing this], then why are they killing Iraqis? I don't blame Iraq or Syria. The Americans are creating a reason to occupy Iraq."

These impressions didn't happen in a vacuum. "We live in a world where a country is judged by more than its actions," wrote Ian Klaus in *Elvis Is Titanic*, based on his experiences teaching English at the University of Salahaddin in Erbil, two years before. "In the age of satellite television and blogs, dictators and mullahs, image can affect perception as much as reality can."

⌒

Shapol Abdullah waited in front of the Mercy Corps house, with Bakhtyar, the driver. We were joining four university professors for lunch, but before that we were stopping for tea with a PUK (Patriotic Union of Kurdistan) politician.

Shapol and her family live around the corner from the Mercy Corps office in relative affluence. Her tentacles of influence spread far and wide among the grandees of Sule. Attractive, with henna-streaked hair and twinkling eyes, handsomely dressed and in her late 40s, Shapol attended a British-run school in Sule that Saddam Hussein closed in 1984 over a spy brouhaha involving a British citizen. Since the 1990s, Shapol has been variously employed by UNHabitat and a Dutch consortium, where she found her voice in 1999 as one of the first employees to work on gender equality programs. She is committed to change.

In many ways, the women's movement in the KRG (and the Middle East), if not the role of modernity in women's lives, has been held hostage to the sectarian and nationalist struggles.

"We still have honor killings. It is important to know how to use the Internet, cell phones, and satellite television," Shapol said, responding to a question about modernity. "My family knows this, but not everyone does. If not careful, sometimes girls are more at risk with their family than they are on the street. Imitating a movie or talking two or three hours on the phone with a boy can be trouble for a girl. Religion affects everything here."

We were in the suburbs, where the home of Awat Sheikh Janab spread like a neocolonial fortress. Sculpted conifers rising in a wall of green columns gave way to an English-style garden. A camouflage-wearing guard met us on the front lawn, while others peered around corners. Awat is a ranking PUK member from a well-to-do family and was mayor of Suleimaniyah from 1992 through 1997. In his stocking feet, with black slacks and a light blue collared shirt, he seated us on bulky new couches in the living room. Though smartly furnished, the room's sterility reminded me of what my father used to call the preacher's room, the unused living room of every 1950s home in America.

Awat's wife appeared for a brief introduction, and then retreated to the kitchen. One of his camouflaged guards served us tea, while I told him of my origins in America.

"I know Americans well. I was a *peshmerga* commander and fought with them in Kirkuk in 2003," he said, running his fingertips across both temples. "That's why my hair has turned gray."

Only minutes after Shapol and I had had a similar conversation, Awat and I were talking about the impact of technology on KRG society.

"The tech sector is like a drug," he said. "Sometimes it can kill you, but it's not manufactured to do so. The Internet and satellite TV are okay here.

Journalists can express themselves freely. They can criticize politicians. We are imitating America and the West, their liberty and the lifestyle. But we are different from people in Basra [Shia south], just start with the clothing. Some people in the KRG are even naming their kids after Americans—Christina, Laura, Howard, Allen, Jimmy. Kurdish people want the same opportunities as the West, and they want peace like in Europe."

As with most Kurds, Awat expressed disappointment, if not jealousy, at all the attention the Arabs get in the south and Turks to the west. No credit, he says, is given to all the progress made in the KRG. When I suggested that, given the democratic reforms of the KRG, only two tribes—the Talibanis and Barzanis—wield real power, Awat drew a parallel with America: "I understand that if Hillary Clinton is elected president, there will be a Bush or a Clinton in the White House for 36 years. Unfortunately, we are doing like America. Even the Islamic party feels like they have democracy here. Kurds here know they can't get rid of each other by war, so we need to make democracy in Kurdistan an example for the whole region."

After three cups of coffee, Shapol was giving me that time-to-go look. We were late for lunch with the university professors.

～

The Saddam-era Abusana Hotel parking lot was filled with Toyota sedans and SUVs. At the entrance to the hotel restaurant, which was partitioned in Chinese screens, we were greeted and seated by a suited-up maître d'. Hanging from the ceiling were crimson- and gold-filigreed Chinese lanterns. Red was the color scheme and scroll paintings, featuring maidens among wispy bamboo fronds, were the motif. In contrast, there wasn't even an egg roll on the menu. "All the furniture and decorations are from China, but the food is not Chinese," Shapol said, while letting go a burst of laughter at the cheesy decor.

Smartly attired, four professors of political science at Suleimaniyah University, Yousef, Anwar, Karaanh, and Rebwar, arrived as we did, filling up an expansive table in the corner. Sharing mezze plates, I explained that I was there to mine their thoughts on America. These agents of change were not short on opinions, nor were they unfamiliar with American NGOs, having consulted on many occasions with UN-funded organizations in conflict mitigation, in hot spots like Mosul and Kirkuk.

"America taught us free speech. We wish they would support us with humanitarian rights and democracy," Rebwar said, choosing his words as carefully as he trimmed his moustache.

"Since we were freed of Saddam, the popular ideas of the people and the private ideas of the politicians are to have one nation," Anwar said. "Kurds are afraid that Bush will get rid of us because of Turkey and the PKK [Kurdistan Workers' Party]. People here don't understand what's going on with America and KRG politicians. We have what America needs: safety. It's important for us to show the world how 'good policy' works, that we are successful in providing security. Otherwise the process of freedom has failed."

On the subject of corruption, Karaanh spoke briefly. "America defends politicians and not people. Iraq is very corrupt, and after 2003 it is worse. You can expect more."

"We don't feel America is coming to support democracy in KRG, although they did so in Iraq," said Yousef.

They all wanted to know what Americans think of the KRG.

"That's an easy question," I said, with a laugh. "The vast majority of Americans don't have a clue you even exist. They couldn't identify Iraq on a map, much less the KRG. As they say in the news business, if it bleeds it leads: Americans read about their soldiers who get killed in Iraq, with little if any analysis. After September 11th, Bush told Americans to go shopping, and they did." The professors went from simmering grins to shameless laughter, at my compatriots' expense.

Shapol confirmed what I said with an anecdote of her own from a recent trip to the States, where she spoke to a high school assembly in Portland, Oregon. No one in the class could identify the KRG on the map, nor did they know it existed.

∼

Later that afternoon Shapol and I went to Dr. Jamal Salish's home, a "million-dollar estate" in a hilly suburban area. Distinguished, dressed formally in a black suit, and imbued with old world manners, Jamal and his wife, Sherien, greeted us in the Western way, with handshakes at the door. Twenty years younger than Jamal, Sherien is also his cousin.

For my part in these opulent digs of cut-glass chandeliers, silk curtains, room-sized Kurdish rugs, leather ottomans, and padded arm chairs, I was still wearing clothes with three days of road dust and badly scuffed shoes and carrying a tattered monk's bag that has traveled widely with me. Jamal didn't pay any attention as we sat in arm chairs and talked while Shapol and Sherien gathered on a couch in Siberia, way across the spacious living room. Their ten-year-old daughter served us high tea, with syrup-dripping filo pastries.

Jamal, portly and gray, is in his late 50s and was educated in graduate and medical schools in England. Upon his return to the KRG, he became dean of the medical school in Sule. Years later, in 1991, he founded KSRO (Kurdish Shelter Reconstruction Organization), a Kurdish human rights NGO. Like many of the KRG's "intellectuals," among which he included himself, Jamal is an agent of change.

I slid down in the armchair before asking him about pressing human rights issues in the KRG, anticipating a double-barreled response.

"The mechanism for corruption is to divide the money [border tariffs and central government distributions] between the two parties and forget the people," he said, knowingly. "They don't help the kids with education, the elderly, or the poor. The budget is hidden from the people. They do a minimum for human rights, only enough to blunt my organization. Until we said something, prisons here were as bad as anywhere in the world. Our goals are to identify inequities," he said, pausing for a deep breath.

Jamal sees corruption in the KRG as the root of all discrimination. "You must have a party affiliation to get a good job [a system known as *wasta*]. Higher jobs—ministerial positions—go to party members. They make you become part of the cycle of corruption like the former communist system. The party leaders asked me to be a minister, but I will not compromise. They give you land, property, cars, extra money, and other perks. So you get used to the system and can't leave it. You must abide by party rules then. [The problem is] if you ignore people and jobs, the youth will turn to radical fundamentalism," he proffered. Without mentioning names, Jamal could have been talking about everyone I had met.

In KRG, it's not uncommon to hear comparisons of corruption before and after the ruinous reign of Saddam. Though there is no love lost for Saddam, many say that, relative to the scale of corruption today, it was cheap to buy his small tribe of family members a big house and a new car every year. Ouja, Saddam's ancestral village near Tikrit, is to Baghdad and Iraq what Dewville is to Dallas. "His relatives didn't know good wine there in Ouja. They didn't even drink, much less go to Paris and spend ten thousand dollars a night," said one local acquaintance. In contrast, the new politicians and ministers— Nouri al-Maliki, Ahmed Chalabi, Jalal Talabani, and Barzani—have been living large out of the country. Their tastes are expensive, maybe even corrupted.

As I scribbled in my diary, Jamal motioned for his daughter to replenish the coffee table, this time with a painted ceramic bowl of bananas and oranges, and silver trays of assorted nuts, macadamias, cashews, and pistachios. Shapol and Sherien cackled like sisters across the way. Meanwhile, I asked Jamal what he expected of the United States.

"We are happy America got rid of Saddam Hussein; however, the U.S. and Europe have no coherent foreign policy on Kurds. We don't like people messing with Kurdistan. In Turkey you cannot even say the word 'Kurd.' America agrees with Turkey that you cannot negotiate [with the PKK]. Military force will not solve the PKK problem. How can you not negotiate?"

Washington's tone has become more tuned in lately, yet it is hard to tell if their words translate to deeds. "Military action alone will not end this terrorist threat," U.S. defense secretary Robert Gates said about the Turkish invasion of northern Iraq, following a meeting with the Turkish foreign minister in Ankara. "Simultaneous efforts should be made with nonmilitary initiatives—economic programs and political outreach. That is the only way to isolate terrorists from the population and provide a long-term solution to the problem."

That was a mouthful of sensible diplomacy, given that Kurds, our most reliable allies in Iraq, view the Turkish invasion as brinkmanship, as a feint to take control of Kirkuk's oilfields, and are unafraid to unleash the battle-tested peshmerga.

Predictably, Jamal favors an American base in the KRG, while at the same time he beat his fist against the table, saying the World War I–era agreements by Europeans should be forgotten. In a word, the KRG should have independence from Baghdad. Kurds, he seemed to say, are waiting for the right moment to make their move.

As I lined Jamal's family up for photos, he put a diplomat's wrap on our visit: "Kurds don't hate anyone. We like all nations, including Israel. We should all capitalize on this. I hope to see more educational exchange with America."

CHAPTER FOURTEEN

~

Saying Boo! to the Bogeyman

Amar Galaly awaited me with Othman Faiq, a fifty-something driver, from a farming village near Halabja. Othman was dressed in traditional costume and comes from a typical rural, agricultural Kurdish family. His father had four wives, who bore him six sons and twelve daughters. Othman was the oldest, with two wives and four sons.

The Kurdish community of Halabja became famous on March 16, 1988. Orchestrated by Saddam Hussein and cousin Chemical Ali, on that warm Wednesday morning the Iraqi air force dropped cluster bombs and cocktails of nerve and mustard agents into the slightly windy skies over Halabja. That day, and in the days that followed, some 5,000 residents perished. Another 15,000 were exposed to the gases, suffering burns, blindness, birth defects, cancers, neurological damage, respiratory diseases, and paralysis.

According to a 1988 audiotape published by Human Rights Watch, Chemical Ali, who was recently hung for his crimes, had forewarned a group of Iraqi officials of a planned gas attack on the Kurds: "I will kill them all with chemical weapons! Who is going to say anything? The international community? Fuck them, the international community and those who listen to them!"

Yet 15 years after the genocidal event, Arkansas rice growers had lost their stroke and Halabja was suddenly imbued with fresh political meaning: it became a central part of the rationale for going to war, to save Iraqis, if not the world, from Saddam Hussein.

In President Bush's Saturday morning radio address, three days before the Iraq invasion, he said, "The chemical attack on Halabja . . . provided a glimpse of the crimes Saddam Hussein is willing to commit, and the kind of threat he now presents to the entire world. He is among history's cruelest dictators, and he is arming himself with the world's most terrible weapons."

On one point he was consistent with American history: all of our foreign wars have been heralded by Washington's wizards as civilizing "missions" to save the world. In *Three Cups of Tea*, the author writes, "In times of war, you often hear leaders—Christian, Jewish, and Muslim—saying, 'God is on our side.' But that isn't true. In war, God is on the side of refugees, widows, and orphans."

On this day, we would visit Amar's aunt and uncle, victims of the gassing, who had only recently returned to Halabja following almost 20 years of exile. Amar last saw his aunt and uncle when he was ten years old, shortly after the genocide, when their families found shelter together in Red Crescent refugee camps in Iran.

There was a pattern emerging here: almost to a person, in all the random encounters I had in Iraq, everyone had been dislocated at one time or another.

⌒

The sky was blue and fresh scrubbed. Soon a raw wind laden with sand blew in and clouds gathered. It was the beginning of the November rains, which, *Inshallah*, would be plentiful through April. We turned off Highway 4 at Arbat, greeted by *peshmerga* and roadblocks, followed by market boys, their heads stacked two feet high with Kurdish flat bread. The Zagros Mountains rose gently to the east, first khaki-colored foothills and then buttery waves of cresting hilltops, lifting and falling imperceptibly into Iran.[1]

"The peshmerga lived in those mountains until 1991," Othman said, pointing across the plains of Sharazoor. "This is the breadbasket of Iraq. It has the most fertile soil in the whole country. Where I am from," he said, sticking a proud finger to his chest. Tobacco, wheat, and cornfields spread in a patchwork in various cycles of cultivation, freshly disked black earth and blond stubble to Irish green, swaying stalks of corn. "Two crops a year we get here," Othman enthused.

The poetry of the plains and mountains seemed timeless. Poets are honored throughout the villages of the KRG, and the statue of 15th-century Kurdish poet Walid Dewana, next to a bustling market, introduced us to the crossroads town of Sayyid Sadiq. There were no such memorials to villains or tyrants. Yet the ancient poets' retreats had been taken over by the redoubts of the PKK

---

1. In 2009, while hiking in these mountains, three Americans, Sarah Shourd, Shane Bauer, and Josh Fattal, were captured by Iranian soldiers. In September 2010, Shourd was released, while Bauer and Fattal were convicted on bogus spy charges and received eight-year sentences. Both were released a year later amid speculation that Iran was posturing for yet another prisoner swap.

(Kurdistan Workers' Party) and PJAK (an offshoot of the PKK fighting for Kurdish rights in Iran).

"Dewana, which in Kurdish means 'crazy,' was an impoverished, homeless shepherd," Amar said. "One day Crazy Walid stopped at a nearby mountain spring to quench his thirst, and came upon Sham, the sister of the Prince of Ardalan, who ruled over this region of Kurdish Iraq and Iran." Amar went on to tell the full legend of monkish reflection and unrequited love.

The shepherd poet fell in love and wanted to marry Sham but was roundly derided as a beggar and a fool by her royal relations. Heartsick, he withdrew into the mountains, which, at the time, were neither Iran nor Iraq, but just the high, ancestral pastures of Kurdish shepherds. There he lived out a meditative life in the twilight of a cave, writing poetry and succored by his wits, with "no friends but the mountains," goes the Kurdish saying.

Walid's star rose brightly after death, as villagers discovered his age-stained parchments of verse, which were published piecemeal as they sporadically surfaced. In the end, he had but one request: the stones of his grave should be as tall as his beloved Sham.

Beyond the plastered likeness of the robed, Greek-like profile of the famous poet was the five-mile road to Iran. We turned to the south, passing the village's cemetery, which advanced like a concretized roll call of Saddam's victims, climbing to a crag of granite overlooking the village. Midway up the tombstone-littered escarp, cordoned by an iron fence, were two tall stones, the height of Sham (perhaps), signaling Crazy Walid's burial site.

Upward, to the top of the ridge, like a sentinel of the ages, was the tomb of Sayyid Sadiq, the village's namesake. Sayyid is a term of respect for religious scholars, or denoting descent from the Prophet. "He was a holy man who came here a long time ago," Amar said. Several women fanned out through the cemetery placing flowers on family plots, while also paying homage to Dewana and Sayyid, with treks to the top.

The trail-wide road morphed into a sprawling new stretch of double-wide asphalt. Given recent protests in Halabja and the mud-hut farm villages in the plains of Sharazoor, the road was widened (something Saddam refused to do, they say, for tactical military reasons). We passed a blown-out bridge, a field of abandoned T-72 Soviet-designed, main battle tanks, 20 or more. It was not hard to imagine that someday the engines would be restarted. "From 1991," Amar said, "the last of Saddam's campaigns was here."

Amar is not alone in calling up 1991 as a red-letter year. Even so, the tanks and demolished bridge were menacing reminders of a time when tables were turned here in the KRG, when the Iraqi army entrenched along the Sayyid Sadiq road, blasting Halabja with artillery shells.

Today life went on along the fresh-tarred roadside. Amid sparse copses of blue gum, wedding parties were setting up rows and circles of plastic chairs and tables, adorned with mounds of food. It was Juma, holy Friday, a day of celebration.

⌒

The spanking new green and glassy agriculture college greeted us on the north end of Halabja. "Green is an Islamic color, the favorite of the PUK [Patriotic Union of Kurdistan]," Amar said. Soon we turned into the long forlorn driveway of the holocaust-like memorial for those who perished on March 16, 1988, and the days that followed. Two lone peshmerga guards signaled us to stop.

Rising before us from the roof of the museum was a modernist architectural sculpture of giant plaster arms pointed skyward, balled at the top in a clasp of fingerlike shapes, a metaphor of harmony and heavenly entreaty. A tattered KRG flag crowning the scorched, bombed-out memorial said otherwise.

On March 16, 2006, politicians from Baghdad to Erbil, along with hundreds of protestors, attended the 18th anniversary ceremony. Violence erupted; one student was killed, while the museum was looted and torched. Artistic and structural relics of the destruction that ensued still litter the once finely groomed grounds, the same force field that once hosted thousands of visitors, often families of victims, in a process of grieving and truth-finding.

Halabja's holocaust tourism, along with justice and tribunals, would have to wait. In the aftermath of the melee, "peshmerga roadblocks took away people's videos and cameras," Amar said. "All the pictures of the [mob] victims and rioting are gone."

As we walked the grounds, snapping photos, I asked Amar how the riot started.

"Ansar al-Islam and the Iranians encouraged everyone to burn the memorial in front of the celebrity politicians. The museum is no longer of interest to anyone here. The locals want real economic assistance," he told me, with an unstated resignation to the volatile nature of politics here (some would say a gestalt of perpetual revolt). Tribal by nature, as is most of the KRG and Iraq, Halabja is as different from Sule as Birmingham is from Boston.

As a potted background, the Kurdistan Islamic Union party was founded in Halabja, with many democratic goals and some not so pluralistic ones, among which is an Islamic state in Iraq. Though looked upon with a wary eye from PUK (Patriotic Union of Kurdistan) and KDP (Kurdistan Democratic Party) officials, the Islamic Union is now a mainstream Kurdish party, garnering 20 percent of the vote in KRG elections; Othman and his family and Amar and his father all support candidates of the Islamic Union, contending that the other parties are too corrupt.

On the other hand, Ansar al-Islam is a Kurdish Sunni Islamist terrorist group. Until 2003—when American Special Forces and peshmerga rooted out several cells—they were running terrorist training camps, hosting many Soviet-Afghanistan war veterans, north of Halabja. Some of those stateless terrorists are said to have included Abu Musab al-Zarqawi, who would eventually lead a campaign of bombings and beheadings, for what came to be known as al-Qaeda Mesopotamia.[2]

Saddam never controlled this border region, not unlike the autonomous Northwest Frontier Provinces of Pakistan today. By mid-March of 1988, Kurdish-Iranian forces had just routed the Iraqi army in Halabja. Indeed, at this time, Iran occupied all the Iraqi border cities. Halabja also was only seven miles from Lake Darbandikhan, a strategic reservoir that supplied Baghdad its water. In a word, Saddam was desperate.

By March 16, Kurdish peshmerga and 1,400 Iranian Revolutionary Guards occupied Halabja. Years later, Mark McDonald of Knight Ridder provided a bracing account of those events:

> All this movement certainly put Halabja in harm's way, although most townspeople hadn't heard that Saddam's troops were using chemical bombs on peshmerga units. But the Iranians knew. The curator of the Halabja museum believes they were setting a trap for Saddam in Halabja, a military ambush of sorts, as if they were daring him to use his gas and chemicals. . . .
>
> Right before the attack, Iranian troops quietly withdrew under the cover of darkness. But they left behind small teams of clandestine agents. The teams wore protective suits and gas masks, and they carried still cameras and video cameras. Tehran knew that pictures and video footage of an Iraqi chemical-gas attack would be a huge public relations victory in its war with Baghdad.

Iranian soldiers and the Red Crescent left the world photos of the grisly aftermath, the bleached and burnt corpses, women and children frozen on doorsteps. "Like a modern Pompei," wrote Samantha Power. Or as Iran's President Al Akbar Hashemi Rafsanjani put it at the time, "people fell like autumn leaves." Innocent civilians were the only ones in Halabja without gas masks and protection, able to smell the rose and garlic scents of the chemical bombs. Even with Western journalists on the ground within days, the fog of war rolled in: Iraq blamed Iran. Soon, American officials and newspapers, whether blind or indifferent, swallowed the plausible deniability of Saddam. After all, even though Iran had lost up to 50,000 of their own to Saddam's chemical attacks, they already had been the American-hating bogeyman for almost a decade. Given the threat of other border cities being attacked with

---

2. In years past, Ansar al-Islam has conducted decapitation campaigns around Halabja.

Saddam's chemical weapons, after Halabja, Iran's Ayatollah Khomeini's zest for apocalyptic war had diminished.[3]

⌇

The shiny green dome of the House of Charity mosque, rebuilt after being barraged by artillery shells and cluster bombs 20 years ago, peeked over Halabja's low-slung skyline. Othman and Amar drew to a stop in a torpid traffic circle at the end of Mokhtar Street. We all got out for a picture, as they bookended a statue of a fallen Kurdish father, Omar Osman, cradling his infant son.

The story behind the statue has become to Halabja what the iconic image of a little girl running down the road in the village of Trang Bang with her skin melting from napalm burns is to Vietnam; and what the charred corpses of Hiroshima and of the Atomic Bomb Dome is to Japan. Through the eyes of victims, the banality of evil knows no national boundaries.

Although obscured beneath a mantle of dust, layered and relayered by rains and daily winds, Amar said Halabja had been rebuilt since the 1988 massacre. "Everything is new," he said, "homes, mosque, shops, schools, fields, crops, trees, goats, sheep, and donkeys." Mercy Corps even built 50 houses here for the refugees returning from Iran and provided diapers and wheelchairs for people with disabilities, who are not hard to spot along the lethargic streets of Halabja.

In front of one municipal building, cluster bomb casings were used as ornamental gateposts, just as you see in bomb-ravaged villages throughout Laos and Vietnam. In a traffic circle next to the House of Charity mosque, a statue of Danielle Mitterand stood, honored for her largesse, for making Halabja a cause célèbre in France, in the immediate aftermath of the genocide (as opposed to 15 years later). There is no such public tribute to George Bush or America.

We turned onto a prosperous street of two-story homes, edging up against a tall security wall along a narrow, walled alleyway. Apricot and pomegranate trees, among the many fruit trees for which Halabja is famous, branched above the masonry walls on both sides of the street. As I hefted myself out of the back seat, Amar explained the various limbs his Uncle Mohammed Sheikh Janfar and Aunt Najiba Mahmudbag occupied in his family tree. "My mother is Sheikh Janfar's first cousin. And because Najiba shared her son's milk with my mother (both born in 1954), their son and my mother are brother and sister, which makes Aunt Najiba my grandmother."

"Then you couldn't marry one of Najiba's other grandchildren, who otherwise might be a cousin?" I asked.

---

3. Some argue that the massacre at Halabja provided Iran with the rationale to develop a nuclear capability.

"That's right, because of the milk. It's in the Koran," he assured me.

"Those are hard family trees to draw. I've seen a few where I come from in the South," I said, drawing self-effacing laughter from Amar.

"Welcome, welcome," Sheikh Janfar said, swinging open the gate, dressed in a dusty blue blazer atop a gray robe. A white prayer cap covered his hairless pate, while he twisted a black-and-white keffiyeh around his neck. "Sheikh" is a term of deference to age and status. Sheikh Janfar and Amar embraced, cheek kissing, each touching the heart; I followed, then Othman.

Arriving from behind the house, Najiba beelined to Amar, and then stopped a short distance away, taking his measure. She regarded his gelled hair shining as bright as his smile; then they pecked on both cheeks. Robed and "hijabed" from head to toe, Najiba's cultural reserve could not hide her familial joy at seeing Amar (whose mother had shared her milk).

In the garden, beneath a pomegranate tree, Najiba arranged red plastic chairs for each of us. Their journey from this address had begun 20 years ago: their home, as well as most houses on the street, was pancaked by Iraqi air force bombs. "They [the houses] were all like this," Sheikh Janfar said, slicing the air with downward-turned palms. Sheikh and Najiba had only lived in their freshly built, beautifully tiled, two-story replacement home for four months, which was when they repatriated.

It was hard not to notice that Sheikh Janfar's hands were thick and meaty, talons of a life of toil. For most of his years he was a farmer, growing everything from watermelons to aubergine, and raising goats, sheep, and chickens. He was also a petty retailer, with a shop that sold rice, vegetables, fruits, and soft drinks, providing for five sons and a daughter.

Their neighborhood is known as *sara*, or the center of government. And like many Halabjans, he was politically driven, if not imprinted, by the Cold War. "Sheikh Janfar was a communist before and not religious, but now he is religious and no longer a communist," Amar said, chortling at the gamelike fragility of geopolitics that Halabjans live with.

"One minute I could see; the next I was blind," Sheikh burst out with an emotive response to a question about how his family was affected. "For two months I was blind. My wife was also blind." Mercifully, his children were not, but they were all sick, suffering from vomiting and fiery red, burning eyes.

"Over 50 people on this street were killed," he said, with a tinge of anger but no self-pity. He did, however, glance to the sky to thank Allah.

Iranian soldiers helped Sheikh's family flee to the border, a half-hour away. There they were given atropine shots, and after two months Sheikh and Najiba had surgeries that cured their blindness. The Janfar family spent two years in the Red Crescent camps before being granted asylum in Bristol, England. (Amar and his family returned to Suleimaniyah at that time.)

Feeling their mortality—though both are a vigorous 76 years old—Sheikh Janfar and Najiba left their kids and grandkids behind in Bristol to live out their days in Halabja.

Najiba served us tea and plates of candied pomegranate berries. Soon my indulgence in the tasty repast caught their eye, prompting Najiba to produce a bottle of the red berry elixir. It's said to keep forever and is good for cholesterol, blood pressure, stomach disorders (and probably erectile dysfunction, says Amar). "I couldn't get it in Bristol," Sheikh complained.

Although he was once hunted by Saddam's henchmen for his affiliation with the Islamic Union and the communists, Sheikh Janfar says he is no longer political. Even so, he is noisy and bare-knuckled. "During Saddam's time the secret police watched what we were doing in the shop and market. Everyone is glad he is gone," he told me, then lashed out at the United States.

"Nothing has changed with the Americans here. They want oil," he said, rubbing his thumb smoothly across the fingertips of his left hand in the universal language that says money. "Americans can control the bombs, but they won't do it. They should just go home."

⌇

My last two days in country were spent in KRG's capital, Erbil. Abbas Lufti, a professor at the University of Salahaddin, played host to me. A journalist friend had introduced us. Abbas is a very dark-skinned Kurd, which he attributes to his family's origins in the Arab south, around Tikrit, near Saddam's home. Sporting a perfectly clipped moustache, Abbas is a smart dresser, always in dark pants and light shirt, with black, shiny, long-toed shoes that point upward, elf-like. His manners are courtly; he enunciates his fluent English with an elder don's certitude, with a hint of a London accent, even though he's never left the country.

Abbas has two wives, the first an arranged marriage with a cousin, the second a love partnership with the deputy dean of the language school at the university. "My cousin and I were married when we were very young, and now we have changed," Abbas told me, delicately explaining a common problem with arranged marriages.

Wives aside, "family ties are more important here [than in America]," he confidently assured me. "I live with my four brothers, sister, and parents. If one of them comes in at midnight, we all get up to see if they are okay. Not like you where you take off and don't check in every night."

Together Abbas and I drove the six-lane boulevards of Erbil, trafficked by a motorcade of old compact Mazdas, Nissans, Toyotas, and more spacious, newer model Opels, Peugots, Humvees, and Chevy Trailblazers.

On a Saturday afternoon we walked up to the ancient citadel of Erbil, claimed by many, especially in the precinct, to be the oldest inhabited city on earth. A stand-alone, gigantic mound at the navel of Erbil, the walled citadel is the mother of all tells. Everyone from the Assyrian scribes who wrote in cuneiform on clay tablets the *Epic of Gilgamesh* and the *Enuma Elish*,[4] the Adam and Eve of literary masterpieces, through the fabled warriors at the Battle of Guagamela (Alexander the Great and Darius III of Persia), to the gallant C-5 Galaxy pilots set to land at Erbil's new $325 million airport have borne witness to the citadel's earthen grandeur.

From the vantage point of the ancient citadel walls, we could see towering in the east like a latter-day Great Wall the 14 towers of Dream City (Naz), where condo units were selling for $180,000. Though the reverse is true more often here in the Middle East, the suburbs of Erbil were much more prosperous than the inner city.

That is not to say urban renewal is over in Erbil. Below us, at the foot of the citadel, the former Choli Bazaar and ancient cemetery were slowly morphing into the Nistiman Mall. Once finished, Abbas says, without tongue in cheek, this garish monstrosity will house 8,000 shops and 4,000 offices, bigger than Istanbul's Grand Bazaar (by no coincidence, I suspect). From boulevards to buildings, everything new in Erbil took on a heroic scale, a wannabe Dubai, they say, in the Iraq desert.

We ate lunch, salad, and kebabs in Ain Kawa, the Christian neighborhood in east Erbil, across the street from St. Joseph's Assyrian church. In 2003, thousands of IDPs fled to Ain Kawa from the south, while others went to camps in Syria and Jordan, abandoning their churches for the first time in 2,000 years. Some say that only half of Iraq's 1.3 million Christians remain in the country. Today, in Ain Kawa, they blend in as renters and house guests. Those who fled here, many from Baghdad's Dora neighborhood, could no longer pay insurgents the *jizya*, a special tax once imposed on Christians and Jews beginning in Mohammed's time, now paid as protection money and used to fund terrorism. The refugees' financial dilemma was only exceeded by the moral Catch 22 of what they were being forced to do. The Ain Kawa neighborhood is a well-defined four- or five-block square with a liquor store or bar on every corner, flanked by blast walls protecting the UN and American NGO compounds.

Abbas, like everyone in the KRG, talked about "before 1991" when the Christians fled to the mountains to avoid being press-ganged into Saddam's army. In the hills they would join up with the peshmerga. "Christians here are

---

4. Predating Israel's prophets and poets, the *Enuma Elish* story tells that in the beginning, according to Elaine Pagels, "God fought against a great sea monster, the dragon of chaos, to bring forth the world." John of Patmos, the Jewish messianic author of Revelation, invoked the same imagery to portray the furor of the end-times as allegory for the conflicts of his own days (as Isaiah and Jeremiah had done over six hundred years before).

not like Christians in America," Abbas vouched. "They are different. They have fought alongside and lived with Muslims for centuries."

Abbas was a crazy driver, understandably so given that he doesn't own a car and rarely gets behind the wheel. But in 2003, when the war began, Abbas was chauffeur and fixer for several American journalists. In those roles, he picked up their slang: "Okie dokie," he says in a southern accent; "Let's rock and roll" is an all-purpose call to action; "Say, bro," "I'm da man," and "Now we're talkin'" he throws out as if in the 'hood. His driving lingo includes (also with a southern accent) "Hang a Ralph," "Hang a Louie," or "Pick your lane, motherfucker." The list goes on, but you get the picture. Abbas pleasures in teaching this slang to his English students.

Abbas recommended that I stay at the Chwarchra Hotel, a couple of blocks from the Sheraton (at $300 a night, a proudly priced knockoff of the American chain). Only two years before, a major terrorist attack took place in front of the Sheraton, killing over 100 people and splattering flesh to its front door. On this Saturday evening, several robed, turbaned, and piously bearded Shia clerics from the south gathered around lobby tables of the Chwarchra. Guns and guards were more common than waiters and water.

After dinner, picking up my key at the front desk, where an evil eye amulet stared back at me, Abbas and I agreed to meet by seven the next morning. On the second floor, as if in a lockup or a psychiatric ward, a camouflaged, bearded guard glared at me, while sitting stock-still at the end of the hallway. My room, number 235, overlooked a bleak tumble of broken concrete in a back alleyway, from which I could hear some knocking around, like the rustlings of a foraging alley cat. After bolt-locking the door, I read a few minutes before falling asleep. That was around ten o'clock.

I've had a bad dream for as long as I can remember, for over 50 years. Now the dream only revisits me every couple of years, whereas at one time it was every few months. Its dark contours are always the same. After hearing footfalls—the intrusive clanging about of someone surely psychotic—a faceless stranger climbs through a window or keys an easy door, creeps up in the dark, and stands over my sleeping, frozen-with-fear body with a knife drawn, poised to waste me. My struggling moans grow louder as the dream progresses and my pulse quickens until I am jolted awake, usually in a sweat, threatened only by what's in my head. For a two-year period, I kept an army .45-caliber pistol in my bedstand, and as the dream unfolded, I would chamber a round and sleepwalk, checking the doors with gun in hand. How had this irrational fear inhabited me for so long?

It's a dream that revealed itself to me at an early age, in small-town America, yet it is not unlike the barbaric reality of everyday life in Baghdad or Baquba. My reflexive response in the dream—fear, sweats, and sleepwalking with a gun—is a human condition that says no such behavior is entirely random or arbitrary: psychologists assert that on average 3 percent of all populations have psychopathic tendencies. Presumably the dream—the conscious mind leaving the body on a night journey—could have been revealed to some dairy farmer in Sweden. Even outside of my somnolent wanderings—whether it's a political fabrication, a religious foreboding, a parental bugaboo, or a real trauma—fear comes from the awareness of a threat and feeling impotent to challenge it. Understanding the dream, or even managing it, and tamping down an overactive amygdala, where fear and aggression reside in the brain, often comes by saying Boo! to the bogeyman.

There at the Chwarchra Hotel, around three in the morning, I was deep within REM sleep. Vaguely, as if in *that* dream, I heard the bolt lock click open, followed by a key twisting the doorknob. As pitch darkness gave way to a seep of shadowed half-light, the low mumble of two men's voices drew closer.

"Hey, motherfuckers," I yawned while stumbling out of bed in nature's glory.

In a flash, the hall light crossed the faces of two men, the first one sporting an Iranian five-day stubble, the other with a full beard and an AK-47. One of the two stammered out something that could have been "sorry." In the same instance, they backpedaled, shutting the door behind them.

It was Iraq, and I was awake.

I threw on shirt and pants and slipped out into the abandoned hallway, and then down the unlighted stairway. The lobby was eerily empty but for a watchman sleeping in a chair, who wouldn't stir even after I kicked the table where his feet rested. Back in the room, sleep was impossible. The cat continued to knock around outside. Three hours later, Abbas arrived.

Incredulous, Abbas asked the desk clerk about the intrusion. Standing next to the head-sized evil eye charm, the fresh-faced attendant had no immediate answers, but as an afterthought, said the intruders must have been with security, mistakenly checking my room. I'm sure that's what it was, or it was whatever you wanted it to be, from falsely freaked out to some late-night gunplay. And although that gerbil down there in my inner-reflex box had slipped a step or two on a cognitive level, it felt as though I had been exorcised of that recurring dream. I had encountered some kind of bogeyman with a real gun and had survived.

That morning, Abbas, who brought along his brother Majeed, and I made tracks for the Turkish border. About 25 miles from Mosul, we crossed the white-stippled waters of the Lesser Zab River at Kalak, where Abbas and Mark McDonald, the American journalist friend who connected me with Abbas, had covered a three-day firefight between Saddam's army and the peshmerga and American Special Forces.

"Right over there a rocket hit," Abbas said, pointing to a gash in a fallow barley field. "We were over here." He pointed to a spot about 50 feet away from the blast. The Iraqi army occupied a looming ridge above Kalak, until they fled after being softened up for two days by American air strikes. "We found toothbrushes, food, clothes, and fresh fires by the river. They left in a hurry," Abbas told me, his words speaking volumes for the devalued state of the Iraqi army at the time.

Two hours later, as I bid adieu to Abbas, his brother Majeed, who served in Saddam's Iraq army, grinned mirthlessly at me and said, "Tell Bush, 'God Bless.'" They were the first words he'd uttered the whole trip.

On this day, a sucking noise was almost audible as Turkish journalists poured across the Iraq border returning home. I met four. They had given up on the invasion, the standoff to end all with the PKK. "Winter is coming. They won't invade until spring," Mahmut Bazarslan of NTV in Turkey, opined.[5]

If Mahmut's camera gear didn't give him away as a journalist, his khaki-pocketed vest and pants and his hiking boots were at least prima facie clues. Waiting together for the border guards to finish their hour-plus lunch, Mahmut imparted that he had run into a *New York Times* reporter in Zahok the night before. The reporter told him he was there to write a travel piece on the KRG, to which Mahmut replied, "Wrong story, wrong place, and wrong time." Ahem!

Mahmut also posited, in a scathing and impersonal tone, that anti-Americanism in Turkey was at record levels but not with Kurds. "Your popularity is going up," he said. "They think you are helping Iraqi Kurds. So they like you more, but everywhere else in Turkey it [popularity] gets worse for two reasons. Turkish people think you support the PKK (and KRG) and that Americans have a problem with Muslims. First you attack Afghanistan and then Iraq. I agree with this."

In Graham Greene's *The Quiet American*, as acts of insurgency and counter-insurgency ravaged a 1950s Vietnam, narrator Thomas Fowler comes to grips with it all when he realizes that taking sides is elemental to our humanity—war or peace? Not surprisingly, the choices in the Middle East can be more labyrinthine than Cold War Vietnam; the more questions I asked on this journey about anti-Americanism, the more that I felt like a cat chasing its tail: that the Venn diagrams one draws, to elucidate in this case religious, cultural, and geopolitical overlays, had turned to scrambled eggs; that the cast of victims and victors were beginning to trip over each other; and that the clarity and compassion inherent in the travel experience was being tested by the timeless nuances of tinderbox tribalism (often torqued by anti-Americanism).

One thing was clear on this day: I was traveling back to the future, to the American dream. Not *that one* you have to be asleep in to believe but the one by which the wizards of Washington live their waking days: that guns, God, and governance by a one-size-fits-all democracy will make the world more prosperous and secure, while taking the terrorists' bulls-eye off Americans.

---

5. As it turned out, Mahmut was wrong: in an attempt to upend the PKK's preparations for the ritual spring offensive, the Turkish army invaded in midwinter, only weeks later.

This self-delusion is beyond parody. Americans, as expats and tourists abroad, are more vulnerable than ever before. As of 2008, al-Qaeda was operating in over 60 countries. And it ain't the ideologies or "isms" that people in developing countries aspire to; it's the idea of hope, the promise of security, and the realization of success.

"They don't want communism," Fowler tells Alden Pyle, the American anticommunist zealot in *The Quiet American*. "They want enough rice. They don't want to be shot at. They want one day to be much the same as another. They don't want our white skins around telling them what they want."

"We invaded not Iraq but the Iraq of our dreams, a country that didn't exist, that we didn't understand," said Charles Freeman, Secretary of State James Baker's ambassador to Saudi Arabia during the U.S.-inspired emergency relief effort Operation Provide Comfort. "And it is therefore not surprising that we knocked the kaleidoscope into a new pattern that we find surprising. The ignorant are always surprised."

～

The Qandil Mountains unfolded around us, the no man's land where Operation Provide Comfort took place, where the Turkish army and PKK continue to battle it out. By no surprise, Efrem, my former driver, was lying in wait in the border parking lot, trying to scare up a customer, hopefully one he could punch like an ATM every time he needed gas or food. I turned down his services (and those obligations) and instead hired what I guessed to be a more time-conscious driver named Osman, who all but swore on mama's grave that we would be in Diyarbakir in three, at most, four hours.

Once on board—gestures filling the void of common words—Osman signaled that he wanted to pack my bag with ten cartons of Marlboro Lights. The cartons were all sealed and felt like cigarettes inside, so I agreed. As expected, once on the Turkish side, inspectors searched my rucksack, randomly opening two cartons. The search was conducted on the Habur Bridge, where a Turkish flag fluttered, while at eye level was a welcome banner that read "Peace at Home and Peace Abroad," an aphorism about hope that the great Atatürk proclaimed for the nascent Turkish republic. On this day it reminded me more of the American Air Force's motto in Dr. Strangelove, "Peace Is Our Profession."

Satisfied that we were a mere brace of petty smugglers, the border police let us pass with our merchandise and without a bribe. We were within the legal limit of smuggled Marlboro Lights, I judged.

What I failed to anticipate was that for the next seven hours the unlikely duo of Osman and this American would become traveling Marlboro Light salesmen. Osman stopped to smoke and barter with every Kurdish shop owner from the border to Diyarbakir, until the Marlboro Lights were "finish," a new word

I taught him in the heat of my protestations. "Finish," he would reply almost mockingly, after each sale and 15-minute stop and palaver. Even as he dropped me two blocks from the Caravanserai in Diyarbakir, there was no bon voyage moment, only "finish."

My guess is that Osman made $30 from the smuggled Marlboros, on top of my generous fare—nothing to sneeze at for a day's hustle. He knew he had one shot at me before I retreated from his catch-as-catch-can, duty-free zone of border chaos. After a restless sleep and an early flight, the next evening I devoured two $30 martinis at the posh Four Seasons bar in Istanbul, about the average monthly income of 4,000,000 Iraqi IDPs and refugees.

Journeys, it is said, begin and end at home; that is, we are products of our environment. On that night in Istanbul my thoughts kept returning to that room in Erbil, the intrusion of the two men with guns, and to the dream that has haunted me since I was an impressionable tyke, where I am powerless from fear. At that bar I recalled in a sudden leap of memory: the dream must have come to me at age 6, when a 28-year-old neighbor, Bobby Joe Burns, decapitated his mother on a Sunday evening and then left her severed head, wrapped in a white sheet, on the altar of the Immaculate Conception Church. My father was out of town when the grisly murder occurred, so while the local police searched for Bobby Joe, my mother, brothers, and I secured all the windows, drew the curtains, double-locked the doors, and jumped at shadows. All the while, a rapt city tuned into the hourly radio news.

Thankfully, Bobby Joe was captured a day later across the Arkansas River in Oklahoma. Once interviewed, while eating candy bars and drinking a soda, he said that he was enacting an Aztec-style sacrifice and, quoting the Book of Revelations, that the orders had come from God. A diagnosed schizophrenic, Bobby Joe spent the rest of his life in the state mental hospital.

So why do my unfulfilled and countless childhood dreams of being a sports star, of performing uncommon feats of valor, not recur with the regularity or nagging persistence of the one that haunts me? It must be that fear, both real and imagined, is the most vulnerable and potent of my—our—emotions. Fear is that inner terror that arises when threatened; that preys on hope, vision, and virtue; and that is the fundamental force behind both the War on Terror and anti-Americanism. For me it is like watching my mind in a bad B movie, while sitting on the edge of my seat, hoping for an intermission. For those 4,000,000 refugees and other Iraqi victims of war, especially the children, mutilated bodies and headless corpses are no isolated neighborhood episode, no dream that dissipates with morning. It is the everyday life they live with and have fled from since the American invasion. It pierces and twists in their guts like a hookworm, the animal spirit intruding.

"This is a farewell kiss, you dog," a shoe-throwing Iraqi journalist said to President Bush one year later. "This is from the widows, the orphans, and those who were killed in Iraq."

PART II

~

A THEOCRACY

CHAPTER FIFTEEN

~

A Wall of Mistrust

November 4, 2008, broke early and fast for me, caught in the slipstream of a Jaguar, zooming across the delta lands of eastern Arkansas at 90 miles an hour. I was traveling to Little Rock from Memphis, where two young white men had just been arraigned for plotting a killing spree against blacks. These self-described white supremacists told police that their rampage was to culminate in the assassination of Barack Obama. While wearing white tuxedos and top hats, the featherbrained duo intended to take the presidential candidate out in a drive-by, blazing away with assault rifles.

Tuesday's Child, Lila Marie, my granddaughter, was born to giddy parents Bethany and Wes, just after noon on that day in Little Rock. A few hours later, next door to Lila Marie's room, another miracle came into the world, Benjamin "Barack" Kimbrough, whose mother is a Little Rock attorney and father is president of the historically all-black Philander Smith College, Little Rock's peer of Atlanta's Morehouse. The Kimbroughs' newborn was named not just for the 44th U.S. president but also for Morehouse president Benjamin E. Mays, who 40 years before had eulogized his most famous student, Martin Luther King Jr., following his assassination on the balcony of the Lorraine Motel in Memphis. In the hospital hallways and our respective rooms and houses, that night the Karbers and Kimbroughs celebrated election returns with tentative fist bumps. And, later, when President-elect Obama gave his acceptance speech in Grant Park to the jubilant, 250,000-strong crowd, who chanted "yes we can," it was silent tears and goose bumps.

There in Little Rock, 50 years ago nine African American students had been turned away at the doors of Central High School. The defiant segregationist policies of Governor Orval Faubus forced President Eisenhower to mobilize the 101st Airborne and federalize the Arkansas National Guard (in which my father served 25 years as an artillery officer and pilot). As a descendant of a 200-year-old, pioneering Arkansas family, the election of Obama was redeeming. Liberating for the majority of Americans and the global community, it was political time travel, from a country lost in fear and hubris in another meaningless war to one that, once again, suddenly held the respect and hope of the world. Instead of the London headline that appeared the day after the 2004 election—"How Can 59,054,087 People Be So DUMB?"—the *Sun* newspaper in Britain borrowed Neil Armstrong's moon-walking quip, describing the election as "one giant leap for mankind."

Nelson Mandela wrote in a letter to President-elect Obama, "Your victory has demonstrated that no person anywhere in the world should not dare to dream of wanting to change the world for a better place."

In Tunisia, the *Al Chourouk* newspaper said, "Today America elects the president of the world." In southeastern Turkey, villagers sacrificed 44 sheep for the 44th president and raised signs smeared in blood that read, "You are one of us." Or as a political science professor in Istanbul put it, "The U.S. needs a facelift and he's the one who can give it."

In general, however, the Islamic world was skeptical, given the ongoing wars and refugee crises in Afghanistan and Iraq, the torturing of Muslim prisoners at Abu Ghraib and Guantanamo, and the blinkered U.S. support of Israel's heavy-handed treatment of Palestinians. In fact, on November 4, with scant attention paid in the international press, Israeli forces, which later claimed the tenuous ceasefire with Hamas had been broken by rocket attacks, raided a beleaguered Gaza and killed six Palestinian militants. After that incursion, violence in Gaza rose sharply, culminating on December 27, with 80 Israeli fighter planes bombing the bejesus out of the 60-year-old refugee camp. Israel Defense Forces then invaded.

In Iran for the first time since the 1979 Islamic revolution, the president sent a congratulatory letter to President-elect Obama. Like America—in which right wingers called Obama the anti-Christ while sales of Bushmasters and armor-piercing bullets surged over fears about gun control ("he'll take my gun . . . bullets first," said one acquaintance)—Iran is a nuanced, paradoxical society, far from one-dimensional: Persian, Shia, tribal, nationalistic, rich, poor, educated, illiterate, secular, theocrat, wise, and foolish. Hardliners in Iran criticized President Mahmoud Ahmadinejad's letter while reformists praised it. "Too many people believe you have to be either for or against the Iranians," said Admiral William Fallon, former head of Central Command over Iraq and Afghanistan. "Eighty million people live there, and everyone's an individual. The idea that they're only one way or another is nonsense."

November 4 was also the 29th anniversary of the Islamist student takeover of the U.S. embassy in Tehran. Fifty-two American hostages were held for 444 days, an embarrassing episode that arguably cost President Jimmy Carter the election to Ronald Reagan. In support of the 1979 Islamic revolution, the students were reacting to the arrival in the United States of the exiled shah of Iran (Mohammed Reza Pahlavi), who had been forced to step down nine months before. The roots of the revolution go back to 1953, when, after ousting the popularly elected prime minister Mohammed Mossadegh, a CIA and British-backed coup restored the shah to power. The plot to overthrow Mossadegh was hatched in the American embassy.

Paraphrasing Ryszard Kapuscinski in *Shah of Shahs*, the American embassy siege happened in an unforeseen moment. The cumulative fear and terror of all those years of torture under the shah's secret police (SAVAK) broke like a fever, followed by a serene sense of liberation and clarity. Then, as always, the oppressor's days were numbered.

For Americans, a wall of mistrust and fear of Iran has existed since the 1979 embassy takeover; for Iranians, the 1953 CIA coup imbues their nationalist psyche with the same organic sentiments. Meantime, staying in the swim is paramount for policy makers on both sides of this 6,000 mile crevasse, and woe betide the career of anyone who suggests a bridge: appeasers of terrorism versus toadies to the Great Satan, goes the Manichean polemic. It's the power of religious conservatives in both countries to dress up myopia in the name of piety, to agitate and keep fear in the minds of their flock. On a more subconscious level, we are all predisposed to hear what we are afraid of or, to a lesser degree, what we hope for. So, as Americans cast their votes for and against Obama, who is open to dialogue with Iran, radical Islamists in Tehran celebrated the anniversary by marching around the American embassy, brandishing "Death to America" placards. "After all, anti-Americanism is among the main features of the Islamic state," said one high-ranking cleric. Frankenstein, it would appear, there in Iran, was off the table once again.

⌒

Two weeks after Obama's election, on a KLM flight from Amsterdam to Tehran, the Dutch stewardess clapped eyes on the book I was soaring through, *Dreams of My Father*, by Barack Obama. "I want to read that," she gushed. "We [the Dutch] stayed up all night to watch your elections. We paid more attention to them than we did our own." The Kurdish-Iranian-Canadian man sitting next to me, tall and broad shouldered as Kurdish men appear next to their Persian counterparts, smiled in agreement. It felt good to once again be an American overseas, as a people to be defined by something other than fear, militarism, and shoddy capitalism.

Only days before I had been in France, where 93 percent of the country favored Obama. Not since 1919 had France been so smitten by an American president. Then it was Woodrow Wilson, who was celebrated on a presidential visit to Paris for the progressive idealism of his 14-point proposal: "The streets were lined with laurel wreaths and flags," wrote Margaret MacMillan in *Paris 1919.* "On the walls, posters paid tribute to Wilson, those from right wingers for saving them from Germany, and those from the left for the new world he promised." While I was in Paris, kudos for America flowed faster than the Bordeaux. At a dinner party given by my Parisian host, attendees, Parisians all, agreed over a tipsy chorus of toasts that France, which has never even had a black judge (nor has any other European country) would not yet elect a dark-skinned minority to the nation's highest position (for example, a Turk in Germany). It had been too many years of having the world's opprobrium heaped on us. A dramatic U.S. election seemed to have put a sharp point on the double-edged phrase "American exceptionalism," coined by Alexis de Tocqueville, in his book *Democracy in America*, to describe our profound differences with other nations.[1]

⁓

Soon we touched down at the Ayatollah Khomeini International Airport 40 miles outside of Tehran. The Kurdish man leaned over and said, "Welcome to Iran. What governments say is rubbish; it's the people who count."

Iranian women, who moments before were dressed sexily, many like Parisian models, and had just finished KLM glasses of white wine, were now chewing gum and complying with the mandatory hijab laws, wrapping their heads in scarves and bodies in *roopoosh*, long coats known by the French term *manteau* (not the shapeless look of a chador, but form fitting). For them, it seemed the paradox of East meeting West was a minor fashion adjustment. Beneath the surface, perhaps, a more culturally complicated turn of some mental dial was taking place. Iranian women, it is often said, bedevil the ayatollahs more than Zionists or the Great Satan of America or even a nuclear war!

The Dutch stewardess said goodbye but not before expressing disbelief that, as an American tourist, I had come to Iran for two weeks. Assuming she wasn't an Islamophobe, her incredulity had merit. Of all nationalities that travel to Iran, only Americans are fingerprinted (and vice versa for Iranians traveling to the United States), are required to have a special visa approved by the Ministry

---

1. In 1919, six months after President Wilson was so widely celebrated in Paris, he returned to the city and found empty streets; his promises of a new world had been scattered to the four winds by a U.S. Congress who didn't share his vision.

of Culture, and must be escorted by a tour guide. No independent travel here for Yanks! So it's natural, as a fresh American arrival, to feel a vague ambivalence of gut fear and gleeful expectation, to harbor more than a few jaundiced assumptions, and most of all, given the news coverage and bellicose modern history between the two countries, to want to avoid too much attention.

Beyond the line of immigration officers' booths, appearing like menacing shadows, were the grim-faced portraits of Iran's two most famous ayatollahs: Ruhollah Khomeini, the patriarch of the 1979 Islamic revolution, and Ali Khamenei, the current Supreme Leader, who, according to the constitution, is elected by an Assembly of Experts. When Khomeini died in 1989, a witness claims to have seen a light pass between the two ayatollahs. Taking my place in the foreigner immigration line in the barnlike terminal, along with five or six others, a thirty-something man in front of me picked up on my American accent. As I oriented, the man bellowed for all to hear, "Are you on a Christian tour? The Prophet Daniel is buried here. The tomb is over 3,000 years old."

"No, no, I'm not," I gasped, in whispered tones, desperate to shut down this stranger's rat-a-tat-tat bombast about my perceived agenda of just visiting Jewish and Christian pilgrimage sites. Dressed in red jogging pants, a Japanese baseball shirt, and a narrow-brimmed, black fedora turned sideways, his togs, his booming voice, and smarmy manners made me think L.A. gangbanger.[2]

"You say no you're not Christian," raising his voice even louder, almost defensively. "Okay, don't go to the Prophet Daniel's tomb. But you should see the ziggurat in Shush (Susa). It's five stories, built 5,000 years ago by the Elamites."

An Iranian man in a yellow golf shirt and blue sports coat, a peer of mine, with his glasses laid professorially across the bridge of his nose, and standing in the line next to us, leaned over to say, "The Elamites were not Aryans [like us Persians]. They were Semites." Lookers-on mumbled in agreement. Suddenly they were all jousting in Farsi and back to English; it felt like Persian history ping pong, and I was the tautly drawn net.

The younger man was indeed from L.A., here for two months on an extended honeymoon with his new Shirazi wife, who would move to the States as soon as her visa was approved. He had done as many Iranian American men do, return to the Islamic Republic for a bride. The choosing was all his: beautiful Iranian women, cousins and others, line up to emigrate to the United States or Europe. These pairings are often arranged in cyberspace. The lure of prosperity and perhaps individual freedoms (shucking the chador) outweighs the lost sense of place and cultural stigma every Iranian feels living abroad. In spite of all the aren't-you-Frankenstein encounters they endure as exiles in the States, Iranians

---

2. Or maybe he was affecting the look of the *laat*, the neighborhood thugs that make up the Basij, the million-strong vigilante force controlled by the Revolutionary Guards.

have a sense of community in places such as L.A., where over one million reside—the result of two generations of postrevolution brain drain. These weren't
boat people like the Vietnamese or Haitians; they all arrived aboard jumbo jets.
After all, Jimmy Delshad, the former mayor of Beverly Hills, is Iranian (or Persian, as they prefer to be described in the United States to blunt the association
with the current Islamic Republic).

Always open to local insights, or introductions, after finally getting a
chance to give more than one-word answers, I told the gathering crowd of
locals and Iranian expatriates that aside from Tehran I would be traveling to
Yazd, Shiraz, and Esfahan. With that, the L.A. guy cut to the chase, "The best
looking women in Iran come from Shiraz." Another man, shouting across the
crowd, who lived in New York, disagreed, "Don't say that. Tehranis are the
most beautiful women."

"I know these things," replied the man from L.A., splaying his hands in an
authoritative gesture. "The best-looking women in China are in Suzhou. I've
been there. I know about beautiful women."

Christian tours, Jewish pilgrimage sites, and objectification of women (which
bordered on men's nooky talk) were not the subjects I had imagined discussing my first few minutes in the Islamic Republic of Iran. Forget about sliding
in under the radar, I thought. But it was a first dose of the trademark Iranian
tendencies to school a stranger on Persian history as a living enterprise, and to
engage in *tarof*, or small talk, which is often contrived to keep up the pretense
of politeness. There it was just as I had been told by travelers before me: Iranians are genetically hospitable and incurably social. A Norwegian friend, who
bicycled 30,000 miles around the world, told me the most hospitable people he
met on his intrepid, two-year journey were from Texas and Tehran! When Iranians see you alone they will ask if you lost your ship and invite you home, for
they are rarely alone. And when Iranians travel they wonder why no one ever
asks them anything. At those times they miss the pleasure of human warmth.
There is a Farsi saying that goes something like "Come in; put your feet in my
eyes. We are honored to have guests."

⌢

It was three in the morning, but I wasn't jet-lagged; my senses now seemed more
sharpened than normal when up in the predawn hours. Mysteriously, I wasn't
detained for fingerprinting, which, by all accounts, takes an hour. The female
customs agent, robed in a black chador, had given me a pass. Beyond the open-
air baggage claim was a buzzing crowd of relatives, family friends, hawkish cab
drivers, and alone, displaying a sign, Mira Mahdavi, my guide for the next two
weeks.

It didn't take long to figure out that Mira is an independent Iranian woman. She has never been married in spite of many opportunities. Mira is hardworking, intelligent, and attractive at 47 years old, with big, lively brown eyes, a reassuring yet self-deprecating smile, and brimming personality; her bleached bangs are rarely covered by the colorful headscarves she wears, which seem to inevitably (perhaps by force of gravity) slide off the back of her head.

Most Iranian men do not accept her lifestyle or job, which is full of financial reward and personal freedoms that she relishes such as escorting English-speaking foreigners around Iran and taking outbound Iranian tour groups to places like India, South Africa, Italy, France, and the UK. The Islamic Republic banned booze but not travel. In her spare time in Tehran, she goes to the Goethe Institute for German lessons and cultural activities, while also corresponding by e-mail with many American friends. She owns a house in trendy north Tehran, where she watches after her parents, both of whom, like Mira, are secular. Having observed many of her friends in miserable marriages or now divorced (at a rate of one in five), and her parents marking time in a loveless relationship, she is content carrying on with life outside of a traditional Iranian marriage. The joy of family comes from her time with her only sibling, a brother, a road engineer, and his wife and children, her much adored nieces and nephews, who live in Nowsud, a Kurdish city near Halabja, on the Iraq border.

Mira would like to travel to the United States but has repeatedly been denied a visa, in spite of recommendations by a number of well-placed Americans. Even with her U.S. supporters, because she is single, those responsible for issuing visas see her as risky, a husband hunter, disfavored in two countries for never being married. Although I was on my own in Iran more than expected, for my two-week windshield tour I would learn about the Islamic Republic through the prism of Mira Mahdavi (and trust her like a big sister).

～

It was misty and chilly on the predawn ride into Tehran. The plaintive tones of a sitar played on the radio. Along the four-lane road there wasn't much illumination, until the four minarets, like giant stems of shiny gold crowned in an imperial haze of emerald, encircling the mausoleum of Supreme Leader Ayatollah Khomeini, came into view. It was hard to make out in the half-light, but next to the mausoleum was a martyr cemetery, in which 36,000 heroes of the Iran-Iraq War are buried. Oil was the prize, beginning with the Iraqi invasion of southwest Iran's oil-rich province of Khuzistan. Tehran paid dearly in this brutal war of attrition that took a million lives, two-thirds of them Iranian. Since Ayatollah Khomeini had dispatched so many young martyrs into the war, often unarmed and unawares, to clear mine fields with their exploding flesh, he chose to be buried next to them.

In the eight-year war, America armed Saddam Hussein and Iraq (until later in the war when the United States tilted to Iran), while Iran received weapons right along from Israel, which saw Persians and the mullahs as less threatening than Saddam and the Arabs. Henry Kissinger coldly summed up the circular drift of our hardware diplomacy: "Too bad they can't both lose."

"Welcome to the Axis of Evil," Mira said, tongue in cheek, as the driver slowed, perhaps deferentially, to pass the mausoleum. I had been to Iraq and North Korea twice but never to Iran. So her words had more meaning to me than she probably knew, but her laughter was not about me or anyone else completing some self-indulgent, travel trifecta known as the Axis of Evil. She was poking fun at the arrogance and ignorance of George Bush's use of the phrase, especially since Iran's borders were calm until the United States invaded two of their neighbors. At the time Bush had used the melodramatic epithet in his State of the Union address—January 29, 2002—Iran's reformist President Mohammad Khatami had just wielded his influence with the Northern Alliance in Afghanistan, which was chiefly composed of Persian-speaking Tajiks and Hazaris, to help defeat the Taliban. We soon found out how much words matter as Obama-the-candidate often asserted during his campaign: Bush's offensive remarks (along with Donald Rumsfeld's bumbling) tilted the focus away from our common interests of Iraq and Afghanistan and ridding the world of the Taliban and al-Qaeda and toward the balance of conservative political power in Iran. There it has remained since the 2005 landslide election of hardliner Mahmoud Ahmadinejad (who won with 62 percent of the vote).

No one likes to be called evil, even those who might be. And only the rare public official sees, at least in real time, the political evil of their governments. For the proud descendants of Cyrus the Great to be linked to the likes of modern-day madmen Kim Jong Il and Saddam Hussein was an offense not taken lightly.

Sleep was fitful that Friday morning, the Muslim prayer day. Mira was off work, and most businesses were not open until late in the afternoon. Staying at the Laleh International Hotel (which was the Intercontinental before the revolution), I joined what felt like a gathering of nations for lunch on the top floor. A million tourists a year come to Iran, but most of the random people I was meeting in the hotel's Internet café, speaking to in the elevators, or just overhearing in the buffet line seemed to be doing business here: Chinese, as Iran's largest trading partner, were most evident. Additionally, there were Russians, Poles, French, Arabs from the Emirates, Turks, South Koreans, Swiss, Spanish, Swedes, Australians, Japanese, British, Germans, Italians, and even a Vietnamese journalist from Ho Chi Minh City. While drinking a Diet Coke, bottled in Iran (Mashad), under a license from the Emirates (sanctions be damned), "Where were the Americans?" was a first impression on my first day in Iran.

That afternoon I walked stretches of Vali-e-Asr Avenue, the longest street in Tehran, and formerly known as Pahlavi Street. The last of Iran's monarchs, Reza Shah Pahlavi and his son Mohammed Reza, built Tehran into a modern city. That it was Friday meant a small breather from the smog and horrendous traffic for which Tehran, a city of 14 million people, is now famous. Plane trees and *joops*, concrete ditches for canalling glacial runoff from the snowy peaks of the foothills of the Alborz Mountains bracketed Vali-e-Asr in the upscale north of the city to the working-class slums of the south. The milky runoff is used to wash carpets and to irrigate parks and gardens along its urban course. Beneath the street, ancient *qanats*, or water channels for irrigation and drinking (which is potable to all), shared space with a modern subway system. Shopping malls, theaters, restaurants, parks, and confectioner shops competed along this modern byway with bigger-than-life portraits of martyrs and ayatollahs, whose turbaned mugs are wallpapered across the buildings of Iran with the same ampleness as a beret-wearing Che is found in the neighborhoods and business districts of Cuba. Just as in the days of the last shah when his portrait appeared on every corner, this tradition may be more about propaganda than popularity. And if importance here is measured by a portraits-in-public standard, President Mahmoud Ahmadinejad, the black-bearded face of Iran, as seen in America, was almost nonexistent (at best, he is a side show, Sancho Panza to the ayatollah's Don Quixote).

∼

When Americans arrive in Paris, they often beeline to the Eiffel Tower, in Rome it's to the Vatican, and so on. Only in Tehran would an American tourist feel the same gravitational pull to their former embassy, now known as the "U.S. Den of Espionage." And who could forget the streaming video of the embassy takeover, firebrand students chanting the revolution's new slogan, "Marg Bar Amrika," or Death to America? To most Americans, it was equal parts terrifying and mystifying. While lowering and burning the cursed American flag, they raised the iconic countenance of a grandfatherly, otherworldly Ayatollah Khomeini, who had recently returned from 14 years of exile, mostly in Iraq via Turkey. The ayatollah's 1963 opposition to the shah's secular reforms known as the White Revolution, which granted women access to the political and bureaucratic realm, landed him in jail; and his 1964 protests against the capitulation laws that gave immunity to American servicemen in Iran (a hot button issue over four decades later in Iraq) raised his political stature geometrically and led to his deportation.

"He [the Shah] did not understand that even though you can destroy a man, destroying him does not make him cease to exist," wrote Kapuscinski in *Shah of Shahs*. "On the contrary, if I can put it this way, he begins to exist all the more. These are paradoxes no tyrant can deal with. The scythe swings, and at once the grass starts to grow back. Cut again and the grass grows faster than ever."

Fifteen years later, and nine months before the '79 embassy siege, the spontaneous turnout for Ayatollah Khomeini's messianic arrival, from his brief residence in the obscure French village of Neauphle-le-Chateau, by a chartered Air France 747, was just shy of what one might imagine if the missing 12th imam (the Mahdi) came whirring through the sky on his return to herald an earthly paradise (as with Jesus). With a crowd of up to four million crushed in the streets for his homecoming, Khomeini raised his hands in appreciation from his slow-moving blue-and-white Chevrolet. The populist struggle of the oppressed against the ruling class had begun. "We are not the people of Kufa," the crowds chanted, an allusion to the 7th-century betrayal of the third imam, Hussein the martyr. Revolutionary tribunals and eight years of war followed.

Spin cycled into the ferment of old anxieties and great expectations, many Iranians thought, including students here and abroad, that they were not only saying goodbye to the oppression of the shah and SAVAK but also welcoming a mainstream nationalist leader. It was a "heady state of utopian promise and practical disorder," reported the *New Yorker*. "The factories were closed. The ministries were in chaos. . . . Everyone was engaged in revolutionary activities, slogans and shouting."

With fear as their bond, what they got was more of the same but this time forged in Khomeini's cruel cast of mind and wrapped in the strict laws of Sharia, which were imposed, against the opposition of the vast majority of Iranian ayatollahs, under a theocratic dictatorship (*velayet-e faqih*). The Islamic republic turned a thousand years of Shia practice and tradition on its head. "Only one party, Hezbollah (the Party of God)," became the catchphrase of hard-core Khomeini followers. For or against, kill or be killed, and God's paradise or the Great Satan was the new order. Not since before Iran's Constitutional Revolution, which occurred between 1905 and 1911, had clerics controlled the legal system. Many universities were closed; intellectuals, writers, gays, minorities, and modern women were treated as a fifth column. Western influences, music, books, haircuts, ham sandwiches, and neckties were banned, while free enterprise and free speech were squelched. It was Kapuscinski's classic example of despotic behavior: strike fast and hard to suppress; then, when forced to, step back and tap into the rational part of the brain.

In 1989, months before the Ayatollah Khomeini's death, his presumptive successor, Ayatollah Hossein Montazeri, was sidelined when he wrote to the Supreme Leader: "Your prisons are far worse than those of the Shah."

Since Khomeini's death, political liberalization has occurred, if only in fits and starts. The Shia concept of *ijtihad* allows flexibility in governance according to changing circumstances. Thus in Iran, civil society and social freedoms remain a constant tussle between modernity and antiquity, and reformers and radical reactionaries. As there have been good and bad popes, the ayatollahs, who wield papal-like influence over Shias, are a mixed bag. Other than the Vatican, Iran is the only nation in the world run by clerics.

⌁

On the tree-lined corner of Moffateh and Taleqani Streets, the embassy, once a fearsome fastness, is now an imperious-looking brick barracks for Iran's Revolutionary Guard. Not unlike the USS *Pueblo*—which was captured by the North Koreans in 1968 and is now parked on the Taedong River, in the center of Pyongyang—the embassy is a trophy piece for the Revolutionary Guard to flaunt. In the crisp air at a mile high, at approximately the same latitude as Washington, D.C., with the Alborz Mountains rising majestically in the background, camouflaged guard towers peered out of the foliage like urban deer stands. The guardians of the Den of Espionage do not allow single-celled monsters, known as foreigners, to enter. The fortified brick ramparts, topped with sharp-tipped steel pickets, are washed in splashy murals and shopworn invective. Like the pithy suras on the sidewalk walls near most public places in Iran, these fighting words might just make today's gunslingers stutter: "The U.S. is too weak to do anything"; "We will make America face a severe defeat"; "Today the U.S. is regarded as the most hated government in the world"; "Under God's grace we shall give in again to the dictatorship of no government even the United States"; or "Portrayal of Great Satan from the States, stroke of 19 August [day of Mossadegh coup in 1953] to November 1998."

With the fervor of a first-time arrival at some Hyde Park rant, I took photos of the inartful denunciations, the Supreme Leader's fearmongering props, unchanged with the election of Barack Hussein Obama. Soldiers, students, mullahs, and the odd couple, abandoned in their own worlds, passed me without notice. Not even a glance was given to the desecrated Star of David or the wall-sized American flag, with a skull-faced Statue of Liberty in place of the stars. Even the house-size banner, depending from the trees, with a portrait of a Basiji martyr branded with the Revolutionary Guard logo—an AK-47 overlaying a globe, sandwiched between Koranic verses—an insignia adopted by Hezbollah, which I had seen so often in Lebanon, didn't appear to stir anyone's interest.

CHAPTER SIXTEEN

~

Coca-Cola and KFC in Tehran

My second day in Tehran, after visiting the former American embassy, Mira Mahdavi and I walked through the cedars and plane trees of Park-e Shahr, not far from the Golestan Palace. In the center of the park, near a fountain and re-flecting pool aligned with the snowy peaks of the Alborz Mountains, we stopped in at a 19th-century tea (*chay*) house, to map out our day. A man carrying a load of stone bread, laid across his arm like a pile of small rugs, seated us on a car-peted divan, rimmed in pillows that we laid against. Softly illuminated kerosene lanterns, shaded with green and red globes, hung from the walls. In a moment, a pot of tea appeared, surrounded by amber sugar crystals and plump dates. A *ghalyoun* (hookah) followed, loaded with Egyptian sweet apple tobacco, which explained the fragrance in the air. Mira abstained but said that even though the clerics forbid hookah smoking by women in public places, said to be too arous-ing for men to watch, more and more women are partaking.

She told me about teahouses during the Qajar dynasty (late 18th century until 1925), a time in which storytellers stretched on the divan with you. Simi-larly to watching an episode of a TV serial such as *Friends*, which is fabulously popular in Iran, you had to go to the teahouse a dozen times to apprehend every fork and fuse of the storyteller's epic novel. In the 1960s and '70s, with the introduction of television, the storytellers disappeared. I was told they are now making a sentimental comeback.

Mira, who was 18 at the time of the revolution, from a middle-class family, spoke with intensity about the impact the ayatollahs have had on her family, women, the economy, and the rest of Iran. "After 30 years I am still not used to wearing the scarf and this coat. As soon as I get home or to the room, I throw them off. Girls must comply with the hijab laws beginning at age 9, the legal

206

age for marriage since Khomeini lowered it from 18 years old." She then echoed words I had heard before: They [clerics] steal your identity and empty you of your own individuality, in an attempt to create models. And as we know, models are just robots, not individuals.

Mira talked about the segregated culture, having to ride at the back of the bus or subway, or often in separate train cars and in separate classes at university; and that the judicial system under the laws of Sharia still allows stoning of women for adultery, while her testimony is given half the weight of a man. "We never expected to have to go back in time like this. My parents, my brother, everyone thought our economic situation would improve. In '79 the Iranian rial was 70 to a dollar; today it is 10,500. A refrigerator costs $70 then, now it is $1,200." Indeed, Iran now has the fourth-highest inflation rate in the world, behind Zimbabwe, Uzbekistan, and Burma.

"So what has happened to the money?" I asked.

"The Revolutionary Guard took the shah's assets, and now they control most of the big business," she said with a wry tilt of the head. "And the *bazaaris* (who were close to the clerics before the revolution) monopolize the export and import trade. We're back to where we were; a few people have all of the money, and there is a lot of corruption." The state and large Islamic foundations (*bonyads*) that are run by the ruling oligarchy of clerics have resisted private enterprise in the same way they oppose free speech.

⌒

While living in Hanoi for five years, I learned that almost every Vietnamese had a tragic family story, borne out of the French and American wars. And, as in Iran, Vietnam's martyr cemeteries were common and crowded, which meant that "corpses" were central to any national vision. In both countries, in the 1980s, citizens were encouraged to turn in neighbors, friends, and family for suspicious activities, a mirror of the Soviet model. "Even today cabbies in Tehran are known for their big ears," Mira told me. "We have a government hotline. You just dial 113 if you think someone is talking or acting suspicious."

In the early 1980s, Mira was denied entry into Tehran University but not because of her academic record, for that was superb. VEVAK (ministry of intelligence and security) agents had called on an old neighbor and discovered that Mira's brother spent time in prison, for guilt by association, during the Iran-Iraq War. Her brother's best friend was executed for his activities with the People's Mujahedin of Iran (PMOI), who fought an armed struggle against the shah and later the Ayatollah Khomeini's Islamic Republic.

Just as in the days of the shah, media or individuals who publicly criticize the government are censored and punished (though the privacy of homes remains sacred). "We can't believe what our politicians say about the world, so now we go to the Internet or listen to the BBC," Mira said. Nabokov, quoted in *Reading Lolita in Tehran* by Azar Nafisi, gave this basic human right philosophical expression when he said that "curiosity is insubordination in its purest form." Iran ranks number three in the world in weblogs (even President Ahmadinejad has one). As fast as Big Brother's firewalls go up, young Iranians, who are eager Internet surfers and social networkers, are building taller ladders, proxies to the forbidden addresses. "I listen to Voice of America on the radio because the government blocks it on the Internet, the same as they do YouTube or Facebook or any women's fashion website," Mira said, while pausing between thoughts. "That's the problem with having a theocracy. Men of God are not supposed to lie. The Koran says lying is a sin. But politicians must lie, so religion and politics don't mix." She admitted, however, that the clerics' hold on this dual sovereignty would take a couple of political generations, at a minimum, to loosen.

Almost all anticolonialist revolutions have paid lip service to the poor and uneducated, known by Stalin as "harnessing the masses." Although full of egalitarianism and leftist ideology, Iran's revolution was different only in its rejection of conventional political models: Khomeini's and the theocracy's appeal, if not that of the radical populist Mahmoud Ahmadinejad, has been its pandering to the working class, antimaterialist crowd; they not only arouse religious passions with Koranic injunctions and promises of justice for the faithful when the Mahdi returns on Judgment Day (a page from every successful evangelical American preacher) but also tap into Persian nationalist tendencies. The ruling class here, Mira said, could care less about the minority opinions of the secular elite of north Tehran (or those who have fled the country). "Villagers rarely question what the clerics say; they just go along with it," she told me. "Now, though, they can only afford meat for their family a few times a week, so they are not happy."

As we were leaving the teahouse, Mira told me that before the revolution villagers and poor urban neighborhoods didn't have good roads, schools, electricity, potable water, and television, but now they do. Even today freedom of speech is far less important to them than employment, food on the table, and equal rights: a sense of justice borne out of Imam Hussein's martyrdom at Karbala 1,400 years ago. For all that time, the Iranian self-image has evolved to that of David fighting Goliath: the elite power, the Great Satan of America, and the suspicious foreigner exploited by the ayatollahs better than any leaders hitherto.

Literacy rates under the shah were 42 percent; today, they are approaching 90, while 65 percent of the enrollment in universities is women, a ticking time bomb for liberation. Ironically, it's because Iran is now an Islamic state that working-class parents are comfortable with sending their daughters away from home to live on their own in a college dorm (unlike the secular days of the shah). It could be said that a penny of progress out there in the provinces has made for a pound of political capital in the palaces of the privileged.

⌒

Five hundred years ago, in the village center of Tehran, first there was a brick and mud citadel, or *arg*, built by the same Safavid rulers who adopted the Twelver Shiite faith as the official religion. (Some would say to further differentiate Persians from Sunni Ottomans, an archenemy.) After the eunuch Agha Mohammad Khan, the first of the Qajar kings, had his Zand predecessor tortured to death (and the eyes of 20,000 followers put out), he moved the Persian capital from Sari to Tehran.[1] The site of the old citadel then became the Golestan Palace.

Holding his AK-47 at port arms, the guard at the Golestan Palace's Gate of Happiness practiced his halting English by asking me where I was from and how I was enjoying Iran; he then welcomed us into the four-walled Persian garden, while professing his love for America. Seventy percent of Iran's population is under 30, and they all have been or will be required to take English for six years, in primary and secondary schools. As I stepped by the guard shack, a class of up to 40 early adolescent girls emerged from the garden, wearing black chadors all, and talking faster than I could respond. "We love America. What do you do? Do you have children? How old are you?" Peering from their closely veiled faces, in a sea of beautiful almond eyes, one girl's sky-blue orbs stood out like those of a Siamese cat.

Golestan translates to "rose garden," but for at least 2,500 years, since the time of Cyrus the Great, the Persian four-walled garden (*chabar bagh*) has been called *pairdaeza*, or paradise. The objective of all Persian gardens, I would learn, went beyond aesthetics to a spiritual realm, a prefiguring of heaven to come. Even predating Cyrus and the biblical account of the Garden of Eden, in nearby Mesopotamia, 6,000-year-old cuneiform tablets were found that recorded the Sumerian god of water, Enki, ordering the sun god, Utu, to "create a divine garden by providing fresh water to transform the parched land of Dilmun . . . into a paradise with fruit trees, green fields and meadows." To Muslims, the number 4 has cosmic importance, so the symmetrical and aesthetic articulation of buildings, reflecting pools, and rills of rippling water and blooming plants gives off a spiritual essence. Garden rills were once used by the wealthy to wash their dead before taking them to the morgue.

The Qajar king, Nasser al-Din Shah, who traveled to Europe in the late 19th century and helped re-create paradise here, blended more than a few secular,

---

1. Castrated at birth, the first of the Qajar kings would die the way he lived: he was beheaded.

aesthetic flourishes that he discovered abroad. Along the palace walls Impressionist hues of pink and yellow Arabesque swirls, along with cameos of bare-breasted maidens and kings bagging lions, outdid traditional Islamic geometric mosaics of Persian blue. A room-sized marble divan—idyllic for coronations, greeting dignitaries, and perhaps opium smoking, an indulgence that remains popular throughout Iranian society—sat on a veranda of vaulted mosaic ceilings and archways that gave way to the rose gardens and reflecting pool. Along with several Qajar kings before him, Reza Shah, the founder of the House of Pahlavi, was crowned here in the Audience Hall.

Until this day, the Shia tradition that upholds an individual's dual persona—conservative political conduct in public and a permissive way of life in private—has its role model in the courts of the Safavid and Qajar kings, who studiously kept their pursuits of pleasure hidden from the eyes of the masses (similar to a G-string and gold finery covered by a chador). When Iran television showed the last shah toasting U.S. president Jimmy Carter with a glass of wine, many Iranians, who often suffered from food shortages at the time (and clinging to their Korans), hit the streets in protest.

Last year, for the first time since the revolution, the Golestan Palace complex, which includes seven regal buildings, was opened to tourists. Even though the Islamic Revolution ostracized all symbols of extravagant wealth, known as *toghouti*, or royalist, thankfully the Golestan was not destroyed in a Taliban-style disregard for historical monuments.

We paused briefly next to the palace complex's Queen Elizabeth II wing (as Mira called it). Built in 1955 for a brief visit by the British monarch, it now serves as a library. Next door was the Hall of Mirrors, a grand vestibule giving way to a stairway of towering walls and ceilings, all covered in geometrically pleasing puzzles of silvery, gilt mirrors. Bracketing the head of the stairs were two eight-foot-tall, scimitar-shaped elephant tusks, which fronted the former harem, now hidden behind a wall of stained glass. The atmospherics were an odd mix of a Gilded Age New Orleans bordello and the fancy glasswork of a Bangkok Buddhist temple, revelry and reverence all in one.

The fabulous luxury displayed at the Golestan Palace, which elevated the status of the monarch, family, and friends but did nothing for the masses, was only matched by the crown jewels found a ten-minute drive away in a basement vault of the former Central Bank of Iran. We parked in the Melli Bank alleyway, and once downstairs, as we proceeded in church-like reverence, alarms went off every time someone brushed a display window. After all, the Safavid and Qajar kings had rummaged from Europe through Asia for these glittering spoils of war. In the 18th century, an invading Afghan ruler stole most of the collection and turned it over to the Mughals of India, who returned it and more when forced to by a Persian army expedition dispatched across the Indus River with a single mission: bring back the jewels. They did, and the jewels that have not since been plundered are at least, if not more, impressive than the collection found in Istanbul's Topkapi Palace.

Entering the dimly lighted vault through a metal detector, with guns and guards more numerous than visitors, we passed the Peacock Throne (aka Naderi Throne). The royal perch is not the original one taken from India but was nevertheless once inlaid with 26,733 jewels. Similarly to the theft of antiquities when Baghdad fell, Mira said rampaging looters had stripped the throne of most of its jewels in the early days of the revolution. Meantime, the whole subterranean room twinkled in iridescent flashes as if one were sky-walking through the aurora borealis. Every facade was of some fanciful design of rubies, sapphires, emeralds, and diamonds; egrets, plates, cups, trays, hookahs, snuff boxes, purses, sabers, ostrich eggs, baby rattles, toy balls, and the shah's and Empress Farah's crowns were all there. Standing somewhere between the jeweled globe, embedded with 51,633 precious stones, and the 182-carat Sea of Light pink diamond, said to be the largest uncut diamond in the world, was a baldish, slightly slumped, sixty-something man; he sported cowboy boots and a western-cut blue blazer, and talked in a suspicious accent. I poked him in the back, and, in my best southern drawl, said, "Hey, cowboy, what brings you to Dodge?"

He wheeled around like he'd heard a ghost, and replied, "Where you from?"

"Fort Smith, Arkansas," I shot back.

"You don't mean it; my mother lives in Fort Smith. I was born in Dardanelle (70 miles away) and have been living in Vicksburg, Mississippi, for the last 30 years."

Don Banks was the first American I had seen in Iran. He was in Tehran for an Asian-sponsored rock mechanics seminar. For 30 years, he was a geologist with the Corps of Engineers but now consults (and knows a whole bunch about why those levees broke in New Orleans). Don told me he'd gone through hell to get a visa, only receiving it two days before his departure, but that the conference was well worth it. "I went to the one in Singapore last year. It was interesting as well," he said. Don knew my wife's cousins down in Vicksburg. We talked a few minutes before he took off to catch up with a field trip, to the outskirts of Tehran, to see bridges, tunnels, and dams. That's what he was here to do. Before leaving he confirmed the obvious, "If you want to know why the revolution occurred, look around."

～

Before dinner we paid a visit to the 19th-century Grand Bazaar, redolent in size, style, and name of the one in Istanbul. Beneath the domes and archways we tunneled through a brisk crowd of shoppers. Only three weeks before the shops were empty, the *bazaaris* had gone on strike and closed up over the value-added tax imposed by President Ahmadinejad and the mullahs. Because *bazaaris* control a sizable portion of Tehran's retail trade and money lending, they got their way.

That evening the nearby Kayam Restaurant was bustling. Mira and I grabbed the last divan next to a long table lined with a family of Iranian Americans from Los Angeles, all drinking Coca-Cola products. The Californians were in Iran for the first time since the revolution for a relative's funeral. When I asked about their trip, aside from the mention of the funeral and thumbs-up for Obama, there was a lot of eye rolling—code for Tehran now versus then. The music of Shahram Nazeri, a Kurdish-Iranian, contemporary classical singer, who wailed the romantic epics of Hafez to the accompaniment of a sitar and drums, played in the background. Around the multilevel room, puffs of fruit-smelling tobacco rose from fresh hookah blasts, curling in clouds to the contours of the vaulted and domed roof. Soon the Californians were lapping up *ghorme sabzi*, a split pea, spinach, and lamb stew served over saffron rice, crusted brown like cornbread. Mira said all Iranians in the diaspora go crazy thinking about this Persian special. We had *ghorme*, too, along with aubergine in a red sauce.

With the election of Barack "Hussein" Obama, namesake to the great Shia martyr, I thought Iranians would be as electrified as the rest of the world. He does, after all, have many close friends and relatives who are Muslim. As a child he lived in Indonesia, the largest Muslim country in the world. As Senator Obama he opposed the Kyl-Lieberman amendment which, by designating Iran's military as a terrorist organization, opened a door for Bush to attack Iran; as a candidate he promised to "engage in aggressive personal diplomacy" with Iran and not seek "regime change." All said, in my mind, President-elect Obama is an aspirational story, one that should be regarded as a role model for all Muslim kids, not least those named Hussein (which means "good" and "handsome" and is so common it is often given to babies from a secular background). Those kids who might otherwise go astray, I thought, now have a fresh alternative to consider.

And that may happen, Mira agreed, but she was only cautiously optimistic. The night before she had listened to the radio and learned that Hillary Clinton was being considered for the job of secretary of state. "She is a very strong woman, not a joke like Sarah Palin. We will see what she and Obama do," Mira told me. During the campaign, candidate Clinton said on *Good Morning America*, "I want the Iranians to know that if I'm the president, we will attack Iran (if it attacks Israel). In the next ten years, during which they might foolishly consider launching an attack on Israel, we would be able to totally obliterate them." Even as liberal as Mira is, why would she not be skeptical? She is Iranian and a realist. Plus, "Iranians are patient," wrote Robert Baer in

The Devil We Know. "They think in centuries, eras—unlike the Americans, who think in fiscal years."

Mira told me that when Arabs invaded the Sassanian Empire in the 7th century, when Zoroastrianism was still the centerpiece of Persian cosmology, women wore white cotton like in India. "At the time, Persians had cool, underground water for dogs and horses while the Arabs were still looking," she said. "The men hid their women when the desert Arabs arrived talking of peace and the new religion. Persians knew what the Arabs were up to and have been hiding the women ever since." The Iranian-against-Arab dilemma was partly resolved 1,400 years ago by Hussein, the martyred grandson of Mohammed, who had a Persian wife.

Dinner ended with tea from a steaming, water-heater-sized samovar, plates of mandarin oranges, dates, and *bamia* (maple-brown spirals of sugar and starch). Before we left, Mira pointed out that, coming from India to Iran in the 19th century, the family of Ayatollah Khomeini's grandfather crossed the path of the many Zoroastrians who settled in India seeking religious freedom. The former Supreme Leader was not pure Persian.

⌒

The next morning, after reading the *New York Times* on the Internet in the hotel's business center, I found a copy of the *Tehran Times*, an English-language newspaper, in the lobby. The headline read, "Iran Executes Mossad Spy." Ali Ashtari, a salesman of electronic devices to Iranian military bases and intelligence centers, who had apparently just been publicly hung, was convicted of selling secrets and giving advice to Mossad. "During the 20-month-period that he was in prison, he elaborated further on his espionage activities, and these clarifications showed what type of information the Israeli intelligence service is seeking inside Iran," an Iranian official told the newspaper, with more than a hint of Guantanamo-like incarceration.

Though Iran (317) ranks second behind China (470) in the world in verifiable executions, with the United States (42) coming in a distant fifth, behind Saudi Arabia (143) and Pakistan (135) but ahead of Iraq (33), I was struck by how the execution of Ali Ashtari was front-page news and not swept under the rug by some "official." After being in Iran a few more days, however, it was apparent from the daily English newspapers that Islamic Republic officials, who control the press, have the heebie-jeebies over Israeli spies. Every day appeared a new Israeli spy caper. And there is a basis for suspicion: the mysterious 2007 demise of nuclear scientist Ardeshire Hassanpour, who worked at the Esfahan uranium plant and was found dead at his home from gas poisoning. Letter bombs and poisoned packages are also all said to be a part of the "dirty war" conducted by Israel. In light of Israel's admission of spying and sponsoring terrorism in Iran, and Iran's backing of Hamas and Hezbollah militias, which many Iranians resent because of the drain on national resources, the Islamic Republic knows how the counterinsurgency game is played.[2]

The rest of the headlines in the Tehran newspaper that day, November 23, 2008, might have appeared in most international papers: "Can Obama Change the Game"; "Iraqi Parliament to Vote on U.S. Pact Wednesday"; "Russia Threatens to Cut Off Gas to Ukraine"; and then there was "No End to IAEA 'Ambiguous Words.'" Iran's speaker of the *majlis* (parliament), Ali Larijani, addressed a seminar of Basij, the million-plus paramilitary force Ayatollah Khomeini organized, and used the news to slam the IAEA (International Atomic Energy Agency) and the U.S. manipulation of international institutions—a means of justifying its adventures, the article alleged.

At breakfast with Mira, I asked her what Iranians thought about the nuclear program, the same one that began with American political and technical support in the early 1970s under the shah as a collateral source of energy. "Everyone is different, but most people I think see it as a right that we have just like India and Pakistan and Israel. We need nuclear for electricity and medicine."

Since the number of centrifuges has grown from a few four years ago to over 5,000 today (with headlines in the *Tehran Times* on another day that said their goal was 50,000 in five years), I asked her about nuclear weapons.

"It's like the eight-year war; the clerics are being hard headed. I don't think it's that important to the people. Iranians just don't like to be told what to do." Indeed, polls show that 60 percent of Iranians are not interested in nuclear weapons (chiefly because of a fatwa issued by Ayatollah Khamenei that says they go against the Islamic precept that forbids killing innocent civilians). With those who are, Mira said it's a Shia justice and self-sufficiency issue; threats only harden their resistance and strengthen their bonds of fear. The clerics, who are sworn enemies of the State of Israel, are wary of American-style diplomacy: carrots and sticks are for donkeys, they say.

During the campaign, Obama proposed that in return for Iran abandoning their nuclear program, as president he would advocate for economic investment in Iran, its admission to the World Trade Organization, and restoration of diplomatic relations between the two countries. Not that Mira was being disingenuous, but with Iran on the verge of launching a satellite, using the

---

2. Iran's suspicions of a Mossad conspiracy in the assassination of Ardeshire Hassanpour has gained merit. Four more scientists have now been assassinated, mostly by limpet mines attached to cars: Massoud Al Mohammadi, a particle physicist (January 2010); Majid Shahriari, a senior figure in the nuclear project (November 2010); Darioush Rezaei Nejad, a nuclear physicist (July 2011); and Mostafa Ahmadi Roshan, a deputy director at the Natanz uranium-enrichment facility (January 2012). In February 2012, Iran responded with attempts to assassinate Israeli civilians and diplomats in India, Georgia, Azerbaijan, and Thailand.

same technology that can deliver a nuclear warhead, leaders in Europe and the United States do not believe the nuclear program is for peaceful purposes such as power generation.[3]

We talked about Iranian hardliners who see a weakened America, given the misadventure in Iraq, the escalating problems in Afghanistan, and the global economic calamity, led by a fast and loose Wall Street. Iran is not an island, immune from it all. "President Ahmadinejad was elected for his economic platform, to improve the common Iranian's life," Mira said. "Holocaust denial and making Iran's nuclear program the cornerstone of foreign policy were never mentioned in his campaign." Four years later, depressed oil revenues, which account for 85 percent of Iran's budget, coupled with inflation reaching 30 percent and unemployment above 20 percent, may prove to be Iran's own Achilles heel and lead to compromise. In the 1990s, when oil plummeted to $10, Iranian leaders were much less independent-minded than when it skyrocketed in 2008 to $147. "Money changes all the iron rules into rubber bands," said Ryszard Kapuscinski, who, as a journalist, witnessed 27 revolutions and coups.

～

Behind oil, Persian rugs are a distant second source of export revenue. A few blocks from the hotel, next to the Museum of Contemporary Art, is the Carpet Museum, both of which were created and dedicated by Empress Farah. Inside, a map of Iran, freckled with blinking green lights, marked the 40-odd villages where carpets are made; it's an industry that goes back 2,500 years to the Achaemenid dynasty. All things Iranian, drawn with both symmetry and minimalism in mind, could be found in the woven images of these carpets: the poems of Rumi, Sa'di, and Hafez; Zoroastrian symbols and the Zodiac; peacocks and nightingales; suras and folktales; and flowers and fruit trees. There were even long excerpts from Ferdosi's *Book of Kings*, the *Shahnameh*, imaginary portraits of the great imams Ali and Hussein and, since the revolution, the face of Mohammed. Motifs of Persian gardens, often laid out in a cruciform shape to depict the life cycle, in which water flows in the four directions, birth, death, life in this world, and the hereafter, were a recurring theme.[4]

---

3. In January 2012, both U.S. secretary of defense Leon Panetta and Israeli defense minister Ehud Barak said that Iran could have a nuclear weapon in one year. What remains unclear, at least by open source estimates, is whether Ayatollah Khamenei has approved the weaponization of Iran's nuclear program.

4. A Persian takeoff on the four rivers of the Bible and Koran that flow from the Garden of Eden: Pishon, Gihon, Tigris, and Euphrates. The Tigris and Euphrates headwaters are in Turkey, and the two rivers come together near Basra, Iraq. Located below the Temple Mount and Dome of the Rock in Jerusalem, the Gihon Spring was the main source of water for the biblical City of David. The location of the Pishon is unknown.

"For Iranians these carpets simulate life," Mira told me. "Not just for the sake of imagery but because of all the weaver labor that goes into each carpet. Before Iranians were interested in carpets for an investment, but now it is more for the love of the work of art. Real estate is for investment."

An hour later we were driving past the former Sheraton, now the Azady (Freedom), and the Independence Hotel, the former Hilton. We were traveling north up Vali-e-Asr Avenue, through Tehran's more upscale neighborhoods such as Elahiyeh and Shemiran, a continuum of economic ease. Given President Ahmadinejad's irresponsible dumping of Iran's cash reserves into the economy, there was a liquidity-driven boom going on, and real estate prices had doubled in the last year. In Tajirish Square, a glassy new high-rise mall and condo complex was going up. New Mercedes and BMWs were not uncommon. An electronic pollution meter stood on the edge of the traffic circle, tracking the current particulate matter in the air. Today, here in the foothills, it was tolerable, but west Tehran was ringed in a rust-colored mushroom cloud. "On bad days people don't go out; schools close," Mira said. "And if they have to go to the store, they wear masks. Ten thousand a year die here from respiratory problems caused by pollution."

Still on Vali-e-Asr Avenue, we turned up what could have been Rodeo Drive, embowered in plane trees and flanked in high-walled estates, European embassies, chic cafés, and luxury retailers: Chopards for fine jewelry, Rolex and Lacoste stores, miniaturist art galleries, yuppie chocolate and coffee shops, Pizza Cafés, and even a KFC takeoff, Kabooky Fried Chicken.

Although I didn't see a SpongeBob SquarePants roller coaster, with this spectacle of opulence and shop-till-you-drop mall mentality in north Tehran, it was evident that Khomeini's anti-Western policies were losing ground, social taboos were being eroded, and *gharbzadegi* (or Westernitis) was in the air. Valentine's is now a day of love for many young Tehranis. Because of rising real estate prices, Tehranis are waiting until their 30s to get married (but not for sex). Along the streets many young men wore spiked hair, one with a Metallica T-shirt. Heavy metal and Iranian nationalism are not incongruous passions here. Women—the modern version of the sensual fair sex written about by Ferdosi almost a millennium ago—showed their curves in garish, tight fitting outfits and scarves that fell to the back of their heads, with tattooed eyebrows, sparkly mascara, and taped noses, a status symbol here. Iran is, after all, number 1 in the world in nose jobs and hymen reconstructions.[5] And, as women's fashion turns more aggressive, tummy tucks and boob jobs may be next; it is undeniable that, at some level, there is a sex revolution going on here.

---

5. "Protective fictions are more important than the truth," wrote Azar Nafisi.

Freedom, as Kris Kristofferson and Janis Joplin sang, is just another word for nothing left to lose. The extreme deprivations imposed by the Islamic Republic are only exceeded by the immoderate reactions of Iranian youth and the 30s and 40s age group of the secular middle and upper classes (many of whom receive remittances from their relatives abroad). Enjoying a love affair with all things Western, not the least among this crowd's indulgences are the wild parties that go on behind the shah-era high-walled estates. Although I was never in attendance (or invited), Mira and others filled in the blanks: drinking bootlegged whiskey and wine; snorting coke and meth; smoking marijuana, hashish, and opium; one-night stands; group sex; and dancing to rock 'n' roll tunes are all in the social cocktail of north Tehran. Given the high unemployment among Iran's educated youth, in which there is reportedly one job for every 100 engineering graduates, drug use is a popular pastime and drug dealing a rising profession. It is a small wonder since it is estimated that over two million Iranians, or 3 percent of the population, are opium or heroin addicts.

A few minutes drive from Tajirish Square, the security was heavy outside the Mellat Palace. The 1,000-acre complex of lakes, fountains, and woodlands of blue spruce, sycamore, and pine was the idyllic setting for the summer homes of the Pahlavi family. Billowy clouds and the snowcapped peaks of the Alborz Mountains formed a natural tiara atop the White House of the shah. Oddly familiar from photos, the palace was built by Reza Shah in the 1930s. Approaching the palace from a long driveway, we stopped by the former 24-foot bronze statue of Reza Shah, now cut off at the knees and only eight feet tall. Imposingly, the self-aggrandizing folly once stood in front of Tehran's central train station but was reconfigured and brought here after the revolution.

The psychic energy expended by Iranians in building and destroying these Pahlavi monuments has been both colossal and comical: up they went when the last shah assumed power in 1941; down they went after democratic elections occurred a decade later; then back up after the 1953 CIA-backed coup restored the shah to the throne; and, once again, torn down after the '79 Islamic revolution.

The palace was filled with European cut-glass chandeliers and porcelains, and bronze busts and portrait paintings of the last shah—not least was him in a Napoleonic pose on a white horse. Vivid murals of Ferdosi's Book of Kings had the royals spearing lions, while the venerable Rostam, the book's celebrated paragon of strength and courage, duels in a two-day battle with Prince Esfandiyar, who had swam in a pool of invincibility. Downstairs, in a spacious office was the (alleged) former desk of Marie Antoinette, from which the shah would deliver his annual Noruz (Persian New Year) address. "The only time we saw the shah was sitting at that desk, talking on television once a year, and then of course, when he was drinking wine with President Carter," Mira said.

Two hours later, we fell down out of the foothills, into the inchworm pace and press of Sunday afternoon traffic. Facing us was the Azadi Tower, the Islamic Revolution's marble-cut symbol of freedom. On one's first sighting of the Tehran landmark, sans the flocking hordes, the architectural sculpture comes off as vaguely familiar, like some bird that you can't quite put a finger on when or where you first saw it: it has the grandeur of the Arc de Triomphe but with a hint of the curves of the Sydney Opera House and the height of Nelson's Column in Trafalgar Square. The modernist, 150-foot structure, which once housed a cinema, was commissioned by the shah in 1971 to commemorate 2,500 years of the Persian monarchy. At the time it was called Shahyad, which means "remembrance of the shahs." Showcased in the center of one of Tehran's busiest intersections, near the shah-era Mehrabad Airport, before the new international airport recently opened, the grandiose tower gave arriving visitors their first impression of the city.

Azadi Square is now one big traffic jam, except for when the festive faithful gather during the Ten-Day Dawn, which commemorates the Islamic Revolution. On February 11, the actual day of the revolution, President Ahmadinejad, always sporting his trademark, working-class beige windbreaker (never a necktie), delivers one of his firebrand speeches to cap off the ten-day celebration. It's the Iranian Fourth of July, charged with nationalistic passion.

Mira made light of the reductive power of the foreign press to breathlessly report on events held here, taking the whole Iranian culture down to the least common denominator of a few, ranting extremists and mad mullahs. Nurturing Islamophobia is titillating, self-reinforcing news: they're radicals, and we're reasonable; they're medieval, and we're modern; and they hate freedom, and we don't, goes the two-dimensional typecasting. Instead of fireworks displays or parades of veterans playing and singing martial music, or wearing hats that say "America Love It or Leave It" or "We Support Our Troops," here they chant and wave anti-Israel/America signs and listen to the Great Satan panegyrics of Ahmadinejad (whose bellicose bombast doesn't hold a candle to that of Israel's Avigdor Lieberman).

It's ironic in the extreme that this ostentatious symbol of freedom and revolution was designed by a Baha'i architect, Hossein Amanat, selected by the shah and whose religion originated in 19th-century Persia but is now banned in the Islamic Republic. The nine lines and windows that score and fenestrate the monument are taken from Baha'i symbolism. Baha'is believe in one God but embrace a universe of messengers: Krishna, Buddha, Zoroaster, Abraham, Moses, Jesus, and Mohammed. A branch of Shia Islam, the founder, Baha'u'llah, is said to be the personification of the "Hidden Imam," or the Mahdi, which is apostasy to the occultation beliefs of the Twelver Shias of Iran.

The light showers ended, but the congested road—mostly of '70s-vintage Peykans, infiltrated by a smattering of newer German, Japanese, and Korean models—remained slick. Lickety-split, in the shadow of the Azadi Tower, a bus rammed into us, taking off the rearview mirror and smashing the minivan's right front door. A much larger van, whose driver abandoned his passengers and hightailed it from the accident scene, had hit the bus from the other side, forcing it into us, narrowly avoiding a cartoon pile up. The driver may have been drunk, Mira suggested. While traffic bottlenecked and exhaust fumes stung the eyes like cinders from a fire, the drivers dialed the police a thousand times. As it turned out, the driver who fled need not have left the scene; the police never arrived, partly due, perhaps, to the impenetrable nature of the traffic. We fled to the nearby Mehrabad Airport.

~

CHAPTER SEVENTEEN

Desert Gardens, Imam Hussein, and the Eternal Flame

Mira and I checked in together at Mehrabad Airport but parted at security into gender-segregated lines. For internal flights, Iran Air uses a fleet of German-made Fokker 100s, but to get around the sanctions the planes and parts are purchased from Russia. "Effective sanctioning of Iran is a dream," wrote Robert Baer, former CIA agent, in *The Devil We Know*. "Iran's regime is still standing after 30 years of sanctions—still able to buy anything it wants from Russia or China."

The stewardess told the pilot that a foreigner was on board, so he gave updates in English instead of Farsi. Upon takeoff my seat fell back in the reclining position; otherwise, in spite of the embargo on spare plane parts, the Iran Air equipment was fine and the flight was short and smooth. Soon we were in Yazd, the Silk Road–era high-desert city, not known for its liberalism, but friendly in a provincial, Mayberry way. As we crossed the tarmac and entered the terminal building, a frightening old harridan, all nose and no teeth, stepped in front of Mira and scolded her about her scarf, followed by an elevator lecture on local mores. In Iran, the penalty for a woman who refuses to cover her hair is 80 lashes. The dress enforcer was of the rural underclass, the favored clients of the revolution. Reluctantly, Mira made a slight forward adjustment with her scarf.

It was after dark when we arrived at the Moshir Garden Hotel. This former family estate, with high adobe walls and an expansive Persian garden, was recently converted to a guesthouse. In the garden, a soccer team of middle-age men sauntered about, sporting team-color warm-ups, taking in the natural beauty as Persians enjoy doing. Meantime, Mira was in an emotion-laced argument with the hotel manager about being paired in a room with another guide and not being appropriately consulted. Iran may have a history of patriarchy, but there was no gender submissiveness in the conversation I witnessed: she gave the man no quarter; piece by piece she diminished him, without a peep from his mouth.

It was dinnertime. Two cockatoos screeched from a perch next to the dining hall, in which we took seats among tables of Taiwanese, Swiss, German, and French. Along with the ever-faithful lamb kebabs, we enjoyed *mirza ghasemi*, a Persian Gulf casserole dish of aubergine, tomatoes, eggs, and garlic. Honoring all nationalities but American, a miniature flag was placed on each table: there was the Swiss red square with bold white cross; the German tricolors of black, red, and gold; and so on, but no Stars and Stripes hoisted on a table for this Yank. Mira was embarrassed by the slight; she considered improvising with a drawn flag.

~

The people of Yazd, where the pace is ponderous and passions run high, are hard workers and religious conservatives, black chadors, blind faith, and babies galore. Wedged between the Dasht-e Kavir desert to the north and the Dasht-e Lut in the south, during the summer the mercury spikes here to 130 degrees Fahrenheit. Water does not flow freely in Yazd, so most residents are centered on the basics, water, food, family, and religion. Water wells are as old as the semimythical Sumerian king Gilgamesh, who survived, together with his companion Enkidu, in harsh desert conditions almost 5,000 years ago, by filling their lambskins with fresh water from the shallow wells they dug. Over the last two millennia, Yazdis have built and maintained an elaborate system of icehouses, cisterns, and *qanats*, aqueducts that provide both drinking water and irrigation. For a thousand years the people of Yazd have constructed "wind catchers," or *badgirs*, for air conditioning. These towers catch the slightest breeze and accelerate it downward to the ground floor and chambers in the basement.

The next morning, fixed like a skyscraper in our line of sight, we drove toward the tallest wind catcher in Yazd, at over 110 feet, set in the middle of Doulat Abad Garden, built in the 18th century by Mohammed Taqi Khan, governor of Yazd. The garden, a meditative, spiritual (and romantic) refuge of shade, water, and vegetative beauty, is encased in mud-brick citadel-like walls, which allow for privacy and protect from the gritty, desert winds and sand drifts. Above the imposing archway entrance—known as the *iwan*, a pre-Islamic architectural feature of walled gardens, which became a hallmark for mosques—an imaginary portrait of Imam Ali greeted us.

In the Koran, there are more than 100 references to the paradise garden. The verses of the Koran, as revealed by Mohammed, transformed the pagan gardens of Gilgamesh's Sumerians and the Garden of Eden, as described in Genesis, to an elaborate celestial paradise. For the Islamic faithful it was written that life ended in a garden paradise: "Abounding in branches, therein fountains of running water, and of every fruit there shall be two kinds." There, believers would be "reclining upon couches lined with brocade, the fruits of the garden nigh to gather; and will find therein maidens restraining their glances . . . lovely as rubies, beautiful as coral."

Noble families who own these stately paradise gardens and residences pass them down from one generation to the next, rarely breaking the chain. Flanked by 40-year-old pines and cypresses, the 300-foot-long reflecting pool linked the summer residence, now a museum under repair after a long abandonment, with the winter pavilion. "Five *qanats* were dug to bring water from Mehriz, 22 miles south of the city in the foothills of the Shirkuh Mountains," wrote Penelope Hobhouse in *Gardens of Persia*. "Only a quarter of the water was needed for the garden and the rest was bequeathed to the town for its use and for irrigating crops."

In full autumn blush, vineyards and orchards of grapes, cherries, and pomegranates grew in perfect Islamic symmetry as I had seen in carpet motifs. Inside the octagonal-shaped residence was a room-size, long reflecting pool that trembled from the cool air circulated through the *badgir*. From the pool, a purdah screen and stained-glass wall looked out into the garden. Next to the wagon-wheel-shaped mouth of the wind catcher, the strong, cool breeze felt fresh and clean, its passive energy giving breath to the desert's dead heat. And romance was in the air: two conservatively dressed couples held hands and took photos of each other standing next to an octagonal fountain, beneath the stained-glass skylight that centers the domed roof. The octagonal design, a circle within a square (or vice versa), is symbolic to Muslims of the circular dome atop a square building. The Dome of the Rock in Jerusalem, from which Mohammed made his ascent to heaven, has a central dome and octagonal base.

A ten-minute drive from the gardened paradise, I found myself escaping the sun's glare on a bench beneath the western entrance to the 12th-century Jameh Mosque. Like many mosques in Iran, it is built over a Zoroastrian fire temple. The intricately tiled *iwan*, or vaulted portal as seen at the paradise garden, gave way to a courtyard brimming with students from the renowned College of Architecture at the University of Yazd. The 160-foot twin minarets rose above the alcove-like *iwan*, which was spectacularly tiled in mosaic stonework of Persian sky blue and desert rust. *Maqurnas*, the stalactite, honeycombed vaults common in Persian architecture, gave way to intense foliation patterns, geometric designs, and swirls of calligraphy, delicately placed and balanced as the cosmos, magnified in the crisp sunlight.

Three sayyids—the black-turbaned clerics who are descendants of Mohammed—walked in single file into the courtyard. At the same time, Eisa Bakhsheshi sat down beside me, asking where I was from, while handing over his business card, which, but for his e-mail address, was in Cyrillic; he was a guide for Russian tourists. His Iraqi friend, Hussein, a salesman of cigarettes, who was from the southern Shia city of Amara, cautiously joined us. Meanwhile, dressed in a white *salwar kameez* and wearing a full beard, a man from the Sunni, independence-minded Baluchistan border region of Pakistan and Iran passed through the portal. And similarly dressed to the Baluch tribesman, a group of young Afghani men stood 30 feet away at the entrance to the bazaar where Mira was upgrading her scarf collection.

Although Yazd felt like a jumping-off point on the Silk Road, today it's wars and employment that are driving migration more than trans-Asian trade. Over one million Afghani refugees, who fled first from the Soviets and later the Taliban, are still living in Iran. They work the menial jobs, in households, the bazaar, guesthouses, or construction, smuggling and drug dealing, anything for money. They come from the Herat region of western Afghanistan, where opium is widely cultivated and has been an area of Persian influence, off and on for 2,500 years. The Iraqis, who control the wholesale cigarette business, stayed after the Iran-Iraq War (or fled here after the 2003 American invasion and the onset of widespread sectarian violence there). Iraqis and Afghanis live in their separate areas around Amir Chakhmaq Square.

Business was slow for Eisa on this day. He reminisced about life in Bishkek, Kyrgyzstan, where he learned Russian six years before. "My friends there were Pakistani engineering teachers and American Peace Corps volunteers," he said. "We all got along. It was a great time to be in Bishkek. We rented a club one night with all the liquor and women you could want. The party went on until daylight." He was frustrated that his American Peace Corps friends could not help him with a visa to the States. As if to soften me up with more Western-friendly notions of paradise, he told me about his holiday exploits in Turkey, an annual destination for as many as two million Iranians. "I go every year. My friends and I split an apartment four ways in Antalya for a month. It cost each of us $200. We drink beer all day and enjoy the Ukrainian women," he said, almost licking his lips as he talked.

At least 20 architecture students stood in a circle in the prayer hall, next to the mihrab niche that indicates the direction of the Kaaba in Mecca. That the Koranic damnation of graven images turned loose the Arabic and Persian passion for meditative, symmetrical art and architecture was richly expressed: the mihrab's bands of calligraphy, revered as the Word of God; the iridescent effect of the metallic blue mosaics; or the arabesques of vines climbing the walls as if in paradise.

Above the gathering students, the dome, a sky-blue web of finely drawn star shapes, invited the viewer into an imaginary heaven (perhaps that of the

Bedouin sky, I thought). Across the inlaid tile work of the mihrab, the *shahada*, or Islamic Creed, was written in Arabic flourishes of yellow: "There is no God but Allah. Mohammed is the Messenger of Allah."

Striking up a conversation, a pimple-faced student, with her hijab drawn tight around her face like a protective helmet, practiced her English, telling me about her school and the Persian architecture that informed historic creations from the Mogul gardens of Humayan's tomb and the Taj Mahal to the sultan's palaces of Zanzibar. I asked naively if she wanted to become a commercial or residential architect, and she replied, "I study only Islamic architecture, to build gardens and mosques." Before leaving, in response to a brief conversation about the mandatory hijab, she told me, "I have no problem covering myself. In fact I like it," finishing with a smile on her face, honor and chastity symbolically secure.

Stepping out of the mosque courtyard, we found ourselves in the narrow streets and alleyways of Yazd's old town, a living history of a medieval desert community. Since the revolution, the old city has received gas and electricity. Otherwise, not much has changed here since Marco Polo arrived in the 13th century, "a very fine and splendid city and a center of commerce," he said. Shafts of sunlight strained to penetrate the maze of mud-brick walls, behind which shops and residences were tidily tucked away. The occasional woman in black chador would swoosh by and then disappear. Well-worn wooden doors were adorned with brass knockers, the circular one for women and the phallic handle for men. Wind towers, tall and square columns, vented at the top like an air filter grille, provided the same skyscape that Polo must have cast his gaze on. Not designed for cars, other than the occasional bicycle and motorcycle that would blow by, and the call to prayer, the old town was graveyard silent. Streets were occasionally marked, and if so, photos of fresh-faced martyrs killed in the eight-year war would often appear alongside them. On one corner was a Basij poster, branded with their trademark globe and AK-47, centered with photos of martyrs, and, at the top, a heavenly fade of roses and nightingales, paradise.

Mira led me up two sets of stairs and out onto a domed roof. Out of a dust-laden sky, towering minarets and the turquoise, egg-shaped domes of mosques sparkled among the city's mud walls and rooftops, many candled with a wind tower. Over there was the domed tomb of the 12 imams, and next to it was Alexander the Great's Prison, made famous in a Hafez poem. Town and desert often of one shade, the drab sweep of Yazd and beyond was broken only by a splash of color here and prominence there all the way to a hazy ring of mountains, the snowcapped Shirkuh range.

Below was an unpaved square named for the third imam, Hussein the martyr, whose actions against injustice inform most Iranians. After leading an uprising against the Ummayad caliph in Damascus, Hussein and dozens of relatives were killed at the Battle of Karbala by Sunni soldiers on Ashura, the tenth day in the Islamic holy month of Moharram, the first in the Muslim lunar year. Muslim funerals occur within 24 hours of death, but a headless Hussein and his family lay in the desert for three days before receiving a proper burial; so penance must be paid as well for his suffering after death.[1]

Yazd, Mira told me, is famous for its Ashura ceremonies, when neighborhoods compete with each other. Black is the color on Ashura: flags hang from homes and businesses, women in their chadors, men in black shirts, and even the *nakhl*, which is only found in Yazd, is cloaked in black. Carried on the backs of the faithful like the cross in the Passion, the *nakhl*, symbolic of Hussein's coffin, is inscribed with Koranic verses and scenes from the Battle of Karbala. Rapturous-faced mothers watch from balcony perches—such as where Mira and I were standing—holding pictures of their martyred sons. *Noheh khanans* (cantors), men of all ages, with beautiful, booming voices, sing the verses commemorating the Battle of Karbala. With drums rumbling in the background, the cantors inspire young men to march and whip their backs with chains, a practice of self-flagellation known as *zanjeer-zani*. This demonstration of grief for Hussein's martyrdom is more about show and machismo than militant fury and drawing blood, which is illegal to do in Iran after Ayatollah Khamenei banned the practice. As Christ died for the sins of Christians, innocence, death, and martyrdom are pillars of Shia Islam. Death with a purpose is a better destiny than just dying.

"Ashura is religious theater," Mira said. "It's like a social event, getting together for a performance, drinking sweetened Ceylon tea, sharing basmati rice, chickpeas, lamb stew, and lime sorbet and rice pudding with rose water and saffron. It's very different than people think in the West." Her descriptions reminded me of a Passion parade, both celebrations somber and festive, full of mystery, inspiring happiness and hope, and embracing transcendence, a trait common to all religions.

~

As historic moments of tectonic change go, in addition to Ashura there are two dates that Persians invoke, each with the same calendric significance as the birth of Jesus: the 1979 Islamic revolution and the 7th-century Arab conquest.

---

1. In his book *Shi'ism: A Religion of Protest*, Hamid Dabashi uses his former professor Philip Rieff's analysis of Freud's theory of collective guilt to partly explain what he calls the "Karbala complex": "Society was based on complicity in the common crime; religion was based on the sense of guilt and remorse attached to it, while morality was based partly on the exigencies of this society and partly on the penance demanded by the sense of guilt." Religion proceeds by "fomenting an increasing sense of guilt." "Man is a remorseful killer, and religion is the history of his guilt," Rieff concluded.

As a result of the latter event, the Sassanian Empire, after Rostam's defeat at Qadesiya and under duress, forsook Zoroastrianism and came to embrace Mohammed and Islam. Thanks though to Ferdosi's *Shahnameh*, a mythical, partly historical tale of Iran that spans from the beginning of time through the Persian Empire to the arrival of Islam, Persians did not forget their past.

Among a medley of rich cultural keepsakes, the Zoroastrian designation for the months of the year are still used, and often preferred as given names; and Noruz, the first day of the Zoroastrian New Year, which occurs on March 21, the vernal equinox, remains the Persian celebration of the end of winter and beginning of spring, or rebirth—a time of vegetative bloom, house cleaning, and wiping the slate (not unlike the Chinese New Year). Chahar Shanbeh Soori, the secular Zoroastrian-era fire festival (which still gives clerics heartburn) occurs throughout Iran the Tuesday night before Noruz, the eve of Red Wednesday. "We have small fires in our neighborhood," Mira told me. "People jump over the flame, singing, 'Your red color is mine; my sickly yellow paleness is yours.'"

Yazd is the stronghold for Iran's 20,000 remaining Zoroastrians (70,000 in India and 200,000 worldwide), who because they until recently rarely intermarried are probably the purest of Persians. Melding custom and metaphysics from east and west, with good going up against evil, in a cosmic struggle of truth against falsehood, the prophet Zoroaster's message was worthy enough that the religion has been around over 2,500 years (some say 3,700). "His religious philosophy hinged on the idea that the purpose of humankind," wrote Azar Nafisi, "like that of all other creations, is to sustain *asa* (a combination of creation, existence, and free will)."

We drove to the outskirts of Yazd and the towers of silence, Zoroastrian funeral grounds. "Thinks well, speaks well, behaves well," Mira said, describing the Zoroastrian creed of active participation in life. "They promote wisdom not sacrifice unless a behavior affects [one's] ability to think clearly. Zoroaster, the prophet, does not say, 'No this, no that, put your right foot down first when you pee,'" Mira told me, mildly venting about the myriad strictures that clerics impose on women here.

Beyond a bustling new hub of glassy apartment and office complexes, Shahriyar, an 85-year-old watchman, stepped out from behind a green metal gate and gave us a toothless smile. His 24-year-old, bony, white-haired donkey brayed impatiently on the other side of the mud-brick wall. Wearing a dusty red-and-black-checkered turban, Shahriyar's desert-brown face was randomly creased like the ruts in a mud road after a hard rain. He has been the caretaker of the Zoroastrian cemetery and towers of silence for 64 years. In the early 1960s, the shah outlawed the ancient Zoroastrian funeral custom of hauling the dead up to the towers of silence, to be fed to birds of prey. Still scored into the hillsides were well-beaten pathways for the priests and bearers. Dressed in white turbans and long white coats, they delivered the wrapped body and performed their funerary rituals.

Leaving Shahriyar to feed his companion, Mira and I set out for the two barren hills in the near distance, each surmounted by perfect-shaped mud-brick roundels. We stopped at the abandoned adobe fire temple and cistern at the foot of the mountain. "You always find fire (*atar*) and water (*apor*) side by side, like the yin and yang," Mira said. Here grieving families held a three-day wake but were forbidden to attend the ceremony at the towers of silence. On top, crawling through a breach in the circular wall, opposite the entrance last used by Zoroastrian priests in the early '60s, we walked to a bone pit in the geometric center, now cluttered in rubble. Mira explained that the bodies of men were placed upright against the perimeter wall, with women next in a concentric array, and then children. While vultures gathered to eat the dead, a practice of purifying the earth not so different from the Tibetan "sky burial," the priest circumambulated the tower, reciting Zoroastrian verses. "By watching the vultures pick apart the corpse, what they ate first or last, the priest could divine the future of the deceased," Mira told me.

Shahriyar and his donkey awaited us at the gate and then led the way to the modern, more conventional cemetery. Still, to avoid polluting the earth and in keeping with their tradition, the graves are elevated and ventilated, above ground. Mazda Ahura, the winged deity of Zoroastrianism, was etched across each marble headstone, along with the three lessons of thinks well, speaks well, and behaves well that Mira had recited. For 30 years, a celebration of remembrance is held on the death anniversary, whereas Muslims mourn for 40 days, pay tribute on the one-year anniversary, and there it customarily ends. Thanks to Puria, the driver, before leaving, we shared hot tea, dates, cookies, and chewy candies with Shahriyar.

At dusk, we parked in a narrow alley at Ateshkadeh, the fire temple located in the center of Yazd. Here, the eternal flame burns. Followers from Zoroastrian enclaves like India and Azerbaijan, where the oldest and largest fire temple is located, pilgrimage here during Noruz. In fact, the only Zoroastrian I had ever met before coming to Iran was from India. He was a U.S. Green Card holder, working as an engineer in the Silicon Valley. On a flight across the Pacific, one Christmas Eve, he told me of the Zoroastrian migration 400 years before from Iran to India, taken from the epic poem the *Story of Sanjan:* "When my ancestors arrived in India, the local rajah, in a meeting with our maji, held up a full glass of milk—signaling there was no room for more people. Our maji responded by pouring sugar in the milk, saying, 'What do you think now?' We have lived in the Gujarati region of India ever since."

It was an Indian Farsi Association that built Ateshkadeh and moved the eternal flame, which, legend says, has been burning since 470 CE. Set several feet behind a glass case, no less than the presentation and power accorded the Hope Diamond, a small flame of apricot and almond wood burns in what appears to be a charcoal brazier. "They worship the light not the fire," Mira said, "just as Muslims don't pray to the mosque but to Allah." Fire is the medium through which wisdom and insight are attained; water is from where wisdom arises. There were a dozen locals, tourists I suppose, in the temple but only one who prayed.

A young couple led me outside for a photo to the edge of the reflecting pool in the paradise garden, with my back to the Mazda Ahura symbol, a frieze that prominently adorns the front of the temple. Stalking me, to practice their English and have some fun with a Westerner, a group of schoolgirls repeated, "cheese, cheese, cheese." It was a perfectly composed picture: my reflection laid over the sunbathed, shimmering waters of the pool like an iridescent hologram, with Mazda Ahura and temple as backdrop, glowing orange like a ball of fire.

CHAPTER EIGHTEEN

~

King of Kings in Wine Country

The next morning we set out to the west and south, rising 3,000 feet to the Abarkuh desert plateau, in the direction of the Persian Gulf. It was a 300-mile drive to Shiraz, the fabled city of singing and dancing, poetry and wine, and flowers and nightingales.

On the outskirts of Yazd we stopped to fill up at a National Iranian Oil Company (NIOC) service station. While the attendant pumped 34 liters, I noticed the spanking new gas pumps were made in South Korea.

As part of the government subsidy, all noncommercial drivers in Iran get their first 120 liters a month for 1,000 rials apiece (or $0.35 a gallon); after that, it goes up to 4,000 rials (or a $1.50 a gallon). Taxi drivers, for example, receive 800 liters a month at the $0.35 a gallon subsidy. Given Iran's diminished refining capacity, they are forced to import 40 percent of their gasoline. Only a year before, when President Ahmadinejad reduced the gasoline ration, protestors took to the streets and burned dozens of these state-owned stations.

Our car filled for less than five dollars, we pushed on, passing Volvo dump trucks, Mercedes eighteen-wheelers, and Peykan buses. Tawny mountains sprang up around us. North of the highway the snowcapped peak of Mt. Sir towered to over 13,000 feet; south were orchards of mulberry and pomegranate. Near a barren walnut orchard, a flock of sheep scratched the ground; a herder wrapped in a dark turban tended them; and a cop, wearing white, knee-high spats, stepped out and aimed his radar gun at us. On we raced, under the radar, at 80 miles an hour.

Soon, as far as the eye could see, was a pale sea of desert cinders, cut by a straight-as-a-string bank of backfill, a new natural gas pipeline. After Russia, Iran has the second-largest natural gas reserves in the world, the majority of which are produced in the nearby South Pars gas field. Due to sanctions, Iran lacks the necessary technology to fully develop those reserves, but that doesn't stop their plans to build pipelines to Pakistan and India in the east and as far west and north as Austria. Amid criticism from the United States over the pipeline to the east, Shiv Shankar Menon, the Indian foreign secretary, said, "Frankly, from our point of view, the more engagement there is, the more Iran becomes a factor of stability in the region, the better it is for us all."

Climbing the southern foothills of the Zagros Mountains, rows of pistachio lined Highway 7. East of the Zagros Mountains we turned off Highway 7, following the signs to Pasagarde. Here in a lush valley of the high plains, Cyrus the Great defeated the Medes, overlords of the Persians, and then built the first Achaemenid capital on the site of the battlefield. Two decades later, Cyrus was buried here, and for two centuries after, his descendants ruled the first world power, the Persian Empire, stretching from the Mediterranean in the west to China in the east.

In the days of Cyrus, the road to the ruins of Pasagarde was said to be shaded in native cypress, white-stemmed poplar, and Asian plane trees. We found an access road rimmed in autumnal-colored elms and passed a fish hatchery on the banks of a tributary of the Polvar River, not so far from where Cyrus's fishponds once teemed. A powder blue sky fell along the brown ridges of mountains that encircled the ancient city in a theater of natural ramparts. Ahead of us, gleaming limestone columns stood in a jumbled symmetry like broken chess pieces on unsteady grounds but orderly enough that the outlines of the great king's palaces were apparent. Beyond, tractors disking a fallow cornfield filled the sky in rooster tails of dust, while sheep dogs tightened the edges of their herd with barks and body. We drank tea and noshed on persimmons, dates, and pistachios in the shade of an elm tree by a shallow pool in an otherwise parched waterway. The well-preserved, six-tiered tomb of Cyrus the Great stood before us, once the center of a lush meadow, with an efficiently canalled paradise garden, forested in fruit groves and arrayed in axial beds of tulips and roses—a prototype for the Persian gardens of today.

In the minds of Persians, Cyrus is held in no less esteem than Moses is to Jews and is often imputed with similar creation myths (like the basket in the bulrushes). Many living historians count his achievements greater than Alexander, who visited Cyrus's tomb twice and was said to be rankled over the lack of care given to the burial site of the godlike king. By all accounts, including those of Herodotus's *The Histories*, Cyrus was a bold and brave conqueror but no less generous and tolerant. By allowing local religions to flourish, even paying homage to their gods, the vanquished became his willing vassals. When Cyrus conquered the Babylonian Empire and issued the Edict of Restoration, which authorized the return of captive Jews to rebuild the temple in Jerusalem, they called him the "Anointed of the Lord." He is the only gentile known to the Jews as a messiah. Many Persians would claim that because of Cyrus's deeds, their DNA makes them immune to accusations of anti-Semitism.

In 2003, when lawyer and human rights advocate Shirin Ebadi gave her acceptance speech for the Nobel Peace Prize, she said, "I am an Iranian, a descendant of Cyrus the Great. This emperor proclaimed at the pinnacle of power 2,500 years ago that he 'would not reign over the people if they did not wish it.' He promised not to force any person to change his religion and faith and guaranteed freedom for all. The Charter of Cyrus the Great should be studied in the history of human rights."

Thirty-two years before Ebadi's speech, the shah of Iran came to Pasagarde in a self-orchestrated celebration of 2,500 years of the Persian monarchy. He spent $120 million on the anniversary, the bulk of which paid for festivities at Persepolis, 20 miles away. "Cyrus sleep well, for we are awake," the shah said, addressing a crowd of dignitaries in attendance. The hoi polloi, at least those with televisions, watched the anniversary events from hundreds of miles away. Mira mocked the shah's speech by saying, "Cyrus sleep well; we are here. We have enough food to eat."

An hour later, with the sun setting, the Koran Gate appeared, announcing the entrance to Shiraz. As has been the practice for a thousand years, it is still considered good luck for travelers headed in the opposite direction to Esfahan to pass beneath a Koran, which was kept in a room at the top of the arched gate, where pigeons now nest. The city of poets came alive with twinkling lights and the steady glow of the turquoise "onion" domes of mosques, unique to Shiraz, the former 18th-century Zand capital.

A few blocks away I found our '70s-era hotel, the Homa, the namesake of the two-headed griffin found at Persepolis and used as the logo for Iran Air. The hotel lobby was abuzz with 135 tour operators from around the world. Most were seated in overstuffed chairs around a tea and coffee bar, looking as if a poltergeist might soon appear with happy hour highballs. While in the elevator, a tall, well-tanned foreigner got on, wearing a long-sleeved T-shirt and blue jeans and carrying a brief case. He was talking to an Iranian friend standing in the lobby. Once again, the accent was suspiciously from southern America. "And what part of the South do you come from?" I asked.

"Birmingham, Alabama," he said, whipping out a business card to finish his sentence. It read, "Donald King, Ambassador at Large," and imprinted above his name, in French and English, was International Institute for Peace through Tourism (IIPT). In his elevator speech he told me that the IIPT promotes travel as a higher purpose, as a way for all nationalities to have face-to-face encounters. "The reason for American's attitude toward the Middle East is the media and Hollywood, given all their violent movies and cardboard-cutout characters. Sure there are terrorists in the Middle East, as well as many good people. One size doesn't fit all. We need a rounder understanding of all the different cultures here." He had warned me that he had a lot to say, so we agreed to continue at breakfast.

By 6:30 the next morning, the exquisite buffet, looking out on a rose garden and Azadi Park, was already an elbowing affair, impeccably laid out and ten minutes later the visage of a food fight. The baked beans (for Brits) and scrambled eggs had landed in the hummus and tomato trays. Donald and his wife Lynn had time for a cup of coffee before catching a group tour bus to Esfahan. While I had sour cherry jam on toast, in short order they told of how they met in the midsixties at Southern Mississippi State. He was on the basketball team and she was a cheerleader. Before becoming a full-time tour operator, he coached for many years at Samford University in Birmingham, a private Southern Baptist institution. Donald still has the long, fit physique of a basketball player, and Lynn the petite good looks and rah-rah passion of a spirit team member. They've worked with refugees from the Balkans to Vietnam to Iran, sacrificing their time and treasure for the good of others. "We come by our values through our Christian faith, but the IIPT is nonsectarian," Donald told me. When I asked Lynn if they were proselytizing, she said, "No, only by our example of helping people."

Donald had been to Iran one other time in the late '90s, when the reformist President Khatami was reaching out to the world. A few weeks before he had flown to New York—on behalf of IIPT—for an hour meeting with the Iranian vice president of tourism (Esfandyar Rahim Moshaei). The goal of the meeting was to attract the largest American tour operators on a junket to Iran, a mission meant to establish Iran as a tourist destination for Americans. "I see some doors opening while others are closing." One of Donald and Lynn's guides joined us. In that warm, fuzzy spirit of peace and cooperation that we were all embracing, the guide told me, "We are a power in the Middle East and the U.S. is one of the world's superpowers. So we must talk and interact. Over the next couple of months Obama will make a difference." Under his breath Donald said, "Obama is naive and has already put his foot in his mouth."

～

An hour later, Qashqai tents gave life to the dull landscape at the gate to Persepolis, the Greek name for Parsa, or the city of Persians. From a distance, it's the 125,000-square-foot terrace, set snugly into Kuh-e Rahmet (or the Mountain of Mercy), and the scatter of limestone columns that spiral above a mature forest of tall pines, cypress, and plane trees, that proclaims the former grandeur of Persepolis. The columns were first built of teak from India and cedars from Lebanon, but when the ancient builders demanded greater size, they resorted to stone. In 518 BCE, Darius I (the Great), who came to power after two sons of Cyrus the Great were killed, moved the capital from Pasagarde and began construction of Persepolis. Given that Persepolis is rarely mentioned in historical records, most believe it was built as a symbol of power for the Achaemenid Empire, and to host celebrations, particularly the Zoroastrian and Persian New Year, Noruz.

Schoolgirls broke the white noise of a rustling wind, raising the pitch to a cacophony of laughter and excited introductions. Like all significant historical sites I would visit in Iran, students were always present. How else do they grow up and become walking encyclopedias on Persian history (and learn English)? On this day, they descended on me as if I was a heat-generating rock star; their chaperones and teachers faked anger while the kids huddled around with their questions in halting English, their pencils writing down addresses, spelling out words that were unclear to all of us.

To one side of the avenue leading to the ruins were the rusted-frame remains of white tents that once billowed with reveling royals and diplomats in attendance at the shah's $120 million, 2,500-year anniversary celebration. At the same moment, as Americans (including myself) protested the Vietnam War, Iranian students across the United States inveighed against the shah and his extravagance, with slogans like "Death to the Shah"; "Iran the Next Vietnam"; and "U.S. Get Out of Iran."

The gathering of nations at the anniversary celebration was redolent of Persepolis' heyday, when they once ate off marble plates and the empire ruled over 23 satrapies, each governed by a king; thus, the Achaemenid ruler became the king of kings (or shah of shahs). It was Darius, after all, who built the 1,677-mile Royal Road from Susa to Sardis (now a natural gas pipeline connecting Iran and Turkey). He also introduced gold coins as currency and instituted the highly efficient satrapy (state) system of administration theretofore unseen.

We walked as kings once did up the shallow steps leading to the Gate of Nations. If we had been here 2,500 years ago, four-foot-long bronze trumpets, with mouths as wide as dinner plates, would have announced our arrival. At the gate, the New Year and spring equinox is depicted in a towering stone carving of a bull, which represents winter, being taken down by a lion, symbolic of spring. In all the statues, friezes, and bas relief of Persepolis, Mira said that, but for a lioness and her cub, not a single female image appears here.

Abdul, a dark-skinned, forty-something Malaysian man, joined us, taking the morning off from making sales calls in Shiraz. He imports latex gloves for medical, dental, and food service and told me that Iran was "a good place to do business." We talked while admiring the bas relief along the staircase of the eastern wall of the Apadana Palace. It was built by Xerxes, featuring elegant stone carvings of Mede guards in dome-shaped hats and Persian soldiers in robes and fluted caps that resembled crowns, each bearing spears and quivers of arrows.

The 23 satrapies were represented on the wall, identified by their artisan skills and costumes: Arabs, Indians, Libyans, Ethiopians, Thracians were but a few; each nationality was separated by a cypress, symbolizing peace and good-will. On an opposing wall was a Persian army of 10,000 soldiers, just as the last shah had the same number of secret police. Cut from gray limestone, Greek columns and capitals, Egyptian doors and carvings, and Assyrian bas relief and statuary were all included in the three areas of Persepolis: the treasury, the military quarters, and the palaces for the king of kings. So how did the ancient glory of Persepolis end?

Xerxes, the son of Darius and Atossa, the daughter of Cyrus the Great, was accused of sacrilege for burning the Athenian temples in 480 BCE, following the Battle of Thermopylae.[1] A century and a half later, Alexander the Great arrived in Persepolis on a campaign of vengeance, one that had begun with his father, Phillip of Macedonia, who was killed in battle in Turkey. Darius III was the Achaemenid king at the time of Alexander's invasion. After crossing the Tigris and Euphrates without resistance, Alexander and the Macedonians defeated Darius and the Persian army in two epic battles.

In the tradition of conquerors of the day, Alexander married Darius's wife, Queen Statira, who, it is said, died in childbirth before the decisive Battle of Gaugamela.[2] Meantime, Darius fled in his chariot, abandoning his 50,000-man army in the field, rendering himself no more than a common fugitive in the end. With Alexander's Macedonian army hot on his trail, Darius was murdered by his Bactrian satrap and dumped on the side of the road; utter ignominy marked the cessation of the Achaemenid dynasty.

Alexander did, however, provide Darius a proper burial in the royal tombs at Persepolis. In the fog of celebration, though sober enough to remove the library beforehand, Alexander's troops torched the palaces of Persepolis, leaving behind the cut-limestone skeletons as reminders: the Apadana Palace of Darius, the palace of Xerxes, the Hall of a Hundred Columns, the Tripylon Hall, and the Imperial Treasury.

Today, near the museum and former harem, the treasury looks like an unmarked cemetery, the stubs of its former columns covered in beige stucco, laid out in almost perfect alignment. Upon Alexander's arrival, Persepolis was arguably the most prosperous city in the world. From the time of Cyrus, for 200 years, gold and silver had been horded. After emptying the treasury and shaking

---

1. The 2007 Hollywood movie *300*, which is based on a novel about the Battle of Thermopylae between Sparta and Persia, gratuitously leaves the Persians looking like barbarians.
2. The backstory alleges that Roxane, Alexander's first wife, from Bactria, had Statira killed.

down the Persian women for their jewels, the ravenous Macedonians hauled 2,500 tons of gold and silver away, on the backs of 3,000 pack camels.

Leaving Mira to enjoy her pistachio ice cream, Abdul and I threaded our way up the hillside to the tombs of Artaxerxes II and Artaxerxes III. Though Abdul is Muslim, in Malaysia the rules are not so rigid; we talked about how great a cold beer would be in the hot sun. In turns we stood on a shallow wall, with the ancient Persian capital and lush Kur River valley as backdrop, for our own conqueror photos. He told me that in "Malaysia we abandoned work on Wednesday morning to watch the election of Obama. We all hope he will succeed." He had to return to Shiraz for a lunch meeting with a new customer, whom he said was on the verge of buying an expanded line of medical supplies. We shook hands and said goodbye.

Mira and I had lunch at Laneh-Tavoos, a family-run restaurant a mile north of Persepolis. The middle-aged owners, two hardworking brothers, made a fuss over our arrival and which table would suit us best. After much ceremony, they set us up around a fountain and pool, with two Mallard drakes swimming and wing flapping and a friendly black-faced Persian cat feeding beneath the table. Autumnal leaves fell on us from a mature canopy of elms, mixed with needles from a stand of tall pines. Breezy, operatic Persian love songs from the 1940s played in the background. Puria, the driver, surprised us with a bottle of his brother's homemade wine. Robert Byron described Shiraz moonshine aptly in *Road to Oxiana*, when he said he preferred "a worse wine with a taste of its own." That it was, but it went down like France's finest with the lingering lunch of lentil soup and Shiraz bread, feta and tomatoes, and aubergine and lamb. Though the comforts and ambiance felt Victorian, we could have just as easily been guests in ancient Persepolis.

⌐

Back in Shiraz, the streets were full and frantic. Twilight was somberly beckoning, when Puria drew to a stop in front of Musalla Gardens, better known as Hafez's Tomb. A bearded man approached us, with a hobbled nightingale on his wrist, and, in the opposite hand, he held a cigarette-pack-sized box that contained thin sheets of Hafez's *ghazals*, a Persian form of rhyming couplets. For a token fee, the trained birds, with their tiny beaks, pluck a poem from the box and give it to visitors. While Mira told me I had drawn a poem about drinking wine and romance, three young army enlistees flashed me the peace sign as I entered the gate. (Or did they mean to say "victory"?)

Buried in a raised alabaster tomb, beneath an octagonal pavilion, the 14th-century Sufi mystic's lyrics about love, wine, the divine, and the moral hypocrisy of monarchs and religious orthodoxy still inspire people from all walks of life: avant-garde couples, women in their monochromatic chadors, middle-aged businessmen, fashion-conscious young women smoking cigarettes, clerics in robes, students with day packs, fortunetellers, young poets, and aging philosophers circulated around the pavilion or fanned out to the private nooks of the paradise garden. In the 14th century, when the king declared the consumption of wine illegal, Hafez, once a court poet, responded,

> Though wine gives delight, and the wind distills the perfume of the rose,
> Drink not the wine to the strains of the harp, for the constable is alert.
> Hide the goblet in the sleeve of the patchwork cloak,
> For the time, like the eye of the decanter, pours forth blood.
> Wash the wine stain from your dervish cloak with tears,
> For it is the season of piety, and the time for abstinence.

The prohibition was soon repealed. In the twilight, by turns Hafez's admirers knelt at his tomb and stood against the pavilion's columns, some clutching a long-stemmed red rose, but all reciting his poetry back to him. That he was most famous for his lyrics of love and romance seemed to attract a disproportionate number of forlorn women. Darkness fell and the garden and pavilion took on an ethereal glow; the singing of Hafez's lyrics wafted through the early evening air, the ghost of a poetic mystic channeling happiness and hope for so many. This ritual-like appreciation goes on 365 days a year.

∼

The next morning, on the Internet and in the local papers the news was all about the global economic meltdown, the war in Iraq to the west and the re-emergence in the east of the Taliban in Afghanistan. And, as if that weren't enough, Pakistani terrorists killed and held hostage American tourists, among other nationalities, in Mumbai, India, while violent protestors in Thailand seized the airports. The Tehran press blamed the British government for the Mumbai attacks. So as it all swarmed around us here in charming Shiraz, remembering all the dire warnings I had received about traveling to Iran, I came to feel as if I had landed in an island of tranquility.

An hour later, we were loafing beneath a grove of sour orange trees on the courtyard steps of the Madraseh-e Khan, a 400-year-old seminary for young men. "Boys enter the school at 15 years old and after 10 years they can wear the turban of clerics," Mira told me. "It's okay for women to become clerics and ayatollahs, but they can only speak in public to audiences of women. In other words, they can be seen but not heard or smelled (no perfume)." She added that there was only one female ayatollah in the holy city of Qum.

Joining us on the courtyard steps were three older sayyids, black turbans all. After a few minutes of small talk, Sayyid Farajollah Jousavi invited us to his quarters, a prison-cell-size cubicle off the courtyard. He was sixty-something, black-skinned, and of medium height; his beard and hair was silver, and he had a high forehead accented by dark, bushy brows. "Ayatollah Khomeini once lived in a room like this and he became the Supreme Leader," Jousavi told me, motioning me on to his bunk.

Known for their cars, cell phones, and satellite televisions, this cleric, at least in his official residence here at the madrassa, was living on the cheap, removed from modernity. A half-eaten plate of food and glass of water lay on the concrete floor. His monastic crib was adorned in posters, redolent of the radical idealism and simplicity of an American '60s-era college dorm room (Abbie Hoffman, Black Panthers, Woodstock, the Vietnam War, etc.). Above the bed Mira and I were sitting on was the sayyid's wall of fame: 4 martyr photos and 13 posters of clerics, most of whom I assume were ayatollahs, including the Grand Ayatollah Sayyid Ali al-Sistani of Iraq; another Iraqi cleric who was apparently assassinated, given the blood pouring from his head; and one young cleric (presumably an ayatollah) being arrested in 1961 by the Shah's secret police. A paradise scene of doves flushing from a garden and a poster of the Basij, which of course included the logo of an AK-47, Koranic verses, and the globe, filled out the sayyid's wall of fame. Opposite, above a small bookshelf that held three Koranic texts and a hot plate, was a poster of the Hajj and the black-curtained Ka'ba. Situated next to the poster was a poem about kindness, which he recited. It went something like "Welcome to my humble home. I have little to offer, but you are welcome to it."

The whole scene—all the adornments, the holy man, and a descendant of Mohammed in his black turban and brown robe—conjured up schizophrenia on steroids. Yet, whether intended or not, as a victim of his (human) DNA, it was a commonsense montage that elegantly blurred the line between hope and fear with existential truth.[3]

Sayyid Jousavi stood and delivered a list of Shia affirmations as if I were his student. "Imam Hussein's message when he was about to die was 'be a man. Don't do this to women and children,'" he said. "We are responsible for what we do here on Judgment Day. No religion believes in invasion and killing. We can never force conversion to Islam." It was hard not to notice that his thick, uneven lips and dark, liquid eyes worked in sync, never betraying a smile or a glimmer of joy, only the rigor of his message. After a pause, I asked him what he thought of Obama.

---

3. At the same time I was visiting with the sayyid, a bill, larded with language about security and religious freedom, was introduced to a Senate committee in the Arkansas legislature that would allow handguns in church.

"How do we know," he said, shrugging his shoulders. "We have to wait and see."

"Do you see any difference between George Bush and Barack Hussein Obama?" I asked, with emphasis on Barack Hussein.

"A name doesn't mean anything," he told me. "We like Americans but not the government."

A pushy man, Mormon-like in black slacks and a white shirt, with a taped nose—that ever-present status symbol of cosmetic surgery here—barged in to say he had a few questions. He had been standing by the sour orange grove in the courtyard, glaring at us. Mira told him we would be finished in a moment, waving him off. Jousavi—whose opaque eyes now sparkled, scouring Mira's cascading hair and body—responded to a question about modernity, how Sunnis and Shias were handling cell phones, the Internet, and satellite television. He heaped praise on Ali as the first Imam and then went into the subtleties of how Shias wash, gesturing from his elbow to the tips of his fingers, from forehead to feet, not otherwise like the Sunnis. Although speaking in generalities now, not addressing the negative attributes of Internet or cable television, he continued, "Shias accept today's technology and the reality that we must have political ties. The clergy is very knowledgeable and must decide issues of modernity if Iran's parliament passes a law. The Supreme Leader must sign off on it."

Without saying it by name, he was alluding to the Shia concept of *ijtihad*, often mentioned by Hezbollah's Hassan Nasrallah in Lebanon. "Ijtihad makes permissible adaptations to the requirements of time and place, permits one to respond to new demands, be they specific or general, upon the individual and community, state and society," said Nasrallah in an interview.

Leaving his monkish quarters and saying goodbye, we followed Sayyid Jousavi into the street. Mira didn't mention the ogling, but she did say that not only do most clerics have multiple wives but also some are just common lechers. We had already talked about the routine practice of clerics granting permissions for temporary marriages, or *sigheh*, to accommodate the male faithful with prostitutes and one-night stands.

That evening on the terrace of a teahouse, sandwiched between the Koran Gate and Shiraz University, and overlooking the fabled city of poets, we smoked hookahs, drank tea, and munched on dates, pistachios, and Persian sweets. A music stall next to the teahouse sold bootleg CDs and posters of Elvis, Marlon Brando, Al Pacino, and Johnny Depp. On a homemade CD, a Metallica-sounding band blasted through the chilled night air. Students, couples, and foursomes gathered on separate divans, broke all the rules of public behavior, smoking, touching, and moving to the music.

CHAPTER NINETEEN

~

Fear and Faith in Paradise

On the way to the Shiraz airport we stopped at the poet Sa'di's tomb. Mira talked about Sa'di as a traveler and philosopher who had wandered a medieval Middle East like Marco Polo at the time of the Mongol invasion and occupation. As an old man, he returned to his birthplace in Shiraz, where he had been educated, long before, by the finest teachers. A forest of cypress surrounded an avenue of persimmon-colored roses that led to Sa'di's milky brown marble tomb, covered in a turquoise dome. Surrounded by turret-topped ridges, a natural spring fed a fishpond next to the colonnaded tomb. While being mobbed by a class of teenage girls, practicing their English, Mira told her favorite story written by Sa'di, from his book *Golestan*.

A padshah was in the same boat with a Persian slave who had never before been at sea and experienced the inconvenience of a vessel. He began to cry and to tremble to such a degree that he could not be pacified by kindness, so that at the last the king became displeased as the matter could not be remedied. In that boat there happened to be a philosopher, who said, "With thy permission I shall quiet him." The padshah replied, "It will be a great favor." The philosopher ordered the slave to be thrown into the water so that he swallowed some of it, whereon he was caught and pulled by his hair to the boat, to the stern of which he clung with both his hands. Then he sat down in a corner and became quiet. This appeared strange to the king who knew not what wisdom there was in the proceeding and asked for it. The philosopher replied, "Before he had tasted the calamity of being drowned, he knew not the safety of the boat; thus also a man does not appreciate the value of immunity from a misfortune until it has befallen him."

Old Sa'di must have been speaking from the grave about September 11, or was it the global economic tsunami, or was it just garden variety fear?

⌒

While I stretched out in the half-empty lobby of Shiraz's airport, awaiting the next flight to Esfahan, I jotted down my journal notes for the day. Pausing briefly, giraffe-like, 20 feet away, in front of the Iran Air check-in counter, the tallest man I had ever seen ambled by, wearing sweats and standing 7'4". Following him were more young men, closer to earth, at 6'7" or maybe 6'5", including two black guys. "Holy shit, that's the Iranian basketball team," I told Mira, springing to my feet to say hello. A few years before, I had read about Americans, who didn't make the cut in the NBA or European leagues, playing basketball in Iran.

"Are you guys by chance a basketball team?" I asked, extending my hand to one of the black guys, who wore a diamond-studded, silver crucifix around his neck that matched his immense stature.

"Yes, we are," said Kevin Johnson, giving me an easy smile. "You sound like you may be from the South." The giraffe was Jaber Rouzbahani, the team's center. They play for Zob Ahan, a steel company in Esfahan, in Iran's Super League, which was started in 1998. Having played college ball at the University of Tulsa, Kevin talked briefly about James "Country" King, who, two weeks before, had been inducted into the Boy's Club Hall of Fame at a dinner I had attended in Fort Smith. Anyone who played at Tulsa knew Country King, who went on to play in the NBA for the Lakers and Bulls, and was on All-Star teams with Bill Russell and Wilt Chamberlain.

Kevin, who is 27 years old, never got an offer from the NBA. Before Iran, he played on teams in Turkey and Lebanon; this would be his last hurrah earning six figures for shooting hoops. He told me there were 13 professional teams in Iran, each limited to two foreign recruits, but only half of the teams can afford American players. The less prosperous team sponsors recruit the less expensive (and talented) Serbian players. "The rivalries here are intense," he said. "In our last game fans were throwing eggs and firecrackers onto the court. Turkey was the worst, though. They don't even wait until the whistle blows. In one game the bleachers emptied during warm-up. Cops were clubbing brawling fans beneath the basket while we were doing practice layups around them."

In the meantime, wearing baggies, with his baseball cap turned sideways, Urfan Nasajour stepped up to introduce himself. At 5'8", he is the shortest player on the Zob Ahan team. Urfan is Iranian, speaks Farsi, but was born and raised in Winnipeg, where he played college basketball before moving to Iran a month ago. At 22 years old, he travels with the team but can't take the court until a Tehran lawyer gets his mandatory military service in Iran waived. Urfan, like most Iranians of the diaspora, has dual citizenship. After his parents divorced, his mother stayed in Winnipeg and his dad, from whom he is estranged, returned to Tehran. He and Kevin have become fast friends.

"There's another guy from Oklahoma I want you to meet," Kevin said, about the time they called our flight. Taking down his cell phone number, before racing to the gate, we agreed to meet for dinner the next night at the Abbasi Hotel in Esfahan.

～

Near midnight in Esfahan, Mira and I were waved to a stop on a dark street by armed civilians: a Basij roadblock; the moral police were out, hitting us with the glare of their flashlights. Seven or eight other cars were already undergoing rigorous searches, doors, hoods, and trunks all wide open. These working-class vigilantes, who are subordinate to the Revolutionary Guard and famous for their human wave attacks in the Iran-Iraq War, were searching for wine, drugs, contraband CDs, insurgents, hijab violators, student dissidents, and anything else they deemed suspicious. "A passage in the Koran exhorted believers to be proactive in maintaining the purity of their communities," wrote Azadeh Moaveni in *Lipstick Jihad.* "The dictum 'Amr be marouf, va nahi be monker' (Promote virtue and contain vice) was embraced by the regime, and gave powers akin to a citizen's arrest to pious, local bullies." The Basij enthusiasm as morality police, handling the bidding of the ayatollahs, shines a light on their résumés when it comes time for that important government job. Mira talked fast, letting them know I was a tourist. After a glance at my passport, within minutes we were pulling into the Abbasi Hotel.

The Hajj season had only just begun: the hotel was booked with over 80 pilots and twice as many stewardesses, who were taking pilgrims on direct flights from Esfahan to Mecca. In the Muslim world, all roads lead to Mecca, fulfilling the fifth pillar of Islam, after which paradise is all but guaranteed. Before oil was king, the Hajj was Saudi Arabia's biggest source of hard currency. In the 1950s, Meccans had a reputation for fleecing pilgrims, who often slept on the streets. By 1973, at the time of the oil embargo, the keepers of the faith had turned the Hajj into a fixed price, package tour: an individual paid $16.76 for general services and $10.64 for lodging at airport villages. By 1987, given the worldwide Islamic revival, galvanized by, among other events, Iran's Islamic revolution, and the coincident rise in popularity of the Hajj, Saudi Arabia had to impose quotas on the number of arrivals each season. "It's big business," Mira said. "Today the package cost of the pilgrimage to Mecca is $1,500 to $1,700 per person." As we checked in there at the Abbasi Hotel, pilots and pilgrims came and went. Fortunately, there were exactly two rooms left in the former caravanserai.

⁓

Waking up with the window open to the Abbasi garden was no less than a flight of fancy. So taken by Shah Abbas the Great's capital of the Safavid dynasty was 16th-century French poet Renier that he extolled its beauty with the famous half-rhyme "Esfahan nesf-e jahan," or "Esfahan is half the world."

"From the eleventh century, architects and craftsmen have recorded the fortunes of the town [Esfahan], its changes of tastes, government and belief," wrote Robert Byron in *Road to Oxiana*. "The buildings reflect these local circumstances; it is their charm, the charm of most old towns. But a few illustrate the heights of art independently, and rank Esfahan among those rarer places, like Athens or Rome, which are the common refreshment of humanity."

It was over 100 steps to the fifth floor of Ali Qapu Palace, the former residence of Abbas the Great. Emerging from a cut-stone stairway, I found myself in a domed room with paintings of fair-skinned maidens; the emphasis on their sensuous curvatures suggested an adaptation of calligraphy to painting. In one corner, musicians once played on a stone divan, hidden behind curtains; they were not allowed to see the cavorting of the shah, his noblemen, and his courtesans. The layered walls of the room, adorned in honeycombed, Islamic shapes and symmetry, were specially designed to absorb sound, to deflect an echo so the hoi polloi in the *maidan* below would not hear the music. It's the Persian leader's manner: publicly damning anyone to eternal hell for debauchery but privately living as a Sybarite.

On the terrace of Ali Qapu Palace, I beheld the incomparable view of Imam Square, fit together like the fine weave of an exquisite Persian rug. Esfahan's *maidan* was formerly known as Naqsh-e Jahan, or pattern of the world. With axial gardens and fountains below, to my left and right, the Qeysarieh Portal, which heralds the entrance to the vaulted hallways of the Bazar-e Bozorg, stands at one end, a third of a mile from the Imam Mosque and its rich Persian blue *iwans*, minarets, and dome, at the other. A wall of arched arcades wraps around the *maidan* in a vibrant belt of artisan shops—miniaturist galleries and enamel painters to hand-printed textiles and gold jewelers. To the east, directly across from my imperial aerie, traced in blue and gold wash runs, was the dome of Sheikh Lotfollah Mosque, one of Byron's few that "illustrate the heights of art independently." Abbas the Great named the private mosque, which has no minarets, for his father-in-law, who was a Lebanese cleric in Esfahan to watch over the royal madrassa and Imam Mosque.

Twice the size of Red Square in Moscow, only Beijing's Tiananmen Square is bigger than Esfahan's sprawling centerpiece, a paragon of Persian architecture. In the day, as the Safavid kings returned from battle, led by horses caparisoned in jewels and cloth of gold, their arrival was signaled not only with trumpets but also with 50,000 oil lamps burning around the square. From this columned terrace, which is centered with a copper pool, the king once watched the Yalda (winter solstice) and Noruz festivities, and on more routine days, polo matches.

The frescos of the nearby Chehel Sotun, built as a pleasure palace, gives a hint of what such a day here might have looked like: princes and viziers, poets and pipe bearers, cooks and scullions, ewer and basin bearers, carpet spreaders, and the controller of the opium box all would have been present, at the king's service. The princes and viziers would have arrived with their own attendants. The royals all dressed in colorful muslin turbans and silk garments, with sashes and swords, and the long, bushy, twisting handlebar moustache was in style along with trim, artfully shaped beards. Conversation was heady; after all, it was a time when Persia wanted to cement relations with Russia and Europe to bolster an alliance against the Ottomans. There was no shortage of music and wine, with revelers passing out drunk, perhaps hidden by a curtain drawn around the columned terrace.

Gone is the polo field; today, the heart of the square is a long pool with fountains and gardens, around which horse-drawn carriages clamor on asphalt to give tourists a real whiff of another era. Whimsically, I chose to picture, instead of a polo match or the steady line of cars crisscrossing in front of the Qeysarieh Portal, a camel caravan circling the *maidan* and turbaned traders unpacking their Bokhara lamb's skins destined for Constantinople, pitching their tents and picketing their animals, with hookah smoke rising and yarns spinning in the air with the florid imagery with which Persians speak.

Leaving the palace onto the square, a short man named Ali, with a large aquiline nose, wearing blue jeans and boots, walked up. "We meet again. Where do you go today?" he said. "Throughout half the world," I told him. We had met the day before on the street a mile from here. He had given me directions. Today, in front of a shop selling antiques, we stood and talked beneath a window poster of Muqtada al-Sadr, the Iraqi political leader and cleric. Ali told me he is a retired petroleum research engineer and has a brother who is a cardiologist, living in San Jose, California. He said he was leaving in a few days for an 18-day, 6-city tour of the United States, costing $12,000 per person; his brother had paid for and arranged it all, including the visa. In the next breath, cynical as Ali was, he talked working-class politics. "Saddam, Bush, Ahmadinejad, Obama, they are all the same. They say this and that but none do anything for the poor. Help the man with the calloused hands," he told me, turning his palms upward to show me patches of thick skin. "Even the ayatollahs have hands like girls. How would they know?" And how would I know who Ali really was?

An hour later I was walking through Qayem Square, also known as Kabuli Square, for all the Afghani refugees living and working here. "Taliban," Mira said, is not a friendly word hereabouts, with Afghanis or Iranians. We stopped for a cup of saffron ice cream before entering the Jameh Mosque through the bazaar and south *iwan*, its murals and stalactite vaults added by 13th-century Mongol rulers. The bazaar and parts of the mosque, which is the largest in Iran, were destroyed by bombing during the Iran-Iraq War. Resiliency, if not asymmetrical harmony, is the cornerstone: from the Zoroastrian fire temple of the Sassanids to the reconstruction by the Islamic Republic after the Iran-Iraq War, successive regimes have made their mark.

From Kabuli Square we wound our way through the bazaar back to Imam Square. Hajji Baba—the cunning protagonist of the early 19th-century novel *Hajji Baba of Ispahan*—was at once ubiquitous and nonexistent in the bazaar's warren of vaulted hallways and shops. By picaresque turns, Hajji Baba becomes a blacksmith, storyteller, barber, traditional healer and bleeder, water carrier for ablutions, carpet spreader (*ferash*), scribe, poet, horseman, bandit, fashion dandy, tobacco vendor, servant to merchant brokers, and dervish. They were all there in the bazaar, but other than the talismans being sold to protect against the evil eye, the Hajji Baba of my imagination, who was full of idealized Persian intrigue, was lost in translation. Instead, old-fashioned, enterprising spirit was the palpable truth.

As it happened, the only professions more visible than *bazaaris* were turbaned clerics, who fell in a steady trickle from madrassas that adjoined the bazaar. Given all the posters of the two Supreme Leaders, the sheer number of clerics clutching their Korans and dawdling around struck me as a colony of fresh-hatched clones. How could one city, in one country, have so many moral avatars? I wondered. What is Qum like with over 500 mosques and the largest seminaries? The bankers and brokers of today hovered in dank rooms off the fairway where one might expect to find the hidden tunnels once used by women to attend the call to prayer or to return to the shah's harem. Small wonder, with the traditional layout of mosque and bazaar adjoining, that Iranian *bazaaris* and clerics are known to have such a cozy relationship.

⁓

Waiting in the hotel lobby when I returned were Kevin Johnson, Urfan Nasajour, and Mike Jones. We agreed to eat from the hotel buffet, which offered every Persian dish imaginable—but not before Mike and Kevin satisfied the curious mob of women, two with medically taped noses, and teenage kids, who had gathered; they all wanted photos of these tall, good-looking African American, Iranian Super League stars.

"If the mullahs would let women show anything but their faces they might not be so focused on getting nose jobs," Urfan said, as we stepped back to watch the commotion. In a perverse way, he was suggesting that liposuction and boob jobs might count for progress here if only women could shed their veils and robes.

Kevin, who is 27 years old, is from Tulsa, Oklahoma, about 90 miles from my hometown of Fort Smith, Arkansas. Mike Jones, who is 33, is from Oklahoma City, where he graduated from Cassidy, a respected prep school that my younger brother attended. I had now met four Americans in Iran, all from the South, and three out of four from near my hometown, with mutual acquaintances—six degrees like hell!

Since leaving TCU (Texas Christian University), Mike has been around the Europe and Middle East leagues: France, Poland, Turkey, Lebanon, and now Iran. "We are lucky. We love playing the game and get paid for it," he told me. "When I was 21, I got my first passport and went to Australia on the under-22 U.S. team. It changed my life and the way I see the world."

I asked about their experience in Iran.

"The hospitality is over the top," said Mike, who is in his second season in the Super League. "There are no problems for us here. We are invited into people's homes every night. Americans are not willing to understand other cultures; that's why they don't like Iran."

Kevin said as much, hospitality was everywhere, and hostility was all in the American imagination. He gave Sarah Palin as an example of those leaders who promote fear against hope, who marginalize Iranians and other cultures in the American consciousness. After only a month here, Kevin was Skype-ing friends and family, dashing their fears, and telling them how great Iranians are. Urfan said he couldn't be happier, other than to say he missed his mother. His plans are to play in the Super League as long as they will pay him.

As we wrapped up our visit in the lobby, Mike and Kevin were once again approached for pictures by women and their teenage sons, who ignored Urfan as if he were the ball boy.

⌒

"Five million Iranian tourists come here each year. They love this city," Mira told me as we left the Abbasi Hotel the following morning. We drove down the city's leafy main street, Chahar Bagh (Four Gardens), passing palaces and parks, gardens and madrassas, three cinemas, and two malls. We circled Revolution Square (Meidan-e Enghelab) and found ourselves along the banks of Zayandeh Rud (or River of Birth), which has its origins to the west in the Zagros Mountains. The Bridge of 33 Arches (Si-o Seh), one of five remaining pedestrian bridges built by Abbas the Great and the Safavids, spanned the river here as if it were a palace moat out of some medieval fairytale. With teahouses at each end, bracketing the arched spaces that form a natural echo chamber for aspiring male singers, it's one of the many crown jewels of Esfahan's living history.

Crossing the Ferdowsi Bridge to the south side of the river, traveling along a boulevard of plane trees, we were in (New) Jolfa, the Armenian Christian district.

Caught in the crossfire of the Ottoman-Persian wars, Armenians arrived here 400 years ago, from the northern Iranian city of Jolfa. After the Safavids adopted Shiism, which threatened the Ottoman caliphate's leadership of the Muslim world, throughout the 16th century, fighting raged across eastern Anatolia. In retreat, employing a scorched-earth strategy to prevent the historic Armenian region from regaining its economic viability, Shah Abbas torched villages and depopulated the area of 250,000 Armenians. Although most Armenians relocated to Iranian Azerbaijan, in 1605, Abbas brought the wealthiest—merchants, artists, and entrepreneurs— to his capital in Esfahan. As local and international traders, free of Ottoman taxes, they flourished, especially in the silk industry, knitting together enterprises from China and Russia to Europe.

In (New) Jolfa, Abbas permitted the Armenians to build Orthodox cathedrals, to make wine, and to have their own courts, elected officials, and traditional elder leaders. Muslims were not allowed to reside in the Jolfa neighborhood, where, at its peak, 50,000 Armenians lived. Today, those numbers have dwindled to 7,000, while 13 churches remain. The '79 Islamic revolution took its toll, but the religious-cultural bonds of Armenians as the first nation to adopt Christianity have allowed them to survive multiple diasporas and to remain intact as a people; their plight may only be matched by that of Jews.

Here in prosperous Jolfa, the streets were wider, the apartments were bigger, and as Mira said, there was less crime and more personal freedoms. We turned down an alleyway leading to Vank Cathedral, capped with an earthen-colored, Persian onion dome (like in Shiraz). This cathedral falls under the oversight of the archbishop of the Armenian Apostolic Church in Beirut.[1]

A memorial to the Armenian genocide in Turkey, dated April 24, 1915, stands at one end of the cathedral courtyard, and at the other is a stand-alone bell tower, beneath which two prominent merchants and church patrons are entombed. Two priests, looking decidedly medieval, wearing long beards and black robes with peaked hoods, led the way into the cathedral. The entrance is painted in motifs of the torture inflicted by the Ottomans on Armenian martyrs. The ceiling of the dome depicts the biblical creation story, including vivid Italian-style oil paintings of the expulsion from the Garden of Eden. Across the courtyard, on a small television in the cathedral museum, streaming video runs with jarring black-and-white images of the genocide: human bone piles and refugees fleeing, emaciated, and near death. And like Gutenberg's Bible in

---

1. Curiously, it was the Shia clerics from Lebanon who were summoned here 500 years ago to instruct the Safavids in their new faith.

Germany and the Maronite clergy, who were the first to use movable type in Lebanon, an antique press was displayed, said to have produced the first book printed in Iran in 1638. Otherwise, the museum held the oddest assortment of memorabilia: a small drawing by Rembrandt; a tear pot for wives and widows to cry into while their men fought and died in wars; and monkish feats such as an Old Testament verse written on a single hair and the smallest book, the size of an AA battery.

Around the corner from the cathedral, we lunched at the popular Pizza Jolfa Armenian Restaurant. Speaking perfect English, the manager of sorts, an Indian man from Mumbai, who had married an Armenian who refused to leave Iran, pulled us out of line and ahead of the crowd. He insisted we have the house specialty, sesame kebabs, with sides of *dolmas*; a delicacy of chopped olives, salads, and pickles; and flaps of fresh bread. But the food was a sideshow: even the houris of Mohammed's paradise would have been jealous of this restaurant's flow of flashy Armenian women, who turned hijab into sexy high fashion, in a country where the morality police, only a few years ago, were confiscating lip gloss and eye liner. The tall black boots and blue jeans, topped with a snug manteau that hung over tight jeans or pants like a miniskirt, and their exposed bouffant hairdos, dark sunglasses, painted nails, collagen-plumped lips, and heavy makeup, were only exceeded in shock value by the sheer number of medically taped noses; the restaurant could have doubled as the waiting room of a plastic surgeon's office.

⌒

In a sylvan river park near the Khaju Bridge, built by Abbas II in 1650, with a sluice gate beneath it, we walked off the heavy lunch. Migrating Mallards and white gulls embroidered the shallow, limpid waters below the bridge of 24 arches. It was Friday, and the banks of the Zayandeh teemed with picnicking families, noshing, smoking hookahs, and taking in the parklike surroundings.

A young man dropped a string and hook into the shallow waters; college-age girls, with the jean and miniskirt look, preened by on rollerblades; and boys played football on an improvised postage-stamp-size pitch. Moein, the famous Iranian singer now living in Los Angeles, and native son of Esfahan, has a popular song about whiling away a day here. Mira sang a few bars: "I'd like to go back to Esfahan, going back again to that Half of the World. Going there, sitting beside the Zayandeh Rud, singing songs and poems from my heart."

In the near distance, on the north shore of the Khaju Bridge, an attractive but modest double-domed mausoleum sits in the center of Professor Pope Park, the garden burial site of two Americans, Arthur Pope and his wife, Dr. Ruth Ackerman, both art historians. Close friends with the Pahlavis, they traveled the world lecturing on such things as Persian bridge architecture. Yet the most

famous Yank buried in Iran is unknown in America: Howard Conklin Basker-
ville, a Nebraska-born, Princeton-educated Presbyterian missionary who, in
1907, was killed in battle in Tabriz while siding with the constitutionalists
against the Cossack brigades of the Qajar despot Muhammad Ali Shah. In 2005,
President Mohammad Khatami unveiled a bust of the Yankee hero, who was
quoted as saying, "The only difference between me and these people is my place
of birth, and this is not a big difference."

⁓

It was Plato who said that only the dead have seen the end of war. A corollary
to those words might be "It is the dead who rule," wrote Chris Hedges in *War
Is a Force That Gives Us Meaning*. "They speak from beyond the grave urging a
nation onward to revenge."

Ten minutes away the taxi dropped us at the martyr cemetery, laid out in the
motif of the four-walled Persian paradise. A man handing out cookies greeted us,
a standard hospitality shown visitors here. Of the 600,000-plus Iranian lives lost
in the Iran-Iraq War, 23,000 *shahids*, or martyrs, are buried here, often with brothers side by side and, just as often, young teenagers. Before charging the enemy in
human waves, many of these malleable souls were given pep talks by commanders, who employed actors to mount white horses to simulate the martyr Hussein's
valorous death charge 1,400 years before. These fallen heroes were each given
a plastic key, a ticket to paradise, to wear around their necks. In total, 123,000
shahids gave their lives in the war against Iraq. In making the gift of death, the
primitive (and modern) mindset says, one will receive the gift of life. Although
the Koran forbids suicide, it rewards the martyr: "Think not of those who are slain
in the cause of God as dead. Nay, they are alive in the presence of the Lord and
are granted gifts from him." There is no mention in the Koran of 72 black-eyed
virgins (houris) awaiting the martyrs, but that doesn't take away the oral histories
that say otherwise and the popular illusion of such a carnal paradise.

Intermixed with rose bushes and fluttering over a matrix of gray, slate tomb-
stones was a candle-like blaze of Iranian flags: green, white, and red. In the center of each flag was the red stylized symbol of Allah and a sword. Bordering the
flag's white stripe, in Kufic script, just like in the Koran, "Allahu akbar" (God
is great) is repeated 22 times. "The green means holy, and red is for the enemy,"
Mira said. Each grave marker was accompanied by a photo of the victim and
listed the age, birth, death date, and name, which was preceded by the honorific
shahid. The twin images of the Supreme Leaders were imprinted at the top of
each headstone, in a cerulean blue sky drawn with wisps of heavenly clouds.
The ayatollahs had made religion one with Iranian nationalism, as nationalism
was an integral part of religion.

The psychological impact of that war on most Iranians was severe; the country was bled white, particularly after the Ayatollah Khomeini took the fight to Iraqi soil. His apocalyptic speculations held that a Muslim Armageddon would occur in Karbala on the "path to Jerusalem." "The clerics could have stopped it four years sooner than they did," Mira told me. After eight years of war, "Iran was a bankrupt country," said Tehran-based political analyst Saed Laylaz. "No infrastructure, empty warehouses, empty stomachs, empty refrigerators, empty houses—empty everything."

A clutch of college students was filming headstones and billboards of Basij martyrs and Supreme Leaders. One student, pointing a video camera in my face, asked in an aggrieved tone if I would mind answering a few questions, such as "What is an American doing here?"

"The Iran-Iraq War is your history," I told her, feeling poorly equipped to fully apprehend or discuss the topic with a perfect stranger. "I am here to learn about and to respect the fallen soldiers." But we were coming from almost opposite psychic realms: they full of faith, real emotion, and loss and me suddenly flipping on my empathy switch. Equally surprised by the presence of an American visitor, a seventy-something, closely veiled woman interrupted to say she hoped that with our new leader relations between the two countries would be better. The student filming me then said that "everyone watched the execution of Saddam Hussein on television" and that "most Iranians were satisfied." Saddam's death was a step forward in the grieving process, which inevitably places a premium on truth finding and justice. Today, she told me, Iranians were less angry at the United States for supplying Saddam with fire power than they are with Germany and France for providing him with poison gas, which he employed on Iranian civilians and soldiers many times.[2]

Several sad-faced old women arrived with chairs, unfolded them in front of a son's grave, washed the stones with rose water, mumbled "praise be to Allah," and wept in silence. Emotion weighted the air like a heavy mist. The primal reality of a child's death must have thundered in their thoughts; the paradox of the atavistic practice that says the lamb is innocent but must be killed, for the lamb brings us salvation, is just as hard to exorcise today as it was in pagan and biblical times. For these martyrs, who were swept from their temporal joys in a concocted storm, the rewards of their holy acts are forever mysterious, airtight in a coffin. Two sayyids moved among the rose bushes. They offered solace to the shrouded figures of gathering women. From a distance, their stark, uniformed bodies struck me more like cutout apparitions than the flesh and tears of mama coming together with the better angels of the departed. And given the universal appeal of piety

---

2. Although she failed to mention it, the Reagan team "not only tolerated but implicitly encouraged" Saddam's use of chemical weapons.

and paradise (and group selection), this meeting of the bereaved and the buried, when viewed through the prism of human instinct, makes it difficult to overlook the seemingly polar dynamics of Darwinism—competition and cooperation—playing out over time.

⁓

Paradise is inherent in all faiths: from sunny Elysian Fields and the Garden of Eden, from that place of idyllic perfection before man's fall from grace to where Jesus promised to meet the Good Thief, to the abode of the virtuous believer and the Koranic heavenly garden. Faith in the goodness of God renders death less intolerable; it stretches "under human destiny like the net below trapeze artists." At the same time, the *Epic of Gilgamesh* and the Hebrew Bible book of Ecclesiastes exhorts us to accept our mortality and enjoy life ("dance and play day and night" and "drink thy wine with a merry heart"). No surprise then that it was the fear of death that fired up the misguided King Gilgamesh to set upon his quest for immortality, which, with great irony, transformed him into a wiser ruler, one, inferentially, informed by the good governance of the gods and the benefits of a less oppressed, more orderly civilization.

Today in the land flowing with milk and honey, fear and faith in paradise has left many followers of the Abrahamic religions, who profess biblical forbearance and a love of mankind, on a benighted course of mutually assured self-destruction. In other words, as with Gilgamesh's often-violent quest for immortality, the means are thought to justify the end. Even Darwin taught us that survival is not just about competition: cooperation is a factor, within family, clans, communities, nations, and networks. "Warfare is ultimately not a denial of the human capacity for cooperation," wrote anthropologist Lawrence Keeley, "but merely the most destructive expression of it."

Absent the guiding force of wise and transformative leadership—those who honestly confront the root causes of global poverty and conflict, and inequality and injustice—the attainment of that higher realm that good and decent people of faith, from Tehran to Tel Aviv to Texas, believe opens the gates to a paradise garden of orchards and flowing streams and final grace, pivots, in their mind's eye, now more than ever, on the mundane outcomes of sectarian, nationalistic power struggles. "Fanatics [and good and decent people] have a dream," said Israeli journalist Amos Elon, "by which they weave a paradise for a sect."

⁓

There are a few ancient communities, as old as the cry of the poet and the prophet and the plaintive pitch of the lyre, that have yet to knuckle under to the Middle East conflicts. Jews have lived in Iran for at least 2,500 years, since the time Cyrus ordered Solomon's Temple to be rebuilt. At the height of the Spanish Inquisition, the 15th-century Safavids welcomed Sephardic refugees here when Western Europe wouldn't. In World War II, Iranian diplomats stationed in Europe helped rescue thousands of Jews. While still in Paris, before returning from exile in 1979, Ayatollah Khomeini issued a fatwa that protected Iran's Jewish citizens; it's now in the constitution.

Today, the Islamic Republic is the most acrimonious, anti-Israel nation in the Middle East, while being home to more Jews than any other Muslim country in the world. The ayatollah's party line seems to be that the followers of the religion of Moses are tolerated, while Zionists are held in the highest contempt, seen as bloodthirsty offenders of Palestinian human rights. Holocaust denial and 9/11 as a Zionist conspiracy are views that are encouraged by President Ahmadinejad and many of Iran's ayatollahs. Although there are still over 30 synagogues in Iran, the Persian Jewish population of perhaps 25,000 souls declines by a few hundred each year, the West Bank and Los Angeles as beacons. Moreover, on this day in Esfahan, the newspaper headlines aimed at a familiar target: "Iran Dismantles Israeli Spy Network."

There was no sign on the green gate of the Keter David Synagogue as we entered, only a black tarp over the underwhelming entrance through a tall security wall. It was seven o'clock Friday night, Shabbat. Muslim style, shoes were lined up outside the door, above which Stars of David were etched on the synagogue walls. Through the cracked door I could see the room filled with men in yarmulkes and women in cheerful scarves, up to 200 in all. Horu, a tall, well-spoken college girl greeted me warmly in perfect English, cautioning me against taking a photo or going inside. A cantor was reading from the Torah.

Fashionably dressed, with a cascade of jet black curls flowing out of her flowery scarf, she talked fast, telling me that she was an accounting major at Esfahan University, that she had another year before graduating and no local possibilities for a job. She spoke of an uncle in Texas whom she would like to go live with but wasn't leaving Iran without her family. Indeed, there are over 125,000 Persian Jews living in the United States, many around Los Angeles.

Moshe Katsav, the president of Israel for seven years, was born in Yazd and lived his early years in Tehran. Like Katsav, over 130,000 Persian Jews have migrated to Israel, often enticed by payments of cash and land on the West Bank. Four years before, in Bokhara, Uzbekistan, I met Mark Dovev, a Ukrainian Jew whose family had recently relocated to the West Bank. It was a move he described as biblical, to Eretz Israel, that is, the land promised to all Jews. He all but taunted me to disagree. Mark was now the envoy in Central Asia and the Southern Caucasus for the World Jewish Agency for Israel, a nonprofit with origins dating to the Holocaust, which resettles Jews to Israel. Today, the whole enterprise smacks more of Zionist organizing and a blank check to biblical Judea and Samaria, the modern West Bank, than of humanitarian assistance. He was in Uzbekistan to entice Bokharan Jews who speak an eastern Persian dialect and claim lineal descent from the Lost Tribes of Israel. When I asked Mark who his donors were, he looked at me as if I were from Mars and said, "Rich Americans."

Horu told me there were 2,000 Jews still living in Esfahan. She wouldn't discuss persecution (if it were a problem). The bulk of emigrants left at the time of the 1948 Arab-Israeli War; then another wave (up to 50,000) exited after the Islamic revolution. This was not a surprise given that Jewish shop owners were initially required to put a sign in their windows identifying themselves as a minority. As with Zoroastrians and Armenians, Persian Jews are currently considered a minority religion, which mandates a seat in parliament for them. They serve in the army; more than a dozen died in the Iran-Iraq War. They travel to Israel via Turkey, but out of caution (especially under Ahmadinejad) their passports go unstamped in Israel. Those few hundred who leave the Islamic Republic each year do so, according to Horu, chiefly for economic and family reasons. Those who remain, she said, are here because they are Persian.

Two couples in their forties threw open the synagogue doors and began ululating, sashaying down the aisle. The energy turned from somber to festive. The congregation stood and clapped and chanted verses from the Song of Songs, a Hebrew love poem, some say an allegory of Israel as a paradise garden, keeping ancient rituals alive. Horu said the couples had married recently and were having a celebration in the synagogue. A renewed strength of faith and group identity has been the result of their isolation here. Drawn closer together, the synagogue is now the polestar of their social life. Or put another way, according to religious scholar Karen Armstrong, "the mythos of confessional religion is unsustainable without spiritual exercises."

Mira said that on the only other occasion she was here, Horu had played the same gatekeeper role—requesting no photos, parrying questions, discouraging any mingling, conversing but with a feigned warmth, and keeping it all on the down low. Or maybe on this evening the congregation just didn't like being treated as some kind of curiosity by a tourist. In a menacing way, it felt like 1933 and the Reichstag Fire had just happened here: These descendants of a 3,000-year-old community, I thought, were huddling and trying to figure out what to do next.

A few blocks away we had dinner at the Shahrzad. With its dark-paneled walls hung with paintings of Qajar court scenes, stained-glass windows, cut-glass mirrors, and floral motifs on the ceiling, the restaurant has an imperious air. Mr. Mehrdad, the gentlemanly owner, who has a noticeable limp and speech impediment, greeted us with menus and showed us to a window table. Impeccably dressed in a dark suit, but without a tie, and in spite of having a full house of prosperous-looking locals, he then took the time to retrieve a guest book for me to sign and had a waiter bring us a complimentary dish of crushed olives in a pomegranate sauce, a restaurant favorite. His Old World manners belied his age (late forties), and as it turned out, he had a special place in his heart for Americans.

Beginning in 1977, Mr. Mehrdad attended the University of Tennessee at Knoxville. While there he was in a horrible car accident, which left him with disabilities not unlike a stroke victim. The emergency care he was given saved his life, and that he had not forgotten. Today, Mr. Mehrdad has a Green Card, sings praises for America, and calls Knoxville his second home. He effused about his many friends in Knoxville and Atlanta. "When I am there each year I love to go to Barnes & Noble, have coffee, and read. Surrounded by all those books, it is one of my favorite things to do," he said, in a whisper, with a self-deprecating laugh. He told me about a cypress tree, the ancient Persian symbol of peace, which had been planted near the university in Knoxville when he was a student, before the accident, at the time of the Islamic revolution. On each visit to Knoxville, Mr. Mehrdad enjoys relaxing on a bench beneath the 30-year-old tree. "Now it's huge," he said, looking up and opening his arms with a smile. "It's interesting; I go there to think about all that has happened in my life here, compared to the one that surrounds the cypress. They are two different worlds. I enjoy them both."

A scrumptious dish of Fesenjan arrived, a chicken breast stewed in more of the pomegranate and walnut sauce, with a side dish of saffron rice and barberry. Mr. Mehrdad circled around to talk and check on the service and quality of the food. "You haven't mentioned Obama," I said. "You must be happy."

"That depends on whether you are Republican or Democrat," he said, leaning over, with a finger pressed to his lips, shushing me. "I'm a Republican, but I wish Obama well." I felt like shouting the popular song lyrics by Radio Head, "How come I end up where I started?"

Why would John "Bomb, Bomb Iran" McCain—who repeatedly trotted out a two-headed bogeyman by accusing Shia Iran of training Sunni al-Qaeda cells and who was often confused during the campaign about the difference between Shia and Sunni faiths—have been a better choice to Mr. Mehrdad than Barack Obama? Like tens of thousands of Iranian émigrés to America, Mira said that the fear of having to endure 30 more years of ayatollahs cramming the Islamic revolution down his throat is perhaps greater than the fear of what John McCain might inspire or actually do. "Many secular Iranians I know in Tehran were for McCain," she told me. "They expect America to lead but we know they cannot do that by imposing their will like Bush did in Iraq."

As it turned out, within 60 days of taking office, President Barack Obama reached out to Russia, calling for a nuclear-free world, and to the "Islamic

Republic of Iran," with a video message offering a "new beginning" of engagement on the first day of Noruz, the Persian New Year. While acknowledging that only actions, not "slogans," could repair the deep hatred of America in the Middle East, on June 4, 2009, at the thousand-year-old Al-Azhar University in Cairo, President Obama delivered a historic speech intended to repair ties with the broader Muslim world.

> It is easier to start wars than to end them. It is easier to blame others than to look inward; to see what is different about someone than to find the things we share. But we should choose the right path, not just the easy path. There is also one rule that lies at the heart of every religion—that we do unto others as we would have them do unto us. This truth transcends nations and peoples—a belief that isn't new; that isn't black or white or brown; that isn't Christian, or Muslim or Jew. It's a belief that pulsed in the cradle of civilization, and that still beats in the heart of billions. It's a faith in other people, and it's what brought me here today.

Less than two weeks after that speech, following Iran's stolen presidential elections, demonstrators from Freedom Square to Vali-e-Asr Avenue and across the country locked arms, wore veils and the green masks of the opposition, brandished protest signs, and intermittently shouted for Obama. At least one protest sign read "Death to Khamenei," until recently an unthinkable act of defiance. "Death to Israel and America" were but a distant echo to the new popular anger of the Green Movement. Old injustices and conspiracy theories, the bread-and-butter policy staple of the ruling ayatollahs, had molded and worn thin. In the days and weeks after the election, on many evenings the Green reformists stood on rooftops across Tehran and chanted, "Marg bar dictator" (Death to the dictator) and "Allah Akbar" (God is great). Peaceful street protesters, a young woman here (Neda Agha-Soltan), two-dozen students over there, were soon struck down, with bullets and batons, by members of the Party of God. Absolute power, in Iran more than anywhere, cannot sustain itself against popular outrage and the courage that never fails: that of Hussein the martyr. "The scythe swings," wrote Ryszard Kapuscinski of the '79 revolution, "and at once the grass starts to grow back. Cut again and the grass grows faster than ever." Then, as always, the oppressor's days are numbered, faith in right triumphs over fear of might.

As Mira and I were leaving the restaurant in Esfahan, Mr. Mehrdad met me at the door. Behind a mischievous grin and in his best southern drawl, he told me, "As they say in Tennessee, y'all come back now."

PART III

~

SHADOW AND LIGHT

An Arab Spring

CHAPTER TWENTY

~

Morocco and the February 20 Movement

Nights in Marrakech often go on longer than they should. On this morning I was feeling a bit woozy, but upon falling into Marrakech's cacophonous medina it felt like I had been zapped to life by a cultural cattle prod. It was a 20-minute walk from Hassan's barbershop to the heart of the Ville Nouvelle, where Joellen and I were meeting Idder Mounier for lunch. Twisting through the open-air spice market and the covered arcade, we sidestepped a gauntlet of beggars and moved aside at the donkey-cart-drivers' call of "balak, balak." Redolent of the Spanish paseo, a steady swarm of women in chic, tropical-bird-colored djellabas and headscarves passed around us. Men sat stoically in the teashops, frozen in ritual. Skirting the bombed and boarded remains of the Argana Café, we emerged onto the modern boulevards of Gueliz.

Tracing Avenue Mohammed V, named for the 1950s-era independence leader, palm and sour orange trees, beeping motorcycles, and Mercedes Benzes replaced the gritty ferment of the medina. The colonial French designed Ville Nouvelle this way, medieval and modernity separated literally by a bold line of rosy ramparts in the sand—and dividing Arabs and Berbers, rich and poor, and French and Moroccans. "If one thought of Gueliz, the modern, Western part of the city, as a trimmed and shaped topiary tree, such as one finds in the gardens of Versailles, the Boulevard Mohammed Cinq was the trunk of the tree," wrote Elizabeth Fernea in *A Street in Marrakech*. "And at the end of the trunk lay the roots, the thousands of tiny, tendril-shaped streets and alleys and sibhas and darbs that converged in some fashion of natural growth rather than imposed design upon larger tendrils, which emerged at last into the trunk again, nourishing, invisibly, the artificial topiary growth beyond."

Idder was waiting for us in front of the Catanzaro Restaurant, off Place du 16 November and Avenue Mohammed V. Joellen, fluent in French, was along to help in case Idder did not speak English. As it turned out, like many in Morocco, he speaks not only excellent English and French but also Arabic and serviceable Berber. At 28 years old, Idder is tall and boyishly handsome, with light brown hair and a stylish stubbly beard. He exudes a self-confidence that stops just short of self-absorption. After attending French schools in Morocco, he completed a graduate degree in finance and strategy at the prestigious Institute of Social Management (Institute de Gestion Sociale) in Paris. Today he works as a consultant and is a regular volunteer with the Circle of Young Moroccan Democrats (Cercle des Jeunes Democrates Marocains). More social movement than political party, the Circle advocates democratic values through nonviolent protest. Boasting a membership of 10,000, it is a cog in the coalition of activists, trade unions, volunteers, academics, bloggers, and political parties who organized the youth-based February 20 movement, the Moroccan version of the Arab Spring. Their Facebook slogan is "We Have a Dream."

Idder ordered a Heineken and steak au poivre, lit a cigarette, and began talking.

"Since independence Morocco has had an opposition force. It started with Mehdi Ben Barka. He stood up for the poor and opposed King Hassan II and the ruling Istiqlal (Independence) Party. For that disloyalty he was forced into exile and later assassinated in Paris. Fifty percent of Berber-speaking people are still illiterate, and Istiqlal would like to keep it that way."

I've traveled across Morocco, and it's not easy for me to tell who is Arab and who is Berber.

"It's not so clear. When the Arabs came they did not bring wives, so they married with the Berbers. Some of the Berbers were Christians, some Jewish, and others animists. The truth is our blood is mixed, but now we are mostly Muslim. My mother is militant about advancing the Berber cause. For a long time she has wanted to make the Berber language an official one along with French and Arabic. She is also working with historians and anthropologists to create a studies program to educate Moroccans on who the Berbers were before the Arabs arrived 1,300 years ago."

Berber rights are a piece of the February 20 movement's platform, but the overarching goal is to force, through a democratic process, the king to give up power.

"The word secular does not exist in Arabic. The Moroccan constitution says that we are a Muslim country and that the king will be an Alawite. We are asking for dignity for all, for human rights and democratic values, such as a parliamentary monarchy in five to ten years. Now the king [Mohammed VI] controls the executive, legislative, and judicial branches of government. The prime minister still kisses his hand," he said, extending his hand across the table for effect. "For two or three years he made reforms, especially after Morocco's Million Signatures campaign that pushed him to improve the lives of women, but then he stopped. Imagine in 20 years if we don't have a working civil society and solid democratic institutions and then a fundamentalist becomes king. Maybe this king has done something for women, but what will the next king do?"

On consecutive Sundays the king's antiriot police forces violently attacked peaceful protestors in Casablanca and Rabat. YouTube videos of truncheon-wielding police left no doubt about what happened. After drawing international criticism, the police backed off, but so did the protestors: they had lost momentum, and their numbers diminished over the following weekends.

"If it weren't for the February 20 movement, the king would not have promised in his March speech a move toward a parliamentary monarchy. On February 20, there were 150,000 people in ten locations, peacefully protesting." Pausing to have a bite and a sip of beer, he continued: "Istiqlal is a typical first-generation revolutionary force: it means independence, but it's really just crony capitalists who surround the king. Political parties in Morocco go the way of the hair, no change. They try to demonize us, saying that we are gay or communist or fundamentalist."

At least half of the million residents of Marrakech were directly affected by the Argana bombing. Several cab drivers told me that they were making four trips a day to the airport before, and now they are lucky if they go once. Flights from Europe are half what they were. Merchants are singing the blues, while the Ministry of Tourism says arrivals are only down 3 percent.

"I was in Rabat with a visiting group of young Democrats from the United States when the attack occurred. First you have to take all the information—what the press says, what the government says, and what people on the street are saying—and deconstruct it, and then rebuild. No question these terrorists were targeting tourists and tourism: mission accomplished; people are hurting. My guess is that arrivals are down by a third, but it is hard to tell because the summer season is just beginning."

Moroccans have no time for terrorists. After the 2003 Casablanca bombings a whole anti-jihadist hip-hop movement became the prevailing taste in music for Moroccan youth (and later across the Arab world). That didn't keep Idder from becoming awkwardly defensive as he continued talking.

"There are 40 million people in Morocco; 90 percent are Muslim, and most of them smoke and drink. In all of Morocco there may be 10,000 fundamentalists but not militant Islamists. This was not their [the fundamentalists] moment to get attention. Moroccans never gave a damn about bin Laden or al-Qaeda.

Anyone can go on the Internet and learn how to make a bomb or read about al-Qaeda. I think that the people responsible for the Argana did just that. But they don't represent Morocco. America was discovered in 1492, the same time as the Inquisition. Islam is not as old as Christianity, so maybe some are still aggressive like in the days of the Inquisition."

A Moroccan invoking the Inquisition should not have been a surprise. Thirteen hundred years ago the conquering Ummayad Syrian Arabs followed the map of the Romans across North Africa: first Jerusalem (638), and then like dominoes, Alexandria (642), Tripoli (644), Kairouan (670), Carthage (698), Fez (711), and finally, accompanied by the armies of the Maghreb Berbers, Gibraltar and up the Iberian Peninsula. In Arabic they called their new Iberian empire al-Andalus. The former Roman city of Cordoba became the caliphate of the Ummayad dynasty, and there, for two centuries, the golden years of active tolerance reigned, in which literature, science, and the arts flourished. At the same time, the Ummayads not only conquered a people and land of plenty but also straddled a religious and cultural fault line. For seven centuries the language of war was at a fever pitch: Christians against Muslims (known as Moors), Muslims fighting Muslims, Arabs versus Berbers, and Muslims and Christians against Jews. Emboldened by the chivalric legend of El Cid and *The Song of Roland*, which aggrandizes Christians fighting Muslims, the Reconquista and Crusades gave way to the Spanish Inquisition: a campaign of blood purity that expelled first the Jews and then the Moors. The nearest and most familiar escape for these refugees of al-Andalus was to Morocco, eight miles across the Strait of Gibraltar; the Ummayads had arrived from across the strait 700 years before. After the 2004 Madrid bombings, this history of Muslim grievance would prompt Osama bin Laden's al-Qaeda deputy to call the expulsion of Muslims from Spain "the tragedy in al-Andalus." Idder is not militant, but he knows his history and the people who surround him.

Three hours later, our lingering lunch ended. As we walked into the street, I asked him what he thought of President Obama.

"He forgot his family past. His mother worked for the CIA and his grandmother worked at the bank that handled CIA accounts. Did you not know this? I just read it last month."

"No, first time I heard that," I said, refraining from telling him it was just another crackpot conspiracy theory. Trusting Obama or the U.S. government, much less the CIA, I thought, is anathema to common sense in the Muslim Middle East.

"He will do whatever the voters tell him to do," Idder replied. "He may change things in form but not in substance. Peace is not in the interest of any leaders. You should read *Shock Strategy* by Naomi Klein. Obama did not deserve the Nobel Prize, but he does give hope to young people in Africa."

～

Retracing our steps up Mohammed V and into the central medina, west of the Bahia Palace and north of the old Jewish quarter, known as the Mellah, we entered Bert Flint's house, Maison Tiskiwin. Bert, a Dutch anthropologist, now in his 80s, first arrived in Marrakech in 1955, smack in the middle of the independence struggle. He came to study Moorish culture in Morocco for a year and never left. His body giving way to gravity, Bert now shuffles more than walks and is hard of hearing, but his mind is sharp and focused on the academic interests that first brought him to Marrakech.

Maison Tiskiwin is more museum than Marrakshi home: its walls and rooms are filled with crafts and artifacts from Burkina Faso, Senegal, Mauritania, Mali, Algeria, Nigeria, Niger, and Morocco. Using carpets and costumes, languages, and caravan route maps, Bert's museum artfully demonstrates the links between the ancient Berbers of Africa. He would prefer calling the recent revolutions in Tunisia, Libya, Egypt, and Morocco the African Spring.

"Moroccans unfortunately identify and are identified more with the Middle East than Africa, in spite of their Berber roots," Bert told me, as his assistant served us mint tea. "The rise in sea trade and desertification separated the Berber tribes of North and West Africa. Still, a Berber in Morocco can still understand a Fulani-speaking Nigerian."

"What percent of Moroccans speak Berber?" I asked.

"Maybe 40 percent can understand it and 30 percent actually speak the language," he told me. "Berber is taught in private schools, but it is difficult for kids to learn three alphabets—European, Arabic, and Berber. The reality is that the Arabic speakers are increasing faster than the students studying Berber."

Moroccans are not burdened by sectarianism, but there is intermittent friction between Arabs and Berbers. So I asked Bert why the vast majority of Moroccans identified with being Middle Eastern.

"You know what's going on in Darfur? I hear Americans don't understand these things."

"Of course I do," I said, brushing off his smugness. "But why don't you tell me."

"The Arabs are doing the same thing there that they did in Morocco 1,300 years ago. It's not because of Islam that Moroccans speak Arabic here. Look at Indonesia and Pakistan. Moroccans speak it because of the conquering Arab tribes."

～

We left Marrakech two days later to explore other parts of Morocco and to hear other voices of the Arab Spring. Turning off the N9 onto a high mountain dirt road, we headed toward Telouet, a former stop on the trans-Saharan caravan route. Before independence we would have been met at this junction by a Berber warlord, but now only a slightly aggressive man in a djellaba selling trilobite fossils attempted to hail us. At times the dirt track (or *piste*) was washed out, and our old Honda was less than inspiring with half the back bumper torn off. We passed through emerald-green, terraced fields of wheat that recalled the pastoral beauty of rice farming in the Far East. Encircled by the ginger-colored, barren ridges of the Atlas, Telouet was bustling. It was market day. Watermelon trucks were rolling in as if it were a competition for who grew the biggest one. Grand taxi drivers, the old Mercedes cars that are shared all across Morocco, and Berber *camionettes* (pick-up trucks) hawked seats and roof space as the market goers dispersed. We drew up next to a plastic table and a circle of local policemen, at Le Palace de Telouet, a cultured name for a countrified truck stop. Mohammed, the multitasking owner, cook, and parking manager, who had waved us into his earthen parking lot cum outdoor restaurant, covered the plastic table in a white cloth and served us a goat *tajine*, a Moroccan stew cooked in an earthenware pot.

The el Glaoui family's power is long gone, but their Kasbah still stands on the outskirts of Telouet as a monument to the warlord, caravan era. That afternoon we followed the old caravan route, meandering down the Telouet Valley, and traveling through geological time zones, each bend a new vista of vertiginous gorges and verdant valleys. Pueblo-like villages, such as Achahoud, were carved from stratified rock faces—blond-colored ones from pale rock, rosy-hued villages from red stone, and so on. Dusty, white minarets crowned these ancient, camouflaged-as-dirt-dauber enclaves. A system of ancient *qanats* irrigated wheat fields and the *palmeraie*, which were mixed with fruit orchards, varying in shades of green for the almonds, figs, apricots, and cherries. But for a few shepherd boys, we sighted only women in the fields and *palmeraie*.

More Hollywood stars have performed in the Kasbah at Ait Benhaddou than it now has residents (perhaps ten families). At the foot of the Telouet Valley, on the banks of the Ounila River, this tranquil, backwater village has provided the set for movies ranging from *Lawrence of Arabia* and *Jesus of Nazareth* to *Sheltering Sky* and *Gladiator*.

A friend in Marrakech had suggested we look up Ait Benhaddou's modern-day Lawrence, Andreas Reinhartz, a German adventurer who, along with his Berber wife Khadija, owns a small auberge. Tall, lean, and worn, Andreas met us at the door in a Berber blue turban, streaked in sunset orange, its tail fashionably wrapped around his neck. For 20 years, Andreas was a Saharan lorry driver, while also guiding adventure tours across the desert. He gave that up a decade ago to settle down with Khadija, who had been his cook on the Saharan tours.

She brought us a pot of mint tea, as her sister looked after their three children. Andreas performed the long Berber pour: the spout elbow's length from the narrow tea glass, it deepens the flavor. We were the only guests in the auberge, the terrace of which overlooked the Kasbah. Nothing moved there.

Berber social structure is tribal and hierarchal. Here they are matrilineal, a wife can choose her spouse. Khadija inherited the land for the auberge, formerly a mill where donkeys ground wheat. Andreas provided the money and contractor skills to build it. Khadija has only three years of education and is 30 years old. If she needs to write a letter, the village scribe does it for her for a small fee. "Why not use a scribe?" Andreas asks. "He needs a job."

Dinner was like breaking the fast during Ramadan, first *harira* (tomato and lentil soup) and dates, sweet to go with spicy. Andreas talked while we ate, delighting in educating us on the realities of rural Berber social structure.

"Moroccans don't trust each other. If you have a meal at a restaurant, everyone gets paid when the customer is finished: the butcher next door and the cook in the kitchen. When I built this house I could not be the carpenter, only the contractor. It's a full employment act, not just for the village but in the family, too. If my brother-in-law is unemployed, then he will steal from me and I can't sue him."

Does the Arab Spring mean anything to Khadija and her family?

"It's different in Morocco than the rest of the Middle East. The king is legal, and he is holy. He is a descendant of Mohammed. He has Baraka. He can touch people like the pope does and they are blessed. He helps poor Moroccans just enough to make them love him."

Idder had touched on corruption at a higher level, and I had had a traffic cop try to extort money from me, but I was curious how it affected villagers.

"Corruption is a big problem in Morocco. I have to pay baksheesh for tax stamps and contracts," he said, as he pulled out his identity card for me to inspect. "Everyone has to have one of these and everyone has to pay a bribe to get it."

In Tangier, Fez, and Marrakech, random people I talked to had bragged about Morocco's 2004 Million Signatures campaign that forced the king to adopt a new family code, the *moudawana*, that improved women's rights. As Khadija filled the table with chicken brochettes and potato pancakes, Andreas spoke with passion about the woman's plight in Morocco.

"Before if a woman was pregnant and not married, she had to give up the child and go to prison for three months. The man had no responsibility. That's why there were 600 abortions a day in Morocco; women have to keep their unwanted pregnancies a secret."

Andreas paused to light another cigarette and pour more tea. "Before, a Moroccan man could say go away three times," he told us, waving his hand like he was swatting flies, "and he was divorced. Now a woman gets 300 dirhams a month and 75 percent of the property. There is a special court for women if there is violence or problems in the home. They deserve protection. If women didn't work here, 50 percent of the men would starve to death."

The next morning as we were loading the car, Khadija motioned us into the dining room for tea, cherry jam, flatbread, and argan oil (produced and sold by women's cooperatives in Morocco). Andreas was having a bowl of *harira*, with his six-year-old son curled up next to him.

We would hear more about Berber women over the next week.

～

At Ouarzazate—a crossroads town at the confluence of the Atlas, Draa, and Dades valleys—we turned northeast on the N10. Sixty miles on, we were greeted on the outskirts of Kelaa M'Gouna by teenagers selling garlands of roses and rose water, reputed to be the best in Morocco. With the windows down, the fragrant aroma of pink roses, hidden in gardens behind the hundreds of miles of hedgerows in and around the Kelaa M'Gouna oasis, permeated the air. By noon we had turned north off the N10 and were flanked by the red rock formations of the Dades Valley. We randomly pulled to a stop in front of a small guesthouse in Ait Oudinar.

Daoud Ochatou, forty-something, sporting a salt-and-pepper Afro and soul patch, said hello in French and English, startling us with his British accent. A musician, who plays traditional Berber folk music, Daoud splits his time between his ancestral home in Ait Oudinar and his Belgian wife in Brussels. Off and on for 20 years he has lived in London and Paris and toured extensively in the United States. Adorning the shelves and walls of his dining room was an impressive collection of traditional instruments: *tan-tans* (bongo drums), *bendir* (goatskin-covered wooden drum), *qarqabas* (metal clackers), and a pear-shaped, intricately painted oud, the instrument for which he is known. After he showed us a photo of him playing in London with Carlos Santana, we acted on the temptation to purchase one of his CDs, ritual music of hypnotic, chanted prayer and poetry often played at weddings and dances.

Daoud's 27-year-old brother Yusef appeared from the kitchen, introduced himself, and sat down in front of the computer. Yusef had been helping his mother prepare lunch for two other guests in this family enterprise. Broad-shouldered, handsome, and with an easy smile, in halting English, he offered to take us trekking in the gorge. We talked about the rains, which had been so heavy this year that the mud huts of the village were starting to melt. He assured us that it wouldn't rain on this afternoon. We wasted no time in jumping in the new family Toyota SUV and driving a couple of miles downstream to Ait Ouiglif.

From the headwaters here the Dades River flows 900 miles, through the Western Sahara, and into the Atlantic Ocean. Berbers built several Kasbahs in the valley because the high valley walls provided a natural defense against invading armies. Yusef called the vertical red folds of the gorge the "hand of the monkey." We crossed the river on a wooden footbridge into the lush and colorful *palmeraie* of almonds and walnuts, roses and oleander, poplars and date palms, stands of bamboo, and a few spiraling plane trees. Above, kids could be heard skylarking on the walls of an abandoned Kasbah. Storks flew low and languorously above the river. Turning into a narrow passage that tapered to a window-size crevice, with an inviting urgency to explore, we waded through a clear pool of water and beyond to a small waterfall. Yusef climbed up between two rocks, planted a foot to be used as a step, and held out his arms: he practically dead lifted me up the rock face. He would repeat this amazing feat of balance and strength for both of us, six or seven times, over the next four hours. The trek was more like spelunking with a skylight. And if it was to rain, and a flash flood occurred, we were goners: we were tracing a rivulet to the top, with no exit until the end.

Until he was 15, Yusef lived as a desert nomad, with almost no formal education. "But nomads have good memories," he said (speaking in French). "They know many languages, and they learn history, folklore, poetry, and survival techniques to use and pass along to their children." He is a man of many hobbies as well: trekking, cooking, playing music, dancing, drinking fig brandy, and smoking hashish. His brother says he is a playboy; the foreign women love him. He struck me as partial to the locals: "Berber women are strong and do all the work. Men drink tea and do nothing. Life is tranquil with a Berber wife."

"What about praying on Friday? Don't men at least do that?" I asked.

"Maybe 20 percent go to the mosque," he said. "The women are much more religious, but in small villages like ours there is no place for them at the mosque. They pray at home and live by Islamic values [dress, education, and social mores]."

The solitude was spectacular. The pungent smell of purple and white thyme, flourishing along the stream and in the mountains, mixed deliciously with the sensation of sandaled feet in cool waters, ringed by branching oleander and nature-imitating-art geology. Then Yusef's cell phone would ring and break the spell. He would laugh out loud about how we had traveled so far to enjoy the solitude of the Dades Gorge, but Berbers would give anything to take in the fast action of New York or Boston. The farthest Yusef had been was Marrakech.

He described Hassan II, the last king, as a despot but said that everyone liked Mohammed VI and that he was good for Morocco. Still, "Berbers and Arabs fight like cats and dogs," he said. "We always have and probably always will.

Berbers are 80 percent of the population." That demographic is a moving target in Morocco, depending on who is providing the statistic. (Bert Flint was probably closer to the right number.)

We climbed nature-carved steppingstones, along the bough of a tree, and into a narrow passage—two massive boulders pressed together. Joellen and Yusef inched through sideways and held their breath while I sucked it up, all but applauding when I emerged. Soon Yusef was pulling us up the last rock face, out of our private adventure into the unknown. From there, we walked the ridge-line overlooking the valley, on the trail of Berber women (one with a baby in a sling), their panniers loaded with herbs (such as purple thyme), animal fodder, and branch wood. We rested where they rested, on long piles of rocks they had stacked, arranged at an angle, where, after a day of gathering in the mountains, they could perch and pause without removing their heavy loads.

～

Arriving in Agdz, after eight hours of driving, we needed to shake the sand off our bodies. We had been in the desert for three days. The night before was spent in the empty and forbidding beauty of the red dunes of Erg Chebbi, where a blue-robed nomad named Mohamed looked after us. Our Berber camp was set in a bowl of silk-smooth sand, protected like a hideout in a box canyon. The camel-and-goat-hair tents were walled and floored in Berber rugs. The desert, beyond the hobbled camels away from the camp, was the restroom for the camp. We drank Berber tea and sat on rugs outside, watching the stars appear, one by one, each an icon unto itself, while Mohamed made a fire and cooked a simple *tajine* of potatoes and goat. Night fell, the fire went out, and there was perfect silence. The sky was now full, the stars brilliant and palpable, their shapes and alignments an existential wonder. Each time I awoke, they were still there but moving across the sky like luminous frames of a slow-motion movie. While a good shower would be enough to wash away the dust of the desert, the memory of that nomad night would linger for a lifetime.

We cleaned up and found ourselves street side in Agdz. Swatting flies with one hand and eating with the other, we watched disgruntled miners march through the main square. With bullhorns blasting, banners waving, and angry fists ripping the late afternoon air, men marched together in a loose formation followed by women, all in hijabs. Many of the protestors were black-skinned. The farther south we traveled, the more people of sub-Saharan origins we encountered—just as Bert Flint had mapped out in his Marrakech museum.

The purpose of the stopover in Agdz was to visit the nearby Berber village of Tamnougalt's 16th-century *ksar* (castle), strategically built at the head of the Draa Valley on the treacherous trans-Saharan trade route from Timbuktu to Marrakech. The journey at the time took 52 days: 1,000-camel caravans plodded the desolate landscape, laden with gold, ivory, salt, sugar, and slaves from West Africa to be sold in Europe and the Middle East. From the *ksar* watchtower, the view was to the south, the better to spot unfriendly Tuaregs arriving through the pass. Mountains surrounded it on two sides and water on the other. In the 16th century, the Beni Saad Berbers ruled from Marrakech to Timbuktu. While local chiefs paid tribute to the ruling Berbers in Marrakech, 4,000 people lived within the mud-brick walls of the *ksar*. Today, only the caretaker families are there.

Hamid Aithssain was a one-man greeting committee as we inched our way through the narrow village gate. Throughout Morocco I had witnessed the separation of men and women, of Jews and Muslims, but never had I seen such a fluid mixing of races. I asked Hamid about the multiracial makeup of the village. "A family might have one brother who is black and the other one not. No one cares and there is no separation," he continued. "There is no racism. The caravans brought us all together. Islam is an organic body that accepts everyone." I took those last words under advisement.

Although the architecture is a subtle mix of Arabic, Andalusian, and Berber Jewish, Hamid said the broader design, in which all radiates from a middle courtyard, comes from the layout of Berber camps. He showed us the well-preserved horse-arched courtyard, open to the sky, often used for public meetings between the ruling *caids* and Jewish leaders. The rooms branching off the courtyard were entered through low-cut doors, not because of the size of people, but to show modesty with a bow. The post office was on the second floor: a corner perch for the carrier pigeons. From the terrace we watched Berber women retreating from the *palmeraie*, crossing a footbridge over a canal. "Water rights here are hereditary," Hamid said. "Each family owns a plot of land for their garden and date palms."

The Mellah (Jewish Quarter) had seen better days, but it was still possible to comprehend the layout of the synagogue. "Jewish people from France and Israel come here and say they are going to restore it," Hamid told us. The mosque dome had disappeared, but we were able to identify the mihrab. Nearby was an ablution fountain and mud-brick bench for preparing corpses for burial. Both the Torah and the Koran require a fast burial; it would show a lack of respect to let the body decompose. Since both religions grew out of the same desert, the similar burial rituals came as no surprise. Hamid explained the burial preparation: a man by older men and a woman by elderly women—washing the corpse, applying oils and perfume, and shrouding it in cotton. Cremation or discussing the state of the corpse was haram, or forbidden, Hamid told us. Death is thought to be Allah's will. The corpse has to be returned to earth, placed on its right side, facing Mecca. After throwing three handfuls of dirt on the grave (similar to the Judaic tradition), a Koranic verse is recited: "We (God) created you from it (earth), and we return you into it, and from it we will raise you a second time."

∼

Two weeks later, we took an early bus from Essaouira to Marrakech, where we caught an afternoon train to Casablanca. We shared a second-class compartment with Khadija, Yusef, and their five-year-old Arwa, a name taken from the aunt of the Prophet that means pleasant and fresh. Indeed, she was reading an Arabic translation of the children's classic *Sleeping Beauty*. Very dark-skinned, Yusef is originally from Er-Rachidia and works in information technology. Khadija, who was wearing a scarf and djellaba, with blue jeans underneath, teaches French at a secondary school outside of Ouarzazate and has recently written a book, *Êtres de sable* (Beings of the Sand). They both speak a salad of languages, and Khadija said she plans on learning Hebrew. "A useful language that is close to Arabic," she said.

Khadija talked all the way to Casablanca, while Yusef took care of Arwa. They were going to Rabat, a trip she makes once a month to see a psychiatrist for postpartum depression. "I just had my second child eight months ago. She is staying with family," she told us. "I am getting better, and my work pays for the trips to Rabat."

She told us about the American movies and television programs she watches on the MBC (Middle East Broadcasting Centre) channels and other pan-Arab TV networks. Bruce Willis, Tom Cruise, Eddie Murphy, and Denzel Washington were but a few of her favorite actors on the 24-hour movie channel. She failed to mention any women, but she does tune into Oprah and thinks Dr. Phil gives good advice on women and children.

"We know all about American culture and elections, but Americans only know Morocco by the Marrakech bombing and the movie *Casablanca*," she blurted out. "There is more to Morocco."

"It's true," Joellen said. We all laughed together.

Khadija—who is named after the Prophet's wife, the first convert to Islam—grew up listening to her grandmother's stories about life as a nomad but doesn't remember her grandfather. He went off in the desert one day and never returned. "The stars didn't show him the way back," she said, wistfully. Encouraged to tell her story by a French painter and photographer, Khadija is traveling to France in September to promote her book. *Êtres de sable* is dedicated to her family and to Mohammed, the Prophet. "Before Mohammed when desert nomads had a baby girl they dug a hole and buried her. Mohammed taught us to love our daughters, not to bury them."

She spoke lovingly about Yusef and how he is an equal partner in parenting. "He always travels with me to Rabat to see the doctor. Berbers respect women. Yet there are a lot of regional differences within Morocco regarding the treatment of women."

I gave Arwa a bag of M&Ms for the ride on to Rabat. Soon we fell into the slipstream of cosmopolitan Casablanca.

∿

More Jewish people live in Casablanca than anywhere else in Morocco. In March of 2009, Islamic fervor and anti-Semitism were endemic in the Middle East. Iranian president Mahmoud Ahmadinejad was throwing fuel on the fire by denying the Holocaust. Yet, King Mohammed VI took a more moderate and courageous course, one that reflected Morocco's history of living side by side with Jews: he gave a speech in Paris, calling the Holocaust "one of the most tragic chapters in history." At the same time, he endorsed the newly launched Aladdin Project, an initiative to spread the word of the Holocaust, which he called "the universal heritage of mankind," to Muslims.

Jews have lived in Morocco for over 2,000 years. After 1492 and the Inquisition in Spain, their numbers surged. Jews (and Christians) were assured safety here under the Koranic injunction known as *dhimmi*—Arabic for the protected "Peoples of the Book." This accommodation existed through the 19th century, as long as a special tax called *jizya* was paid. During the years of Nazi persecution, before and during World War II, Morocco (and Tunisia) became a safe haven, protected by King Mohammed V—who, to the chagrin of fascist-leaning French colonialists—wrote "equality for all" into the constitution. Since World War II, though, Morocco's medieval Mellahs have emptied. Three pivotal events triggered this emigration now known as the "trek through the desert": the 1948 creation of Israel, the 1962 ascension of King Hassan II to the throne, and the 1967 Six Day War. It also is difficult to measure what effect Zionist organizing, set against local attitudes and persecutions (boycotts, assassinations, and press campaigns), had on shrinking the Moroccan Jewish population from 300,000 at the end of World War II to a mere 7,000 today. Those families who stayed now live predominantly in Rabat or Casablanca, where there are 42 synagogues.

When I stopped by the Verdan Place synagogue on the Sabbath, Simon the caretaker, now in his 80s, told me they had had 60 worshipers that day; their total membership was 250. He grew up in Er-Rachidia but moved to Casablanca in 1965. "No more rabbi or synagogue. No one to worship with," he told me, after I asked him why he moved. "Then my kids left for school and never came back. I was there alone and decided to move to Casablanca." Symptomatic of the '60s in Morocco and those early days of Hassan II's rule, the rabbinate was not invited to the Feast of the Throne, the annual national celebration of the king's ascension that historically included Jews, Christians, and Muslims.

I had visited Mellahs and synagogues in almost every city I traveled to in Morocco—Tangier, Fez, Casablanca, Marrakech, Essaouira, Meknes, and so on. Most of the synagogues are closed or have become museums, funded by former members or their descendants. Even the Sephardic Museum (which I also visited) in Cordoba, Spain, has a room paid for by the Israeli Community of Marrakech and Essaouira.

Simon Levy, a longtime political activist and general secretary of the Foundation of Jewish-Moroccan Cultural Heritage, wrote about the one million Jewish Moroccans throughout the world: "We Jews of Morocco were never expelled from our country of origin. Just like the four million expatriate Moroccan Muslims, whenever we want to, we can return to Morocco, go home to where our parents lived. That's what 'globalization' means."

～

We walked west of the medina to the American Language Center, a school sponsored by the U.S. government for young Moroccans to learn English. All the high walls and heavy security made it no less attractive to the throng of students in the hallways and classrooms. I was there looking for a Paul Bowles novel in the bookstore. Ten minutes later I was standing on the street corner working out directions to Casablanca's Jewish museum, the only one in the Muslim world. Bilal Abdellah pulled up two feet away, leaned out the window of an aging SUV, with a cigarette in hand, and asked if he could be of help. After a brief vetting, I was sitting shotgun.

Abdellah, as he liked to be called, is from Zagora in the south. After 20 years in the city, he hasn't lost his country boy manners. Dark-skinned as his ancestors who no doubt came from sub-Saharan Africa way back in the mists of time, he weaved through Friday's traffic snarls, chatting and chortling, "People are crazy in the city. They are much better behaved in the south." Twenty minutes later we were inching by a crush of men, crossing the street next to the Gare Oasis, leaving a mosque after Friday prayer. Soon we turned into a wealthy neighborhood of walled homes and winding streets. We passed the museum twice before noticing two guards stepping out from behind an unmarked gate. After all, a Jewish community center was targeted in the 2003 bombings. The guards, all Muslim, showed us in, while they shared with Abdellah a plate of their couscous, the traditional Moroccan meal after Friday prayer.

Three rooms of the museum featured religious and family life, with shadow boxes of Torahs, period costumes, and Chanukah lamps; one room served as a mock synagogue. Simon Levy is the founder, and Zhor Rehihill is the curator. Dressed in jeans and a tight-fitting blouse, Zhor is short, attractive, and, as a Muslim, effervescent about her beliefs in a multicultural Morocco and Middle East. Educated as an anthropologist, she is fluent in French and English, and speaks and writes classical Arabic.

"We reach out to all schools in Morocco—French, American, and Moroccan—and to Christians and Muslims, with a message about our work here," she told us. "Jews, Christians, and Muslims in the Middle East worship the same God. The similarities between us in our religious, linguistic, and cultural traditions are everywhere. Many Muslim families in Morocco have Jewish names; and 800 years ago they were Jewish," she continued. "Even in my family we have certain traditions which are Jewish. Where did that come from?"

She handed us a museum brochure that sketched out the closeness between Judaism and Islam: single God, common prophets, circumcision, *qibla*, prayer, burial, halal food, ritual slaughtering, and sacrifice.[1] Further, many local traditions are now common to both Jews and Muslims, relating to marriage (the use of henna), family celebrations, the evil eye, the cult of the saints (*moussem*), and *mimouna*, a day when Jewish families receive their Muslim friends. Having recently attended an exhibition on the three Abrahamic religions, I brought up a few broader commonalities: revelation through individuals or groups, scriptures communicated to human authors, public and private prayer and worship, the spreading of the word, and an afterlife that ranges from a messianic era of universal harmony to eternal heaven and everlasting paradise. For better or worse, the three faiths also believe that heaven and earth come together in Jerusalem: the Temple Mount, where God's divine presence descended; the Dome of the Rock (also the Temple Mount) from which Mohammed ascended; and the Church of the Holy Sepulcher, where Jesus was crucified, buried, and resurrected.

Oren Kosansky overheard our discussion with Zhor and introduced himself. We stepped into Zhor's office; other tourists had arrived. An associate professor of anthropology at Lewis & Clark College in Oregon, Oren received a grant from the National Endowment for the Humanities to digitalize Judaic Moroccan documents from the 18th century forward—known as the Rabat Genizah Project. That Oren speaks French, Arabic, and Hebrew facilitates his work with the thousands of documents written in Judeo-Arabic, an Arab dialect written in Hebrew script. Having just toured the museum—which left me with the distinct

---

1. Against the belief of the early messianic Jews who followed Christ, including Jesus's brother James and disciples Peter and John, the apostle Paul preached a "gospel" that "dropped all Torah requirements." A generation later, John of Patmos, author of Revelation, was outraged at Paul for not following the hereditary sexual, social, and dietary practices. Five centuries later, Islam would adopt many of the Torah traditions.

impression that Morocco was accommodating to Jews and other cultures—I asked him why then did the vast majority of Moroccan Jews emigrate?

"Zionist organizing was part of it," Oren said. "Remember, however, that Zionists were originally socialists, and most Moroccan Jews were not socialists."

"Yet they were often given land and money to emigrate," I suggested, after explaining that my own ancestors had migrated to the United States over two centuries ago for money, land, and a better future.[2]

"If you give your average 19-year-old Moroccan money and a passport, do you think he is staying in Morocco? Look how many are in Europe. The 20th century was characterized by migration and globalization," he continued. "After the Holocaust and the '67 war, fear was a factor, but neither fear nor the enticements offered by Zionist organizers were dominant reasons. I would argue that liturgical reasons, that Jews pray to Jerusalem, played a bigger part than fear."

"So it was faith," I said.

"Yes." After a moment of reflection, he finished, "Because they were Moroccan—and culture often precedes religion—their departure was not bittersweet, but bitter and sweet. It was a complex matrix of reasons."

⌒

The much-anticipated king's speech finally came at 9:00 p.m. on June 17, 2011. On television he spoke for 25 minutes in Arabic, followed by 25 minutes in French (perhaps for all those Moroccans living in France). We were still in Casablanca, leaving for Tunisia in two days. We had seen glimpses of the speech on TV in Arabic but had gone to bed by the time he finished in French. It wasn't long before Casablanca's neighborhoods were thronging with revelers. The celebratory street parties went on until four in the morning (at least that's when the commotion below our window died out).

In a referendum on constitutional reforms a mere ten days later, the government claimed a 70 percent voter turnout, 98.5 percent of whom voted for the king's proposals. The February 20 movement boycotted and called the vote result a masquerade. On paper, the king's birthright of absolute dominance had been reduced: greater power was ceded to the prime minister and parliament, the judiciary system was overhauled, gender equality was spotlighted, and Berber was recognized as an official language. The king lost his "sacred" status in the constitution but is still regarded as the "Commander of the Faithful." Reading between the lines, however, there are many reasons to be dismayed: the king remains, directly or indirectly, the "supreme arbiter" of political and institutional life in Morocco.

---

2. There are studies of the settlement of Israel that assert that 30 percent of immigrants are ideologues, and 70 percent arrived for economic reasons.

Protests by the February 20 movement have continued on Sundays in most major cities. Though reports suggest they have lost momentum, Facebook users in Morocco have grown from 800,000 in 2009 to three million today. The country remains a test case for other Middle East monarchies, which have scant history of bowing to popular will. The king's father, "Hassan II, was amoral, a classic Machiavellian," said exiled journalist Aboubakr Jamai at a seminar I later attended. "This means he was wise enough to give a little when necessary, cracking the door open to the Islamist PJD [Justice and Development Party], to human rights groups, and to unions." It was this kind of "social intermediation" in which civil society stakeholders feel like they are a part of the decision process that prevented Morocco from erupting like Tunisia and Egypt. Further, in 1994, Aboubakr said, King Hassan II gave passports to everyone and did not block the borders to illegal immigrants. Today, those immigrants send home up to seven billion dollars a year, mostly going to poor families. These remittances are a stabilizing force for Morocco, masking the state's failings in areas such as housing and education. The king, Aboubakr says, is "the optimizer" of conservatives and progressives, of rich and poor, paying lip service to all.

The next day Abdellah was invigorated by the king's speech. He saw it as closure to the bombing in Marrakech and the weekly protests that had taken their toll on his tourist business. Like most Berbers I had met, Abdellah has nothing negative to say about the monarchy. The food and fuel subsidies Mohammed VI provides are important to Abdellah's family of five.[3] He praised the king—often called the monarch of the poor—for his prior reforms when he raised the salaries of the police, military, and gendarmes. "Before they would stop me and say give me 50. Now any baksheesh and they go to jail."

We drove to the massive Hassan II Mosque, on the waterfront. Topped by a laser-beam that shines toward Mecca, the 650-foot minaret makes it the tallest building in Morocco. More importantly, it's the third-biggest mosque in the world, after Mecca and Medina. Pilgrims from around Morocco call it the Casablanca Hajj, a Moroccan version of the fifth pillar of Islam. Built to commemorate Hassan II's 60th birthday, and paid for mostly by public donations, it took 13 years and over half a billion dollars to complete. Taking in the ablution room with 41 marble fountains, the hammam with an Olympic-size pool, and the prayer hall with a sliding roof (like Dallas Cowboys Stadium) and 56 chandeliers from Venice, I was reminded of what Aldous Huxley had to say about extravagance in the name of faith: "The most convincing way of proving that a given place is holy is to make it so grand and so beautiful that when they see it, people catch their breath with astonishment and awe. Fine architecture is one of the visible embodiments of mana."

---

3. Most of the subsidies come from the Mohammed V Foundation, which each year raises funds from businesses with ties to government. Recipients must tow the line or receive nothing.

Abdellah then drove toward Rabat, through the slums and shantytowns north of Casablanca that called up the sad-sack townships of South Africa. Many had been bulldozed and replaced by social housing. "This is where the terrorist bombers of 2003 came from," he said, pointing to a cluster of ramshackle homes. "The king has promised to get rid of all of these by 2015."

We passed through affluent bedroom communities, such as Mohammedia, where condos cost $300 a square foot. Upscale retreats such as the Bahia Golf Course and Country Club and the Kasbah Bouznika dominated the flag-lined roadway all the way to the king's palace in Rabat, where modernity and ambitious planned development conjured up Dubai or Singapore. Founded 800 years ago by the Almohads, a Moroccan-Berber dynasty, but rescued from decline by Christian corsairs fleeing Spain with the Muslims in the 17th century, the Kasbah and medina of Rabat overlook the mouth of the Oued Bou Regreg and the Atlantic Ocean. Hassan's tower, the unfinished red sandstone minaret begun in 1196 by Sultan Yacoub al-Mansour, and its open hypostyle terrace, the Roman ruins, and the Merenid necropolis of Chellah all paled next to the Rameses-like building that is currently underway. Bringing together Rabat with its sister city of Sale, the 150-foot-wide Hassan II Bridge is part of a spanking new tram system, with 31 stations and, so far, 12 miles of track. On the banks of the river, yachting marinas have been added, along with a grandiose theater designed by an Iranian architect, hotels, public buildings, skyscrapers, and Parisian-like boulevards and green spaces. Only a Sovereign Wealth Fund, a Chinese planned economy, or a Moroccan king could make such a spectacular public works program come to fruition.

"Look, look," Abdellah said, pointing to a tram that pulled up next to us. "It has a woman driver." Further along, on the palm-lined Avenue Mohammed V, in front of Parliament, were 30 or 40 protestors with a sign that read, "We love our king. We want [the] rights of war prisoners [a reference to political prisoners]."

"All parties are afraid of the king," Mustapha, a retired state finance employee of 32 years, told me at dinner a few nights before. "If he wants a business, his people come and take it. The king is the biggest landowner in the country; he controls the biggest bank and the largest insurance and telecommunication companies. Most people would like him to just stay out of business."

Unaffordable monuments to faith, eradication of urban slums, huge gaps between the rich and poor, the medieval facing off with the modern, gender equality,[4] human rights violations, civil society, corruption, equitable justice

---

4. Even with the new constitution's shout-out for gender equity, women in Morocco remain vulnerable: Apart from fears over the November 2011 parliamentary elections that handed the (moderate) Islamist Justice and Development party a victory, the family code (*moudawana*) adopted in 2004 changed the law but not repressive social customs and mores. Rape and domestic violence complaints are routinely mishandled by an untrained police force and by an unfriendly judiciary. Further, official numbers show that 41,000 marriages to minors occurred in 2010, up 25 percent from the year before.

and the king's broad powers, and inestimable wealth are all ingredients in the murky gumbo of 21st-century Morocco.

Abdellah gave us a ride to the airport the next morning. On the way, Joellen translated aloud an interview with Benjamin Stora, author, historian, and expert on North Africa, by Renaud De Rochebrune in *Jeune Afrique*, a Paris-based magazine. I summarized the article in my notes while Joellen and Abdellah talked.

Since independence 50 years ago it is not reality that has been the object of debate but ideology: it has been anticolonial and anti-imperial, a rejection of the West while embracing Arab nationalism and Islamism. When it's all focused on ideology you don't talk about real problems: jobs, the economy, effective relations with the West, and how one's own history favors ideas of conspiracy and secrecy.

We were Tunisia bound, to the fountainhead of the Arab Spring.

CHAPTER TWENTY-ONE

~

The Jasmine Revolution

Concertina wire, tanks, soldiers, and police were strung along the pedestrian parkway of the Ville Nouvelle from the Place de Independence to the Place du 7 November 1987, which is centered by a clock tower and commemorates the day President Ben Ali took power. Joellen and I were staying a block away, next to the medina. A couple of days after arriving in Tunis we found ourselves pressed against the concertina wire, angling for a view of French and Tunisian actors on set in front of the corn-colored Cathedral St. Vincent de Paul. Directed by French filmmaker Alexandre Arcady and based on a novel by Yasmina Khadra, *What the Day Owes the Night* (*Ce que le jour doit a la nuit*) is based on events that took place in the 1930s in Algeria (the tanks and concertina were not props). Famously, *Star Wars* was filmed in the desert of Tunisia over three decades ago, but more recently the film industry here has been in the doldrums.

Zied Jallaili, a 25-year-old graduate of the University of Tunis, Carthage, working as a production assistant on the film, introduced himself to us from the other side of the ropes. "It's cheap to film here, and we have competent people," he told us, adding that his father was an executive producer. We watched several takes of a car scene with French police, while dueling smartphones were drawn and we became Facebook friends. His favorite musicians were Americans Wynton Marsalis, Joe Bonamassa, and Matt Savage, and Syrian jazz singer Lena Chamamyan. He watches the *Daily Show* and NessmanTV, a Maghreb channel that features sitcoms on politics, Arab history, and Islamic culture and an Arab version of *Who Wants to Be a Millionaire?*

Zied told me that he had attended a protest in Sousse, 85 miles south of Tunis, on January 14, the day President Ben Ali was ousted, ending a 23-year dictatorship. Amid a noisy backdrop, for a few minutes Zied and I discussed the people and events that seeded the Jasmine Revolution. We later elaborated that conversation by e-mail.

"I remember having seen a documentary about the collapse of communism. In Eastern Europe the frequency of political jokes and cartoons and protest songs had increased over time," Zied said. "El General's [a hip-hop singer] song ("Rais Lebled") was one of those indicators that fed the mood of anger and frustration in Tunisia and helped create other [songs]. These last years Tunisians started to criticize Ben Ali's regime openly at universities and in cafés. The [palace] scandals and [corruption] were talked about among Tunisians long before their publication in WikiLeaks or foreign newspapers."

Zied spoke about how the Arab Spring reached critical mass—or that Eureka moment when Gene Sharp, nonviolent protest guru and author of *From Dictator to Democracy*, says people cast off their fears and dictatorships tumble.

"The Tunisian revolution was started by unfortunate people who had nothing to lose. That's known as Kahneman's loss aversion. [So] they decided to protest," Zied said. "And then Facebook came in. People started to see what happened to [Mohamed Bouazizi] and that was outrageous. So the shrinking middle class and the rich started to join the movement. The tipping point was reached and everyone joined."

Zied told me the weeks after January 14 were all fun and love—like Valentine's Day all the time. Then the Libyan refugees arrived, which he described as a spectacular moment of solidarity. Some people left their homes to let Libyan families stay in them. At one point he said the NGOs had to ask people to stop donating food, drugs, blankets, and money.

Before Zied resumed his work, he pointed to the crowd and said, "Don't take my word. Everyone will talk openly about the revolution. They will all offer their own opinion about it." He was right. Tunisians' openness would turn out to be palpably different than the Moroccans'. We walked toward the Ministry of Interior, the epicenter of the Jasmine Revolution.

A block away, Mohammed Salem Abou complimented me on my purchase of a Free Libya T-shirt from a Tunisian kiosk owner who was showing solidarity with her neighbors. Mohammed and a friend, both Libyans, had arrived by car the day before from Tripoli. He handed me his business card from KCA Deutag, an oil services company with offices in Tripoli. "Pipelines are shut down. No one is working," he told me. "We are here to get supplies and a visa at the Italian embassy. We will return to Tripoli in a few days."

Mohammed wasn't a gun-carrying rebel, but as a purchasing manager at KCA Deutag, he told us he had police connections and logistics skills. "We are from the Tajura neighborhood where the fighting started in Tripoli," he told us. He couldn't talk fast enough about being on the brink of a free Libya, but Gaddafi wasn't gone yet.

"Have Tunisians been welcoming?" I asked.

"Yes, but there are spies all around us," he told me, casting a glance in each direction to see if any were watching or listening. "The embassy here is on the side of Gaddafi. We have to be careful you understand."

Mohammed invited us to come by the Grand Hotel de France (nothing grand about it), room number 14, and talk more. At that moment I realized he and I had exchanged pleasantries in the hallway that morning. We were staying in room 15.

Promising to meet at the hotel later, Joellen and I walked further up Avenue Habib Bourguiba to the Jasmine Café, next to the Ministry of Interior. We had a cup of tea and people watched, with the tanks and soldiers 20 feet from us. It was easy to conjure the iconic image of the revolution sent around the world: human rights lawyer Leila Ben Debba, commanding the podium from about where the soldiers now stood, waved a flag of hope to an electrified crowd. It was January 14. Six hours later Ben Ali fled to Egypt. The banners, the marching bands, and the teashop conversations do not give full account of the buzz of freedom in the Tunis air then or now.

We took the train to Carthage that afternoon and walked up Byrsa Hill through wealthy bougainvillea-draped neighborhoods. Above the thematic white homes trimmed out in Mediterranean blue was the scenic promontory overlooking the Gulf of Tunis that attracted the seafaring Phoenicians to make Carthage their center of power. A Who's Who of empires and gods has since inhabited this hilltop: Greek, Roman, Vandal, Byzantine, Arab, Berber, Ottoman, and French. Standing in the ruins of the Roman forum, where Augustus Caesar might have walked, over there was the Punic residential quarter where Hannibal once lived. Four centuries after Hannibal, another Carthaginian, Tertullian, who was a leading voice in the New Prophecy movement, inspired by the new Jerusalem of Revelation, wrote prodigiously in a nearby basilica and made his famous observation: "The blood of the martyrs is the seed of the church." Beyond the Punic port and the Roman Amphitheater was a cruise ship arriving, following in the ancient wake of Punic warships and Roman triremes. Rising above where I stood is what was formerly a French cathedral dedicated to Louis IX, the crusader saint-king. "A man who spends his life visiting Carthage will discover a new wonder everyday," wrote 11th-century geographer El Bekri (now etched in stone atop Byrsa Hill), at a time when Carthage had gone to seed. After the Arab conquest, the Ummayads ruled from Tunis.

～

I fell asleep before Mohammed and his friend returned to the hotel that night. I was up and out at 5:20 a.m. A passel of men perched on stools in front of our colonial-era hotel, smoked *shishas* (hookahs) and sipped espressos. Following the medina wall, I turned right at the Porte de France and walked through the empty arcades on Avenue Habib Bourguiba to the Place de Independence. Each night while I was in Tunis, I watched the army band march this pedestrian parkway and sing the national anthem. Spontaneous crowds would gather, imbued with the afterglow of fresh-found liberty and celebrating the people's partnership with the army. I turned right at the French embassy, and two blocks on was the train station. I was going to the refugee camps in Tunisia's Libyan frontier.

"It's too early to be getting on this train," I said to the man in front of me who was placing his mother's luggage in the rack above her seat. "Not too early," the affable man said. "It's noon in Japan."

The man's name was Abdel Mottaleb Ovederni, a 56-year-old professor of chemical engineering at Gabes University. He received his doctorate in Toulouse, France, and afterward spent a year in Paris doing postdoctorate work in physics. His wife teaches theology in high school. Aside from spending time with family, he still likes to go boar hunting in the pine forests of the high mountains of Croumerif along the Algerian border. On this day, he was returning to Gabes with his mother and daughter, who wore djellabas and hijabs and were seated across the aisle. When I told him that I was going to the refugee camps, he switched seats and our conversation began.

"We are hosting 12,000 refugees in Gabes," he said, and then went down a map I was studying, pointing to other host cities: Mendenine, Tafaouine, Remada, and Ben Guerdane. "It was spontaneous hospitality," he continued. "We put families in our homes, children in schools, and babies are being born in our hospitals. It doesn't matter if they are pro-Gaddafi or prorevolution, but most of them are flying the flag of the revolution."

He then told a story of clashes between the two Libyan sides on the nearby resort island of Jerba (said to be the Land of the Lotus Eaters from Homer's *Odyssey*). Wealthy Gaddafi supporters were there, enjoying the drinking and women, and then the less privileged anti-Gaddafi refugees from Libya's Western Mountains region showed up and there were fights. Finally, the Tunisian army had to step in.

We discussed what the driving forces were that united the Jasmine Revolution protestors: high youth unemployment, corruption, food inflation, Internet censorship (second only to Iran and China), trade union repression, and the marginalization of Islamic parties. The fate of the revolution, it came out, was sealed when the military no longer supported the president.

"Ben Ali did not like the military, and the military didn't like him. He was a policeman, who never went to university," Abdel said. "The revolution was not planned. Opposing factions came together for a moment in time. Mohamed Bouazizi was a poor man who sold fruit in the market to support his family.

He did not represent young people in Tunisia. When he refused to pay the policewoman a bribe, she took his scales and vegetable cart and insulted him. In desperation he burned himself. Privileged young, educated people, who use the Internet and speak English and French and travel abroad, were horrified. Suddenly, two classes normally opposed converged on January 14. And now they diverge again," he said, as he bumped his fists and then symbolically pulled them apart.

"All these people Ben Ali did not like. He hated the army, the Islamists, the labor unions. He created these opponents—almost the whole country—who killed [not literally] him. It's ironic that Ben Ali introduced the Internet but tried to control it, and it was Facebook, Twitter, WikiLeaks, and smartphones that brought him down. His own hands destroyed him. I'm an engineer so I believe in natural laws. Compress a plastic bottle enough and it will explode."

I was curious about Abdel's political activism during the Stasi-style police state of Ben Ali.

"As a student in the late 1970s and early 1980s I spoke out, but not since," he said, gesturing a zip of the mouth or else a slice of the throat. I got the message. He goes on. "I've never voted in an election because I didn't think they were democratic. We have a good constitution; it just needs to be reformed, with less power to the president and more to the people, parliament, and the courts. The authorities never let me exercise my rights under the constitution—that is the compression of the bottle."

"What were you doing on January 14?" I asked.

"At five in the morning I was still awake. I had stayed up all night. I called a friend and told him that I was happy to be alive on this day. I could die tomorrow and everything would be okay."

I tried to link the goose-bump moment many Americans shared when President Obama was elected. He was nice enough to agree, but that led to more talk about the United States.

"Tunisians like to know what is going on in the world. When I taught at the University of Oregon I learned that Americans only want to know about America," he told me. "For the first few weeks we thought Obama might be different. But America is America, is what they say, whether it's Clinton, Bush, or Obama, especially when it comes to Israel."

Like many in the Middle East and North Africa, Abdel's take on U.S. policy around Israel and the Palestinians is through the prism that says Jewish people own all the banks and media organizations and therefore are the guiding force in Washington. They certainly have a strong voice and some have deep pockets, but that's not the whole story. He knew about AIPAC (American Israel Public Affairs Committee) and their disproportionate influence on American elections. He had not apprehended the Christian-based breadth of Israel-firsters (Democrats and Republicans) in the U.S. Congress, who campaign and vote on their loyalty and obeisance to a foreign government (Israel) and not to the security and vital interests of their own country. In fact, about the time we were talking and training south in Tunisia, passing donkey carts and olive groves, Benjamin Netanyahu was in the United States, blasting President Obama's proposal for peace talks. The U.S. Congress gave the blustering prime minister, who has no proposal on the table, 29 standing ovations, four more than President Obama had received only months before at his State of the Union address.[1]

Although there are likely more "love thy neighbor as thyself" American Christians who support a two-state solution, that day I elaborated for an hour on the Christian Zionists who are complicit in holding American foreign policy hostage to Israel by voting as they do. With 66 books in the Bible, morality (and "afterlife" geopolitics) can be interpreted according to the rigidity of one's prejudices. As many as 40 million Americans think the rapture and end times will occur before 2050. Most of them do not give credence to evolution or the geological ages but instead swear by the Ussher chronology of Genesis that says the world began Sunday morning, October 23, 4004 BCE. Moreover, their rigid take on the Bible says that when the rapture occurs, Jewish people must be in the land of Israel, and, after Armageddon and a rally in the sky, they too can go to eternal heaven if only they convert to Christianity—in effect seizing the legacy of God's chosen people. Since I was talking about superstition, and emotion trumping reason, I pointed out that at least one poll says that 30 percent of Americans are convinced of the presence of UFOs. We both laughed, but it really isn't a laughing matter. It did, however, bring to mind the famous quip of the Pogo cartoon character: "We have met the enemy, and it is us."

While in Tunis a friend had told me that Saudi Arabia was pouring money into the Islamist parties in Tunisia.

"I haven't heard that," Abdel said. "But Islamists here have much more than money. They have the mosque. Tunisia is a Muslim country. I am a Muslim, a modern one, but a Muslim who tries to live my life by the ethics of the Koran. I don't judge you or your religion. My wife is more conservative than I. We are a mixed country. First we were Berbers, then Phoenicians and Romans, followed by Arabs, Turks, and French. We are all those things. Some Tunisians drink wine and whiskey; others don't. Some choose the hijab. Others wear almost nothing. In the same family you might have an Islamist, a Nationalist, a Marxist, and a European—that is Tunisia."

---

1. Two months later, as bad news sent the U.S. economy near a tipping point, 81 members of Congress visited Israel as guests of AIPAC. In 1996, President Bill Clinton called Netanyahu's interference in American politics "scandalous electioneering."

Three days before, Joellen and I had attended Ben Ali's trial in absentia in Tunis. He and his inner circle of family and friends are facing 93 charges that cover the waterfront: embezzlement, money laundering, and theft of archaeological artifacts right on up to torture and murder. We talked to several lawyers (advocates) outside room 10 of the Tribunal de Premier Instance (Court of First Instance). As officers of the court, they were dressed in black robes, and each one we talked to said they practiced human rights law. At one point a distressed woman interrupted us to request help from lawyers in finding her husband who was a political prisoner. Another approached us with a picture of a missing daughter, and several were turned away at the doors with petitions. Meanwhile, Mohammed Ben Smida, one of the lawyers, told us that the defense's whole argument was that Tunisian law did not allow a trial in absentia. We squeezed in the crowded courtroom for an hour. Two of the five judges were women. The trial was conducted in Arabic; we couldn't understand a word and left.

As it turned out we left too soon. The trial lasted all of a day, truth and reconciliation it wasn't. Ben Ali and his wife, Leila Trabelsi, who are now living in Jeddah, Saudi Arabia, were convicted of embezzlement and misuse of funds and sentenced to 35 years in prison and fined 66 million dollars. More trials are to follow.

"It means nothing. It was all a show," Abdel said, throwing his hands in the air at the absurd thought of a one-day trial. "He is gone, but his wife's family, the Trabelsi clan, are a mafia. They controlled everything everywhere. Some have been arrested. Her brother fled to Canada, and others are in Europe. They have networks in government offices, in customs, and with the police. Now it's a big job to clean up. It will take five to ten years."

Reports had also been emerging that Gaddafi was the linchpin in keeping the dictatorships of Egypt and Tunisia alive. Before the civil war there were over 50,000 Tunisians living and working in Libya. One story alleged that Ben Ali received a monthly payment from Gaddafi.

"I have heard some of the same. In any case, it's important that the revolution succeeds in Libya. Having a dictatorship in the middle of two new democracies would reduce our chances of success," he said. "The Libya crisis hurts Tunisia for two reasons. Security is good here, but tourists are afraid to come. And the Tunisian business investment in Libya is huge. Now that suffers."

As the train arrived in Gabes, I asked Abdel one last question before he showed me the way to the bus station. Given that I had been to Iran two years before and seen the sprouts of the Green Movement, did the grassroots movements that have occurred in North Africa and the Middle East, now known as the Arab Spring, really start in Tunisia?

"Yes," he said flatly. "Iran still has a dictator. Again, I have a brain like an engineer. Think of a pipe that runs through the Middle East and it has shut off valves where the fluid cannot go backwards. Tunisia is where the pipe begins."

⟳

It was a 20-minute walk to the main Gabes bus and *louage* (shared taxi) station. A bus was ready to depart for the coastal resort of Zarzis, where UNHCR had set up temporary headquarters to handle refugees from Libya. A two-hour scheduled ride across a desert landscape turned into three. I was on a milk run. Stopping every five to ten minutes, soldiers in olive drab and a black-booted policewoman boarded. Several Libyans sat near the front, returning to Tripoli I was told. Colorfully dressed Berber women, accompanied by men who wore straw hats with chinstraps that made me think of Mexico or Guatemala, rode for a short way. The Berber women laid their produce in the aisles. One older lady sat next to me on what may have been her first bus ride. She gripped the seat and hung on like she was on a circus ride and about to throw up. When she got off, I noticed that she had pulled the ashtray off the back of the seat in front of her.

Those people and the landscape were the frontier tapestry I had anticipated, not the Odyssee Resort Zarzis, where Firas Kayal, the press liaison with UNHCR, had told me to meet him in the late afternoon. "I don't know anyone who travels to Zarzis by train or bus," he told me over the phone two days before. "We fly into Jerba, then take a UN vehicle to the Odyssee." The cab dropped me at the back of the hotel, like a servant's entrance. I passed two of the four palm-fringed swimming pools before I got to the hotel beach, where half-naked French and Belgian tourists were sunning and riding ponies. Rented sailboats crisscrossed the dazzling blue waters of the Mediterranean. "Animation team" members, who wore matching shorts and identifying blue T-shirts, were teaching several Speedo-and-bikini-clad couples in a poolside amphitheater how to dance a polka. With umbrella drinks in hand, they stepped out the rhythms of "La Bamba." Once inside, I passed the hookah bar and the Odyssee Thalasso Oriental Spa, which offered up, among other things, a "revitalizing massage or a typical Tunisian therapy based on ancient wisdom."

Several well-dressed, pro-Gaddafi Libyans sat in the lobby. The desk clerk told me they were here to buy medicines. I stopped by the UNHCR "war room" to see if Firas had arrived. He wasn't there, but I soon found him in the lobby bar. "My apologies. We don't normally stay in places like this," he said, as we sat down. "No need to apologize. You didn't pick the place," I told him. He pulled out his laptop and we ordered espressos. Like at least 15 of his coworkers, who were having beers on the terrace, Firas was kitted out safari-like in a

UNHCR khaki vest. In his mid-40s, and of Syrian nationality, Firas graduated from Washington University Law School in St. Louis. He married an American girl from California who, he said, loves the Middle East. They live in Dubai. UNHCR is his career.

He pulled up a Google map of the region and identified the refugee camps' locations, pointing out which ones were for Libyans, and which for the third country nationals. Fighting was raging in the Western Mountains. Two weeks before, the Berber rebels had taken control of the Dehiba border post, where refugees from the mountains are crossing.

There were 1.5 million third country nationals working in Libya when the fighting began. Gaddafi and Libya's oil money sponsored them, which made them the first to lose their jobs. Fleeing in all directions—Tunisia, Egypt, and to the sea—they were mostly single, middle-aged men from Egypt, Bangladesh, Sudan, Eritrea, Ethiopia, Chad, Mali, Niger, and Nigeria. Firas showed photos he had taken in March of the first wave of refugees at the Ras al-Jedir crossing (which is where I was going the following morning): tens of thousands, a sea of humanity, a crush of bodies often submerged beneath a duffel bag or suitcase atop their heads. "Over half a million refugees have arrived in Tunisia so far," Firas told me.

"Tunisia was in the middle of its own revolution. It was amazing that they opened up the way they did. Most countries freak out and lock their borders," he continued. "Initially, personal initiatives were the dominant source of food and water and shelter. Tunisians strung up banners that said, "Welcome our Libyan brothers." At one point, a big group of Malians were trying to cross but didn't have passports. Officials from Tunis arrived and stamped them through."

"Why such hospitality?" I asked.

"Good question. They are neighbors; they are both Muslim, there is a lot of cross-border trade, and it's the humanitarian spirit coming out. At first the refugees were sleeping beneath trees, but within five days the Tunisian army had leveled the ground at Shousha, and UNHCR had set up tents to house 20,000 refugees."

We discussed the burden developing countries have of taking care of refugees. Firas was a font of statistics: Pakistan has 1.9 million refugees from Afghanistan, Iran has 1.1 million from Afghanistan, and Syria has 1.3 million, mostly Iraqis.[2] The extreme irony is that, in Firas's home country, Syrians are now fleeing in droves to Turkey, escaping the wrath of Bashar al-Assad's police and army while Palestinian and Iraqi refugees are sitting tight!

Firas had been generous with his time. He had been transferred to Geneva and was on his way to his farewell party, after which, he would be leaving in

---

2. Palestinians are not included in those statistics.

a few days. My last request was to show me a picture of UNHCR Goodwill Ambassador Angelina Jolie. He beamed, as he should have. One ping later she was on the screen, dressed in a stunning evening dress, with Firas all suited up standing next to her. She had been to Shousha camp two weeks before.

I was at the back gate before eight the next morning, waiting for Tahir in his yellow taxi. Shousha camp was an hour away. For insurance reasons, Firas told me I couldn't ride in UNHCR vehicles, so the night before I had worked out a fare with Tahir.

As we drove through Zarzis, Tahir pointed out the black tags with white lettering of the Libyan cars parked in front of private homes and guesthouses. In some neighborhoods they accounted for a third of the cars. This contrasted with the camel herds, olive groves, trucks piled high with wheat, glimpses of the ocean, police and military checkpoints, and desert bleakness we passed on our drive to Ben Guerdane, along the Tripoli highway.

Ben Guerdane is a dusty trading village and smugglers paradise, the last stop before the Ras Jdir crossing. Moneychanger shops, no more than a booth, with a small desk, a calculator, and a man waving a wad of bills—dollars, dinars, and Euros—at everyone who passed, lined the main street for two or three blocks. Just as I had seen on the Turkey-Iraq border, profiteering in diesel and gasoline was a vibrant business: 55-gallon drums and plastic jerry cans were being loaded in cars and trucks headed for Libya. Oil had given Gaddafi his power, but now the taps were shut off. Tahir said the contraband fuel, which was coming from Algeria, was being sold here for one dinar per liter. It would go for five times that in Libya. International sanctions against fuel imports to Libya, which include a NATO naval blockade, are intended to break Gaddafi's hold on power, but the profits are too high for fuel traders to back off. In this border town chaos, traders are on the side of the trade and could give a damn about sanctions or who is buying. Meanwhile, opposition forces were getting closer to cutting off this supply route to Tripoli.

Arriving from Libya were cars loaded down with cheap electronics and trucks packed with Daewoo air conditioners and refrigerators. The closer we got to the border, the more I saw Libya-bound flatbed trucks stacked high with bags of wheat and cases of Coca-Cola. Tahir pointed to the empty desert and said that many trucks hauling contraband avoid the Ras Jdir border station. At a checkpoint just before the border, police were roughing up a young Libyan driver—throwing him in a headlock and shoving him to the ground in front of a line of cars. A few miles further on, with a camera around my neck, I got out at Ras Jdir to observe who was crossing. Two nonuniformed men rushed me, screaming in Arabic. It was not the place to look suspicious. Tahir intervened, and after searches and a passport check, they shooed us away like stray dogs. We doubled back to the Shousha camp.

In front of the UNHCR tent a bus had just arrived from the border. Thirty or more sub-Saharan Africans, mostly from Sudan, Eritrea, and Ethiopia, lined up and began processing into the camp. I left Tahir parked beneath one of the few shade trees for miles and trudged through the sand to the barn-size World Food Program tents. Three men, all from Ben Guardane, stood at the entrance, check-listing food stocks and water as it left the tent. "What do Americans think of Shousha?" one of the men asked me. "They don't," I said, walking across the way to the kitchen. Twenty vats of rice and stewed tomatoes and onions were cooking, stirred with canoe-paddle-size ladles. "We prepare three meals a day, plus provide milk for the babies," one of the cooks told me. It was midmorning, but people were already lining up for lunch. There is little else to do here.

Dwana, a Somalian, told me he arrived at Shousha on March 22. He had been working construction in Tripoli, sending money home to his wife and son. Now he can't go back or he will be killed. I asked him how the food was. "Pasta and rice, pasta and rice; the same thing every day. No books, no medicine, just the Sahara," he said, turning toward the blazing sun and bleak landscape. A Sudanese man told a similar story. I left the food line and walked through the camp.

In the Eritrean section six young men sat at a makeshift store that sold Coca-Cola. I joined them, crouching in the sand beneath a tent flap. They were cheered when I told them I had traveled in Eritrea. We talked about Asmara, and the train to Massawa on the Red Sea coast. Merhowi was 25; Aron and Arawat, 27; and Daniel Fisseha, the best English speaker, was 31. They were all from near Asmara, seeking asylum in another country, all at least twice refugees. Long before the Libyan civil war broke out, these young men had already paid a high price of personal suffering. Daniel's nine-year saga as a refugee had more twists of fate than Homer's Odysseus.

Eritrean president Isaias Afewerki came to power in 1993. For most of the last 18 years he has been a paranoid, brutal dictator. Eritrea no longer has a free press (ranked behind North Korea as the worst), a meeting of over seven people requires permission, there is no political opposition, the Internet is censored, and conscripts in the army are used as forced labor for public works projects. Daniel was a shovel-swinging, rock-breaking conscript in the Eritrean army for two years, until 2004. Defying a shoot-to-kill order, he deserted and crossed the desert to Sudan. He eventually found a job as a waiter at the Grand Holiday Villa Hotel, in Khartoum, at the confluence of the White and Blue Nile rivers.

"The money was good, but the Sudanese looking for jobs weren't happy," he told me. "They kept attacking me until it wasn't worth it anymore."

Two years later he paid human traffickers 500 dollars to put him in the migrant's pipeline to cross the Sahara from Khartoum to the oasis village of Kufra, Libya. Colluding with Libyan police and human traders, two months later he made the 950-mile ride in a tarpaulin-covered truck to Tripoli. Like many young Eritrean men, he worked as a slave laborer in the Tripoli vegetable market. He was making money, so he wasn't complaining. In the meantime, the European Union was pressuring Libya to clamp down on the human trafficking: many like Daniel were crossing the Mediterranean to Europe. Daniel had been in Tripoli a year when the police stopped him and put him in prison for not having a visa. Later he was moved to a migrant detention camp two hours south of Tripoli, one of a dozen or more such camps in Libya. Aid workers found Daniel's English to be exceptional. As a result, two and a half years later he left the camp and went to work in Tripoli as a translator for UNHCR.

On February 15, 2011, almost nine years into Daniel's odyssey, peaceful protestors across Libya, inspired by the Tunisian and Egyptian uprisings, were met by violent Gaddafi police forces. February 17 was scheduled to be a "Day of Rage," to commemorate a protest in Benghazi five years before. Gaddafi security forces fired live ammunition into the crowds, who then went on a rampage, burning public buildings from Benghazi to Tripoli. The National Transitional Council (NTC) was formed on February 27, uniting anti-Gaddafi forces.

Gaddafi was using sub-Saharan Africans—mainly from Mali and Niger—as his frontline fighting force. Daniel and his Eritrean roommates were afraid of being mistaken for mercenaries and thus being attacked when they went into the streets. "We didn't see it happen," he told me. "But we heard about it several times."[3] Eventually thugs posing as police came to them. "They stole our money, television, and cell phones," he said. "They had guns and knives. We had nothing. We left on March 20 and arrived here that day. We have been here ever since."

Security problems for Daniel and his fellow Eritrean's didn't end at Shousha camp.

"A month ago the Nigerians blocked the road and wouldn't let cars or trucks pass. Traffic was backed up on both sides. Then they came after us. We [the Eritreans] ran that way for two or three kilometers," he said, pointing to the road toward Ben Guerdane. "They burned our tents and killed four Eritreans. The Tunisian army and the people from Ben Guerdane saved us. The Tunisian

---

3. In fact, while pro-Gaddafi Libyan fighters are now free to go home, black Africans suspected of supporting Gaddafi are held in fetid jails.

merchants were upset because their business with Libya was interrupted. The Tunisian army fired on the Nigerians. Now the Nigerians blame us."

Two-thirds of the Shousha camp was destroyed during the course of those events. Now rebuilt, security fences have been erected to separate the different nationalities of sub-Saharan Africans. Everyone at Shousha camp is glad the security has improved, but there are still 4,000 asylum seekers with no host country.

Daniel has hope, if not wishful thinking. He told me he had heard that the Eritreans might be sent to a resettlement camp in Romania. He probably knows more about the Schengen Agreement, which allows travelers passport-free movement in Europe, than the people who wrote it. Many refugees, mostly Tunisians, have perished at sea trying to escape the unrest of the North Africa revolutions. Crossing the Mediterranean and establishing a foothold in Europe beats staying in yet another refugee or detention camp. A few days before, on World Refugee Day, UNHCR high commissioner Antonio Guterres visited Shousha camp. From here, he symbolically followed the path of the refugees to Tunisia's Jerba Island and on to Lampedusa, an Italian island and gateway to Europe.

"If one person makes it across, he will call his friends back in Tunisia or Tripoli [or the camps], and off they go," Firas assured me the day before. So far Europe has experienced an influx of 25,000 immigrants, mostly unemployed Tunisians. This relatively small number when compared with the millions housed in developing countries created a dustup between Prime Minister Silvio Berlusconi in Italy and President Nicolas Sarkozy in France. In June, Sarkozy prevented a train from Italy with Tunisian immigrants from entering France. That one should admire the emotional and physical resilience of Daniel and others in the Eritrean diaspora, in the face of blatant racism, does nothing to take the bull's eye off of immigrants during a worldwide financial meltdown. In a phrase, they are to a political upheaval what purgatory is to religion: people in limbo.

Before leaving, I asked Daniel what he thought of the Arab Spring.

"It should spread to Eritrea and end the dictator. Then I could go home to my family."

Tahir was still asleep in his taxi beneath the shade tree. "How was it?" he asked when he heard me open the door. "Many stories and problems," I said. "C'est la vie," he replied. And off we went to the Odyssee Resort Zarzis.

~

I got off the Tunis train at El-Jem. Joellen and a friend from Paris, Pascale Brudon, were waiting at the station with a young man, Wassim Zaghdane, who drove them there. We had a late lunch in front of the well-preserved Roman coliseum. Not only is the grandiose 30,000-seat amphitheater a reminder of the fleeting nature of empire, but the underground passageways and stalls that held the animals and the gladiators also recalls the timeless, red-in-tooth-and-claw nature of humanity—men acting like beasts and beasts acting like men.

Over lunch Joellen and Pascale told me about a conversation they had had the night before with a 50-year-old accountant employed in Tunis. He told them that Tunisians are undisciplined, don't like rules, and are out for themselves. No wonder there are more than 60 recognized parties in Tunisia and another 100 that have not yet obtained recognition. Dictators have destroyed all sense of sacrifice for the common good. "The Arab Spring will take 30 years," he concluded. "I won't benefit, but my children will."

We spent the afternoon drive to Tunis talking to Wassim. A 25-year-old graduate student in aeronautical engineering, Wassim works part time ferrying tourists around Tunisia. For that he dresses smartly, as if he were in a commercial cockpit, sporting black slacks and a long-sleeve white shirt, with a blue-gray tie and aviator shades. He is enthused about blues, jazz, and rock and roll, and is a fan of the Tunisian hip-hop scene, especially the invigorating role their protest songs played in the revolution. When they can get gigs, he plays guitar in a band on weekends. In Tunis, Wassim's office is directly across from the Ministry of Interior, ground zero of the revolution. After a long day of street demonstrations, Wassim was leaving his office when the police arrived and roughed him up. Suspecting Wassim of photographing their attacks on protestors, they confiscated his Nikon Digital SLR camera (which is why he kept admiring my newer model).

One look at Wassim's Facebook page and it is apparent that his love for music and action movies is only exceeded by the sweetness of freedom the Jasmine Revolution has spread. Most recently, though, he posted a photo of an Israeli soldier with his foot on the chest of a young girl, with his rifle pointed toward her face. He urged friends to circulate the disturbing photo. Still buoyant with that revolutionary esprit, Wassim tempers his optimism and rejection of extremism in a real-world context.

"This is where the Arab Spring started," he said proudly. "Students and young educated and underemployed people like me were mobilized through Facebook and Twitter. But now the elections have been postponed until October. We weren't prepared. There are 81 parties in Tunisia. So today there is no danger of fundamentalists taking over. If there is economic chaos and conflict the Ennahda Party will get more votes. Right now they won't receive over 30 percent."

The Ennahda Party—with old ties to the Muslim Brotherhood in Egypt—was banned in Tunisia until March, after the fall of President Ben Ali. The

Tunisian politics of secular versus Islamic go way back. Habib Bourguiba, educated at the Sorbonne in Paris, was the founder and first president of the Republic of Tunisia. His pluralist, secular policies are often compared to those of Turkey's founding father Mustafa Kemal Atatürk. Abdel had told me on the train that Bourguiba spent the first half of his life in the independence struggle against France, and the next half trying to mold Tunisia to be more like France. For 31 years, Bourguiba suppressed Islamic fundamentalism and championed rights for women in Tunisia, actions and efforts unmatched in any other Arab country. Not only did he outlaw polygamy and legalize abortion, but also he abolished Sharia courts, closed down religious schools, and outlawed the hijab in the workplace. In 1987, an aging and out-of-touch Bourguiba lost power in a bloodless coup led by then prime minister Zine al-Abidine Ben Ali.

Bourguiba's ousting came at a moment when he was about to execute Islamist extremists. Although the extremists had been convicted of attempting to overthrow the government, the political winds did not favor that kind of overreach. After a period of grace, in 1991, Ben Ali took up Bourguiba's heavy-handed tactics, defiantly imprisoning as many as 25,000 Ennahda Party activists. Rached Ghannouchi, the Sorbonne-educated founder of the Ennahda Party, who was twice jailed under Bourguiba, fled and has lived in exile in England for the last 20 years. In March he returned as Ennahda's leader. Wassim's fear, along with other secularists, is that while Ennahda—the best-organized political party in Tunisia—has moderated in their time in exile, and advocates a pluralistic secular government, once in power, it would impose Islamic law.

Wassim detoured through the Cape Bon resort town of Hammamet, with over 120 hotels. There were far more bikinis than hijabs in this European and progressive upper-class Tunisian playground. Similarly to Egypt, tourism has plummeted since the revolution began. Occupancy rates in Hammamet are in the tank.

Wassim wanted to show us the Lela Baya 247-room resort, formerly owned by Ben Ali's family. Set on seven acres, with three swimming pools and access to a golf course, the hotel faces the turquoise waters of the Mediterranean. The wealth of Ben Ali and the Trabelsi clan (known by WikiLeaks as "The Family") is reported to include not just tens of millions of dollars tucked away in secret accounts in France, United Arab Emirates, and Switzerland—and behind bookshelves in the royal palace—but also apartments in Paris, villas on the Cote d'Azur, and a chalet at Courchevel. We had walked around the compound walls of his presidential palace in Carthage, one of many such royal residences just in Tunisia. The personal hijacking of their national economies and the ill-gotten, in-your-face fortunes of al-Assad in Syria, Gaddafi in Libya, Mubarak in Egypt, and Ben Ali in Tunisia, for no other reason, made the region ripe for unrest—and for a transfer of power from dictatorship to democracy.

∼

Internet access was sketchy at our downscale hotel between the medina and the Place de Independence. It was our last night in Tunis, and Joellen had walked down Avenue Habib Bourguiba to the more high-priced New Africa Hotel to have coffee and access WiFi. She wasn't gone long when I received a series of text messages: "There is a demonstration near the hotel. No one can tell me who it is. People have left the sidewalk café. The café is removing chairs and tables from the streets. Be careful when you get closer."

I raced down the stairs and out the door into an eerily quiet and empty street. It was Sunday night. Two young men in beards ran in the opposite direction, in a state of high dudgeon, shouting at me. A crowd gathered in front of the New Africa, next to the Jasmine Café and the Ministry of Interior. They stood behind a phalanx of riot police, who were wielding tear-gas guns and truncheons slowly advancing down the side street. Paddy wagons arrived. Police motorcycles raced through the alleys and back streets. Tanks and armored personnel carriers rolled up—no longer adorned with the flowers of the Jasmine Revolution. I stood next to a banner in front of the New Africa Hotel. It advertised a conference on religion in democracies (Les religions dans les democraties), sponsored by UNESCO and the Konrad Adenauer Foundation. Attendees filled the lobby with trepidation.

Minutes earlier up to 100 Salafists, young bearded men carrying black flags and crying "Allahu akbar" (God is great), had stormed the Africa Art Theater next to the hotel. They were members of Al-tahrir, the Tunisian Salafist party, which advocates a return to a caliph-run Islamic state. Protesting modernity and freedom, they chanted, "Tunisia is an Islamic state." The film being presented by director Nadia el Fani was *Neither Allah nor Master* (*Ni Allah ni Maitre*), a progressive documentary that addresses secularism and respect for religious beliefs. Armed with long batons and tear gas bombs, reported *La Presse de Tunise*, the Salafists roughed up the projectionist and the ushers and threatened to kill the director and viewers. Seven people were hospitalized. Six of the attackers were arrested, while the rest scattered like rats through the streets.

Joellen and I skipped out of the hotel and walked to the Opera House restaurant a block away. We sat away from the street and watched the paddy wagons and tanks roll by. After an hour, we moved quickly down the middle of Avenue Habib Bourguiba, followed by the Tunisian army band playing the national anthem.

When I contacted Abdel, the professor at Gabes University, about the attack, he wrote back: "I'm struck by the Salafist protestors' violence and reaction to the film. This is not our conception of freedom. This event and similar [ones] may be explained by the residual tension in Tunisian society [left over] from the Ben Ali regime. Hoping that the social climate will be better after the elections. I hope you and your wife enjoy your stay in Tunisia and discover the beautiful sides of our country."

Two months before the attack, Salafists had mounted a Facebook campaign against director Nadia el Fani. In an interview at that time with a local television station, she explained her views that the Salafists found offensive: "The problem with our constitution is that article 1 states that the religion of the republic is Muslim, but what about those who are atheist, Christian, Jewish, Buddhist—and who are also Tunisian? We should not have to declare that we are only Muslim. We are many other things as well and everyone has the right to live in peace here and express her/himself as he/she wishes."

Like all emerging democracies, the future here is uncertain, clouded by emerging factions, Islamic politics, crime, corruption, and unemployment. The common enemy—Ben Ali—is gone. In spite of that uncertain future a stronger civil society has to develop and expectations must be managed. Tunisians have to be tolerant and embrace the common good: everyone in Tunisia has a story to tell; everyone is a walking, talking, living history; and everyone therefore has a sense of entitlement, a feel-good superiority of personal piety that fails to justly remember the past and foils the recovery of whatever harmony and wholeness existed in Tunisia on January 14. "A social movement that only moves people is merely a revolt," wrote Martin Luther King Jr. "A movement that changes both people and institutions is a revolution."

~

Epilogue

David Holdridge, who is now president of Bridging the Divide (an innovative nonprofit organization working to make the world safer by connecting Americans with communities from Egypt and Lebanon's Bekaa Valley to Iraq), sent me a dispatch from Egypt's Tahrir Square on February 18. "It was bone to bone, beating heart to beating heart. Poor, middle class, families and teenagers. All there to be a part of history, which is what they told me in various ways. If Arab pride must precede Arab renaissance—and I believe it must—then this was that heretofore 'elusive' podium. . . . As one man told me when I asked him if this was properly called a 'pro-democracy revolution,' he responded, 'it is a pro-dignity revolution.'"

He continued, "Thermidor [when power slips from revolutionary leaders] is beckoning, and they know that. You can see it in their eyes, if you look deep enough. They know that the pervasive grinding poverty and illiteracy were not created in a year, and will not retreat in a year. They know that corruption is baked in our DNA and will never be excised to the extent they would like. 'We are watching them,' one activist told me, placing her forefinger on her lower eyelid and putting it wide open."

David concluded his dispatch by saying, "Yet still, Thermidor is a law of nature which cannot be denied. It will come, and the Friday celebrations of dignity will become memories. Beyond Tahrir, as Arab pride sweeps all before it—from the Maghreb to the gates of Jerusalem and Jeddah—renaissance will slam up against America's vital interests: oil and Israel. For inevitably, Arab pride, now set loose, will not allow for the kings and the emirs of the Gulf to speak for them or for the continued humiliation of the Palestinians."

~

Slam up against Israel they did. Six months later, in September 2011, Egyptian protestors unleashed their long-suppressed frustrations over the stalemate on Palestinian statehood—the totem of all democratic movements in the region—and stormed the Israeli embassy in Cairo. Though there were no casualties, the demonstrators crossed the line of peaceful protest, endangering the lives of many embassy staff members. The same week protestors forced the evacuation of the Israeli embassies in Ankara, Turkey, and Amman, Jordan. Turkey, America and Israel's closest regional strategic ally, expelled Israel's ambassador because Tel Aviv refused to apologize for last year's commando raid that killed Turkish civilians on a Gaza-bound aid flotilla. Sustaining the apartheid-style status quo—in which a Palestinian earns, on average, one-thirtieth of his Israeli neighbor living only a few meters away—goes against the rising tide of the Arab world.

Consistent with Zionist political thinking, the Arab Spring, coupled with the political paralysis in the United States, has moved Israel to hunker down, to grant no concessions, in what some are calling Israel's "winter hibernation." In doing so Israel passes up geopolitical opportunities with the new Arab democracies, which, if there were a true Palestinian peace process, might be supportive against an Iranian threat. Instead, Israel has built new security fences on the Egyptian and Jordanian borders, ratcheted up defense spending, increased the settlements in the occupied territories, shut down the peace process, and sounded the drumbeat for war with Iran. Many Middle East experts suggest that the dog that hasn't barked, which would provide a wake-up call to the drowsy peace process, would be a unified Palestinian civil disobedience campaign—Hamas, Fatah, the refugee camps and diaspora in sync—shaking up Israel's status quo with sustained disorder. Apartheid ended in South Africa because civil unrest, boycotts, divestment campaigns, and UN resolutions eventually made the country ungovernable. When will that tipping point arrive with Palestine and Israel?

~

Since December 2010, the majority of civic protests and movements for change in North Africa and the Middle East have been guided by self-determination. Libya was a special case: after the popular uprising turned into civil war, the Arab League supported NATO intervention to thwart Gaddafi forces in their attempt at slaughtering civilians. Early in the war, Misurata, on Libya's Mediterranean coast, was subjected to aerial bombardment and tank and heavy artillery shelling. Genocide was avoided—but savage vengeance was not when Misurata militiamen captured Colonel Muammar el-Gaddafi.

On October 20, 2011, a NATO airstrike of French fighter jets and an American Predator drone piloted from Las Vegas decimated a loyalist convoy of battlewagons departing Sirte, Gaddafi's hometown and last stronghold of loyalist forces. In the aftermath, Misurata rebel fighters tracked down Africa's "king of kings" hiding in a drainpipe. Emerging from piles of rubbish with a Kalashnikov in one hand and a silver pistol in the other, a disoriented Gaddafi was quoted as saying, "What's wrong; what's happening?" He then pled for mercy. None was given. Within minutes, a militiaman sodomized him with a metal rod. Al Jazeera video then shows a blood-drenched, dazed Gaddafi being paraded down a street on the hood of a Toyota truck, while frenzied NTC (National Transitional Council) fighters tugged at his famous locks and cried "Allahu akbar" (God is great). Next, the viewer sees his bloodied corpse, scarred by a bullet hole above the left eye, in a Misurata home, surrounded and manhandled by a mob of rebels, bouncing his lifeless head up and down in triumph. The corpses of Gaddafi and his son, Muatassim, who, in April 2009, had been hosted as a valued ally by Hillary Clinton at the State Department, were then displayed in a Misurata shopping center meat locker. For three days, residents lined up to pose for photographs with the corpses, waving the victory sign and shouting "Allahu akbar"!

Was this savage conclusion to Libya's civil war a Misurata interpretation of circular revenge—atrocity canceling out atrocity—or final justice, the vampire of Libya's nightmares vanquished?[1] Was the rebel's combustible compound of repressed rage and riotous celebration not the ultimate expression of fear? And how do the leftovers from civil war and the cultural insanity visited upon Libya for 42 years get cleaned up after the NTC militias go home?

Capturing, executing, and defiling the corpse of the unhinged despot, in God's name, no doubt was cathartic, but the NTC now has the troublesome task of keeping Libya's 50 new political parties and 140 tribes and religious sects on the same page—while building a civil society from scratch. The transition from revolution and vicious mob assaults to functioning government will take a radical recalibration of the mindset and, at the very least, outside material and moral assistance. The principal NATO allies—France, Britain, and the United States—are already getting their piece of a post-Gaddafi Libya (as well as Egypt and Tunisia)—while also promoting democratic institutions.

～

All revolutions, they say, are local. The October 23, 2011, elections in Tunisia boasted a high turnout and widespread praise for legitimacy: the Ennahda Party received 41 percent of the vote—and leadership of a unity government composed of secular allies. "This is the mistake [not governing by coalition] that happened

---

1. In 1945, after Italian dictator Benito Mussolini was executed, not only did the masses demand to see his corpse, but they also kicked and cursed it and hung him by his heels in the main square of Milan.

in Algeria when the Islamists won 80 percent of the vote but they completely ignored the influential minority of secularists, of the army, of the business community," Rached Ghannouchi, Ennahda's "intellectual leader" and cofounder, told *Foreign Policy* magazine. "So they did a coup d'état against the democratic process and Algeria is still suffering from that. This is why we always insisted on a national unity government." Tunisia's constitutional history and Europeanization over the last half-century, many would argue, positions it as a kind of laboratory for the broader reconfiguring of governments in North Africa and the Middle East. As demonstrated by the solidarity enjoyed during the Jasmine Revolution, Zine al-Abidine Ben Ali alienated all constituencies—students, the military, women, unions (the UCCT), small business owners, and even his own political party, the RPD—paving the way for the mass mobilization that crossed class boundaries and political divisions. There were not even counter-civilian protests in Tunisia, unlike, for instance, in Syria, Libya, or Egypt. "The Egyptian equation is much more complicated than the Tunisian equation," Ghannouchi told *Foreign Policy* interviewer Mark Lynch. "There are religious minorities and ethnic minorities in Egypt. There is a strong salafi movement. The role of the army is different in Egypt than it is in Tunisia."

So, given the differences from country to country, it's anyone's guess how, in the current state of flux, the rage, revolts, and crackdowns in the wider Arab awakening will tumble forward. After the Syrian army began its brutal crackdown in July 2011, the country pivoted from an Arab Spring of nonviolent protests to an Arab Winter of burgeoning civil war. Disaffected soldiers deserted the Syrian army and formed the vanguard of armed resistance, the Free Syria Army. The city of Homs, largely a Sunni enclave with a minority of Alawites and Christians, who are pro-Assad, has come under relentless government bombardment, killing thousands, with Sunni neighborhoods roundly reduced to rubble and ash.

Geography alone makes a Syrian civil war an international affair: Iraq to the east, Lebanon to the west, Israel and Jordan to the south, and Turkey to the north. When asked by Fareed Zakaria about military intervention, General Martin Dempsey, chairman of the Joint Chiefs of Staff, described a relatively sophisticated Syrian army and air defense system before saying it would be a big mistake to think of this as another Libya. Although President Bashar al-Assad is in an existential struggle for survival, not unlike Gaddafi, there remain unanswered questions as to who all the players are in the internal opposition and what their divisions might be. The cracks in the 310-member Syrian National Council, the main political opposition group, dominated by Sunnis, appear to cover the waterfront: young, old, militant fighters, grassroots organizers, urban, rural, rich, poor, exiles, educated, sectarians, Islamists, and secularists.

A Sunni friend of mine from Aleppo (who doesn't want to be named) says that his family and friends are divided, not by their opposition to al-Assad, but over the decision to destroy the country in an all-out civil war in order to have democracy. He falls into the group that wants to play it safe, sit on the fence, and pray for an end to the violence.

Externally, with Russian warships providing weapons while docking at their Mediterranean naval base in the Syrian port of Tartus, it's certainly not as simplistic as Sunnis, supported by Saudi Arabia, in a Middle East proxy war with Shia Iran and al-Assad. Syria has long been a safe haven for Hezbollah and Hamas, as well as a conduit for weapons from Iran. But now Hamas has broken the geopolitical alliance and opposes al-Assad, while the Sunni resistance is trashing the once popular Sheikh Nasrallah and Hezbollah posters, a lost symbol of Sunni-Shia, anti-Israel unity. Qatar, Saudi Arabia, Lebanon, and Turkey have chosen to arm the resistance, as have Sunnis from Iraq (all of whom are weapons clients of the United States).

A small, cohesive group of Assad cronies controls all the institutions of Syria, including the army and public and private sector assets: Makhloufs, Shalish, Shawkat, Najib are but a few names of the power elite. They are as clannish and thick as thieves as the opposition population is heterogeneous and breakable. "The regime-business alliance took shape over decades, and it is unlikely to snap until the very last moment," wrote Middle East scholar, author, and filmmaker Bassam Haddad. "Public defections by big businessmen would be a fair indicator that the regime's days are numbered."[2]

Clocking forward, if the Syrian democratic movement goes forward, will the Sunni majority there turn on Shia Iran for their support of the al-Assad regime? Will Iran in turn increase its influence in a Shia-dominated Iraq? Will Sunni Saudi Arabia ever allow the Shia majority to rule in Bahrain? How will the centrifugal forces of ethnicity and faith play out in Libya? Can Ennahda, the Muslim Brotherhood, the JDP in Morocco, and other Islamic parties become trusted partners in a secular government that respects minority and women's rights? It may be that these sectarian Venn overlays of the region foretell the future. What we know for certain is that recent events in the region have triggered a chain reaction from which there is no going back.

⌒

As shown by the experience in Iraq, democracy does not always produce liberal outcomes. In fact, there are no words in Arabic for secular, liberal, and democracy. So when the election results in Egypt favored the Muslim Brother-

---

2. But the instability doesn't end with the Assads, crony capitalism, battlefront atrocities, economic sanctions or even a ceasefire: Syria (and Yemen, Iraq, Libya and across the Middle East and North Africa) are undergoing critical water shortages and rising food prices; since 2003 droughts in Syria have gotten progressively worse. Creeping immigration from rural areas to the already crowded cities of Aleppo and Damascus has contributed to higher unemployment, greater income inequality and rising tensions and insecurity.

hood and the Salafist Al Nour Party with 65 percent of the vote, apprehensive Westerners and the country's Egyptian Bloc, a coalition of liberal parties, should not have been surprised. The Brotherhood, which is 50 percent women, has been providing social services to Egypt's poor for years while, leading up to the election, Al Nour handed out meat and medicines to the rural and urban poor.

A year to the week after the Tahrir Square revolution, I attended events sponsored by the Middle East Initiative at Harvard's John F. Kennedy School of Government. On consecutive days Mona Eltahawy and Wael Ghonim were featured guests. A columnist for the *Toronto Star*, the *Jerusalem Report*, and Denmark's *Politiken*, Eltahawy, an Egyptian American, is a vocal feminist and human rights activist. She wore casts on her left arm and right wrist, both broken two months before by riot police in Cairo, who beat and sexually assaulted her. "Initially, I assumed my experience was random," she wrote in the *Guardian* shortly after the attack, "but a veteran human rights activist told me they knew exactly who I was and what they were doing to my writing arms when they sent riot police conscripts to that deserted shop."

Wael Ghonim, who is head of marketing of Google Middle East and North Africa, is an Egyptian Internet activist who was a member of the Facebook group that planned and organized the antigovernment protests. Although many credit Ghonim for the success of the Tahrir Square revolts, he does not accept that: spontaneous, reactive, ground up, people's power, and no single leader is how he describes the Egyptian revolution. A year before, Ghonim was a handcuffed and blindfolded captive of State Security, "not knowing if I would live or die," he told the group at the Kennedy forum. As a means to instill fear, Ghonim says that he was "slapped, kicked and cursed" before being interrogated. Under pressure from family, friends, and human rights groups, State Security released him after 11 days. From his jail cell he returned to Tahrir Square. His fearless defiance stirred protestors to a critical mass—in which a transcendent spirit of liberation became their new weapon. President Mubarak fled Cairo three days later. "Egypt revolted because people were oppressed by a dictator, not because of a Facebook page," Ghonim assured us.

Acknowledging that the "will of the people" trumped their personal politics, Eltahawy and Ghonim, both devout Muslims, dismissed American fears of an imminent anti-Western, patriarchal theocracy. The logic against such an outcome is that, unlike Saudi Arabia and Iran, which are dominated by fundamentalist regimes, Egypt does not have the luxury of oil to placate the 80 percent who are poor and unemployed—or to snub interaction in a multicultural globalized world. "If the Brotherhood doesn't produce, they will be held accountable," Eltahawy said. "Forty percent of Egyptians live on less than two dollars a day," Ghonim explained. "Secularists and Islamists arguing about ideas while someone poor is lying on the floor sick and has no medical care makes no sense. . . . Your average taxi driver wants to see the [economic] problems of the country fixed and not to have the government tell people what to do with religion."

During the protests, Ghonim placed quotes from the film *Gandhi* on his Facebook page, *Kullena Khaled Said* (We are all Khaled Said), named for a 28-year-old who was murdered by two police officers in Alexandria. One excerpt has Gandhi addressing a crowd in South Africa: "But we cannot lose. We cannot. They may torture my body, break my bones, even kill me. Then they will have my dead body—not my obedience."

Eltahawy and many other Egyptian women are living proof of those who are not giving their obedience. She talked about the "virginity tests" and the unchecked assaults on women by police, the military, and Egyptian men: "This was not just a political revolution, it was a revolution of the mind—social, cultural, and even sexual," she asserted, the words tripping off her tongue with a fiery passion. She expressed solidarity with the thousands of female demonstrators who are using the democratic movement to demand systemic changes in the chauvinistic behavior that plagues Egyptian culture. "Listen, brother, I don't need you to protect my honor. I will be in charge of my honor and feminism," paraphrasing Eltahawy's recollections of a recent conversation she had with a traditional Egyptian man who offered to protect her.

In response to a question about the 19 American NGO workers who were arrested in Egypt for allegedly trying to affect the political process to benefit their donors, Ghonim just shook his head, and succinctly said that America should stay out of Egyptian politics. In his book *Revolution 2.0: The Power of the People Is Greater than the People in Power*—with a hat tip to Martin Luther King—he warns that revolutions are processes and not events. The next chapter of this story is only beginning to be written.

⌒

It's true that the United States and European countries were, at best, reactive and slow to give up the devil they knew in Tunisia and Egypt. What's important going forward is that they are playing a supportive role in those countries' social and democratic initiatives. The formation of the Deauville Partnership of G-8 countries to facilitate a "transition towards free, democratic and tolerant societies" in Arab countries was a well-timed engagement. Moreover, in a May 19, 2011, address, President Obama pledged a billion dollars of debt relief to Egypt, and he has called on OPIC (Overseas Private Investment Corporation) to make available monies for private investment and the European Bank for Reconstruction and Development to provide transitional assistance in the private sector as they did for Eastern Europe after the fall of the Berlin wall.

"The great transfer of goods, services and capital from Americans can now 'go direct,'" David Holdridge wrote. While Joellen and I were in Tunis, a delegation from the United States organized by John McCain arrived with executives from Marriott, Boeing, Coca-Cola, and General Electric. Money seeks opportunity. The days of Ben Ali's family demanding a pig's share of all foreign investment opportunities are in the rearview mirror. With youth unemployment rates ranging up to 70 percent in some parts of the region, jobs are a priority.

It was no coincidence that, while staying in the medinas of Morocco, on four occasions, I witnessed bloody street brawls: unemployed boys and young men with nothing better to do. I watched one teenager back up three thugs by breaking a Coke bottle in half. He then swung it wildly at their throats. In Essaouira, on two consecutive nights, I hung out my second-story *riad* window and watched young men, definitely drunk and probably on drugs, beat each other bloody while a scrum of women screamed and struggled to pull them apart. In Marrakech, a well-dressed man in his early 20s who demanded money from me and wouldn't take no for an answer tried to force his way into the private *riad* where I was staying. I had to push him back through the doorway. More than once, Joellen and I encountered unruly juveniles making trouble for everyone on the trains in Tunis. The average educated, fully employed young man, from Kansas to Cairo, has better ways to spend his time.

In addition to jobs, organizations such as Bridging the Divide are connecting people to people—promoting tolerance and dialogue through social media and networking technology. It's no revelation in our globalized world that what goes down in the Middle East, at some level, bears upon Europe and America, just as how a person votes or spreads his views in the United States or Europe has far-reaching consequences. Moreover, insularity on both sides of the Atlantic is diffuse and also dangerous.

As one example of the insularity in the United States, Lefty Palmer, a 82-year-old retired railroad worker, recently joined my uncle and me for breakfast at a small-town café in Arkansas. Given the abysmal state of the local timber business, most of the coffee klatch sitting across the room was unemployed (or underemployed)—hardworking, religious, "Jacksonian" patriots all. Lefty, who couldn't have been more courteous and sincere, writes fearmongering editorials about the imminent dangers of Sharia law in a weekly paper sponsored by a right-wing evangelical preacher. In this small town in Clark County where my family roots run deep, I've never seen an African American or a Jew. In fact, I don't recall meeting any Catholics.

"Are there a lot of Muslims passing through here?" I asked.

"Not unless they're lost," deadpanned my uncle.

Lefty didn't laugh but quickly interjected, "What about Dearborn, Michigan? Have you heard about that?" Lefty, of course, has never been to Dearborn but was fairly certain that, with all the people of Middle East descent he had read about living there, honor killings must have become the rule of law. I thought, if only my new friend could actually meet and spend a day with a person of Islamic faith, his post-9/11 obsessive fear of a Muslim threat would go away. Or just tune in to *All American Muslim*, a reality show set in Dearborn about the everyday lives of five Muslim families.[3]

Like Lefty, " . . . most people in the world believe that they are the People," wrote Paul Theroux in the *Tao of Travel*, "and their language is the Word, and strangers are not fully human—at least not human in the way the People are. . . . " Today, insularity (and imagining foreign monsters) in rural Clark County, Arkansas, and beyond, is more often a choice—one steeped in custom and creed and distorted by fear—than a mere circumstance of geographical isolation. Lefty bought my breakfast and went jauntily on his way, knowing unflinchingly what he wants to believe.

Comfortably (and culturally) removed from the living situations of the Middle East, Lefty and his small-town audience of sympathetic readers are nevertheless critical cogs in a vicious circle of geopolitics. Loosely stitched together, tacitly bound by fear and faith, they are indispensible to the mission of a network of U.S.-based anti-Muslim hate groups. According to the Southern Poverty Law Center (SPLC), a nonprofit civil rights organization, most of these groups sprang up after 9/11 and are on the increase. Their raison d'être, to put it politely, is to demonize Muslims and their faith as an irrational, monolithic conspiracy of freedom-hating terrorists, set on undermining American jurisprudence with Sharia law.[4] David Yerushalmi, a lawyer and Hassidic Jew from New York, has been instrumental in fostering the fear of a creeping Sharia menace across the United States for over five years. He and his network of anti-Muslim cohorts—such as the Reverend Terry Jones, instigator of "International Burn a Koran Day," and Robert Spencer, who runs the *Jihad Watch* website—are bright stars on SPLC's Hate Map. To be map worthy, groups must meet the following criterion: have beliefs or practices that attack or malign an entire class of people, typically for their immutable characteristics. Working behind the scenes, Yerushalmi has drafted legislation and filed lawsuits, while successfully influencing politicians in Oklahoma and Tennessee to ban Sharia. Old as time, and nothing more than bogeyman politics, the Tea Party has picked up on the hysteria embedded in the likes of Yerushalmi's rhetoric. Presidential candidate Rick Santorum says Sharia is an "existential threat"; candidate Newt Gingrich has called for a federal law to ban it. Just as 19th- and 20th-century Europe marginalized Jews as a fifth column for practicing Judaic law, Lefty, Yerushalmi, Santorum, Gingrich, and their fellow fearmongers have targeted Muslims.

---

3. After a protest from the evangelical group Florida Family Association, in an act of "naked religious bigotry" (according to Senator Ted Lieu), retail giant Lowe's Home Improvement pulled advertising from *All American Muslim*.

4. According to the CIA fact book, in 2011 Muslims make up six-tenths of 1 percent of the U.S. population.

Fear and faith wins elections and, more often than not, determines U.S. policy in the Middle East. With unprecedented success, Ronald Reagan tapped into the political mother lode of fear and faith politics. His union with the Committee on Present Danger, a hawkish interest group noted for faulty analysis and false frights, and the Moral Majority, the nascent right-wing evangelical organization led by Reverend Jerry Falwell, also obsessed with foreign monsters, made the actor president's road to the White House less arduous. Once there, while morphing himself into the "family values" president (though he was divorced, was not a churchgoer, and had rocky relationships with his kids), Reagan appointed 33 officials from the Committee on Present Danger to his administration.

George W. Bush discovered new faith in God after losing a congressional race in a conservative district in Texas. Washington's "C Street" Bible group and governors Sam Brownback of Kansas and Rick Perry of Texas have gone through similar public transformations. Perry, a 2012 candidate for president, created and organized—using state resources in his official capacity as governor—a 30,000-strong evangelical fast and prayer rally at Reliant Stadium in Houston. In the shameless fashion of 19th-century tent preachers, seducing evangelical constituents by attacking science and knowledge and bringing to bear willful ignorance on U.S. Middle East policy are hallmarks of these politicians. Candidate Perry, in a presidential debate in South Carolina, in which 65 percent of Republican voters are evangelical, referred to Turkey, America's 60-year NATO ally, as a country ruled by Islamic terrorists. Santorum, Mitt Romney, and Gingrich, all of whom chose not to serve in the military, get their biggest applause lines when they mention military buildups and bombing Iran. Gingrich, the former House speaker—who is bankrolled by casino magnate Sheldon Aldelson, a staunch supporter of Israel whose money has also bought him close counsel with Prime Minister Benjamin Netanyahu—now calls Palestinians an "invented" people. Santorum, the favorite candidate of American fundamentalists, claims that colleges are "indoctrination mills" and that Satan has his sights set on America. But Santorum really gets spun up when his pants-on-fire rants turn to the Middle East: "The idea that the Crusades and the fight of Christendom against Islam is somehow an aggression on our part is absolutely anti-historical," he told a South Carolina audience in February 2011. "And that is what the perception is by the American left who hates Christendom. . . . What I'm talking about is onward American soldiers."[5]

The vicious circle continues its spin. The market for political consultants who specialize in selectively interpreting the Bible to justify religion in gov-

---

5. I was reminded of Santorum's zealotry when Zied Jallaili, whom I interviewed in Tunis, sent me a postelection update from Tunisia: we now have a polarization between "democrats" and "conservatives." You can also see an unhealthy competition among conservatives: who is more Muslim than the other. It's dividing the country.

ernment and foreign policy is booming. It is hard not to think of them as the "assumed audience" addressed by English poet William Blake when he wrote: "Both read the Bible day and night; but you read black where I read white." In Aledo, Texas, David Barton, who graduated from Oral Roberts University and is an advisor to the Republican National Committee on outreach to evangelicals, is the darling of aspiring right-wing politicians. Conservative grandees and Israel-firsters like Mike Huckabee, Newt Gingrich, and Representative Michele Bachmann have sought his counsel for their campaigns. "I never listen to David Barton without learning a whole lot of new things," says an enthralled Gingrich. Breaking down the wall between church and state is the stated goal of Wallbuilders, the organization Barton founded. According to the *Economist* in an article titled "The Faith (and Doubts) of Our Fathers," Barton was an advocate for getting the Texas Board of Education, which is heavily stacked with evangelicals, to order up textbooks that lay out "the idea that America was established as a Christian state (known as the 'Christian nation' theory). Given the size of the Texas market, school book publishers across the country often follow its lead." When I read about Barton, who blames secularists and the Supreme Court for the ruin of America, I imagined that if the birth lottery had placed him in Tehran and not Texas, he would be advising the theocratic dictatorship of President Mahmoud Ahmadinejad.

～

The same week we left Tunisia, Ander Behring Breivik, primed by American Christian extremists, went on a murderous rampage in Oslo, Norway, that left 92 people dead. With that disturbing news we were all reminded of Timothy McVeigh and the Oklahoma City bombing. Breivik wrote profusely about his fears of Islam, liberal Marxists, and multiculturalism. His unarmed victims, as young as 16, were at a Labor Party island retreat. Heavily influenced by the anti-Islamic fearmongering in the United States, Breivik's writings and postings on Facebook are telling: in his manifesto, he quoted American blogger Robert Spencer's *Jihad Watch* 64 times. Paraphrasing one consultant on terrorism, al-Qaeda emerged from the writings of Salafist extremists, just as Timothy McVeigh was inspired by a racist Jew-hating manifesto, *The Turner Diaries*.

The distance between cause and effect is a short one. Words matter, and what we do on the Internet or in the voting booth or at the coffee shop, we do to ourselves—to humanity. Yet liberals and Muslims should no more make a right-wing Christian fetish out of a wacko like Breivik than conservative Christians should label Islamic people of good faith as suicide bombers or Sharia monsters. It is fair to say, however, that disrespecting Muslims and their faith is often consistent with the Christian fundamentalist fervor over the furious end-times of Revelations—as opposed to embracing the lessons of forgiveness, compassion, and peace revealed by Jesus in the Sermon on the Mount. David Holdridge's vision of a way forward is through citizen-to-citizen interactions, though I doubt that the 82-year-old Lefty is going to start tweeting friends from Iraq any time soon. The old ways of violent jihad, the War on Terror, and wars of choice have failed, but from these failures it is not difficult to envisage an Arab-to-American Spring, in which Lefty's great-great grandchildren are sitting in an elementary school classroom, learning geography for the first time, by networking with a school in the Bekaa Valley. Through interactions such as these, American and Arab children will learn together that paradise is in another world—or in what we make of this one—not in an arid tract of real estate in the Middle East.

On March 2, 2010, almost a year before the Jasmine Revolution, prominent Pakistani television cleric Mohammed Tahir ul Qadri declared a jihad against terrorism. He was not the first, but his words sent a clear message to bloodthirsty martyrs. In a 600-page fatwa, ul Qadri denounced al-Qaeda and attacked Osama bin Laden for leading Muslims into "hellfire." "They're not going to have paradise, and they're not going to have 72 virgins in heaven. They're totally on the wrong side," ul Qadri thundered. It would be hard to imagine the most wanted and feared man of the 21st century as anywhere but dead—and where he should be: in the shrineless, shivering abyss of the Indian Ocean.

~

Notes

Prologue

xv   "No revolution is executed": Martin Luther King Jr., *Why We Can't Wait* (Boston: Beacon Press, 1964).

Introduction

1   "Anglo-Saxons as the 'true Israel'": Jessica Stern, *Terror in the Name of God* (New York: HarperCollins, 2003).

2   "Every single fundamentalist": Karen Armstrong, *The Case for God* (New York: Anchor Books, 2009).

4   "alien customs and morals": Barry Rubin, *Islamic Fundamentalism in Egyptian Politics* (New York: Palgrave Macmillan, 2002).

5   "But that, as it turned out": Lawrence Wright, *The Looming Tower* (New York: Knopf, 2006).

Chapter 1

14   "The Crusader's God": Armstrong, *The Case for God*.

20   "The Koran was not meant": Karen Armstrong, *A History of God* (New York: Ballentine, 1994).

22   "Britain to the Persian empire": Marius Kociejowski, *The Street Philosopher and the Holy Fool: A Syrian Journey* (Gloucestershire, UK: Sutton, 2004).

23   [He] was involved in social work: Marius Kociejowski, *The Street Philosopher and the Holy Fool: A Syrian Journey* (Stroud, Gloucestershire, UK: Sutton, 2004).

24   "the conduct of nations": Edward Gibbons, *The History of the Decline and Fall of the Roman Empire*, abridged ed. (London: Penguin, 1788).

Chapter 2

27 "God, guns, and government": Robin Wright, *Dreams and Shadows* (New York: Penguin, 2008).

Chapter 3

38 Go back as far: Mark Twain, *The Innocents Abroad* (New York: Modern Library, 2003).

41 "radically inventive exegesis" (fn 1): Armstrong, *The Case for God*.

44 "Syria will be one": Wright, *Dreams and Shadows*.

46 "90.3 percent of the sample": quoted in Mary B. Anderson, *Do No Harm* (Boulder, Colo.: Lynne Rienner Publishers, 1999).

47 It is the fear that turns: Michael Ignatieff, *The Warrior's Honor: Ethnic War and the Modern Conscience* (New York: Metropolitan, 1998).

Chapter 4

56 "As I looked at those": Wright, *The Looming Tower*.

59 "overwhelmingly suicide-terrorist attacks" (fn 3): quoted in Armstrong, *The Case for God*.

59 "I could at least conceal": T. E. Lawrence, *Seven Pillars of Wisdom* (London: Penguin, 1935).

Chapter 5

69 "Along the great escarpments": Robert Fisk, *Pity the Nation* (New York: Thunder's Mouth Press, 1990).

72 "For the Maronites": Kamal Salibi, *A House of Many Mansions* (Berkeley: University of California Press, 1988).

76 Pity the nation: Kahlil Gibran, *The Garden of the Prophet* (New York: Knopf, 1995).

77 "they saw the mountain": *The Epic of Gilgamesh* (New York: Penguin Classics, 1960).

Chapter 6

79 "If it succeeded": William Lederer, *The Ugly American* (New York: Norton, 1965).

79 "In the days of hashish": Neil Macfarquhar, "Cattlemen in Lebanon Miss Lucre of Hashish," *New York Times*, April 5, 2001.

79 "a village of chickens": Fisk, *Pity the Nation*.

Chapter 7

89 [Jacksonians] believe that: Walter Russell Mead, "The New Israel and the Old," *Foreign Relations* (July/August 2008).

89 "Eighteen years of unforgiving war": Robert Baer, *The Devil We Know* (New York: Crown Publishers, 2008).

95 "What we did was insane": Meron Rappaport, "IDF Commander: We Fired More than a Million Cluster Bombs in Lebanon," *Haaretz*, September 12, 2006.

95 "There is a danger": quoted in John Mearsheimer and Stephen Walt, *The Israel Lobby and U.S. Foreign Policy* (New York: Farrar, Straus and Giroux, 2007).

96 "the United States intervened": Robert Kagan, *The Return of History* (New York: Knopf, 2008).

96 "We are offering the wrong": Lederer, *The Ugly American*.

99 "The experience of war": Anderson, *Do No Harm*.

99 "When a French patrol": David Halberstam, "The History Boys," *Vanity Fair* (August 2007).

100 "It will happen when the U.S.": Michael Kinsley, "What Bush Isn't Saying about Iraq," *Slate* (October 24, 2002).

101 "qualitative military advantage": David Cloud, "U.S. Set to Offer Huge Arms Deal to Saudi Arabia," *New York Times*, July 28, 2007.

Chapter 8

103 "a decent democratizing example": Thomas Friedman, *New York Times*, "Dog Paddling in the Tigris," *New York Times*, July 3, 2007.

107 "alienated from the East": Orhan Pamuk, *Istanbul: Memories of the City* (New York: Knopf, 2005).

108 "At some point Turkey": Samuel Huntington, *The Clash of Civilizations and the Remaking of World Order* (London: Touchstone, 1998).

108 "Of the 33 new Turkish" (fn 2): Soner Cagaptay, "The Empire Strikes Back," *New York Times*, January 15, 2012.

110 The Latin soldiery: Speros Vryonis, *Byzantium and Europe* (New York: Harcourt, Brace & World, 1967).

112 "The agency devoted": James Traub, "Persuading Them," *New York Times*, November 25, 2007.

112 "Europe is boosting": Parag Khanna, "Waving Goodbye to Hegemony," *New York Times Magazine*, January 27, 2008.

112 "It simply does not have": quoted in Nicholas Kristoff, "Make Diplomacy, Not War," *New York Times*, August 10, 2008.

Chapter 9

119 "People chose armed struggle": quoted in Aliza Marcus, *Blood and Belief* (New York: New York University Press, 2007).

123 "Prisoners were sodomized": Marcus, *Blood and Belief*.

Chapter 10

132 "It's the money pit": quoted in Richard Oppel, "Five Years In: Iraq's Insurgency Runs on Stolen Oil Profits," *New York Times*, March 16, 2008.

Chapter 11

145 "back to Jerusalem": Stephen Farrell, "Baghdad Jews Have Become a Fearful Few," *New York Times*, June 1, 2008.

146 "I have enjoyed great satisfaction": Greg Mortenson and David Oliver Relin, *Three Cups of Tea* (New York: Penguin, 2006).

147 "If we truly want": Mortenson and Relin, *Three Cups of Tea*.

148 "Civil war is development": Paul Collier, *The Bottom Billion* (Oxford: Oxford University Press, 2007).

153 "Except for the Islamic": Ali Alwandy, "My Trip to Masfa Alwand in 2003," accessed February 28, 2012, www.alwandy.110mb.com/.

Chapter 12

159 "Yet about a year": Thomas Ricks, *Fiasco* (New York: Penguin, 2006).

161 "I am saddened": Alan Greenspan, *The Age of Turbulence: Adventures in a New World* (New York: Penguin, 2007).

165 "I would not eat": Amit Paley, "For Kurdish Girls, a Painful Ancient Ritual," *Washington Post*, December 29, 2008.

Chapter 13

167 "American forces": Damien Cave, "Militant Group Is Out of Baghdad, U.S. Says," *New York Times*, November 8, 2007.

168 "Americans don't understand": quoted in Barbara Bedway, "Profile of McClatchy's Leila Fadel," *Editor and Publisher*, February 20, 2008.

171 "Geography is the most" (fn 4): Nicholas Spykman, *The Geography of Peace* (London: Gazelle Book Services, 1966).

172 "We live in a world": Ian Klaus, *Elvis Is Titanic* (New York: Knopf, 2007).

177 "Military action alone": Mark Mazzetti, "Robert Gates Advises Turkey to End Incursion Soon," *New York Times*, December 8, 2008.

Chapter 14

179 "In times of war": Mortenson and Relin, *Three Cups of Tea*.

182 All this movement: Mark McDonald, "Halabja Is Eager to Try Man behind Gas Attack," Knight Ridder News Service, June 20, 2004.

182 "Like a modern Pompei": Samantha Power, *A Problem from Hell* (New York: Harper Perennial, 2003).

186 "God fought against": Elaine Pagels, *Revelations: Visions, Prophecy, and Politics in the Book of Revelation* (New York: Viking, 2012).

190 "They don't want communism": Graham Greene, *The Quiet American* (London: Heinemann, 1955).

190 "We invaded not Iraq": quoted in Peter Galbraith, *The End of Iraq* (New York: Simon and Schuster, 2006).

Chapter 15

196 "You are one of us" and "The U.S. needs a facelift": Alan Cowell, "Election Unleashes a Flood of Hope Worldwide," *New York Times*, November 5, 2008.

196 "Too many people believe": Seymour Hersh, "The Administration's Secret Iran Campaign," *New Yorker* (July 7, 2008).

198 "The streets were lined": Margaret MacMillan, *Paris 1919: Six Months that Changed the World* (New York: Random House, 2002).

202 "Too bad they can't": Peter Galbraith, *The End of Iraq* (New York: Simon and Schuster, 2006).

204 "He [the Shah] did not": Ryszard Kapuscinski, *Shah of Shahs* (New York: Vintage, 1992).

204 "heady state of utopian": Laura Secor, "The Rationalist," *New Yorker* (February 2, 2009).

Chapter 16

212 "Iranians are patient": Baer, *The Devil We Know*.

213 "During the 20-month": "Iran Executes Mossad Spy," *Tehran Times*, November 23, 2008.

215 "Money changes all": Kapuscinski, *Shah of Shahs*.

216 "Protective fictions are more" (fn 5): Azar Nafisi, *Reading Lolita in Tehran* (New York: Random House, 2003).

Chapter 17

220 "Effective sanctioning of Iran": Baer, *The Devil We Know*.

222 "Five *qanats* were dug": Penelope Hobhouse, *Gardens of Persia* (Hong Kong: Kales Press, 2004).

225 "Karbala complex" (fn 1): Hamid Dabashi, *Shi'ism: A Religion of Protest* (Cambridge, Mass.: Belknap Press, 2011).

226 "His religious philosophy": Azar Nafisi, *Things I've Been Silent About* (New York: Random House, 2008).

Chapter 18

231 "I am an Iranian": Shirin Ebadi, "Award Ceremony Speech," Nobel Peace Prize, December 10, 2003, www.nobelprize.org/.

235 "a worse wine": Robert Byron, *Road to Oxiana* (Oxford: Oxford University Press, 1937).

236 Though wine gives delight: Hafez, *The Poems of Hafez* (Bethesda, Md.: Ibex, 2006).

238 "Ijtihad makes permissible": Eqbal Ahmad, "Encounter with a Fighter," *Al-Ahram*, August 5, 1998.

Chapter 19

241 "A passage in the Koran": Azadeh Moaveni, *Lipstick Jihad* (New York: Public Affairs Books, 2005).

242 "From the eleventh century": Byron, *Road to Oxiana*.

248 "It is the dead": Chris Hedges, *War Is a Force That Gives Us Meaning* (New York: Anchor Books, 2003).

249 "Iran was a bankrupt": quoted in Secor, "The Rationalist."

250 "under human destiny": Rebecca West, *Black Lamb and Grey Falcon* (New York: Viking Press, 1941).

250 "Warfare is ultimately": Lawrence H. Keeley, *War before Civilization* (New York: Oxford University Press, 1996).

250 "Fanatics [and good and decent people]": Tony Judt, "Amos Elon (1926–2009)," *New York Review of Books*, June 25, 2009.

252 "the mythos of confessional": Armstrong, *The Case for God*.

254 It is easier to start wars: Barack Obama, "A Moment of Opportunity" (speech), U.S. Department of State, 2011.

254 "The scythe swings": Kapuscinski, *Shah of Shahs*.

Chapter 20

257 "If one thought of Gueliz": Elizabeth Warnock Fernea, *A Street in Marrakech* (New York: Anchor Press/Doubleday, 1976).

270 "We Jews of Morocco": Simon Levy, "Untitled," Foundation of Jewish-Moroccan Cultural Heritage, Casablanca, 2011.

271 "dropped all Torah requirements": Pagels, *Revelations*.

273 "The most convincing way": Aldous Huxley, *Beyond the Mexique Bay* (Chicago: Academy Chicago Publishing, 1985).

274 41,000 marriages: Afua Hirsch, "Morocco Grapples with Women's Rights after Raped Bride's Suicide," *Mail & Guardian*, London, April 4, 2012.

Chapter 21

292 "A social movement": King Jr., *Why We Can't Wait*.

Epilogue

295 "This is the mistake": Mark Lynch, "Rached Ghannouchi: FP Interview," *Foreign Policy* (December 5, 2011).

297 "The regime business alliance": Bassam Haddad, The Syrian Regime's Business Backbone, Middle East Research and Information Project, Washington, D.C., Spring 2012.

297 "Initially, I assumed": Mona Eltahawy, "Bruised but Defiant," *Guardian*, December 23, 2011.

301 Committee on Present Danger: Rachel Maddow, *Drift: The Unmooring of American Military Power* (New York: Crown Publishers, 2012).

302 "the idea that America": "The Faith (and Doubts) of Our Fathers," *Economist*, December 17, 2011.

303 "They're not going to have paradise": Christian Caryl, "Sheikh to Terrorists: Go to Hell," *Foreign Policy* (April 14, 2010).

Bibliography

Acocella, Joan. "Prophet Motive." *New Yorker*, January 7, 2008.

Agha, Hussein, and Robert Malley. "The Arab Counterrevolution." *New York Review of Books*, September 29, 2011.

Ahmad, Eqbal. "Encounter with a Fighter." *Al-Ahram*, August 5, 1998.

Alwandy, Ali. "My Trip to Masfa Alwand in 2003." Accessed February 28, 2012. www .alwandy.110mb.com/.

Amnesty International. "Israel/Lebanon: Need for Investigation into Violations Committed during Israel/Hizbullah Conflict." July 24, 2007. www.amnesty.org/.

Anderson, Jon Lee. "The Battle for Lebanon." *New Yorker*, August 7 and 14, 2006.

———. "Can Iran Change?" *New Yorker*, April 13, 2009.

———. "The Implosion." *New Yorker*, February 27, 2012.

Anderson, Mary B. *Do No Harm*. Boulder, Colo.: Lynne Rienner Publishers, 1999.

Armstrong, Karen. *The Case for God*. New York: Anchor Books, 2009.

———. *A History of God*. New York: Ballentine, 1994.

———. *Holy War*. New York: Anchor Books, 1988.

Bacevich, Andrew. "Surge to Nowhere." *Washington Post*, January 20, 2008.

Baer, Robert. *The Devil We Know*. New York: Crown Publishers, 2008.

Baker, Luke. "Israel Engaged in Covert War inside Iran." Reuters, February 17, 2009.

Bakri, Nada. "6 UN Peacekeepers Killed in Lebanon." *New York Times*, June 25, 2007.

Bandon, Doug. "Terrorism: Why They Want to Kill Us." *Huffington Post*, February 17, 2012.

Barnes-Dacey, Julien. "Even with Sanctions, Syrians Embrace KFC and Gap." *Christian Science Monitor*, January 11, 2008.

Barr, Andy. "Santorum: Left hates 'Christendom.'" *Politico*, February 23, 2011.

Barr, Cameron. "Petraeus: Iraq Leaders Not Making Sufficient Progress." *Washington Post*, March 14, 2008.

Bedway, Barbara. "Profile of McClatchy's Leila Fadel." *Editor and Publisher*, February 20, 2008.

Bender, Bryan. "US Is Top Purveyor on Weapons Sales List." *Boston Globe*, November 13, 2006.

Bennhold, Katrin. "Women's Rights a Strong Point in Tunisia." *New York Times*, February 22, 2011.

Bergman, Ronan. "Will Israel Attack Iran?" *New York Times Magazine*, January 25, 2012.

Bloom, Jonathan. *Islam*. New Haven, Conn.: Yale University Press, 2002.

Boulden, Ben. "The Burns Murder." Accessed January 24, 2012. www.fortsmithhistory.org/.

Bozarsian, Mahmut. "Police Hold Four over Deadly Bombing in Turkey." Agence France-Presse, January 4, 2008.

Bromvich, David. "The Republican Nightmare." *New York Review of Books*, February 9, 2012.

Brooks, David. "The End of Philosophy." *New York Times*, April 7, 2009.

Burke, Andrew. *Iran*. Footscray, Vic., Australia: Lonely Planet, 2004.

Buruma, Ian. "Ghosts." *New York Review of Books*, June 26, 2008.

Butler, Paul. "Annual Report to USAID: Suleimaniyah, Iraq," USAID, September 30, 2007.

Byron, Robert. *Road to Oxiana*. Oxford: Oxford University Press, 1937.

Cagaptay, Soner. "The Empire Strikes Back." *New York Times*, January 15, 2012.

Calafi, Farnaz. "Iran's Yankee Hero." *New York Times*, April 18, 2009.

Caputo, Philip. *Acts of Faith*. New York: Vintage, 2005.

Caryl, Christian. "Sheikh to Terrorists: Go to Hell." *Foreign Policy*, April 14, 2010.

Cave, Damien. "Militant Group Is Out of Baghdad, U.S. Says." *New York Times*, November 8, 2007.

———. "Nonstop Theft and Bribery Are Staggering Iraq." *New York Times*, December 2, 2007.

Chivers, C. J. "Threats and Responses." *New York Times*, February 3, 2003.

"City on the Hill or Just Another Country? The United States and the Promotion of Human Rights and Democracy." *Hearing before the Subcommittee on International Organizations, Human Rights, and Oversight of the House Committee on Foreign Affairs*, 110th Cong. (May 22, 2008) (statement of Kenneth Roth, executive director of Human Rights Watch).

Clammer, Paul. *Morocco*. Footscray, Vic., Australia: Lonely Planet, 2009.

Cloud, David. "U.S. Set to Offer Huge Arms Deal to Saudi Arabia." *New York Times*, July 28, 2007.

Cockburn, Patrick. "How Picture Phones Have Fuelled Frenzy of Honour Killing in Iraq." *Independent* (London), May 17, 2008.

Cohen, Jared. *Children of Jihad*. New York: Gotham Books, 2007.

Cohen, Roger. "What Iran's Jews Say." *New York Times*, February 29, 2009.

Cole, Juan. *Engaging the Muslim World*. New York: Palgrave Macmillan, 2009.

———. *Informed Comment* (blog). Accessed February 20, 2012. www.juancole.com/.

———. "McCain Runs on Iraq in Michigan." Salon, January 15, 2008, www.salon.com/.

Collier, Paul. *The Bottom Billion*. Oxford: Oxford University Press, 2007.

Dabashi, Hamid. *Shi'ism: A Religion of Protest*. Cambridge, Mass.: Belknap Press, 2011.

Dagher, Sam. "Turkish Raid Strains U.S.-Kurd Ties." *Christian Science Monitor*, February 25, 2008.

Dalrymple, William. *From the Holy Mountain*. New York: Henry Holt, 1997.

Damrosch, David. *The Buried Book*. New York: Henry Holt, 2006.

Ebadi, Shirin. "Award Ceremony Speech." Nobel Peace Prize, December 10, 2003. www.nobelprize.org/.

Economist. "The Faith (and Doubts) of Our Fathers." December 17, 2011.

———. "A Very Small Step." July 9, 2011.

Elliot, Andrea. "Behind an Anti-Shariah Push." *New York Times*, July 31, 2011.

Eltahawy, Mona. "Bruised but Defiant." *Guardian*, December 23, 2011.

Engelhardt, Tom. "Tomgram: Bombs Away over Iraq; Looking Up." *Tomdispatch.com* (blog), January 29, 2008. www.tomdispatch.com/.

The Epic of Gilgamesh. New York: Penguin Classics, 1960.

Erlanger, Steven. "Israel to Get $30 Billion in Military Aid from U.S." *New York Times*, August 17, 2007.

Esposito, John. "Influential Pakistani Cleric Issues Fatwa against Terrorism." *Washington Post*, March 5, 2010.

Fahim, Kareem, Anthony Shadid, and Rick Gladstone. "Violent End to an Era as Qaddafi Dies in Libya." *New York Times*, October 21, 2011.

Farrell, Stephen. "Baghdad Jews Have Become a Fearful Few." *New York Times*, June 1, 2008.

Fattah, Hassan. "Dozens Slain as Lebanese Army Fights Islamists." *New York Times*, May 21, 2007.

Fernea, Elizabeth Warnock. *A Street in Marrakech.* New York: Anchor Press/Doubleday, 1976.

Fisk, Robert. *Pity the Nation.* New York: Thunder's Mouth Press, 1990.

Flynn, Stephen. "America the Resilient." *Foreign Affairs*, March/April 2008.

Friedman, Thomas. "Dog Paddling in the Tigris." *New York Times*, July 3, 2007.

Fuller, Graham. "A World without Islam." *Foreign Policy*, January/February 2008.

Galbraith, Peter. *The End of Iraq.* New York: Simon and Schuster, 2006.

Ghonim, Wael. *Revolution 2.0: The Power of the People Is Greater than the People in Power.* Boston: Houghton Mifflin Harcourt, 2012.

Gibbons, Edward. *The History of the Decline and Fall of the Roman Empire.* Abridged ed. London: Penguin, 1788.

Gibran, Kahlil. *The Garden of the Prophet.* New York: Knopf, 1995.

Global Public Square. "Fareed Zakaria Interview with General Dempsey." February 20, 2012.

Gokoluk, Selcuk. "Turkey's Kurds Angry after Blast." Reuters, January 8, 2008.

Goldberg, Jeffrey. "After Iraq." *Atlantic*, January/February 2008.

Goodman, David. "Lowe's Pulls Ads from TV Show about US Muslims." Associated Press, December 12, 2011.

Goodwin, Liz. "In Interviews, American Muslims Say They Reject Separate 'Sharia' Law System." *Lookout*, January 31, 2012.

Gore, Rick. "Who Were the Phoenicians?" *National Geographic*, October 2004.

Guillame, Alfred. *Islam.* New York: Penguin, 1954.

Greene, Graham. *The Quiet American.* London: Heinemann, 1955.

Greenspan, Alan. *The Age of Turbulence: Adventures in a New World.* New York: Penguin, 2007.

Haass, Richard. "U.S. Foreign Policy in a Nonpolar World." *Foreign Affairs*, May/June 2008.

Haddad, Bassam. The Syrian Regime's Business Backbone. Washington, D.C.: Middle East Research and Information Project, Spring 2012.

Hafez. *The Poems of Hafez.* Bethesda, Md.: Ibex, 2006.

Hafidh, Hassan. "Oil Majors to Resume Talks on Iraq Tech Pacts." Dow Jones Newswires, February 8, 2008.

Hajaj, Claire. "Holding Back Cholera in Iraq to Protect Thousands at Risk." UNICEF, September 27, 2007. www.unicef.org/.

Hajdari, Ismet. "Pro-Americanism 'a Must' in Kosovo." *Turkish Daily News* (Istanbul), November 15, 2007.

Halberstam, David. "The History Boys." *Vanity Fair*, August 2007.

Hamilton, A. M. *Road through Kurdistan.* London: Taurus Park Paperbacks, 1937.

Hedges, Chris. *War Is a Force That Gives Us Meaning.* New York: Anchor Books, 2003.

Hersh, Seymour. "The Administration's Secret Iran Campaign." *New Yorker*, July 7, 2008.

Hertzberg, Hendrik. "Follow the Leaders." *New Yorker*, December 10, 2007.

Hirsch, Afua. "Morocco Grapples with Women's Rights after Raped Bride's Suicide." *Mail & Guardian* (London), April 4, 2012.

Hobhouse, Penelope. *Gardens of Persia.* Hong Kong: Kales Press, 2004.

Holguin, Jaime. "Iran: Nose Job Capital of World." CBS News, February 11, 2009. www.cbsnews.com/.

Huntington, Samuel. *The Clash of Civilizations and the Remaking of World Order.* London: Touchstone, 1998.

Huxley, Aldous. *Beyond the Mexique Bay*. Chicago: Academy Chicago Publishing, 1985.
Ignatieff, Michael. *The Warrior's Honor: Ethnic War and the Modern Conscience*. New York: Metropolitan, 1998.
International Organization for Migration (IOM). "IOM Emergency Needs Assessments." Biweekly report. February 15, 2008.
Iran News. "Iran Dismantles Israeli Spy Network." November 27, 2008.
Isachenkov, Vladimir. "Old Rivals Unite versus U.S. Plans." Associated Press, May 24, 2008.
Issenberg, Sasha. "Slaying Gave US a First Taste of Mideast Terror." *Boston Globe*, June 5, 2008.
Jay, Martin. "Police Violence Reaching New Levels in Morocco with Sunday Beatings." CNN World, May 30, 2011. http://articles.cnn.com/.
Jolly, David. "Anti-Islam View: Attacks' Toll Is Put at 91." *New York Times*, July 24, 2011.
Jones, Gareth. "Turkish Parliament Lifts University Headscarf Ban." Agence France-Presse, February 9, 2008.
Judt, Tony. "Amos Elon (1926–2009)." *New York Review of Books*, June 25, 2009.
Kagan, Robert. *The Return of History*. New York: Knopf, 2008.
Kamber, Michael. "Shame of Imported Labor in Kurdish North of Iraq." *New York Times*, December 29, 2007.
Kaplan, Robert. *Eastward to Tartary*. New York: Vintage, 2000.
Kapuscinski, Ryszard. *Shah of Shahs*. New York: Vintage, 1992.
Keeley, Lawrence H. *War before Civilization*. New York: Oxford University Press, 1996.
K. F. "Ombre et lumière." *La Presse de Tunisie*, June 27, 2011.
Khanna, Parag. *The Second World*. New York: Random House, 2008.
———. "Waving Goodbye to Hegemony." *New York Times Magazine*, January 27, 2008.
King, Martin Luther, Jr. *Why We Can't Wait*. Boston: Beacon Press, 1964.
Kinsley, Michael. "What Bush Isn't Saying about Iraq." *Slate*, October 24, 2002.
Kirkpatrick, David. "Ex-Tunisian President Found Guilty, in Absentia." *New York Times*, June 20, 2011.
Klaus, Ian. *Elvis Is Titanic*. New York: Knopf, 2007.
Kociejowski, Marius. *The Street Philosopher and the Holy Fool: A Syrian Journey*. Stroud, Gloucestershire, UK: Sutton, 2004.
Kristoff, Nicholas. "Make Diplomacy, Not War." *New York Times*, August 10, 2008.
———. "A Prison of Shame, and It's Ours." *New York Times*, May 4, 2008.
Ladek, Dana Graber. "Iraq Displacement: 2007 Year in Review." International Organization for Migration (IOM), 2007.
Lahcen, Mawassi. "Police Disperse Casablanca, Tangier Protests." Magharebia, May 31, 2011. http://magharebia.com/.
Lando, Ben. "Analysis: Petraeus Makes Iraq Energy Calls." UPI.com, March 18, 2008. http://upi.com/.
Larrabee, Stephen. "Turkey Turns to the Middle East." *Foreign Affairs*, July/August 2007.
Lawrence, T. E. *Seven Pillars of Wisdom*. London: Penguin, 1935.
Lederer, William. *The Ugly American*. New York: Norton, 1965.
Levy, Simon. "Untitled." Foundation of Jewish-Moroccan Cultural Heritage, Casablanca, 2011.
Lewis, Bernard. *Islam and the West*. New York: Oxford University Press, 1993.
Lipton, Eric. "With White House Push, U.S. Arms Sales Rise Sharply." *New York Times*, September 14, 2008.
Lynch, Mark. "Rached Ghannouchi: FP Interview." *Foreign Policy*, December 5, 2011.
Lyons, Alistair. "Bush Jabs Shi'ite Radicals." Reuters, January 24, 2007.
Macfarquhar, Neil. "Cattlemen in Lebanon Miss Lucre of Hashish." *New York Times*, April 5, 2001.

Mackintosh-Smith, Tim. *Travels with a Tangerine*. New York: Random House, 2001.

MacMillan, Margaret. *Paris 1919: Six Months that Changed the World*. New York: Random House, 2002.

Maddow, Rachel. *Drift: The Unmooring of American Military Power*. New York: Crown, 2012.

Majd, Hooman. *The Ayatollah Begs to Differ*. New York: Doubleday, 2008.

Makdisi, Jean Said. *Beirut Fragments*. New York: Persea Books, 1990.

Malouf, Greg. *Syria and Lebanon*. Melbourne, Australia: Lonely Planet, 2004.

Marcus, Aliza. *Blood and Belief*. New York: New York University Press, 2007.

Mazzetti, Mark. "Robert Gates Advises Turkey to End Incursion Soon." *New York Times*, December 8, 2008.

McDonald, Mark. "Halabja Is Eager to Try Man behind Gas Attack." Knight Ridder News Service, June 20, 2004.

McIntire, Mike, and Michael Luo. "The Man behind Gingrich's Money." *New York Times*, January 28, 2012.

Mead, Walter Russell. "The New Israel and the Old." *Foreign Relations*, July/August 2008.

Mearsheimer, John, and Stephen Walt. *The Israel Lobby and U.S. Foreign Policy*. New York: Farrar, Straus and Giroux, 2007.

Mekhennet, Souad. "Chaotic Lebanon Risks Becoming Militant Haven." *New York Times*, July 7, 2007.

Menocal, Maria Rosa. *Ornament of the World: How Muslims, Jews and Christians Created a Culture of Tolerance in Medieval Spain*. New York: Back Bay Books, 2002.

Moaveni, Azadeh. *Lipstick Jihad*. New York: Public Affairs Books, 2005.

Morier, James. *Hajji Baba of Ispahan*. New York: Random House, 1937.

"Morocco's Holocaust Recognition Rare in Islam." Associated Press, July 25, 2009.

Mortenson, Greg, and David Oliver Relin. *Three Cups of Tea*. New York: Penguin, 2006.

Moschos, John. *The Spiritual Meadow*. Kalamazoo, Mich.: Cistercian Publications, 1992.

Muller, Jerry. "Us and Them." *Foreign Affairs*, March/April 2008.

Musharbash, Yassim. "Likely Terror Attack Strikes Popular Tourist Café in Morocco." *Spiegel Online*, April 28, 2011. www.spiegel.de/.

Nafisi, Azar. *Reading Lolita in Tehran*. New York: Random House, 2003.

———. *Things I've Been Silent About*. New York: Random House, 2008.

Obama, Barack. *The Audacity of Hope*. New York: Three Rivers Press, 2006.

———. *Dreams of My Father*. New York: Three Rivers Press, 2004.

———. "A Moment of Opportunity" (speech). U.S. Department of State, 2011.

Okafor, Anwulika. "Jordan's Queen Rania Issues UNICEF's Worldwide Call to Action to Aid Iraqi Children." UNICEF, May 23, 2007. www.unicef.org/.

Oppel, Richard. "Five Years In: Iraq's Insurgency Runs on Stolen Oil Profits." *New York Times*, March 16, 2008.

Packer, George. "Knowing the Enemy." *New Yorker*, December 18, 2006.

Pagels, Elaine. *Revelations: Visions, Prophecy, and Politics in the Book of Revelation*. New York: Viking, 2012.

Paley, Amit. "For Kurdish Girls, a Painful Ancient Ritual." *Washington Post*, December 29, 2008.

Pamuk, Orhan, *Istanbul: Memories of the City*. New York: Knopf, 2005.

Pollack, Andrew. "China's Need for Metal Keeps U.S. Scrap Dealers Scrounging." *New York Times*, March 13, 2004.

Power, Samantha. *A Problem from Hell*. New York: Harper Perennial, 2003.

Rappaport, Meron. "IDF Commander: We Fired More than a Million Cluster Bombs in Lebanon." *Haaretz*, September 12, 2006.

Rashid, Ahmed. "Jihadi Suicide Bombers: The New Wave." *New York Review of Books*, June 12, 2008.

Ricks, Thomas. *Fiasco*. New York: Penguin, 2006.

Riedel, Bruce. "Al Qaeda Strikes Back." *Foreign Affairs*, May/June 2007.

Rochebrune, Renaud De. "Benjamin Stora." *Jeune Afrique* (Paris), June 11, 2011.

Ross, Dennis. "The Art of Peace." *Utne*, July–August 2007.

Rubin, Barry. *Islamic Fundamentalism in Egyptian Politics*. New York: Palgrave Macmillan, 2002.

Ruthven, Malise. "Divided Iran on the Eve." *New York Review of Books*, July 2, 2009.

Rutter, Jill, and Crispin Jones. *Refugee Education: Mapping the Field*. Stoke on Trent, UK: Trentham Books, 1998.

Salibi, Kamal. *A House of Many Mansions*. Berkeley: University of California Press, 1988.

Schjeldahl, Peter. "All Souls." *New Yorker*, November 5, 2007.

———. "All Together Now." *New Yorker*, October 8, 2007.

Schleifer, Yigal. "Why Turks No Longer Love the U.S." *Christian Science Monitor*, November 1, 2007.

Schmidt, Michael. "Suicide Bombs in Iraq Have Killed 12,000 Civilians, Study Says." *New York Times*, September 2, 2011.

Sever, Megan. "Oil and Politics in Iraq." *GeoTimes*, February 2008.

Seal, Jeremy. *A Fez of the Heart*. London: Picador, 1995.

Secor, Laura. "The Rationalist." *New Yorker*, February 2, 2009.

Shane, Scott. "Killings in Norway Spotlight Anti-Muslim Thought in U.S." *New York Times*, July 24, 2011.

Slackman, Michael. "Israeli Bomblets Plague Lebanon." *New York Times*, October 6, 2006.

Spolar, Christine. "On Turkey-Iraq Border, Rumblings of War, Trucks." *Chicago Tribune*, October 25, 2007.

Spykman, Nicholas. *The Geography of Peace*. London: Gazelle Book Services, 1966.

Stark, Freya. *East Is West*. London: John Murray, 1945.

Steinback, Robert. "The Anti-Muslim Inner Circle." Southern Poverty Law Center, *Intelligence Report* 142 (Summer 2011).

Stern, Eliyahu. "Don't Fear Islamic Law in America." *New York Times*, September 2, 2011.

Stern, Jessica. *Terror in the Name of God*. New York: HarperCollins, 2003.

Stockman, Farah. "Bush Brings Faith to Foreign Aid." *Boston Globe*, October 8, 2006.

Stohl, Rachel. *The Small Arms Trade*. Oxford, UK: One World, 2007.

Takeh, Ray. *Hidden Iran*. New York: Henry Holt, 2006.

Tehran Times. "Iran Executes Mossad Spy." November 23, 2008.

Theroux, Paul. *The Pillars of Hercules*. New York: Fawcett Books, 1995.

———. *The Tao of Travel*. New York: Houghton Mifflin Harcourt, 2011.

Totten, Michael. "The Kurds Go Their Own Way." *Reason*, August/September 2006. http://reason.com/.

Traub, James. "Persuading Them." *New York Times*, November 25, 2007.

Twain, Mark. *The Innocents Abroad*. New York: Modern Library, 2003.

UNHCR: The UN Refugee Agency. "Iraq Situation Report." February 2008. www.unhcr.org/.

———. "Lebanon: Stop Detaining Syrian Refugees." May 20, 2011. www.unhcr.org/.

———. "Southern Tunisia: Dehiba/Remada UNHCR Update #11." June 4, 2011. www.unhcr.org/.

———. "Southern Tunisia: Weekly Update." August 15, 2011. www.unhcr.org/.

Vryonis, Speros. *Byzantium and Europe*. New York: Harcourt, Brace & World, 1967.

Wade, Nicholas. "We May Be Born with an Urge to Help." *New York Times*, November 30, 2009.

West, Rebecca. *Black Lamb and Grey Falcon*. New York: Viking Press, 1941.

Wheeler, Donna. *Tunisia*. Footscray, Vic., Australia: Lonely Planet, 2010.

Williams, Timothy. "With Need Dire and Aid Scant, Iraq's Widows Struggle." *New York Times*, February 23, 2009.

Wright, Lawrence. *The Looming Tower*. New York: Knopf, 2006.

———. "The Rebellion Within: An Al Qaeda Mentor Rethinks Terrorism." *New Yorker*, June 2, 2008.

Wright, Robin. *Dreams and Shadows*. New York: Penguin, 2008.

Yildiz, Kerim. *The Kurds in Iraq*. Ann Harbor, Mich.: Pluto Press, 2004.

Young, Michael. "Hezbollah's Other War." *New York Times Magazine*, August 13, 2006.

Zakaria, Fareed. "Why the United States Will Survive the Rise of the Rest." *Foreign Affairs*, May/June 2008.

Index

~

About the Author

Phil Karber is an award-winning travel writer whose passion to see the world and experience other cultures began as a young man in the army, stationed for two years in northern Thailand during the Vietnam War. He has traveled to over 125 countries, most of them in the developing world. He began writing in 1996 after a successful career in business. As a fifth-generation native of Arkansas, he has been greatly influenced by coming of age amid the social injustices of the Jim Crow South. Devoted to fighting world hunger, poverty, and disease through writing and his involvement with World Neighbors, where he was formerly a trustee, Karber has lived in Nairobi, Kenya; Hanoi, Vietnam; Bangkok, Thailand; and East London, South Africa. He currently resides in Cambridge, Massachusetts. When not traveling, he spends time with his four granddaughters, Parker, Suzi, Lila, and Mabyn.